Dragon Eye
Volume 2

Kairi Fujiyama

Translated and adapted by Mari Morimoto

Lettered by North Market Street Graphics

Ballantine Books · New York

Dragon Eye volume 2 is a work of fiction. Names, characters, places, and incidents are the products of the author's imagination or are used fictitiously. Any resemblance to actual events, locales, or persons, living or dead, is entirely coincidental.

A Del Rey Books Trade Paperback Original

Published in the United States by Del Rey Books, an imprint of The Random House Publishing Group, a division of Random House, Inc., New York.

Publication rights arranged through Kodansha Ltd.

First published in Japan in 2006 by Kodansha Ltd., Tokyo

ISBN 978-0-345-49883-0

Printed in the United States of America

www.delreymanga.com

987654321

Translator/Adapter: Mari Morimoto
Lettering: North Market Street Graphics
Cover design: Yo-Yo Rarandays (Suzuki Yo-Yo, Kawai Rara)

Contents

Honorifics Explained V

Dragon Eye, volume 2 I

Translation Notes 190

Preview of *Dragon Eye*, volume 3 193

I've finally mastered
the main character's
hairstyle. But there is still
a lot that I don't know.
Most of these things have
to do with hairstyles...

Honorifics Explained

Throughout the Del Rey Manga books, you will find Japanese honorifics left intact in the translations. For those not familiar with how the Japanese use honorifics and, more important, how they differ from American honorifics, we present this brief overview.

Politeness has always been a critical facet of Japanese culture. Ever since the feudal era, when Japan was a highly stratified society, use of honorifics—which can be defined as polite speech that indicates relationship or status—has played an essential role in the Japanese language. When you address someone in Japanese, an honorific usually takes the form of a suffix attached to one's name (example: "Asuna-san"), is used as a title at the end of one's name, or appears in place of the name itself (example: "Negi-sensei," or simply "Sensei!").

Honorifics can be expressions of respect or endearment. In the context of manga and anime, honorifics give insight into the nature of the relationship between characters. Many English translations leave out these important honorifics and therefore distort the feel of the original Japanese. Because Japanese honorifics contain nuances that English honorifics lack, it is our policy at Del Rey not to translate them. Here, instead, is a guide to some of the honorifics you may encounter in Del Rey Manga.

-*san:* This is the most common honorific and is equivalent to Mr., Miss, Ms., or Mrs. It is the all-purpose honorific and can be used in any situation where politeness is required.

-*sama:* This is one level higher than "-san" and is used to confer great respect.

-*dono:* This comes from the word "tono," which means "lord." It is an even higher level than "-sama" and confers utmost respect.

-kun: This suffix is used at the end of boys' names to express familiarity or endearment. It is also sometimes used by men among friends, or when addressing someone younger or of a lower station.

-chan: This is used to express endearment, mostly toward girls. It is also used for little boys, pets, and even between lovers. It gives a sense of childish cuteness.

Bozu: This is an informal way to refer to a boy, similar to the English terms "kid" and "squirt."

Sempai/Senpai: This title suggests that the addressee is one's senior in a group or organization. It is most often used in a school setting, where underclassmen refer to their upperclassmen as "sempai." It can also be used in the workplace, such as when a newer employee addresses an employee who has seniority in the company.

Kohai: This is the opposite of "sempai" and is used toward underclassmen in school or newcomers in the workplace. It connotes that the addressee is of a lower station.

Sensei: Literally meaning "one who has come before," this title is used for teachers, doctors, or masters of any profession or art.

[blank]: This is usually forgotten in these lists, but it is perhaps the most significant difference between Japanese and English. The lack of honorific means that the speaker has permission to address the person in a very intimate way. Usually, only family, spouses, or very close friends have this kind of permission. This is known as *yobisute,* and it can be gratifying when someone who has earned the intimacy starts to call one by one's name without an honorific. But when that intimacy hasn't been earned, it can be very insulting.

Dragon Eye

Kairi Fujiyama

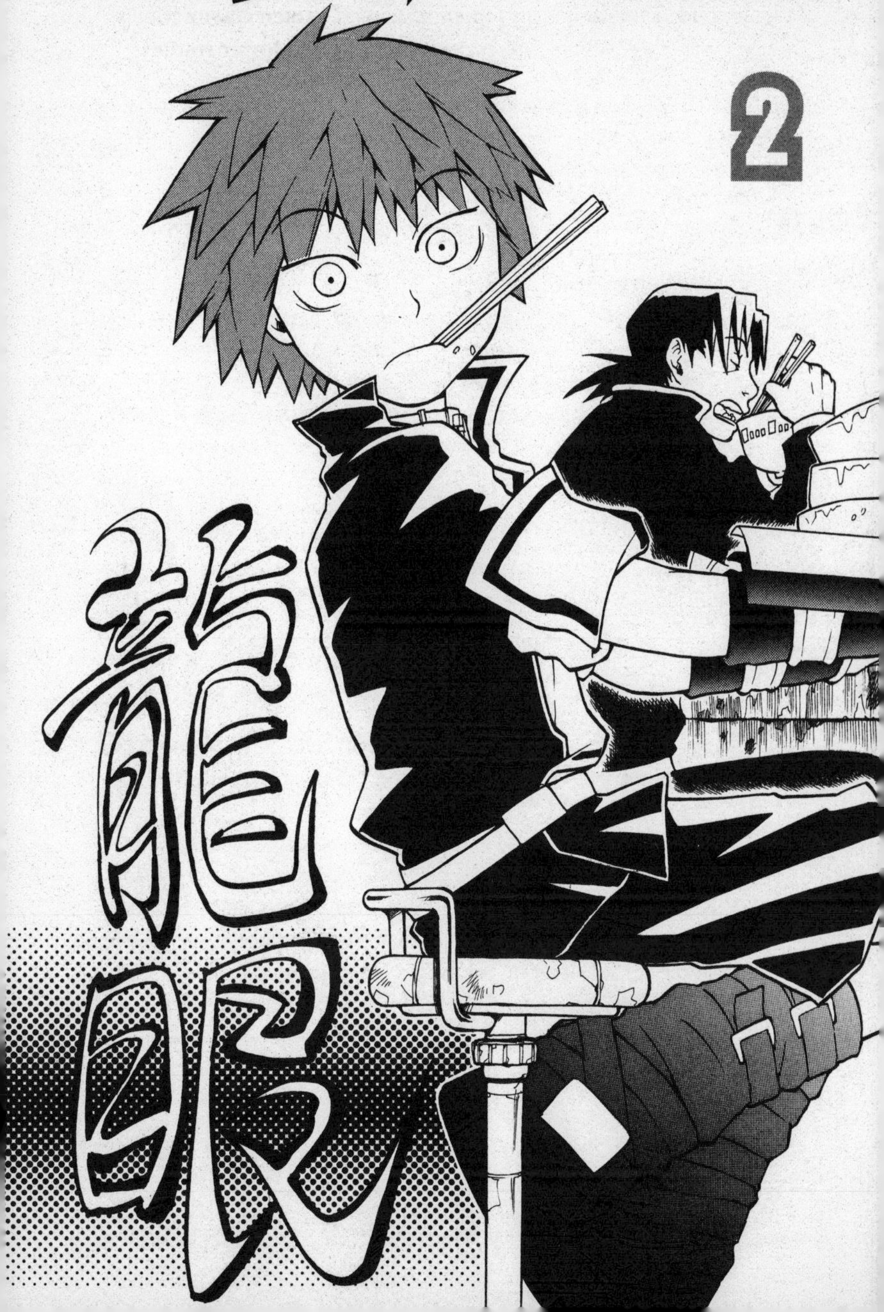
2
龍眼

Story of DRAGON EYE

龍眼物語

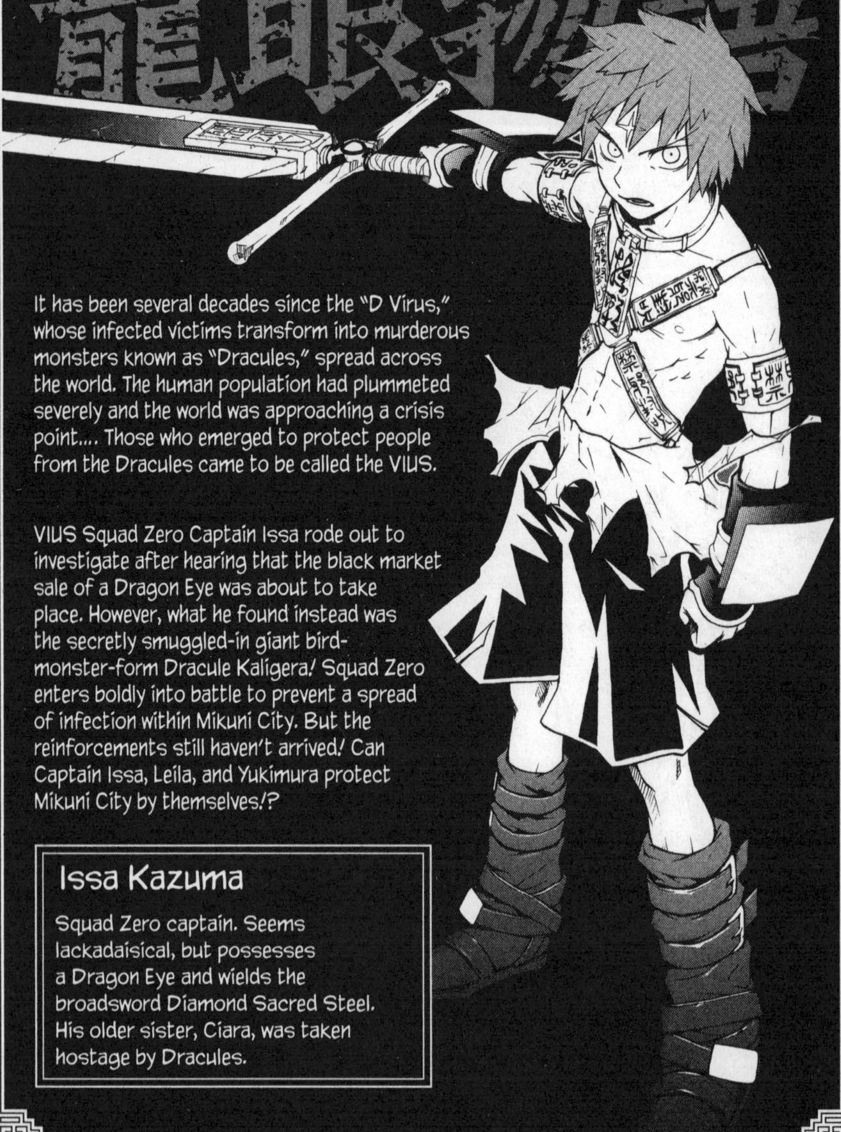

It has been several decades since the "D Virus," whose infected victims transform into murderous monsters known as "Dracules," spread across the world. The human population had plummeted severely and the world was approaching a crisis point.... Those who emerged to protect people from the Dracules came to be called the VIUS.

VIUS Squad Zero Captain Issa rode out to investigate after hearing that the black market sale of a Dragon Eye was about to take place. However, what he found instead was the secretly smuggled-in giant bird-monster-form Dracule Kaligera! Squad Zero enters boldly into battle to prevent a spread of infection within Mikuni City. But the reinforcements still haven't arrived! Can Captain Issa, Leila, and Yukimura protect Mikuni City by themselves!?

Issa Kazuma

Squad Zero captain. Seems lackadaisical, but possesses a Dragon Eye and wields the broadsword Diamond Sacred Steel. His older sister, Ciara, was taken hostage by Dracules.

Sôsei Yukimura

A former Squad Five member currently on temporary reassignment to Squad Zero. Believes Issa killed his twin sister—and so he wields twin blades in her memory and secretly plots for vengeance.

Leila Mikami

Newly inducted VIUS member. When she was little, both of her parents were killed by Dracules. She was, however, saved by a man with a Dragon Eye—which is why she joined VIUS.

Hyûga

Assigned to the Intelligence Corps. Does not have a lot of battle experience but idolizes Issa—perhaps because his first mission was with Issa's squad.

Masamune Hibiki

Squad Six member. Volunteers on missions with the shorthanded Squad Zero. Appears to be young but is quite an accomplished warrior.

[Dracule] Kaligera

A Dracule smuggled into Mikuni under the guise of black-market goods. Although in bird monster-form, he is capable of human speech. Kaligera is very swift and packs a powerful punch. His body is armored by Diamond Skin.

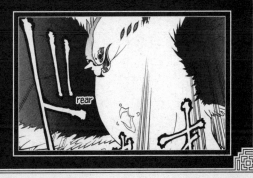

rear

Mission ◉ Four
The Forgotten Promise
5

Mission ◉ Five
The Captain Demoted!?
69

Mission ◉ Six
The Battle on the Lines
127

Extras
188

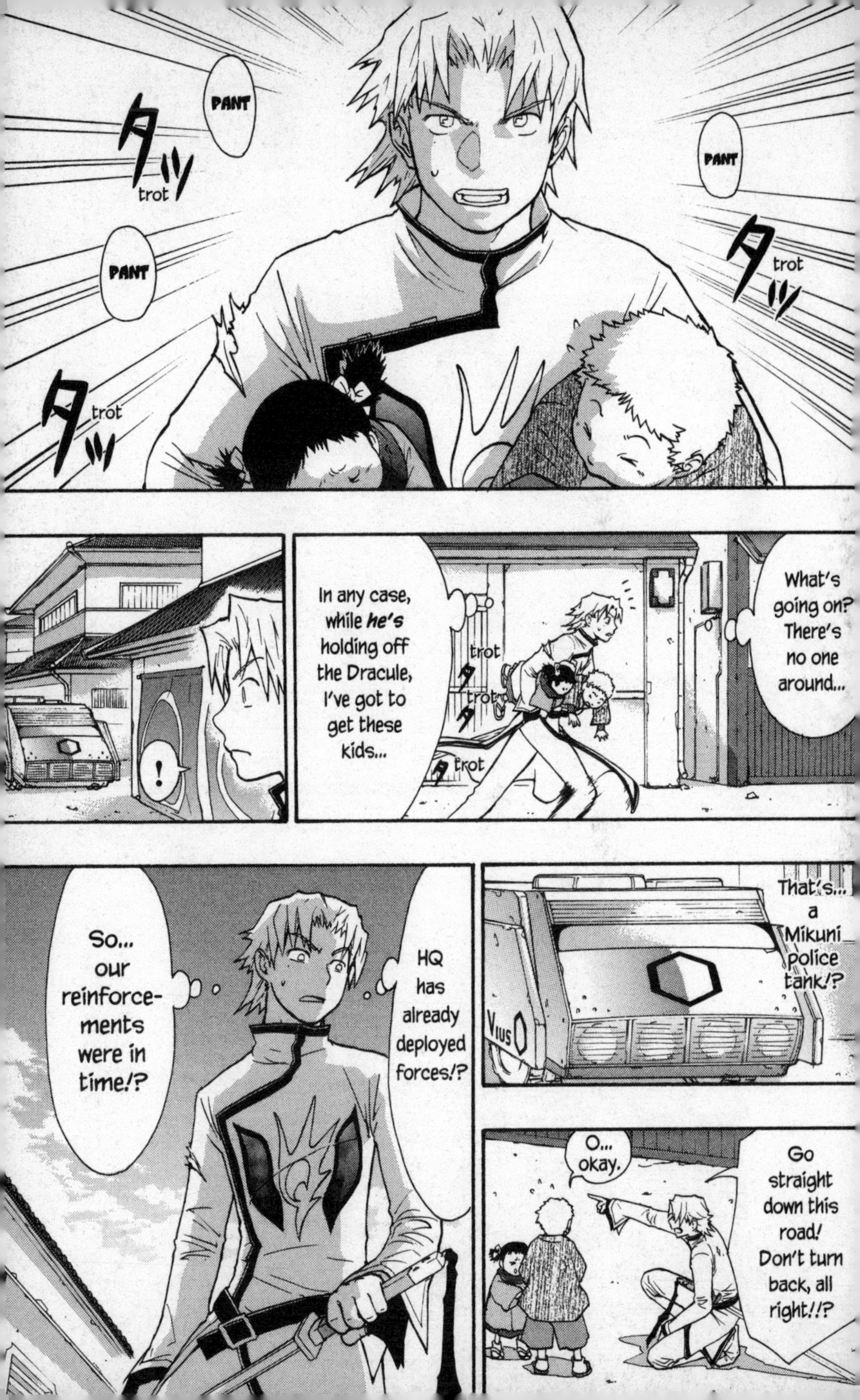

PANT
タッ
trot
PANT
PANT
タッ
trot
タッ
trot
What's going on? There's no one around...
In any case, while *he's* holding off the Dracule, I've got to get these kids...
タ trot
タ trot
タ trot
!
That's... a Mikuni police tank!?
VIUS
Go straight down this road! Don't turn back, all right!?
O... okay.
HQ has already deployed forces!?
So... our reinforcements were in time!?

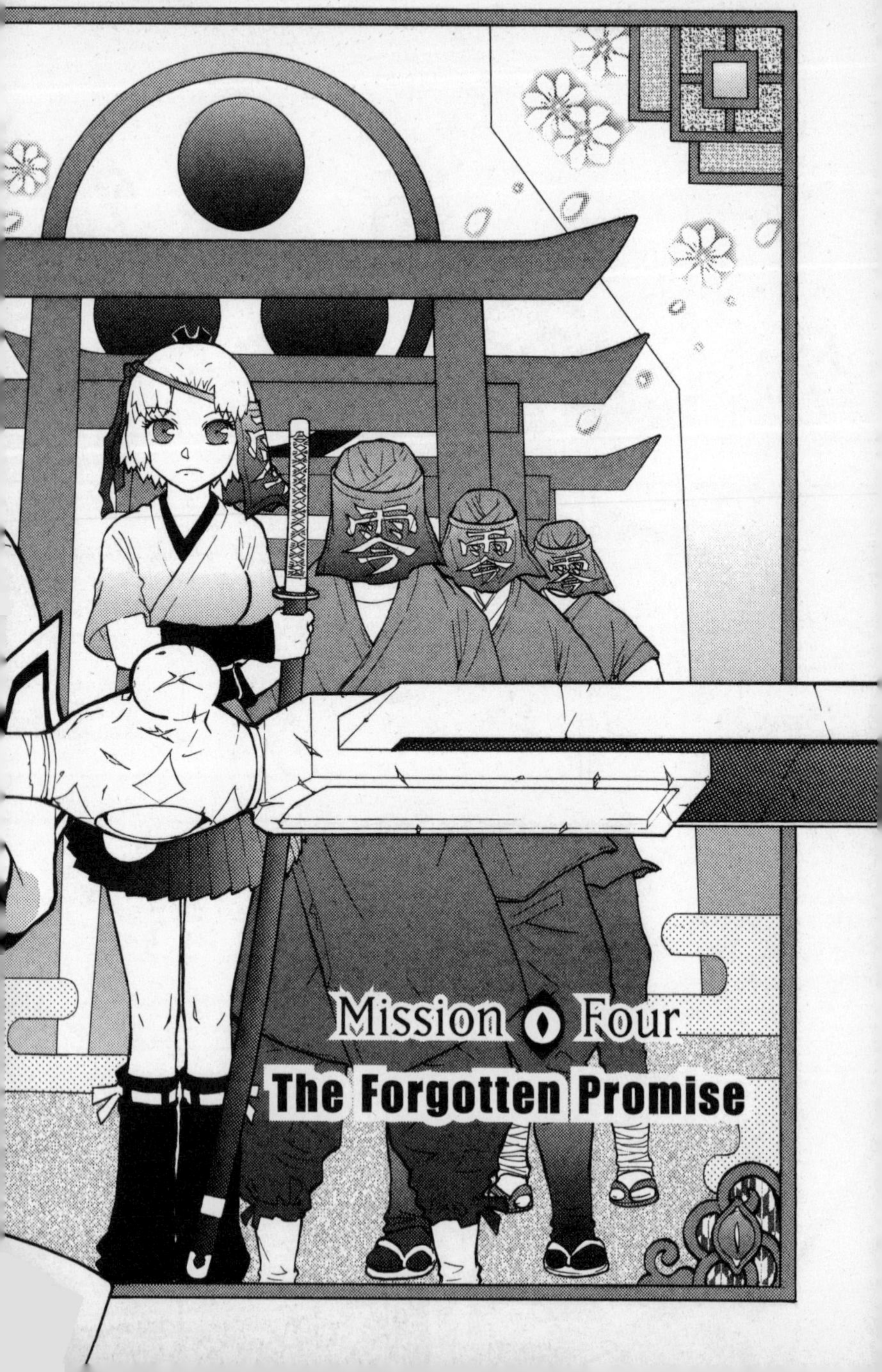
零
零
零
Mission Four
The Forgotten Promise

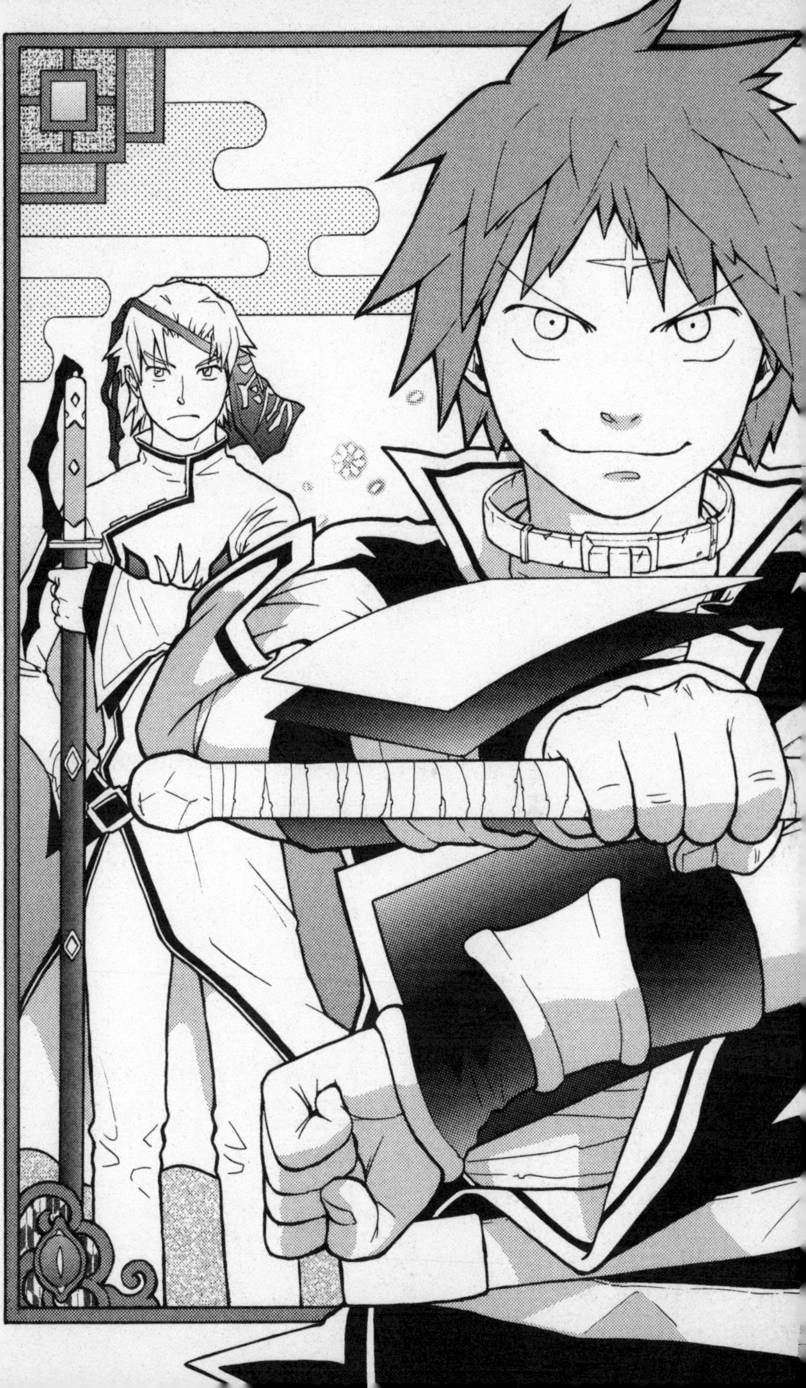

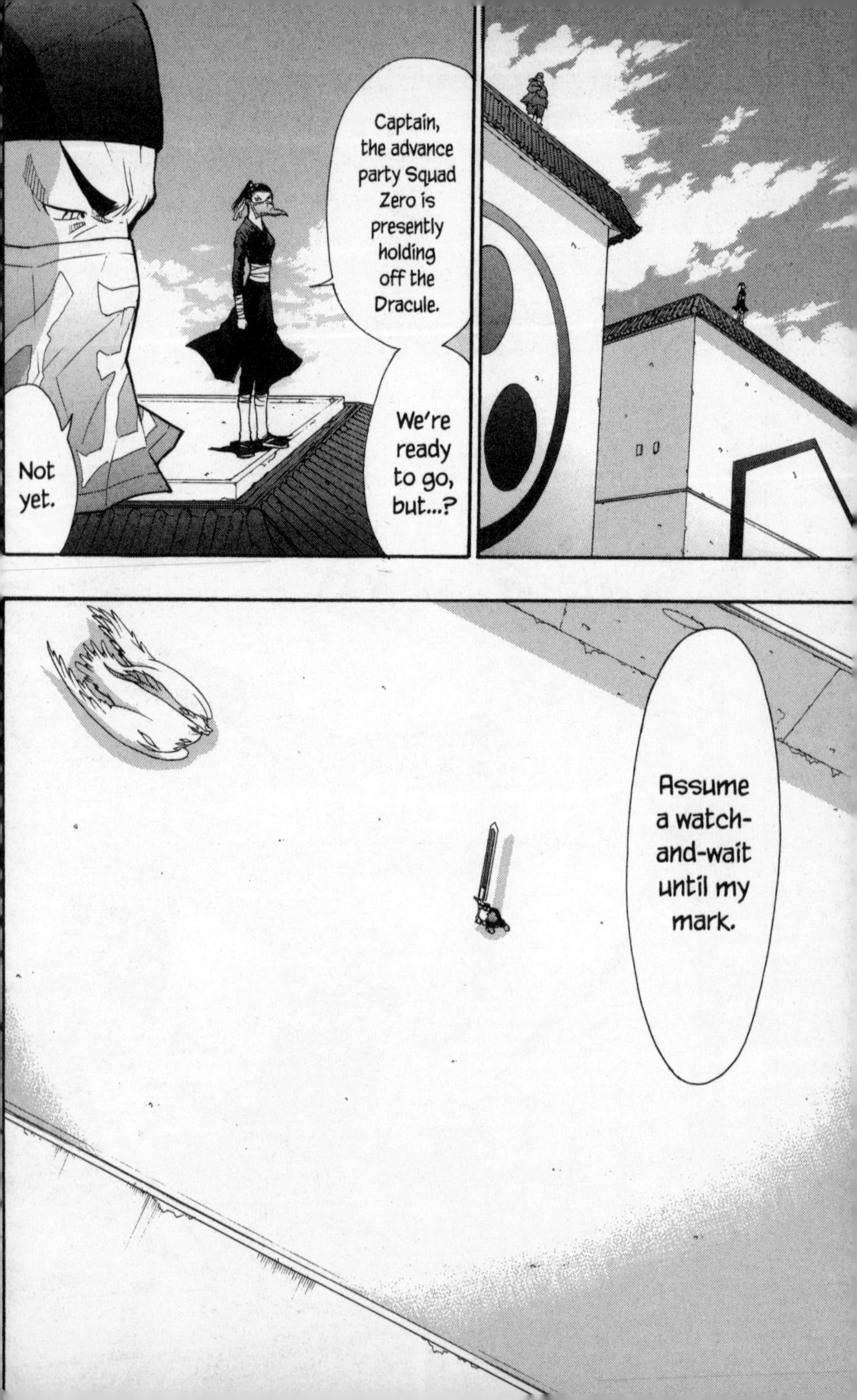
Captain, the advance party Squad Zero is presently holding off the Dracule.
We're ready to go, but...?
Not yet.
Assume a watch-and-wait until my mark.

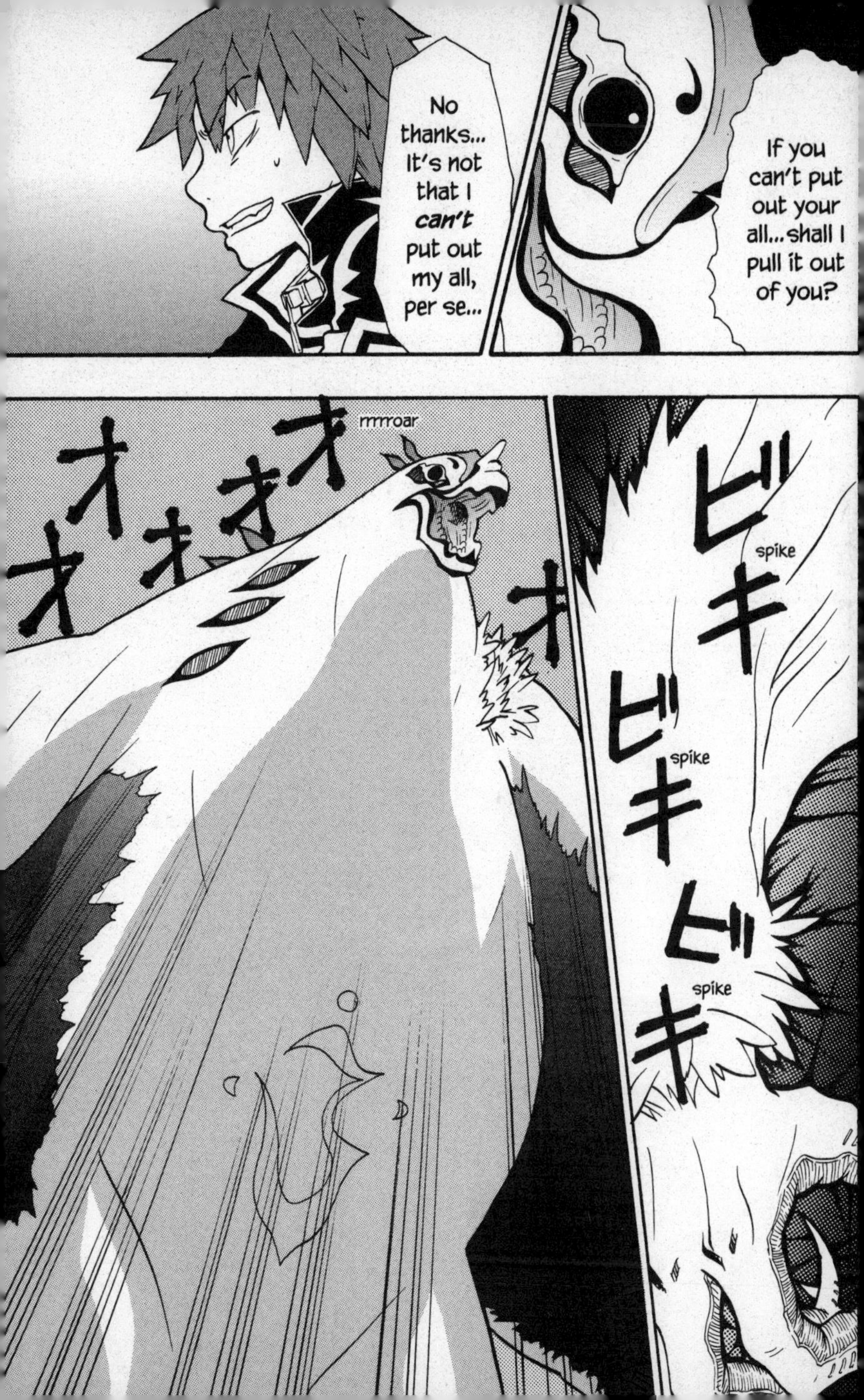
If you can't put out your all...shall I pull it out of you?
No thanks... It's not that I *can't* put out my all, per se...
ビキ
spike
ビキ
spike
ビキ
spike
オオオオオ
rrrrroar

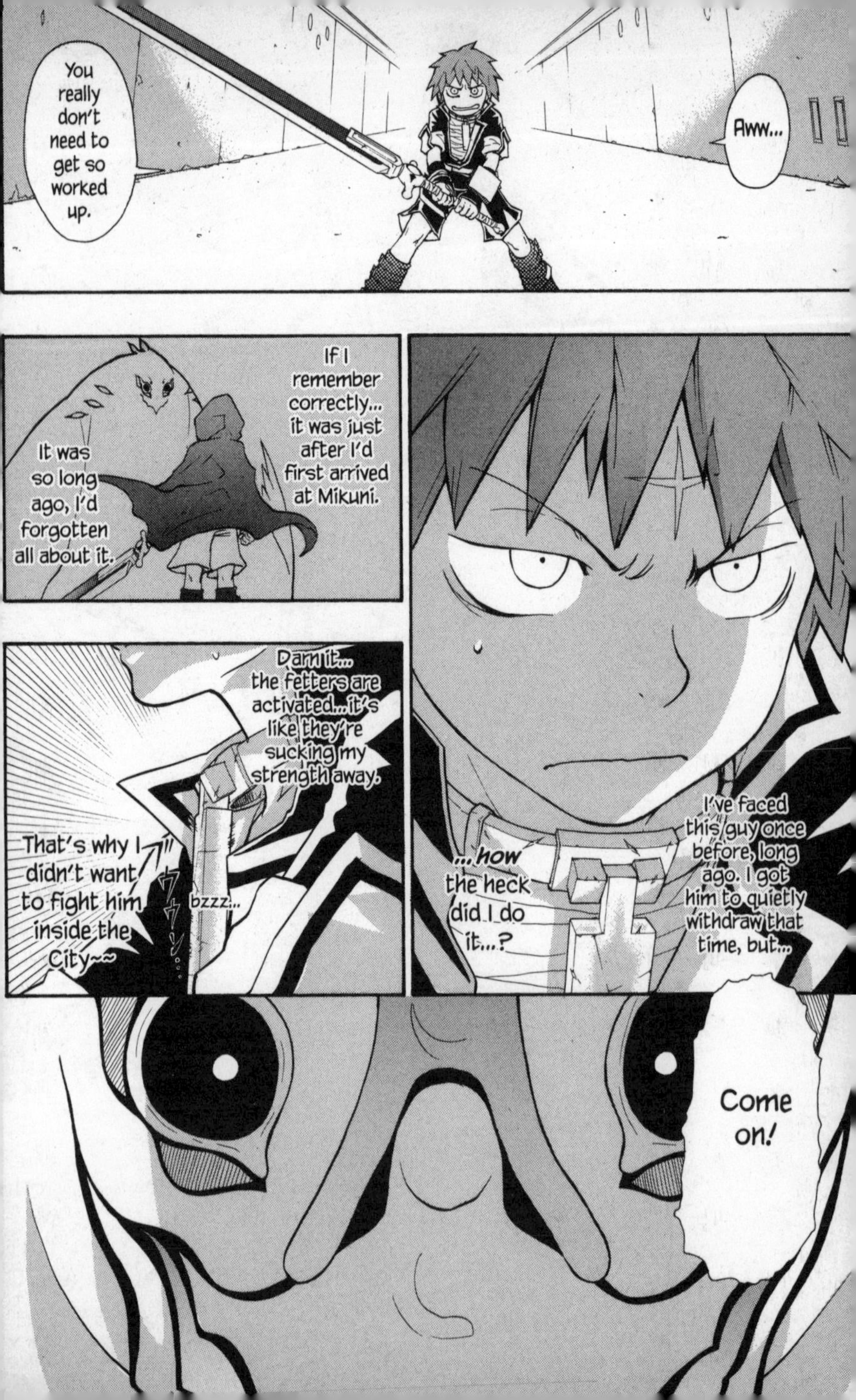
Aww...
You really don't need to get so worked up.
I've faced this guy once before, long ago. I got him to quietly withdraw that time, but...
...how the heck did I do it...?
If I remember correctly... it was just after I'd first arrived at Mikuni.
It was so long ago, I'd forgotten all about it.
Darn it... the fetters are activated... it's like they're sucking my strength away.
That's why I didn't want to fight him inside the City~~
bzzz...
Come on!

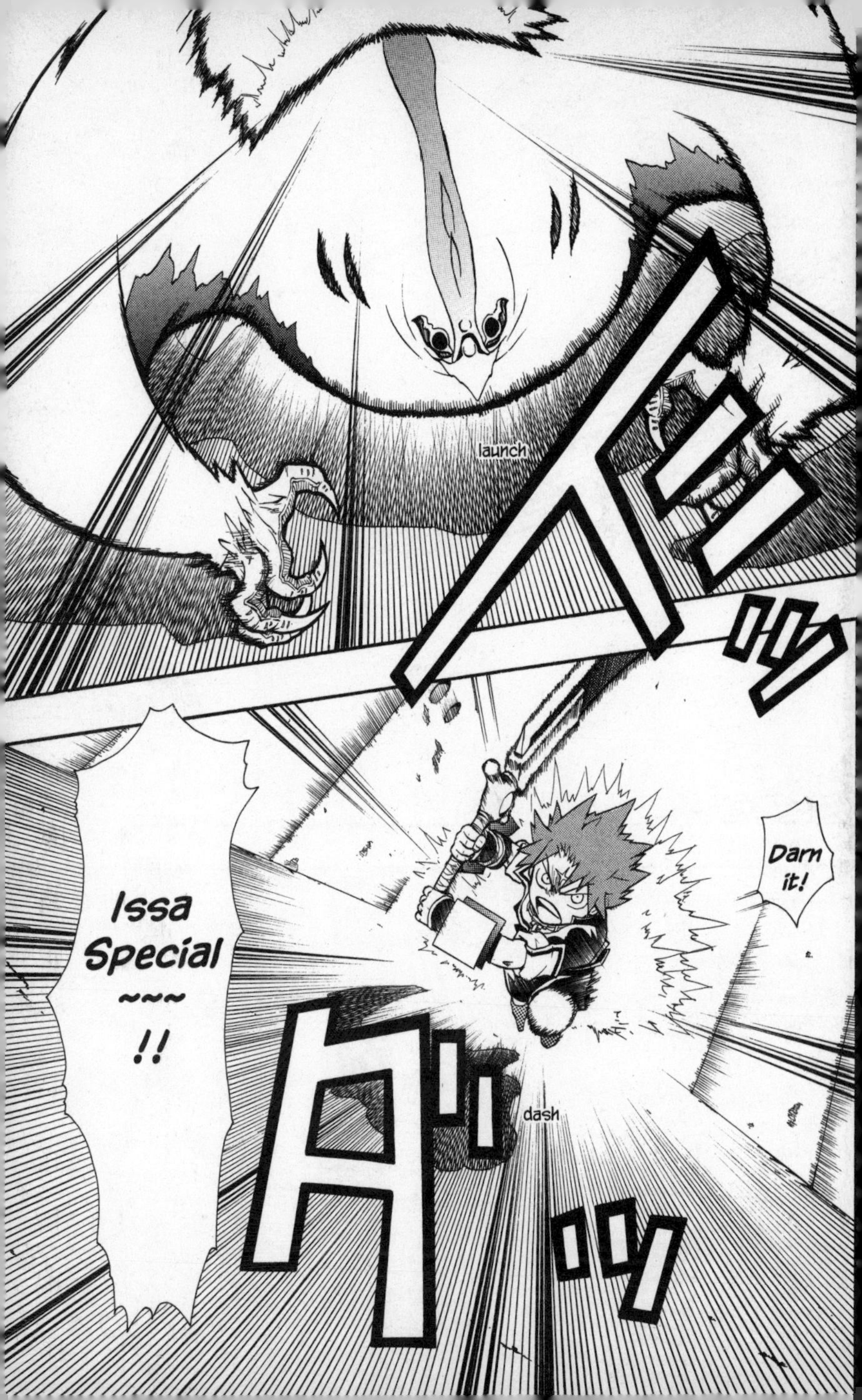
launch
Darn it!
dash
Issa Special ~~~ !!

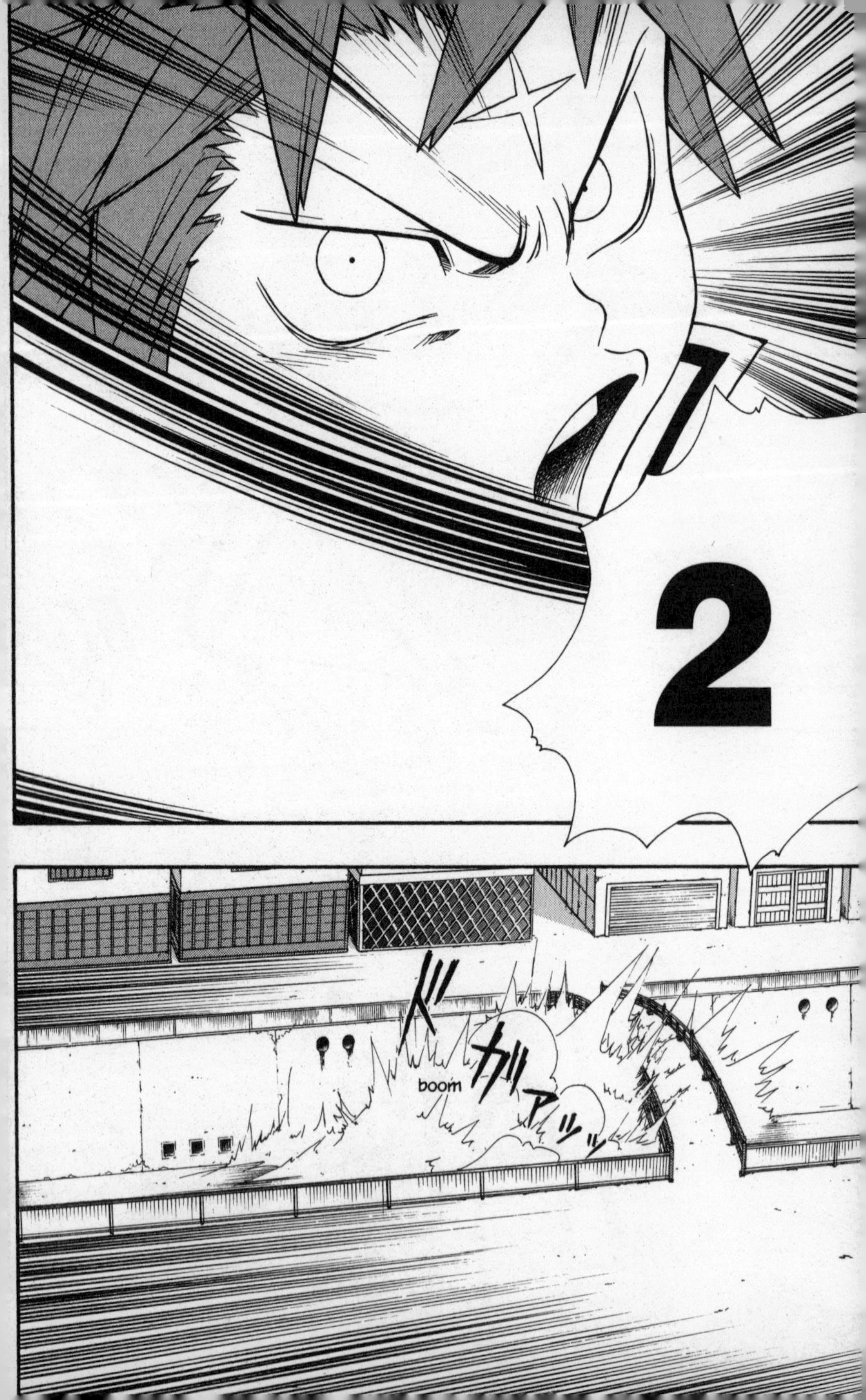
2
ドガアッ
boom

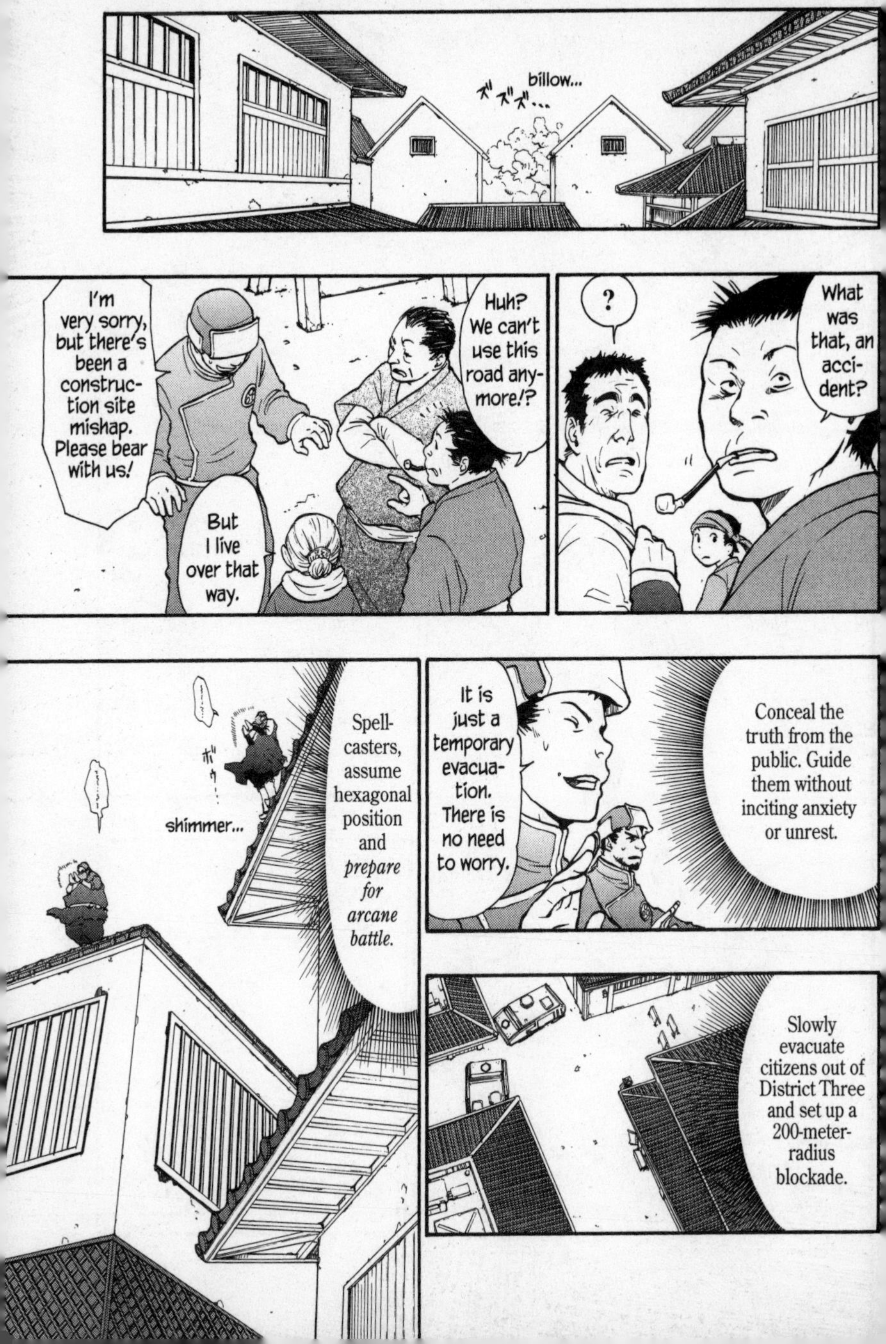
ズズズ...
billow...
?
What was that, an accident?
Huh? We can't use this road anymore!?
I'm very sorry, but there's been a construction site mishap. Please bear with us!
But I live over that way.
Conceal the truth from the public. Guide them without inciting anxiety or unrest.
It is just a temporary evacuation. There is no need to worry.
Slowly evacuate citizens out of District Three and set up a 200-meter-radius blockade.
Spell-casters, assume hexagonal position and *prepare for arcane battle.*
ボゥ...
shimmer...

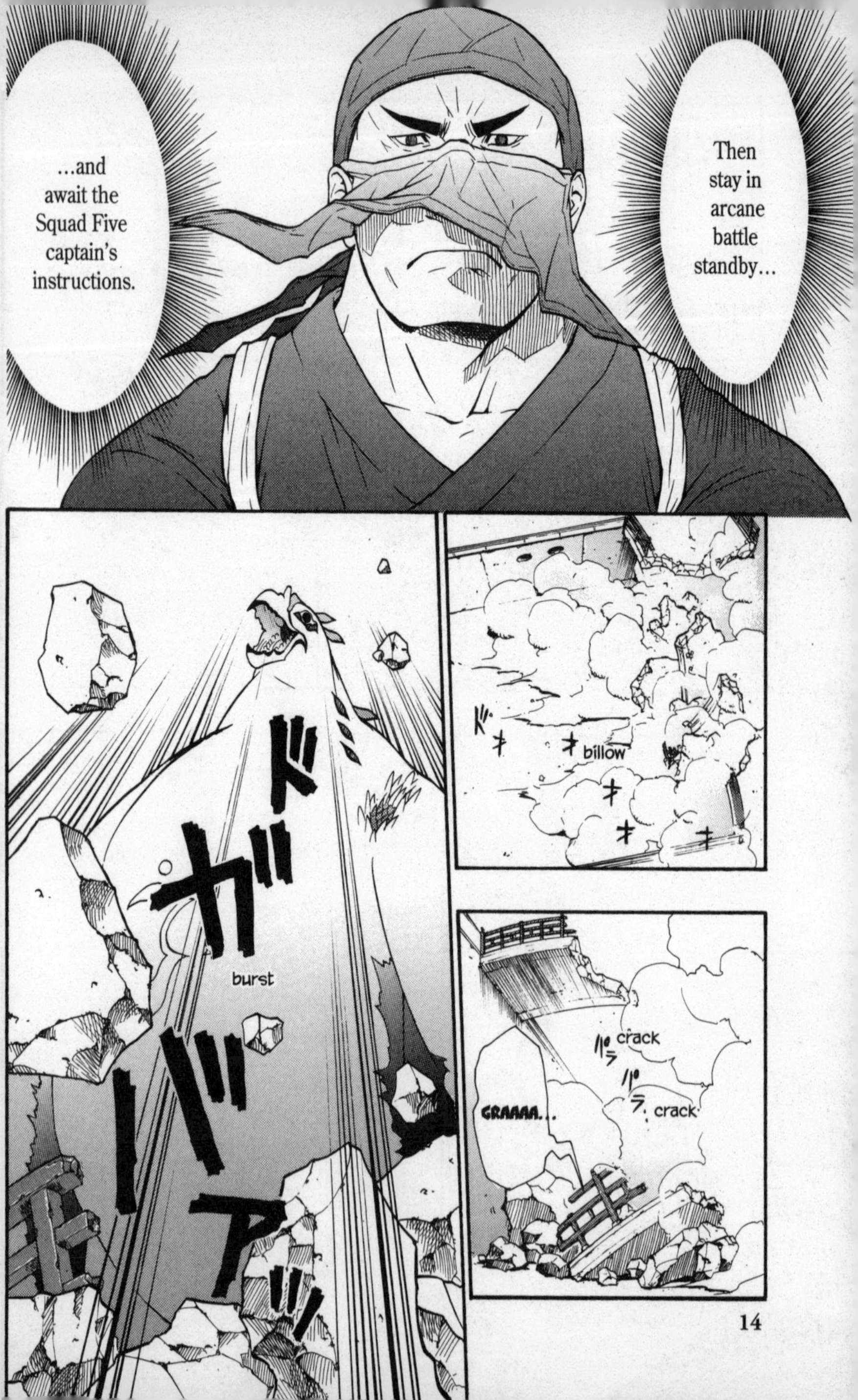

Then stay in arcane battle standby...
...and await the Squad Five captain's instructions.
billow
crack
crack
GRAAAA...
burst

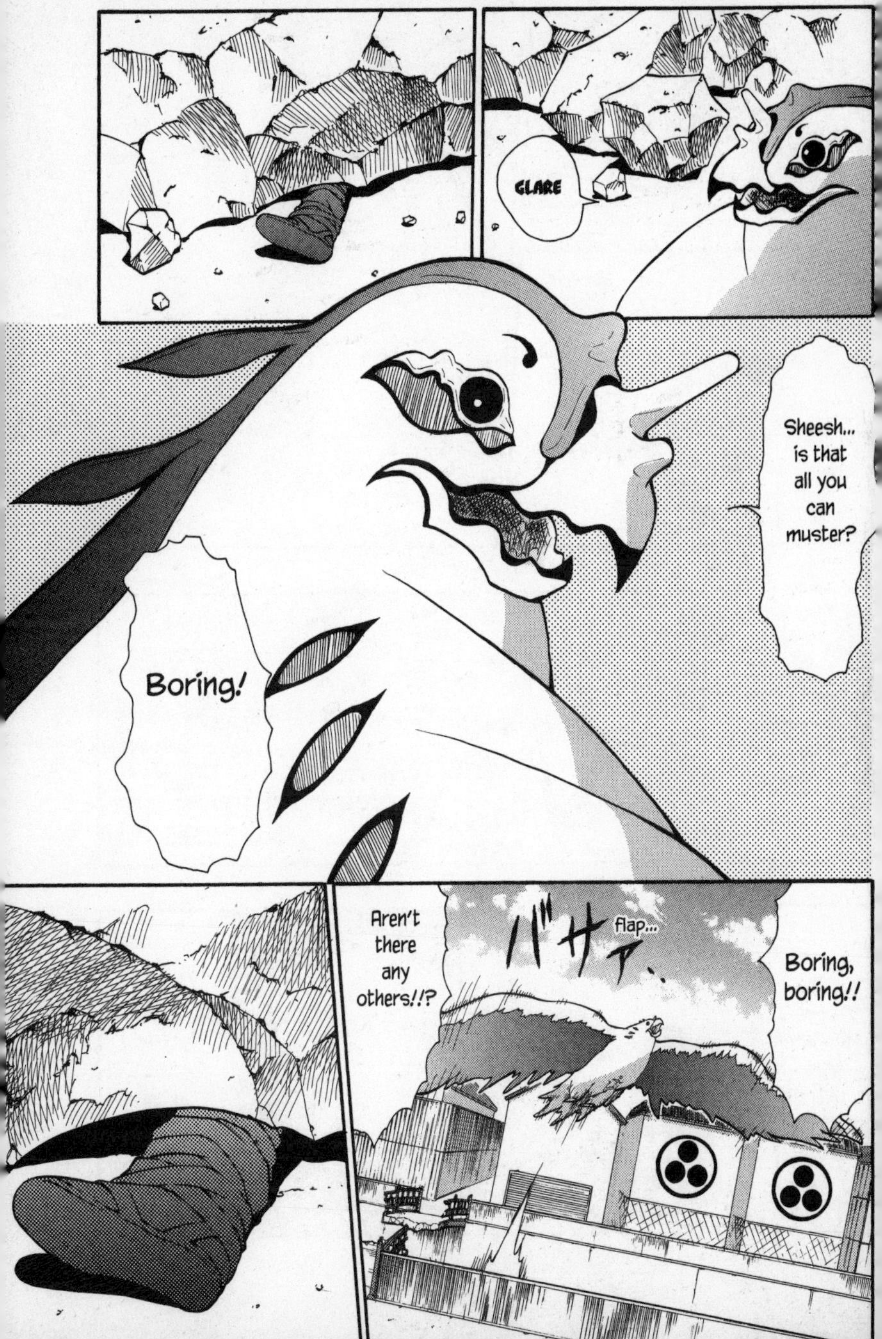
GLARE
Sheesh... is that all you can muster?
Boring!
Boring, boring!!
バサァ
flap...
Aren't there any others!!?

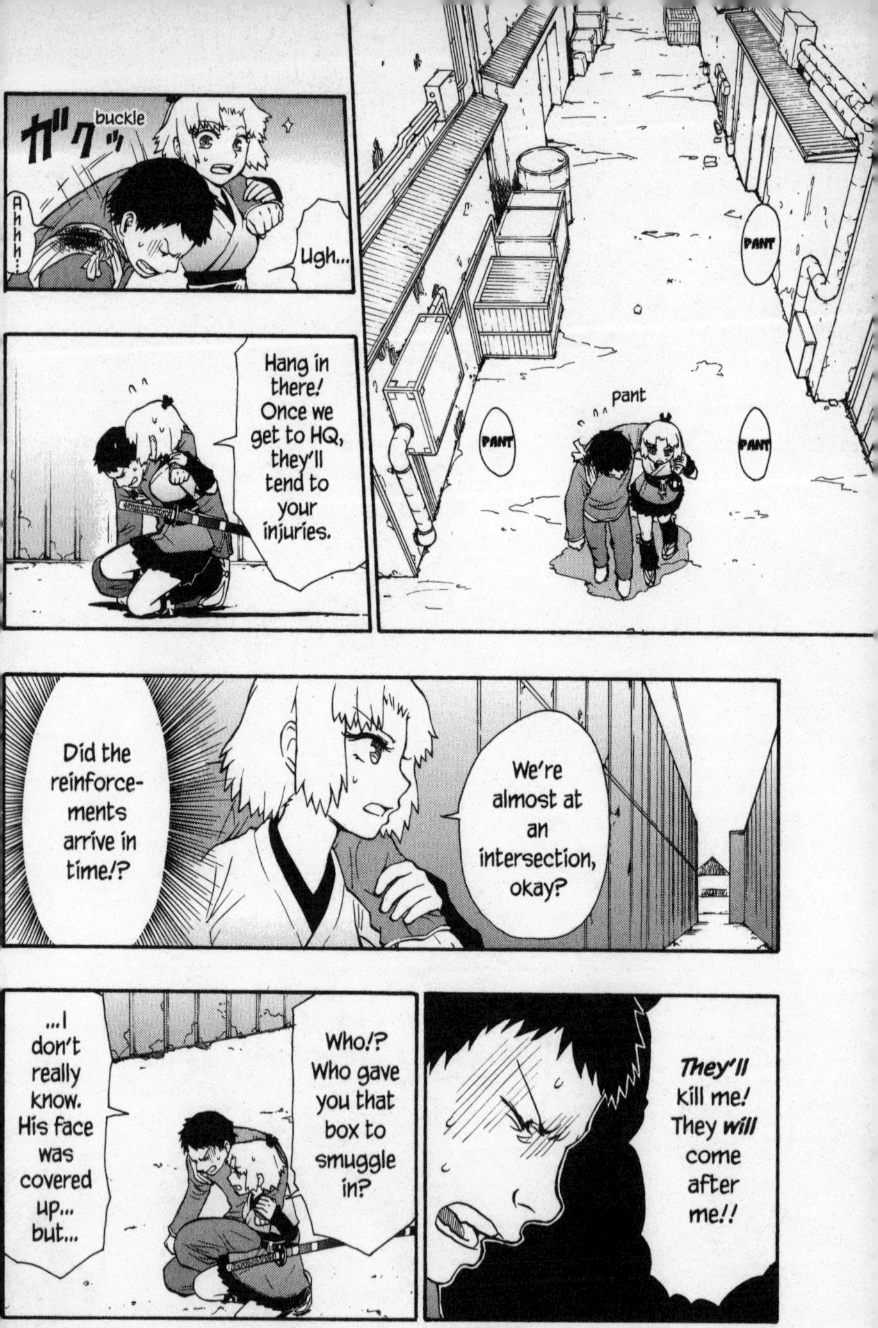
PANT
pant
PANT
PANT
Ugh...
ガクッ
buckle
Ahhh...
Hang in there! Once we get to HQ, they'll tend to your injuries.
We're almost at an intersection, okay?
Did the reinforcements arrive in time!?
They'll kill me! They *will* come after me!!
Who!? Who gave you that box to smuggle in?
...I don't really know. His face was covered up... but...

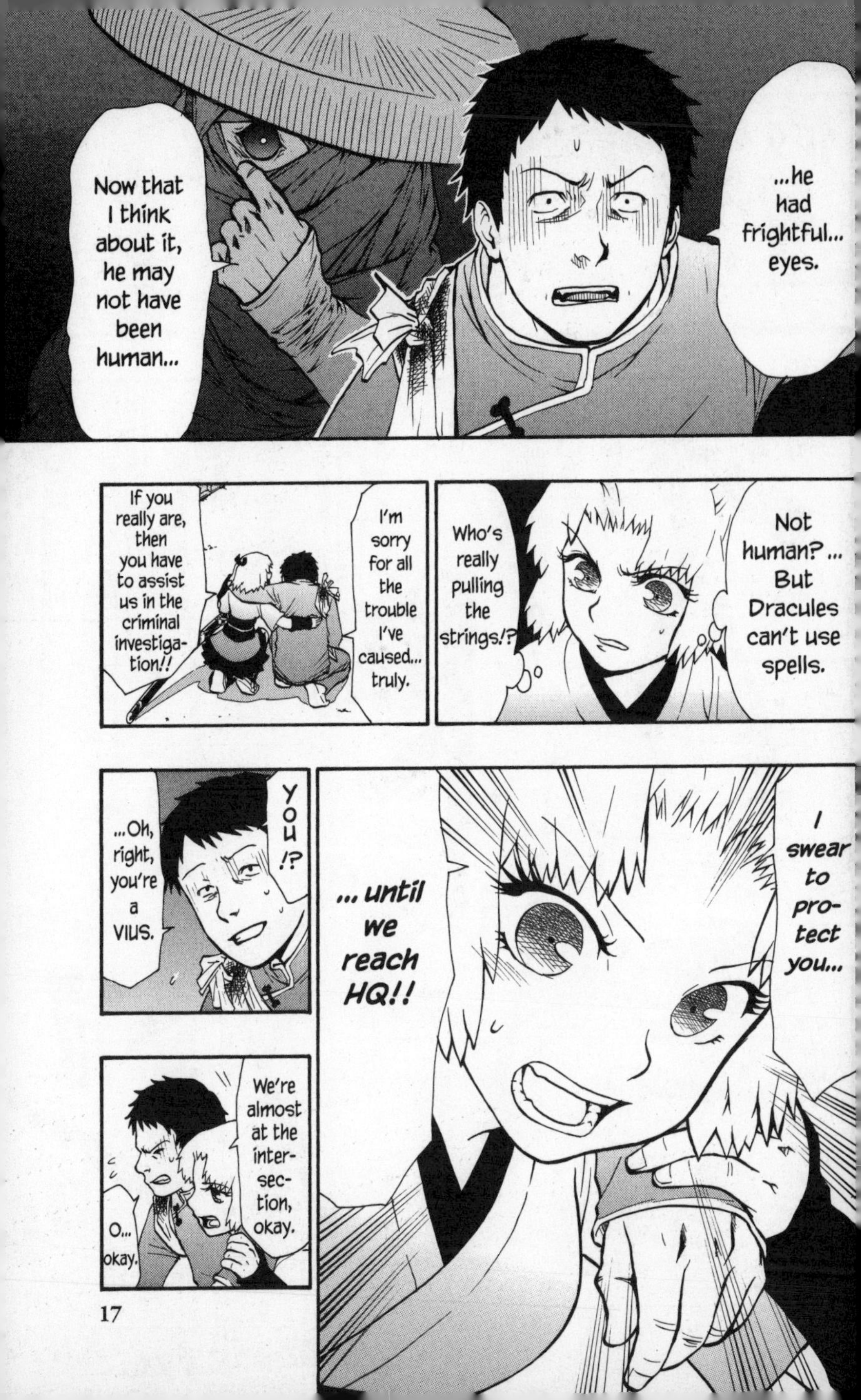
...he had frightful... eyes.
Now that I think about it, he may not have been human...
Not human? ... But Dracules can't use spells.
Who's really pulling the strings!?
I'm sorry for all the trouble I've caused... truly.
If you really are, then you have to assist us in the criminal investigation!!
I swear to protect you...
... until we reach HQ!!
You!?
...Oh, right, you're a Vius.
We're almost at the intersection, okay.
O... okay.

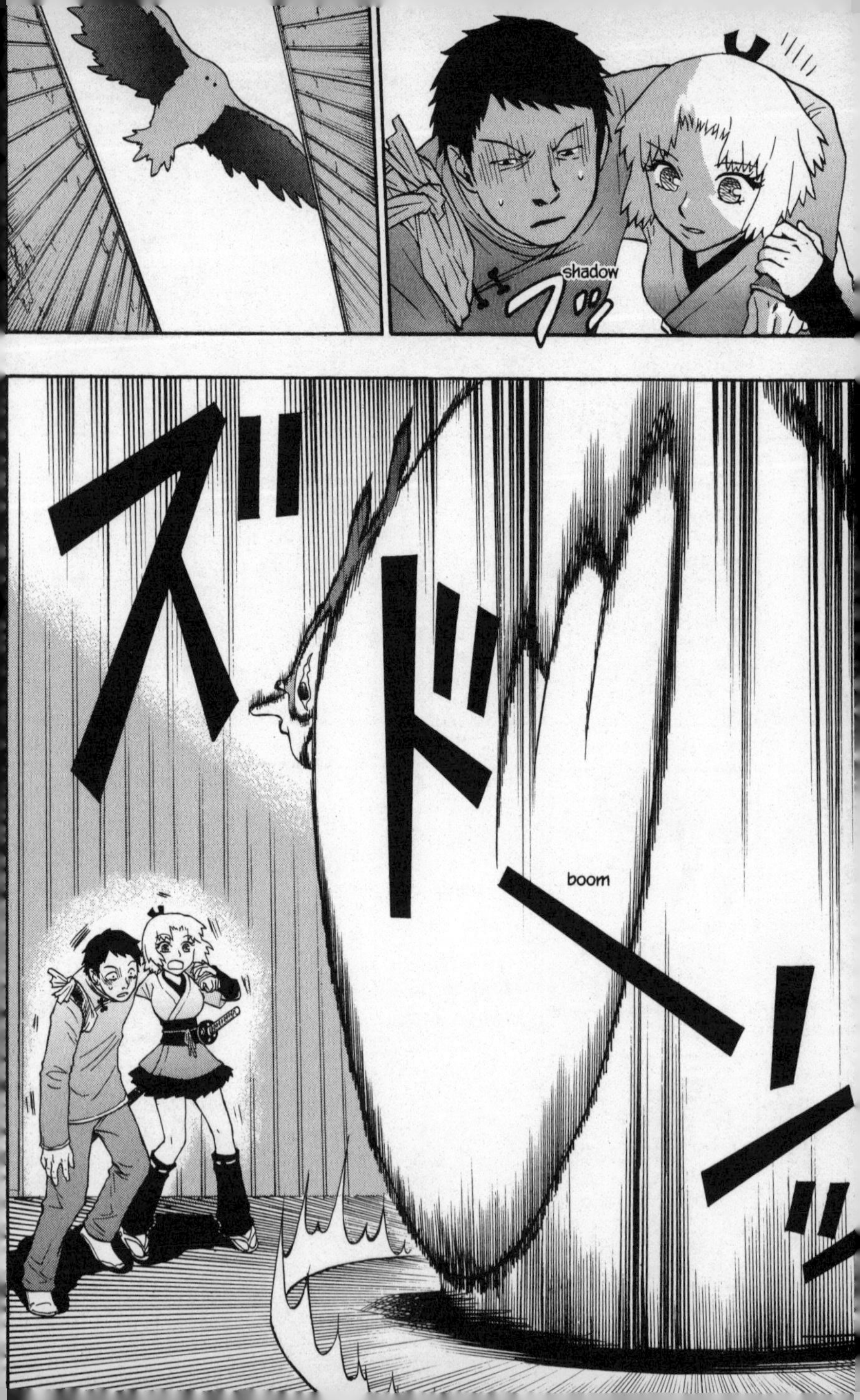
フッ
shadow
ズドーン
boom

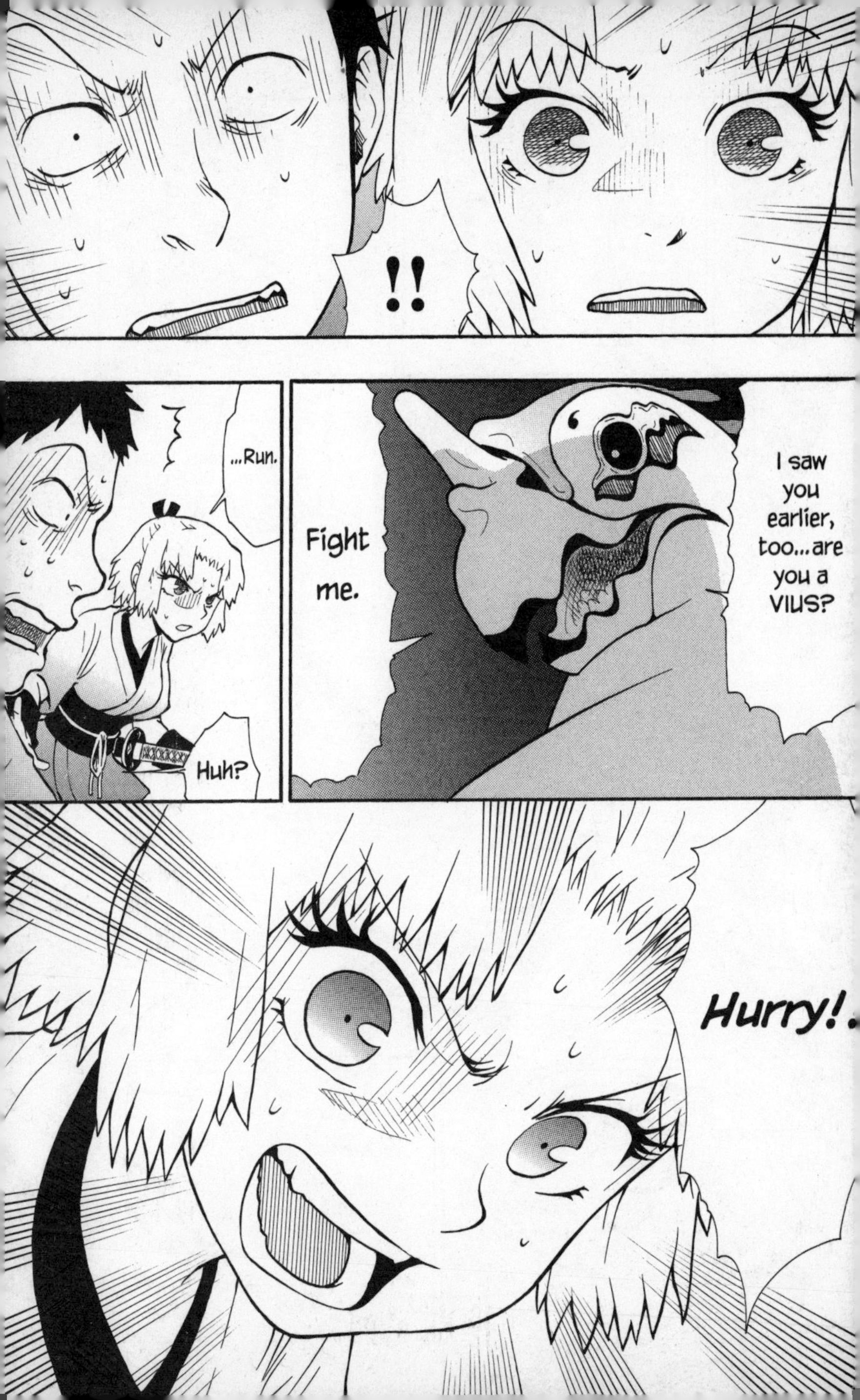
!!
I saw you earlier, too...are you a VIUS?
Fight me.
...Run.
Huh?
Hurry!.

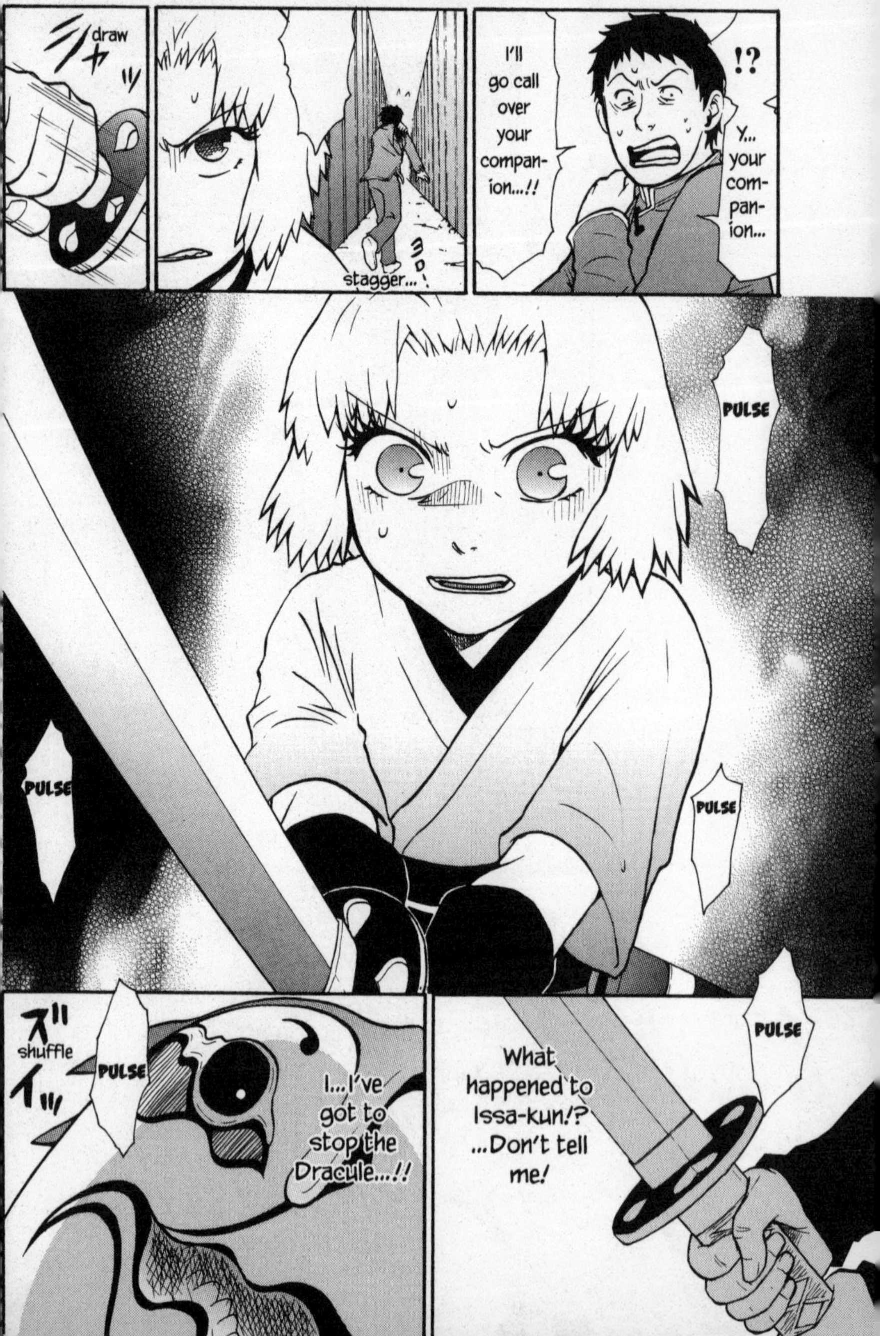
!?
Y... your com-pan-ion...
I'll go call over your compan-ion...!!
stagger...
draw
PULSE
PULSE
PULSE
PULSE
What happened to Issa-kun!? ...Don't tell me!
I...I've got to stop the Dracule...!!
PULSE
shuffle

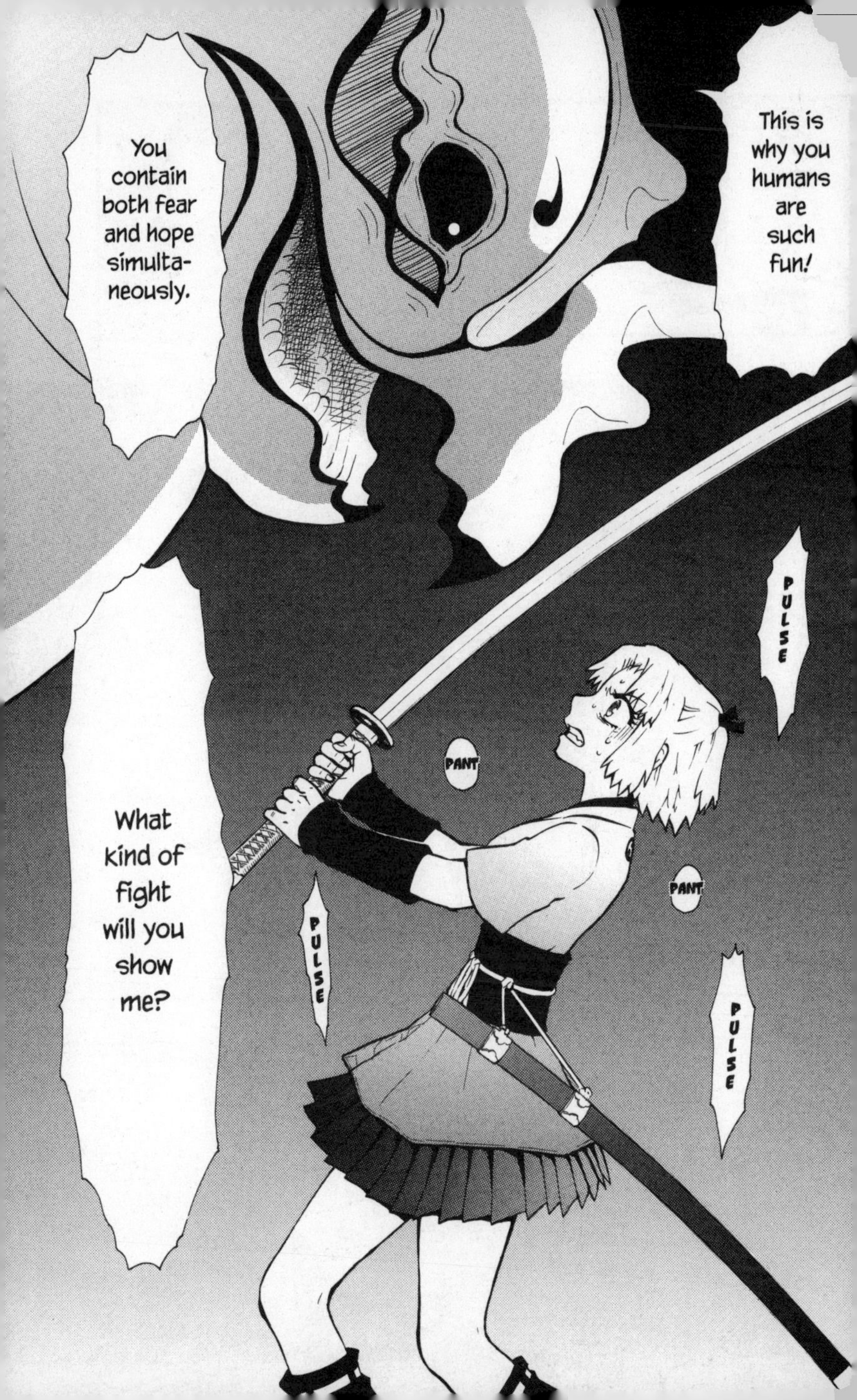
This is why you humans are such fun!
You contain both fear and hope simultaneously.
PULSE
PANT
PANT
PULSE
PULSE
What kind of fight will you show me?

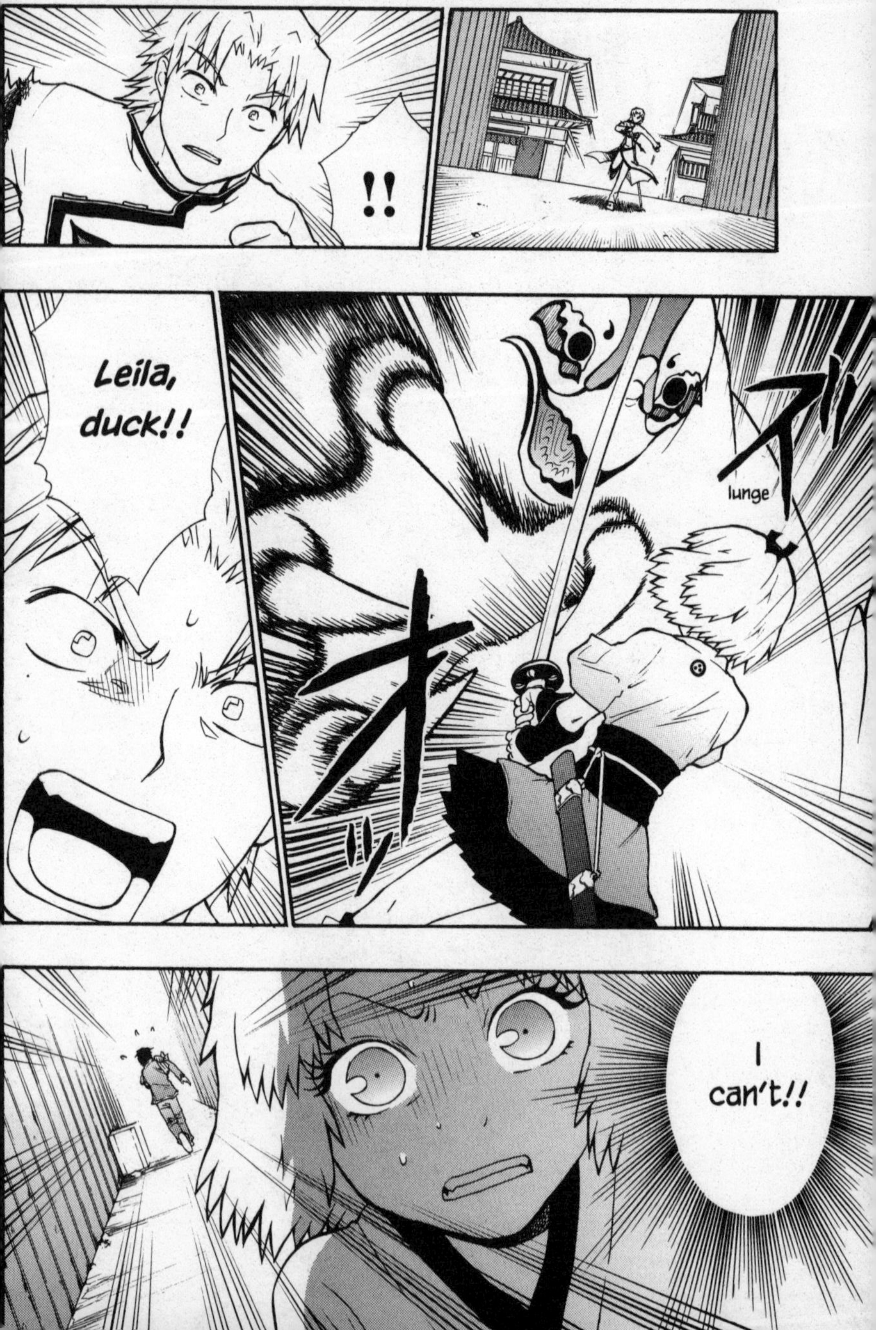
!!
lunge
Leila, duck!!
I can't!!

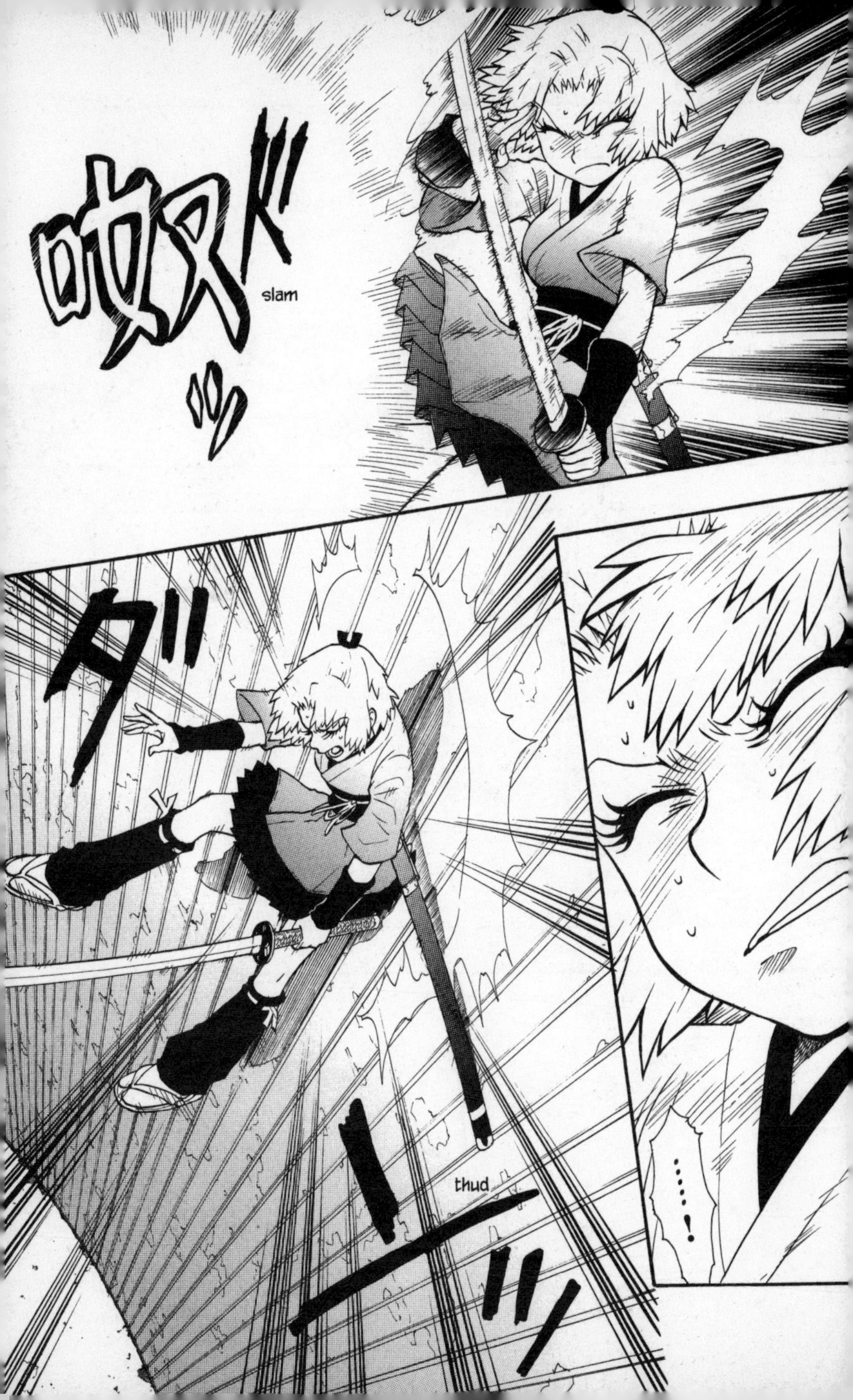
slam
......!
thud

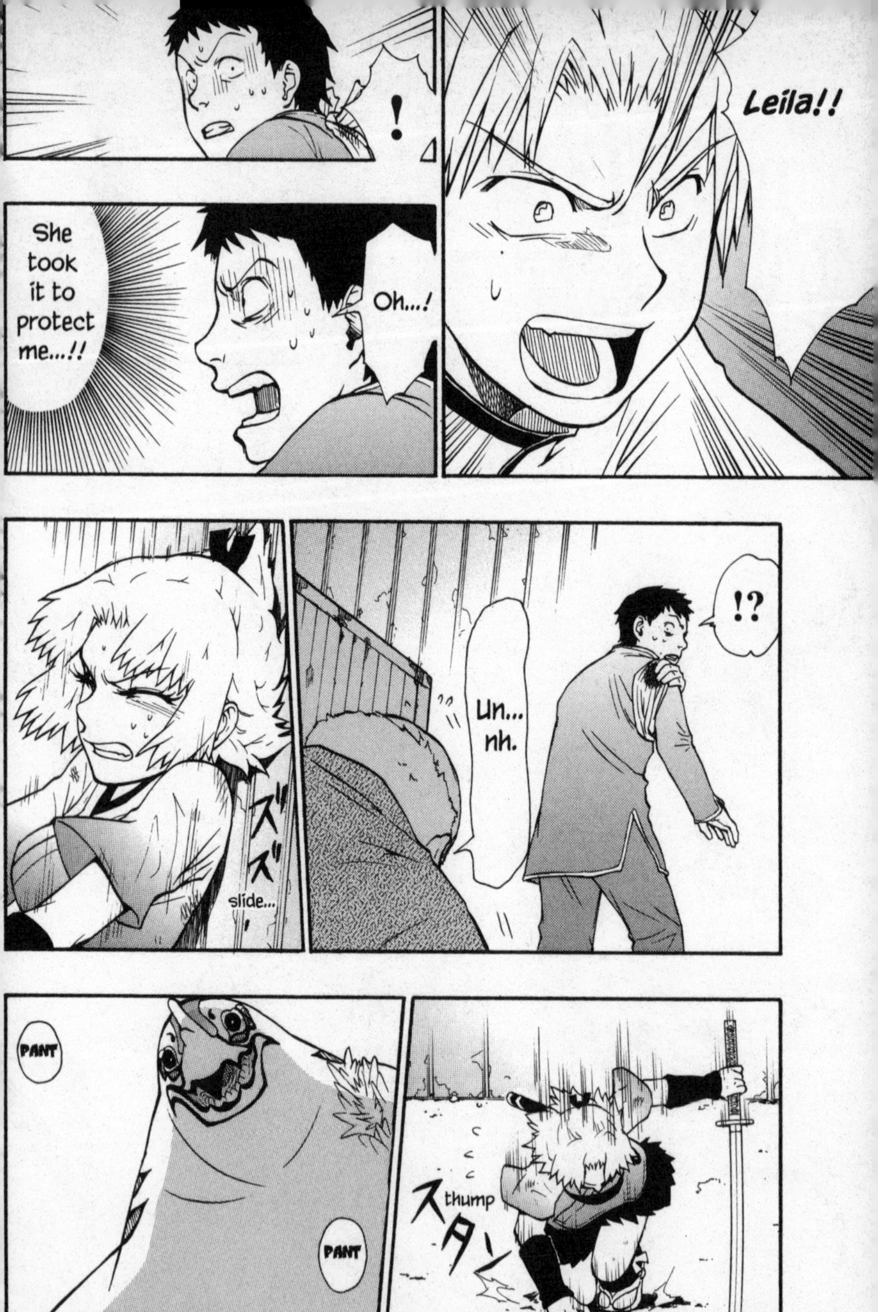
Leila!!
!
Oh...!
She took it to protect me...!!
!?
Un... nh.
ズズ
slide...
スタン
thump
PANT
PANT

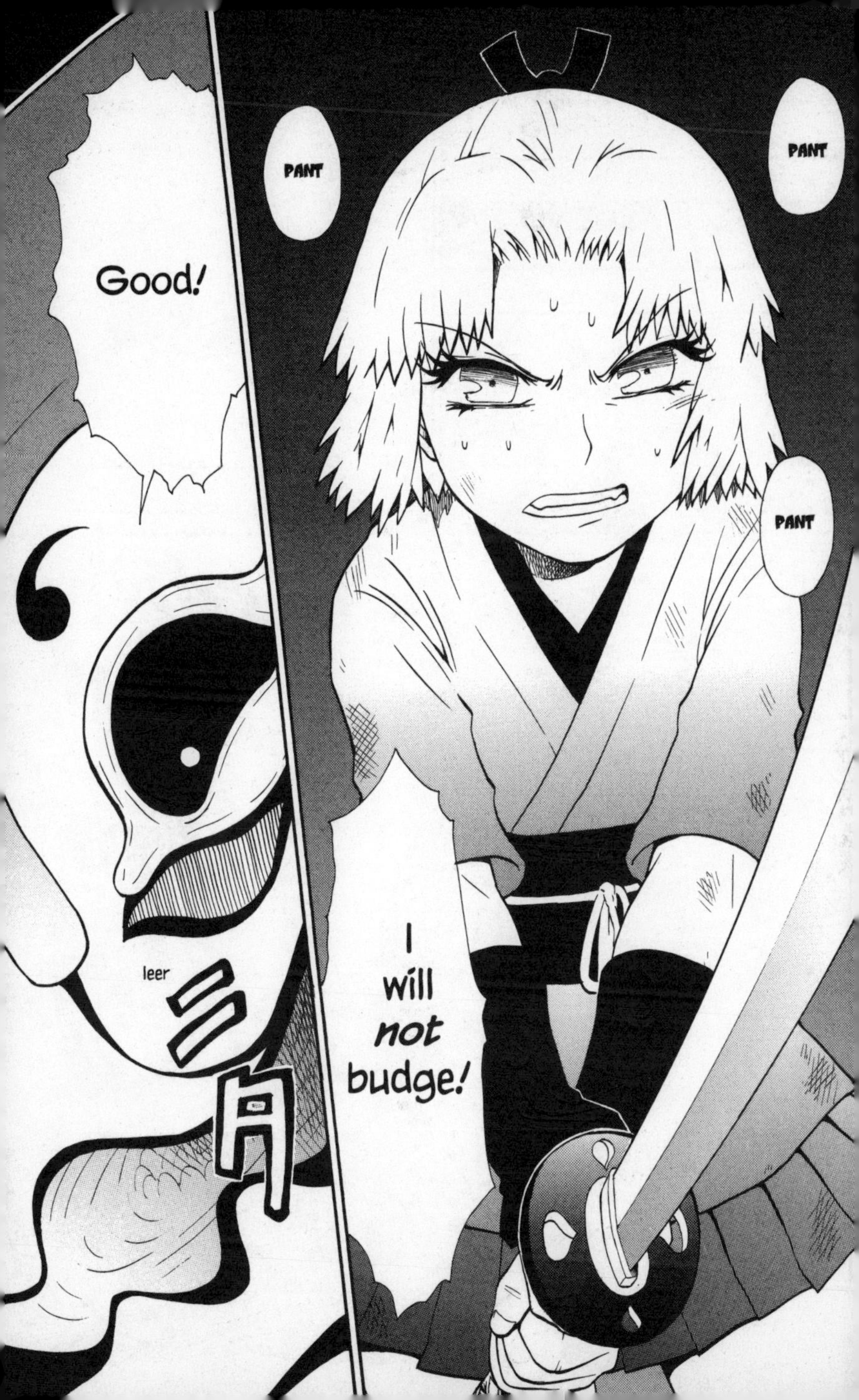

PANT
PANT
PANT
I will *not* budge!
Good!
leer

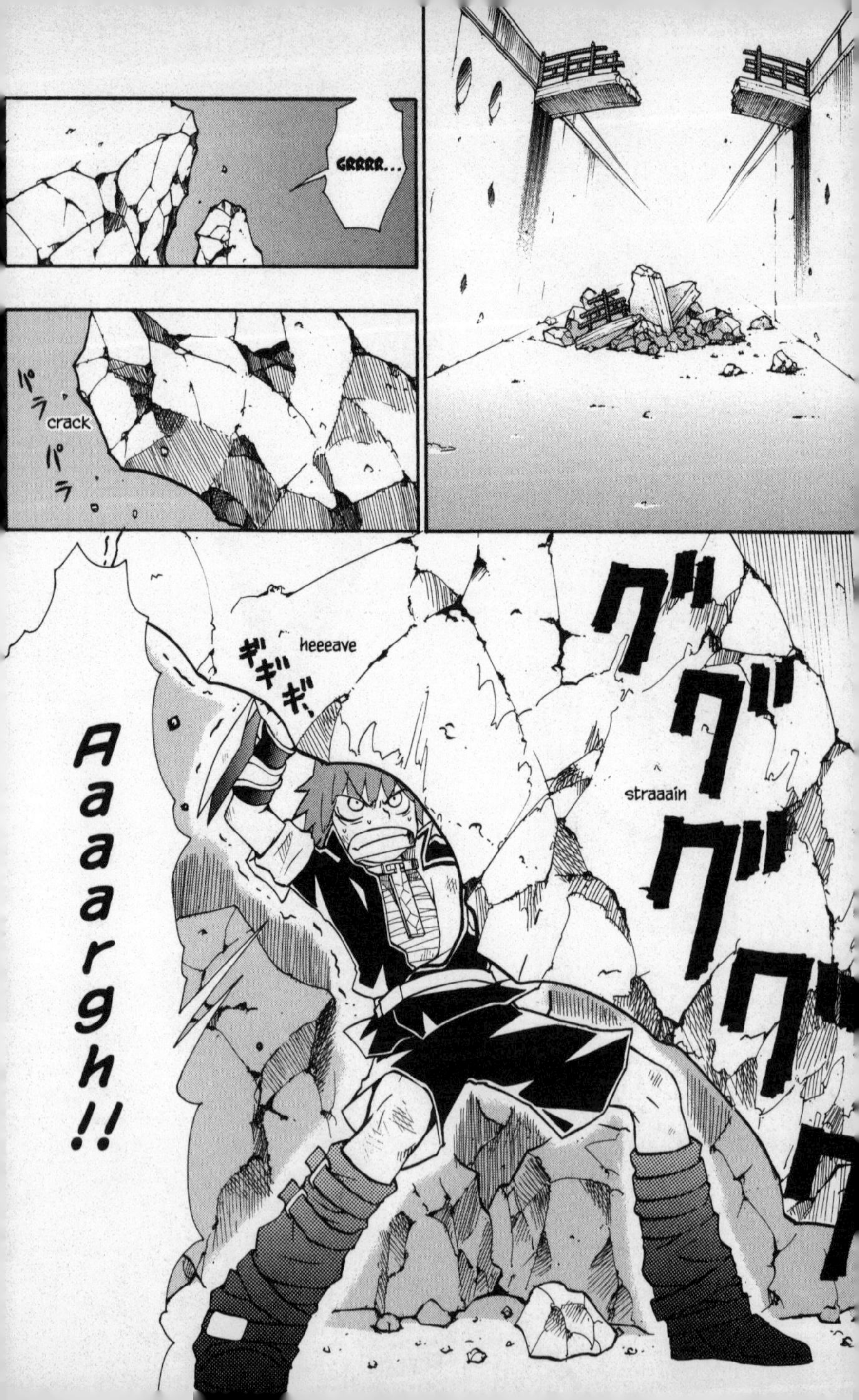
GRRRR...
パラ
crack
パラ
グググ
straaain
ギギギ
heeeave
Aaaargh!!

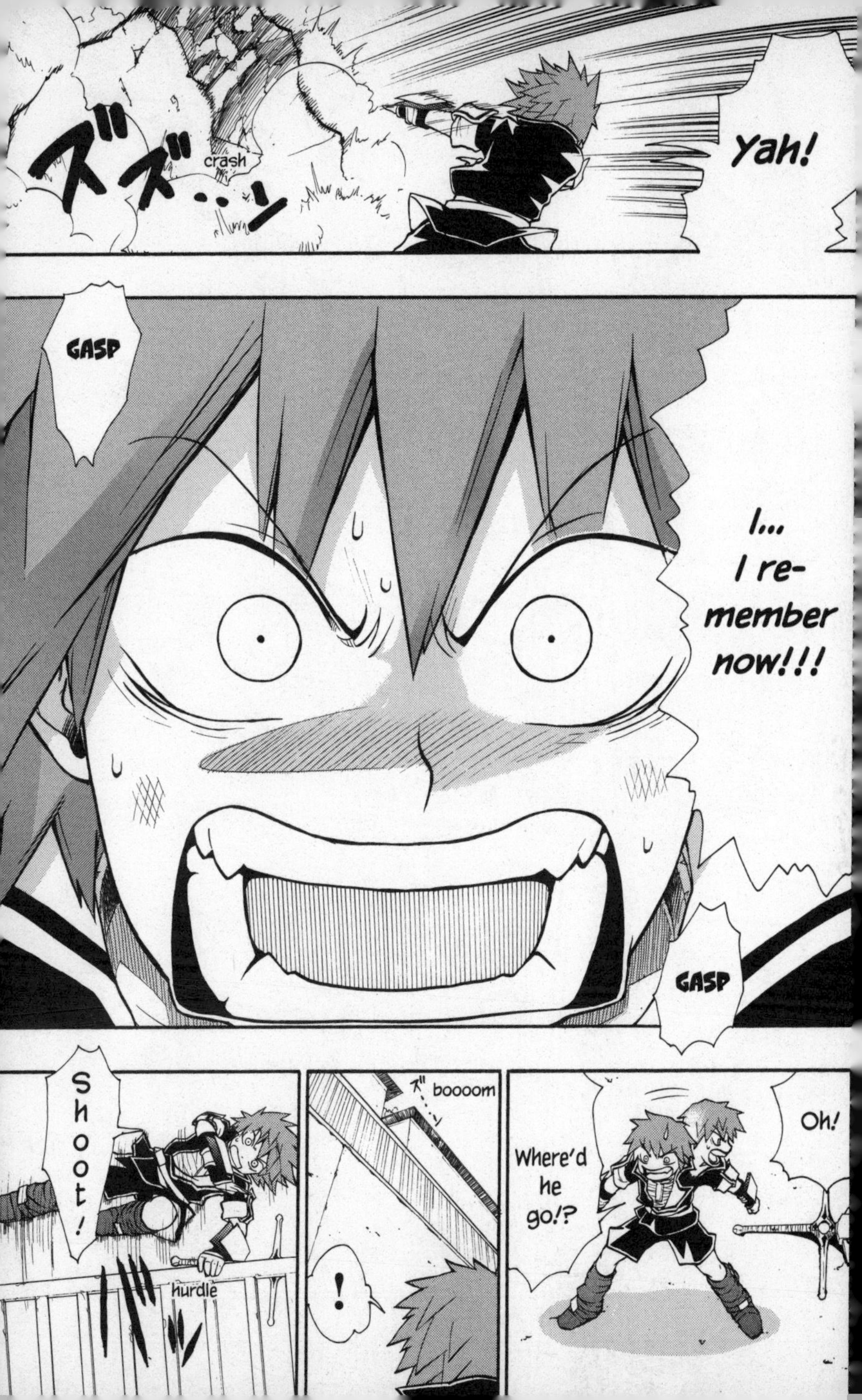
Yah!
ズズ…ン
crash
I... I re-member now!!!
GASP
GASP
Oh!
Where'd he go!?
ズ…ン
booom
!
Shoot!
hurdle

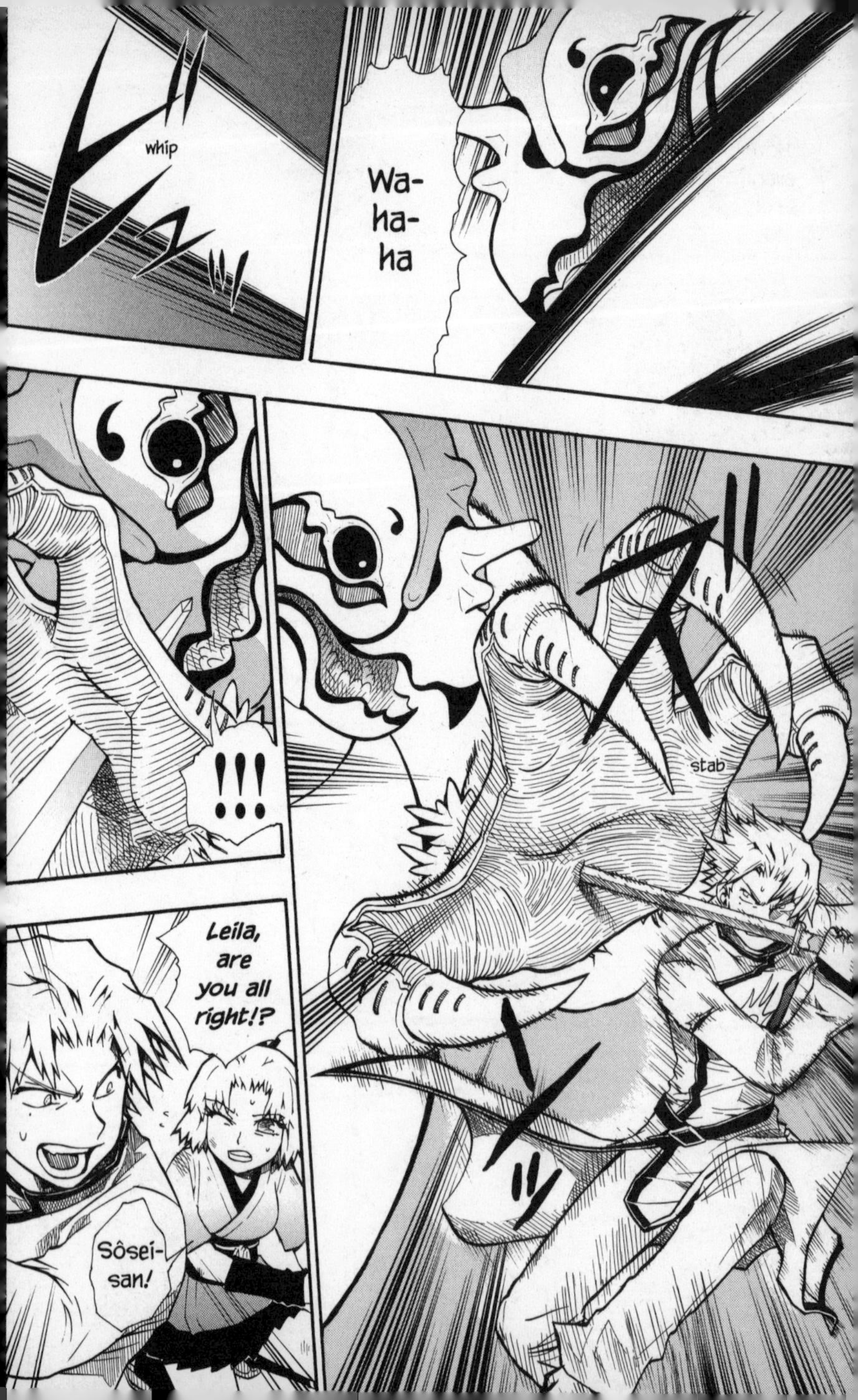
Wa-
ha-
ha
whip
stab
!!!
Leila, are you all right!?
Sôsei-san!

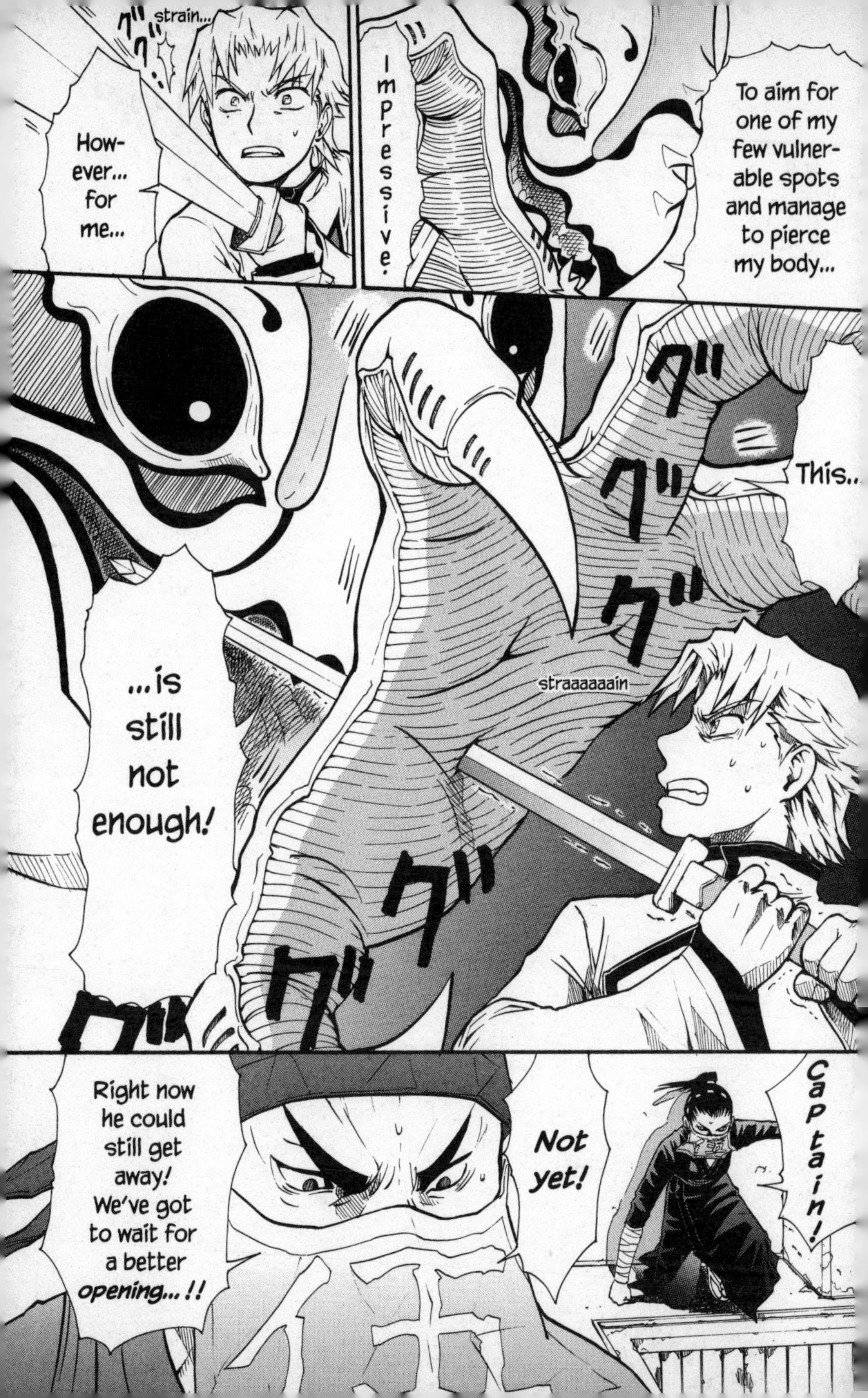
To aim for one of my few vulner-able spots and manage to pierce my body...
Impressive.
strain...
How-ever... for me...
This...
...is still not enough!
straaaaaain
Captain!
Not yet!
Right now he could still get away! We've got to wait for a better opening...!!

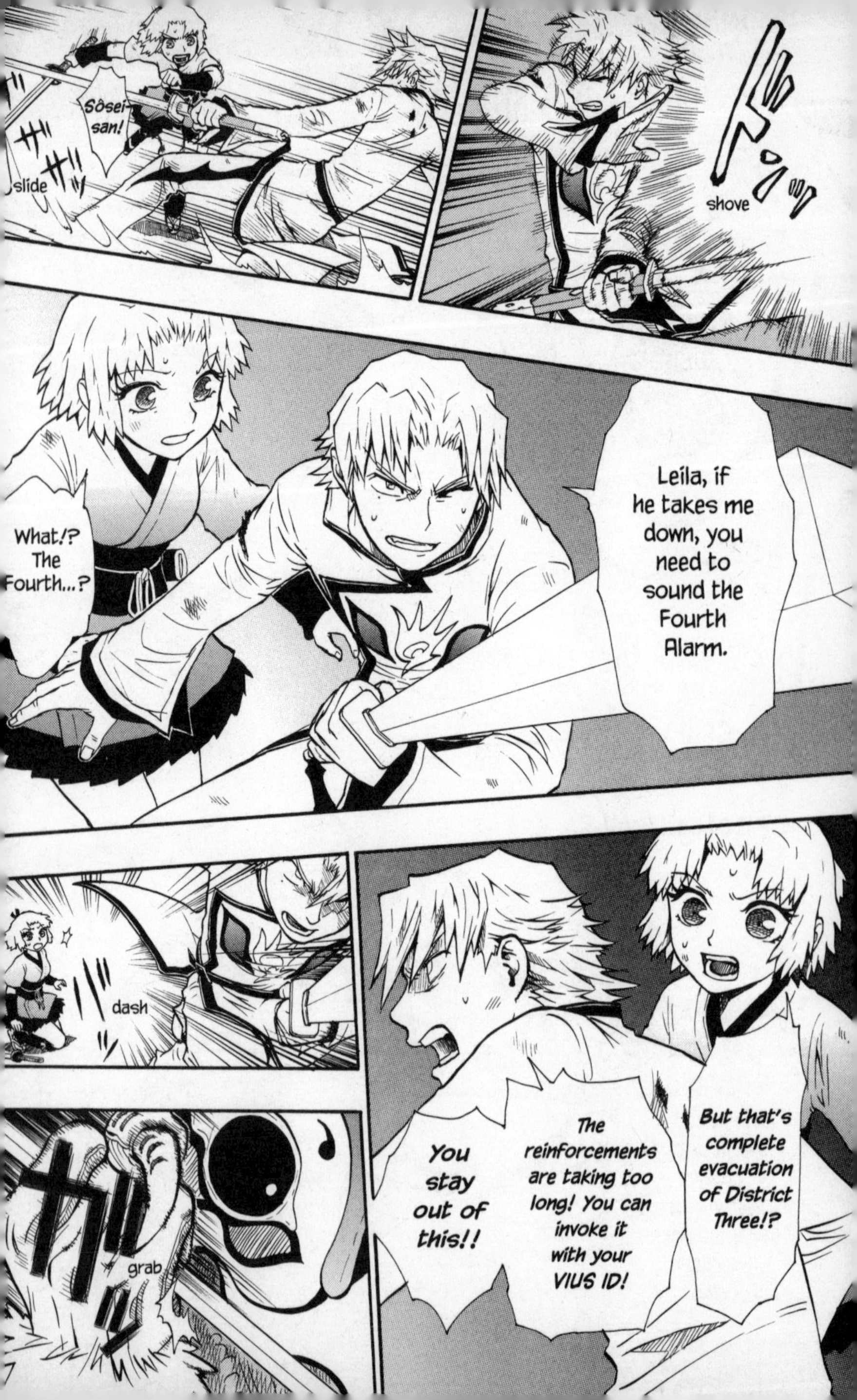
shove
Sôsei-san!
slide
Leila, if he takes me down, you need to sound the Fourth Alarm.
What!? The Fourth...?
But that's complete evacuation of District Three!?
The reinforcements are taking too long! You can invoke it with your VIUS ID!
You stay out of this!!
dash
grab

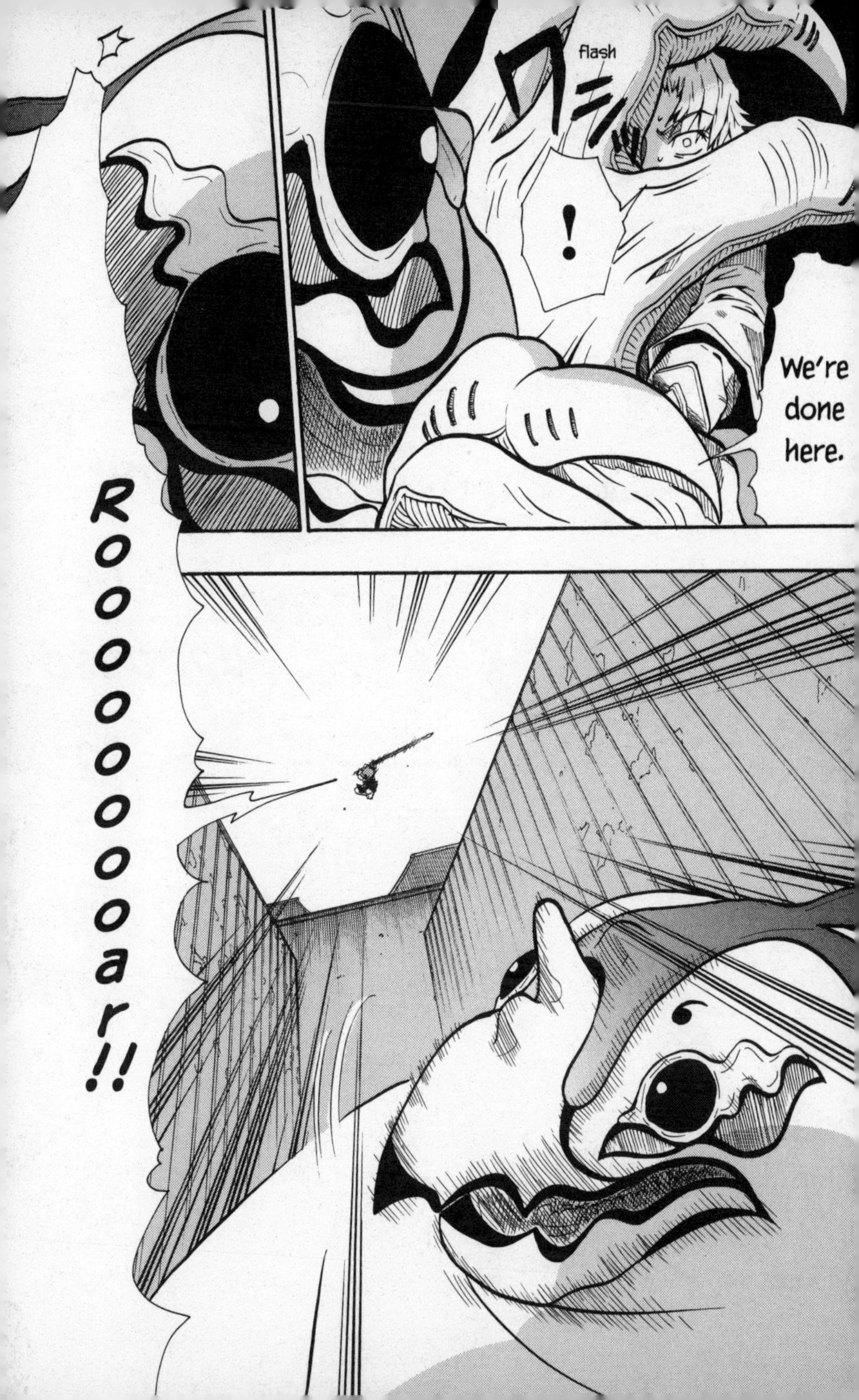

flash
!
We're done here.
Roooooooooar!!

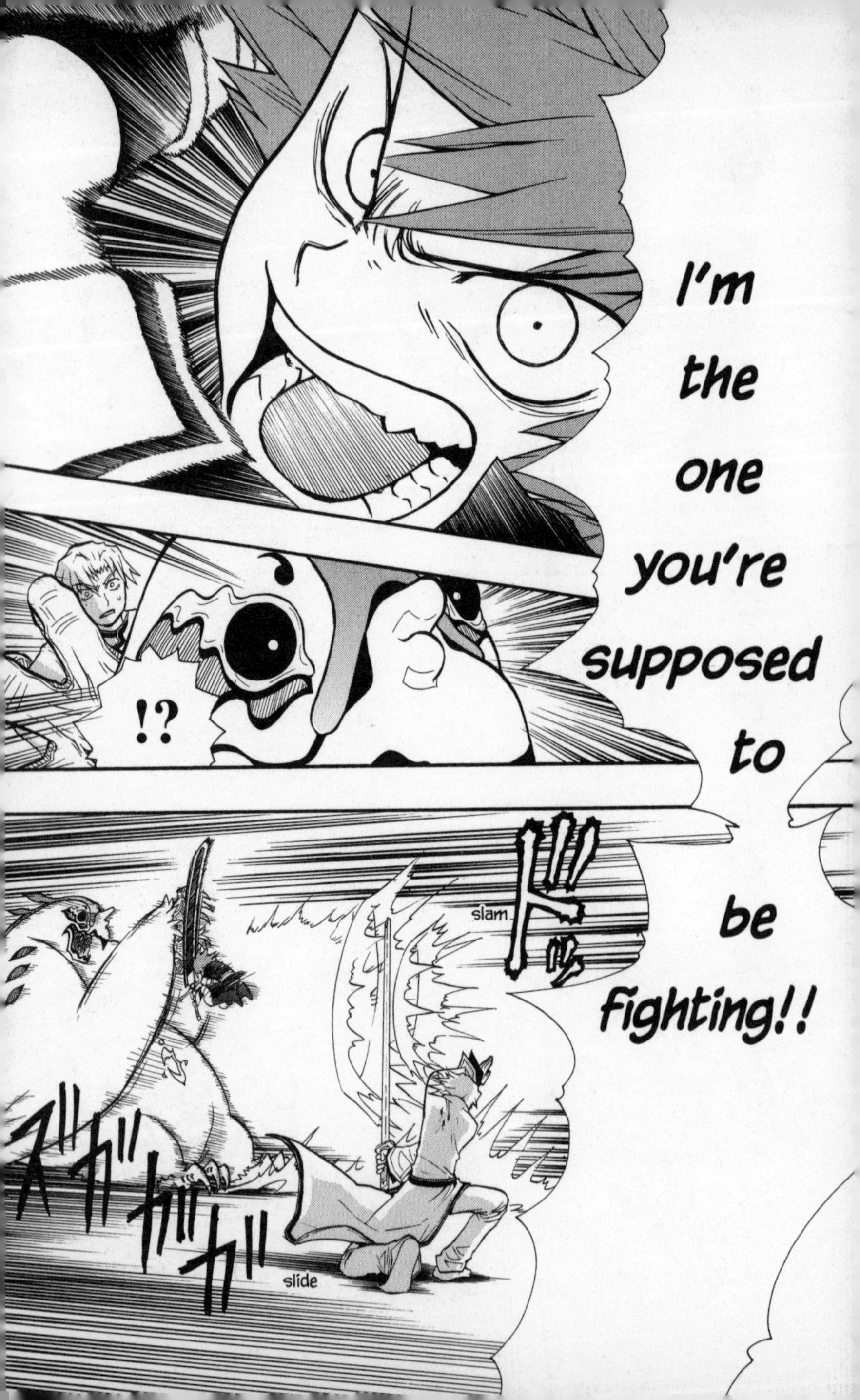
I'm the one you're supposed to be fighting!!
!?
slam
slide

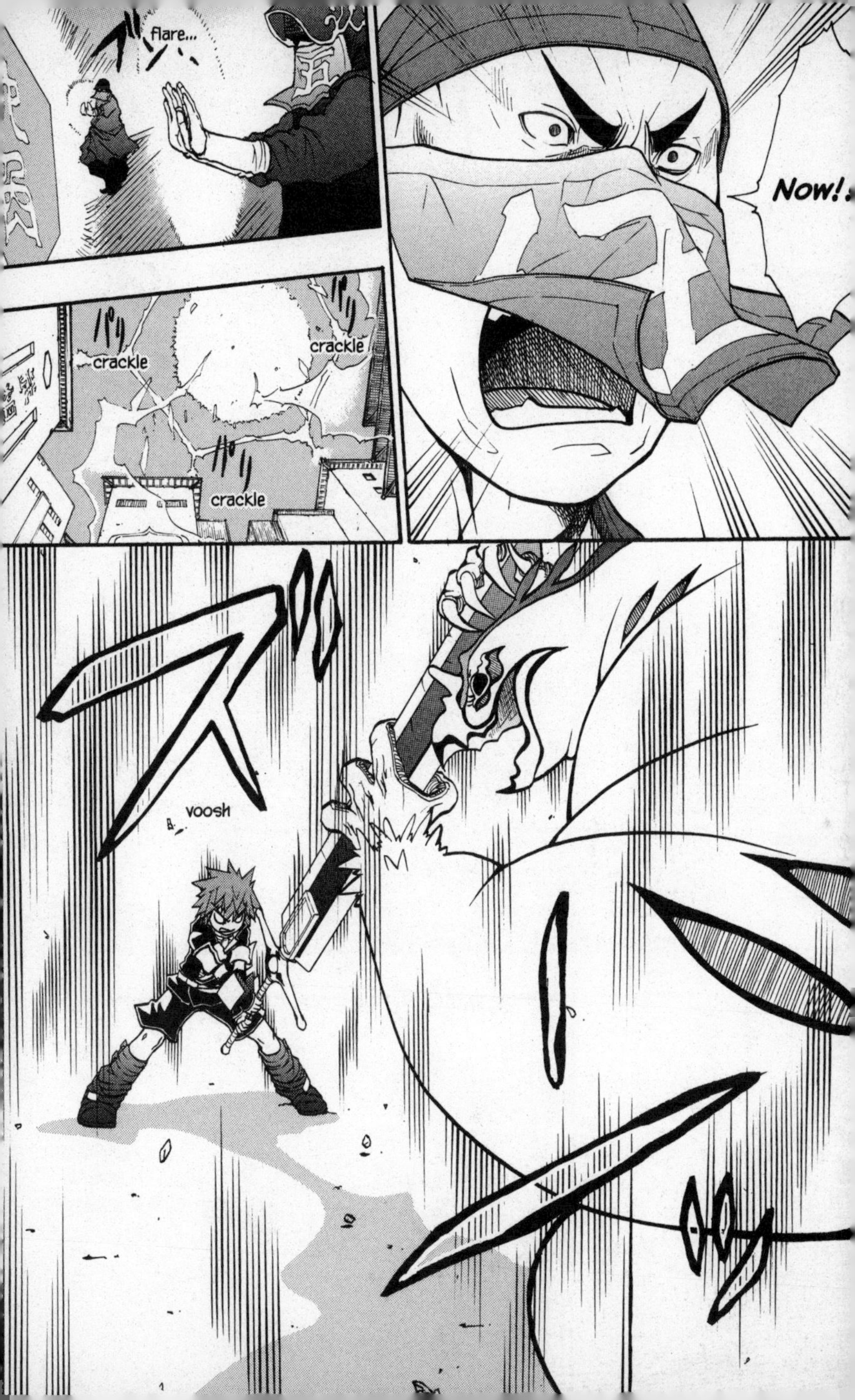
Now!
flare...
crackle
crackle
crackle
voosh

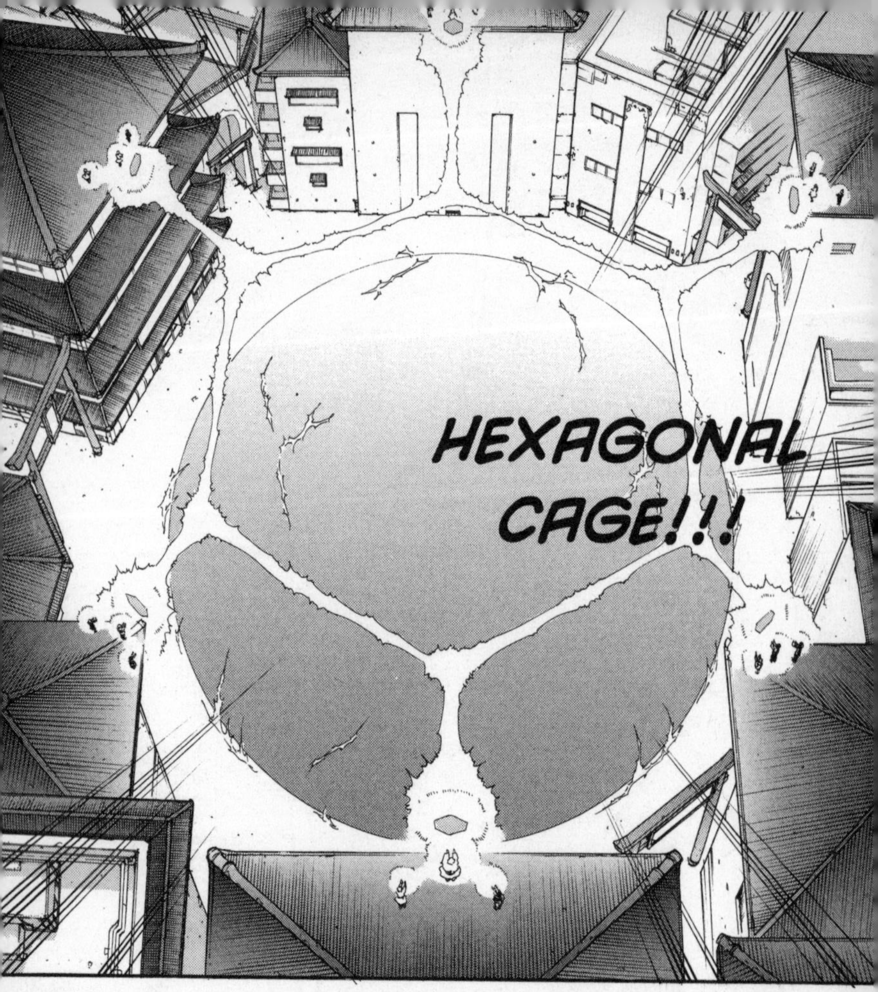
HEXAGONAL CAGE!!!

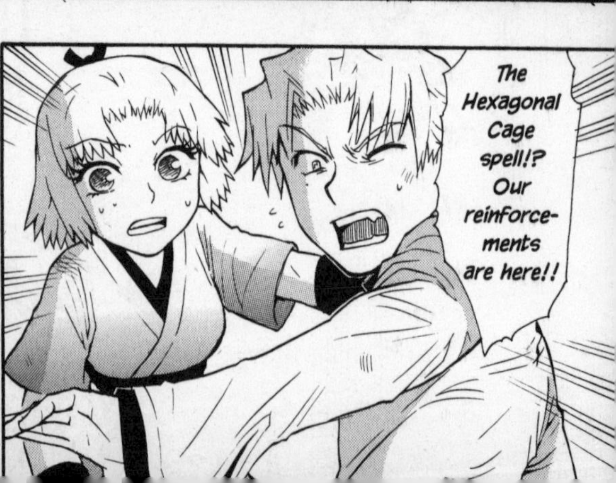
The Hexagonal Cage spell!? Our reinforcements are here!!

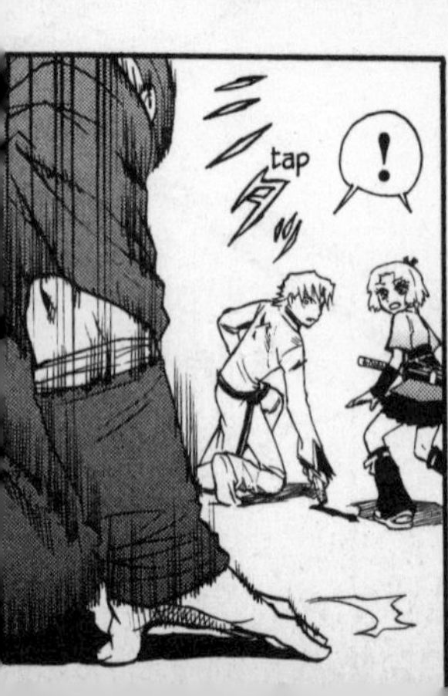
!
tap

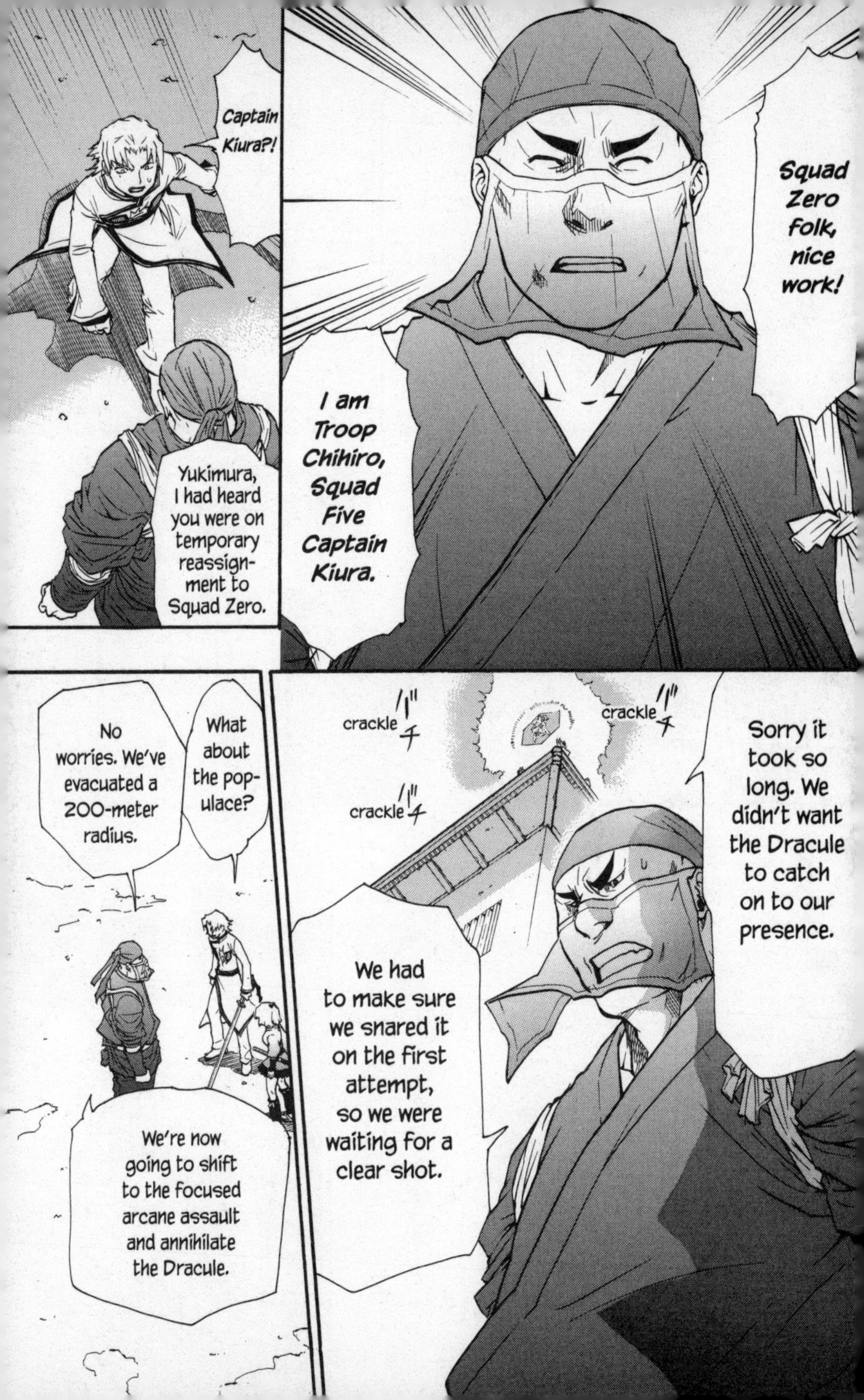
Squad Zero folk, nice work!
I am Troop Chihiro, Squad Five Captain Kiura.
Captain Kiura?!
Yukimura, I had heard you were on temporary reassignment to Squad Zero.
crackle
crackle
crackle
Sorry it took so long. We didn't want the Dracule to catch on to our presence.
We had to make sure we snared it on the first attempt, so we were waiting for a clear shot.
What about the populace?
No worries. We've evacuated a 200-meter radius.
We're now going to shift to the focused arcane assault and annihilate the Dracule.

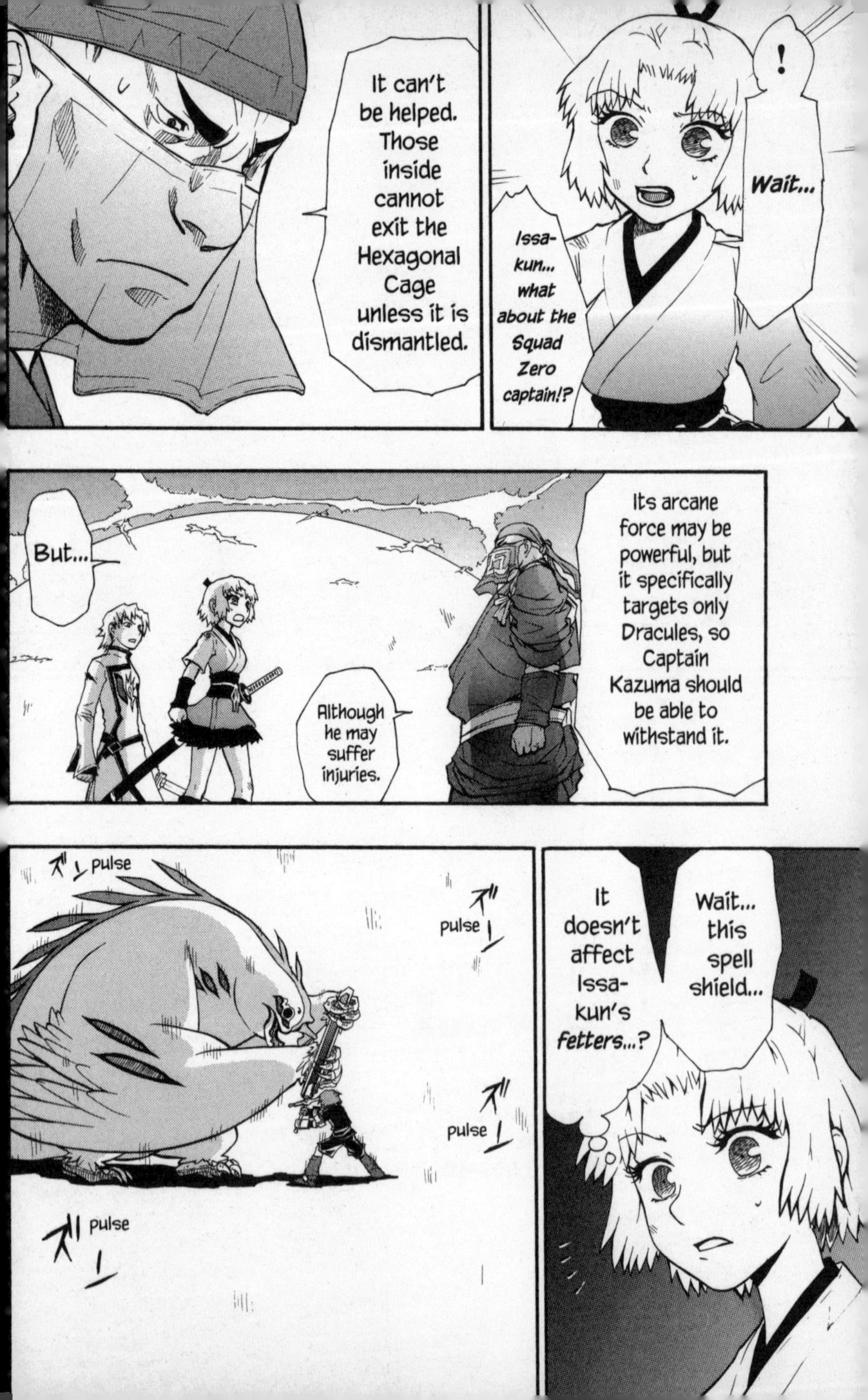
!
Wait...
Issa-kun... what about the Squad Zero captain!?
It can't be helped. Those inside cannot exit the Hexagonal Cage unless it is dismantled.
Its arcane force may be powerful, but it specifically targets only Dracules, so Captain Kazuma should be able to withstand it.
Although he may suffer injuries.
But...
Wait... this spell shield...
It doesn't affect Issa-kun's fetters...?
pulse
pulse
pulse
pulse

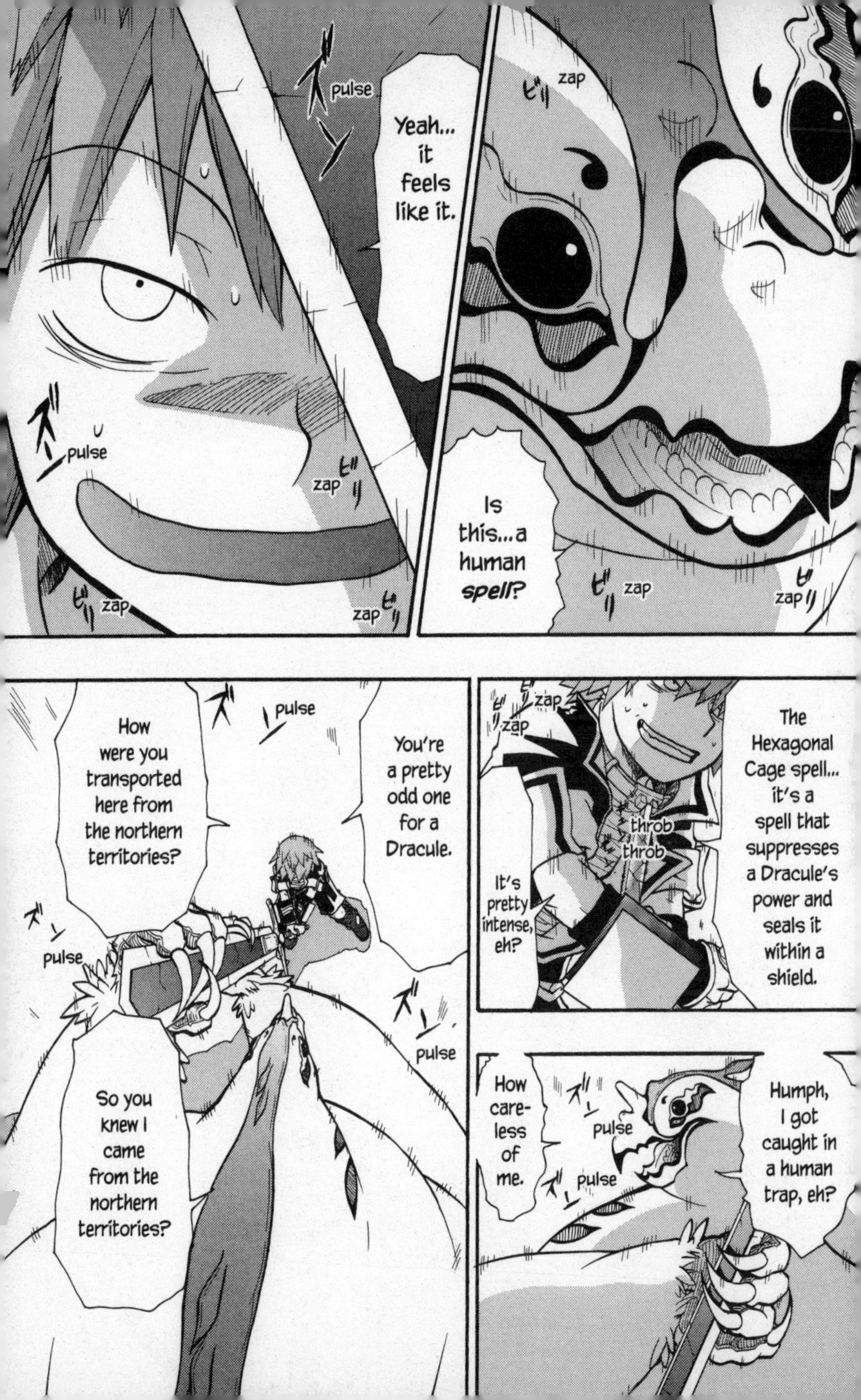

zap
Is this...a human spell?
zap
zap
pulse
Yeah... it feels like it.
pulse
zap
zap
zap
zap
zap
The Hexagonal Cage spell... it's a spell that suppresses a Dracule's power and seals it within a shield.
throb
throb
It's pretty intense, eh?
Humph, I got caught in a human trap, eh?
pulse
How careless of me.
pulse
pulse
You're a pretty odd one for a Dracule.
How were you transported here from the northern territories?
pulse
pulse
So you knew I came from the northern territories?

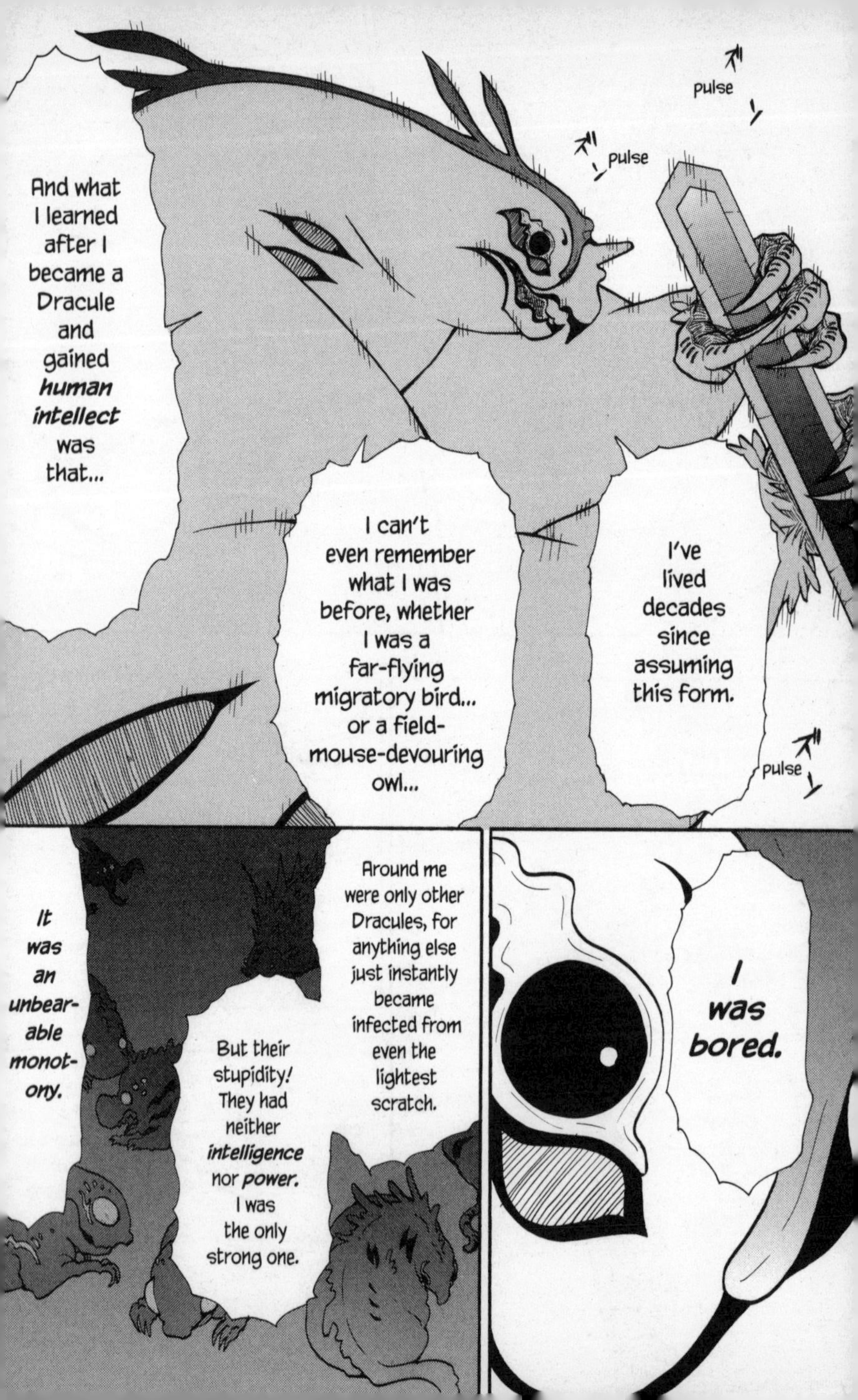
pulse
pulse
I've lived decades since assuming this form.
pulse
I can't even remember what I was before, whether I was a far-flying migratory bird... or a field-mouse-devouring owl...
And what I learned after I became a Dracule and gained **human intellect** was that...
I was bored.
Around me were only other Dracules, for anything else just instantly became infected from even the lightest scratch.
But their stupidity! They had neither ***intelligence*** nor ***power.*** I was the only strong one.
It was an unbearable monotony.

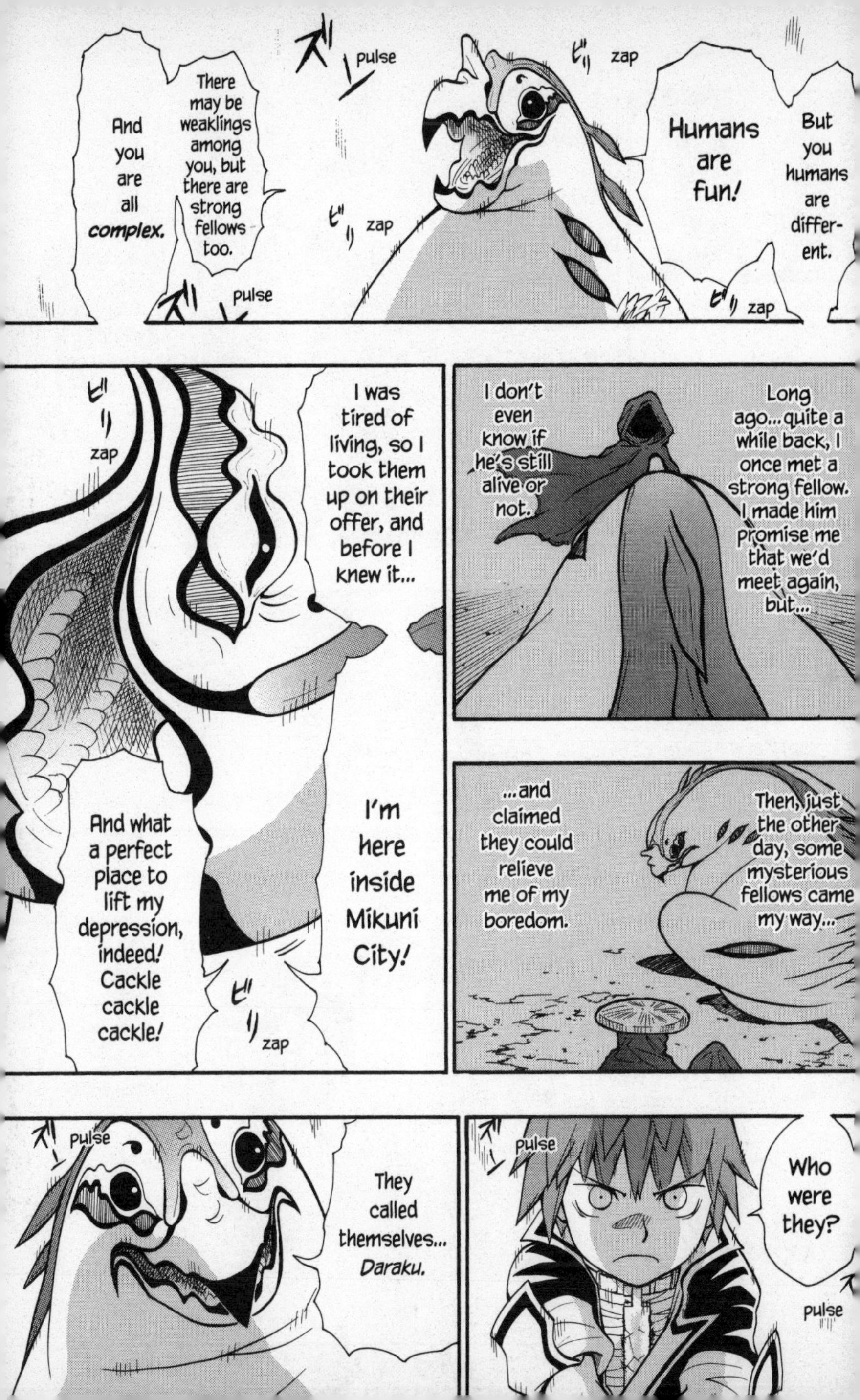
zap
But you humans are different.
Humans are fun!
zap
pulse
zap
There may be weaklings among you, but there are strong fellows too.
And you are all *complex.*
pulse
Long ago...quite a while back, I once met a strong fellow. I made him promise me that we'd meet again, but...
I don't even know if he's still alive or not.
Then, just the other day, some mysterious fellows came my way...
...and claimed they could relieve me of my boredom.
I was tired of living, so I took them up on their offer, and before I knew it...
zap
I'm here inside Mikuni City!
And what a perfect place to lift my depression, indeed! Cackle cackle cackle!
zap
Who were they?
pulse
pulse
They called themselves... *Daraku.*
pulse

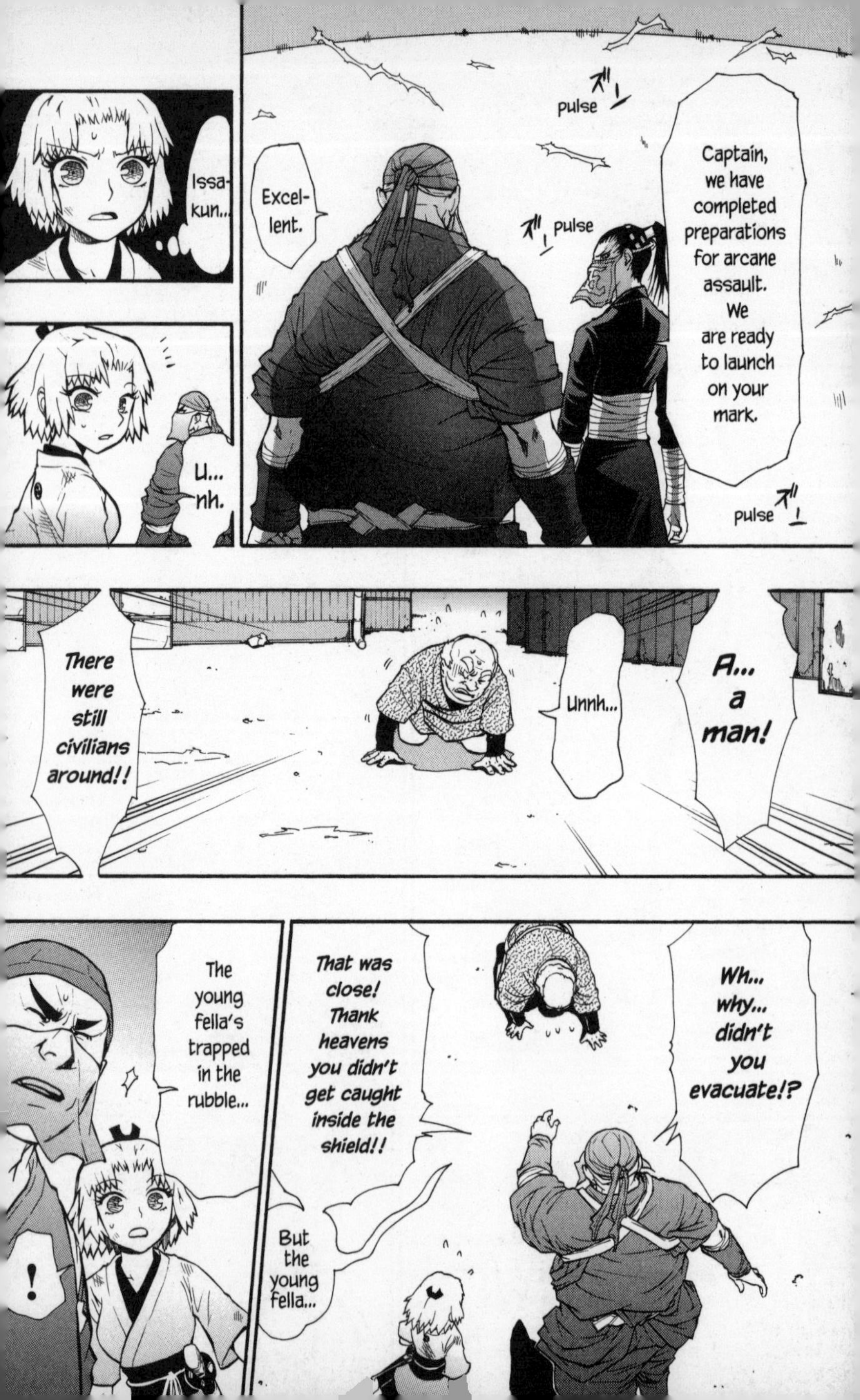

pulse
Captain, we have completed preparations for arcane assault. We are ready to launch on your mark.
pulse
Excel-lent.
pulse
Issa-kun...
U... nh.
A... a man!
Unnh...
There were still civilians around!!
Wh... why... didn't you evacuate!?
That was close! Thank heavens you didn't get caught inside the shield!!
But the young fella...
The young fella's trapped in the rubble...
!

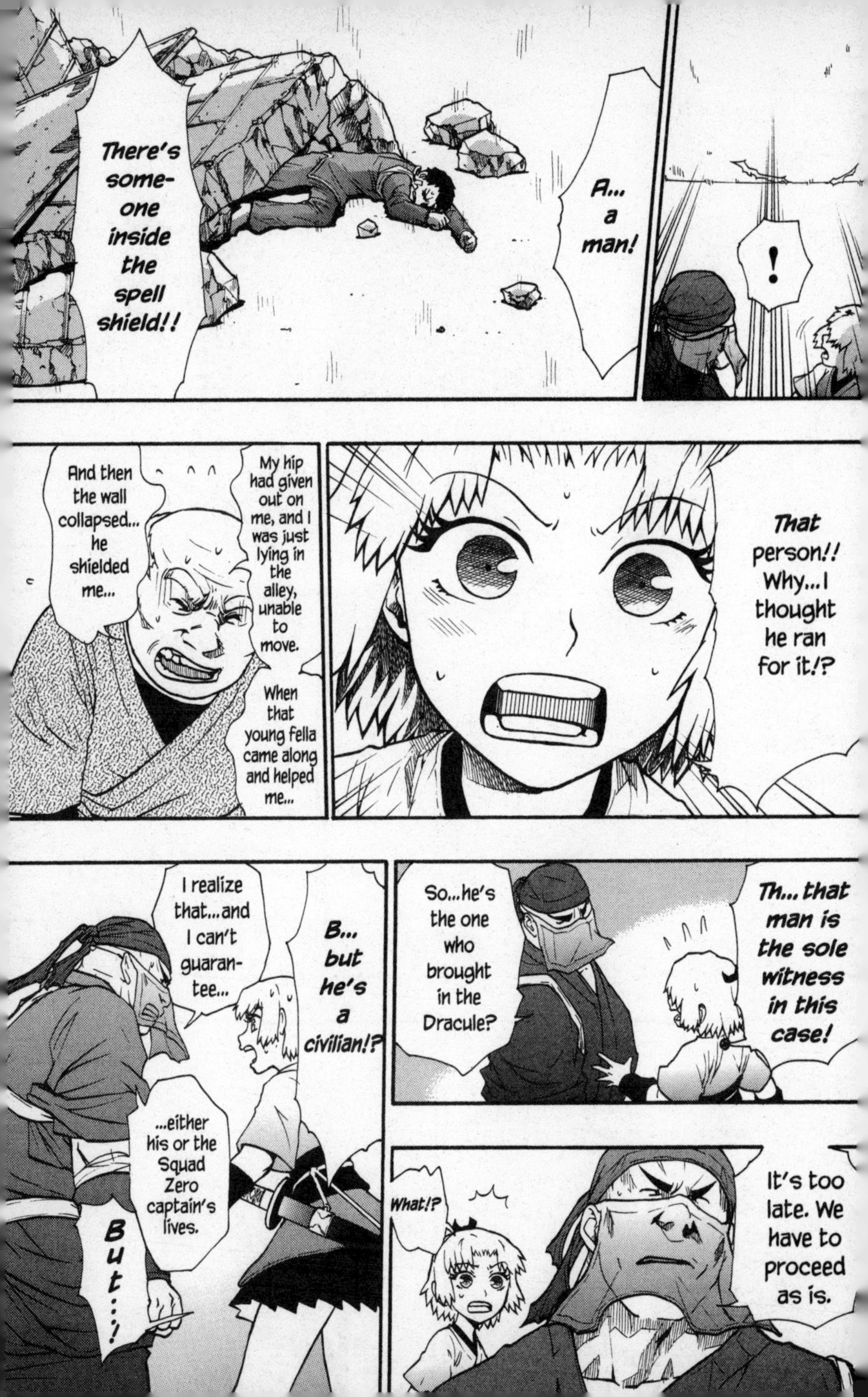
!
A... a man!
There's some-one inside the spell shield!!
That person!! Why...I thought he ran for it!?
My hip had given out on me, and I was just lying in the alley, unable to move.
When that young fella came along and helped me...
And then the wall collapsed... he shielded me...
Th... that man is the sole witness in this case!
So...he's the one who brought in the Dracule?
It's too late. We have to proceed as is.
What!?
B... but he's a civilian!?
I realize that...and I can't guaran-tee...
...either his or the Squad Zero captain's lives.
But...!

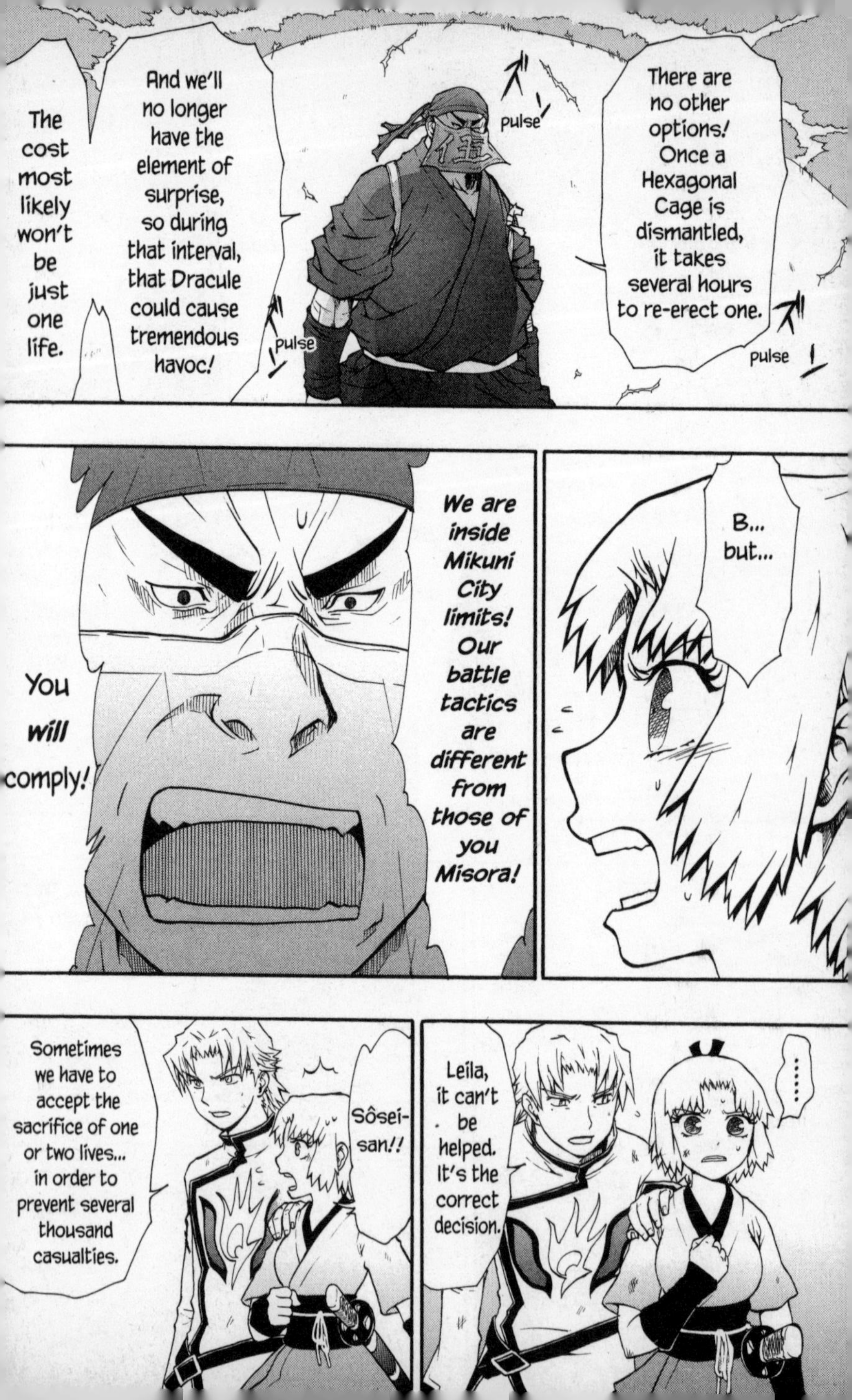
There are no other options! Once a Hexagonal Cage is dismantled, it takes several hours to re-erect one.
pulse
pulse
pulse
And we'll no longer have the element of surprise, so during that interval, that Dracule could cause tremendous havoc!
The cost most likely won't be just one life.
B... but...
We are inside Mikuni City limits! Our battle tactics are different from those of you Misora!
You will comply!
......
Leila, it can't be helped. It's the correct decision.
Sôsei-san!!
Sometimes we have to accept the sacrifice of one or two lives... in order to prevent several thousand casualties.

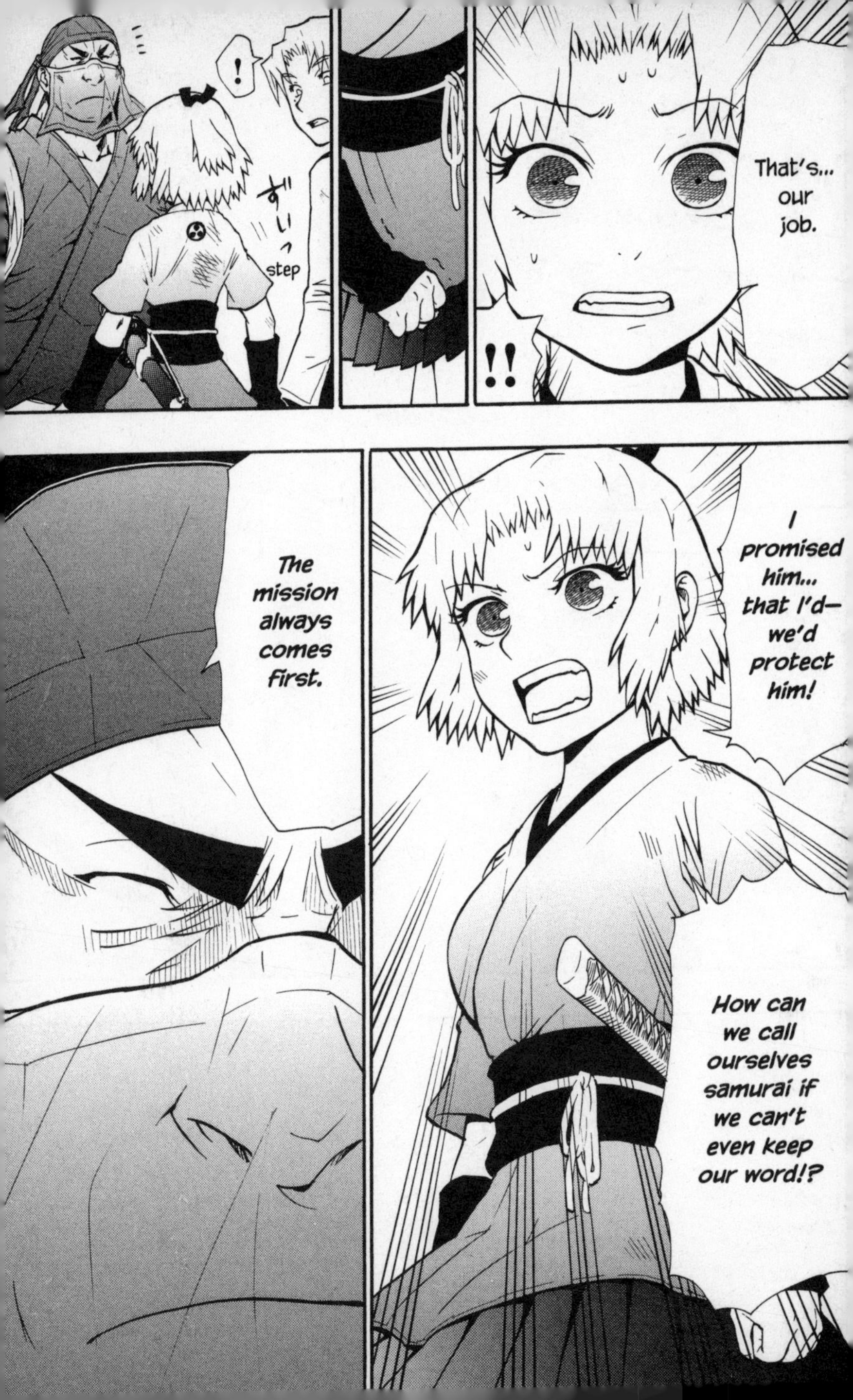
That's... our job.
!!
!
ずいっ
step
I promised him... that I'd— we'd protect him!
How can we call ourselves samurai if we can't even keep our word!?
The mission always comes first.

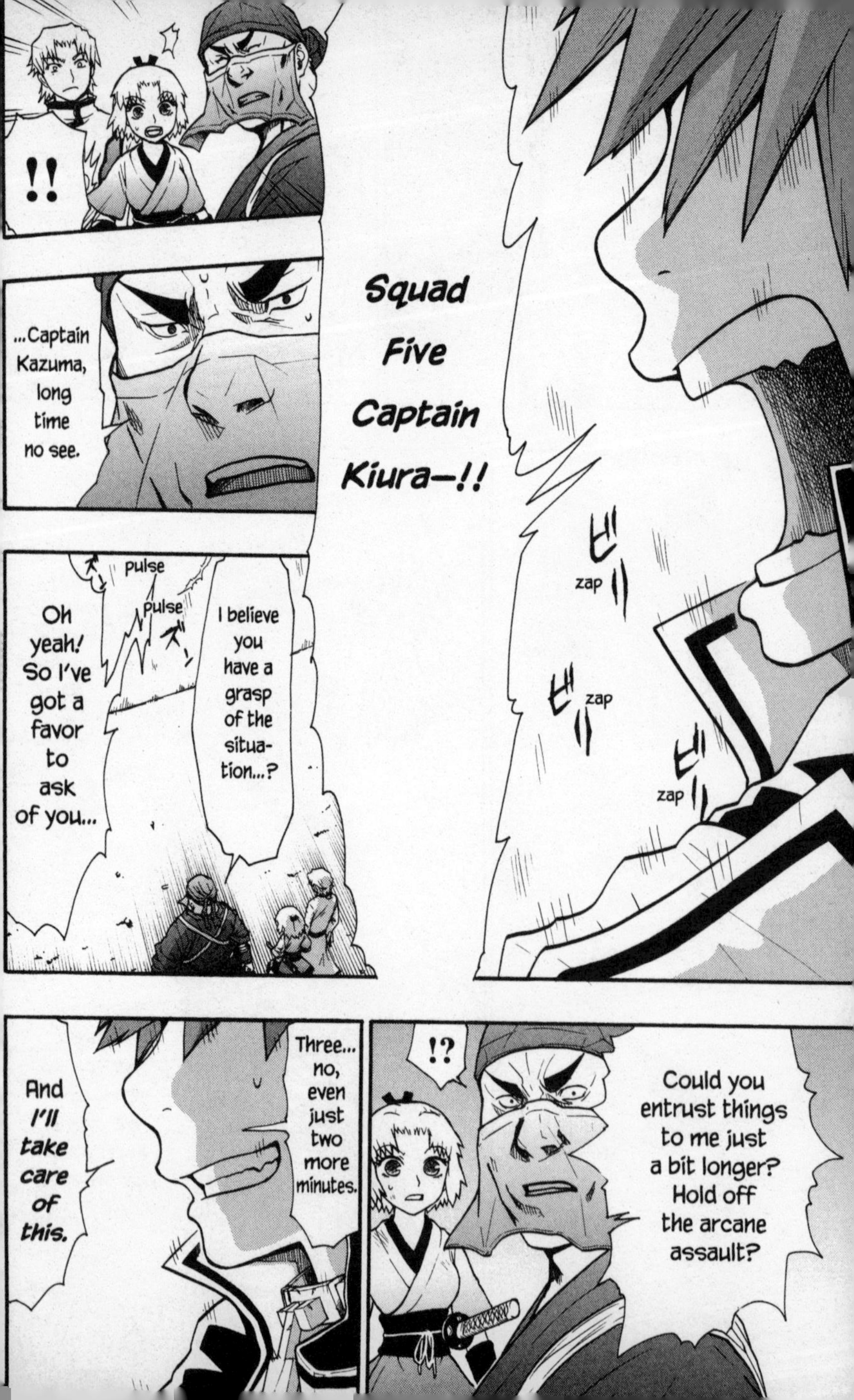
Squad Five Captain Kiura–!!
zap
zap
zap
!!
...Captain Kazuma, long time no see.
I believe you have a grasp of the situation...?
pulse
pulse
Oh yeah! So I've got a favor to ask of you...
Could you entrust things to me just a bit longer? Hold off the arcane assault?
!?
Three... no, even just two more minutes.
And *I'll take care of this.*

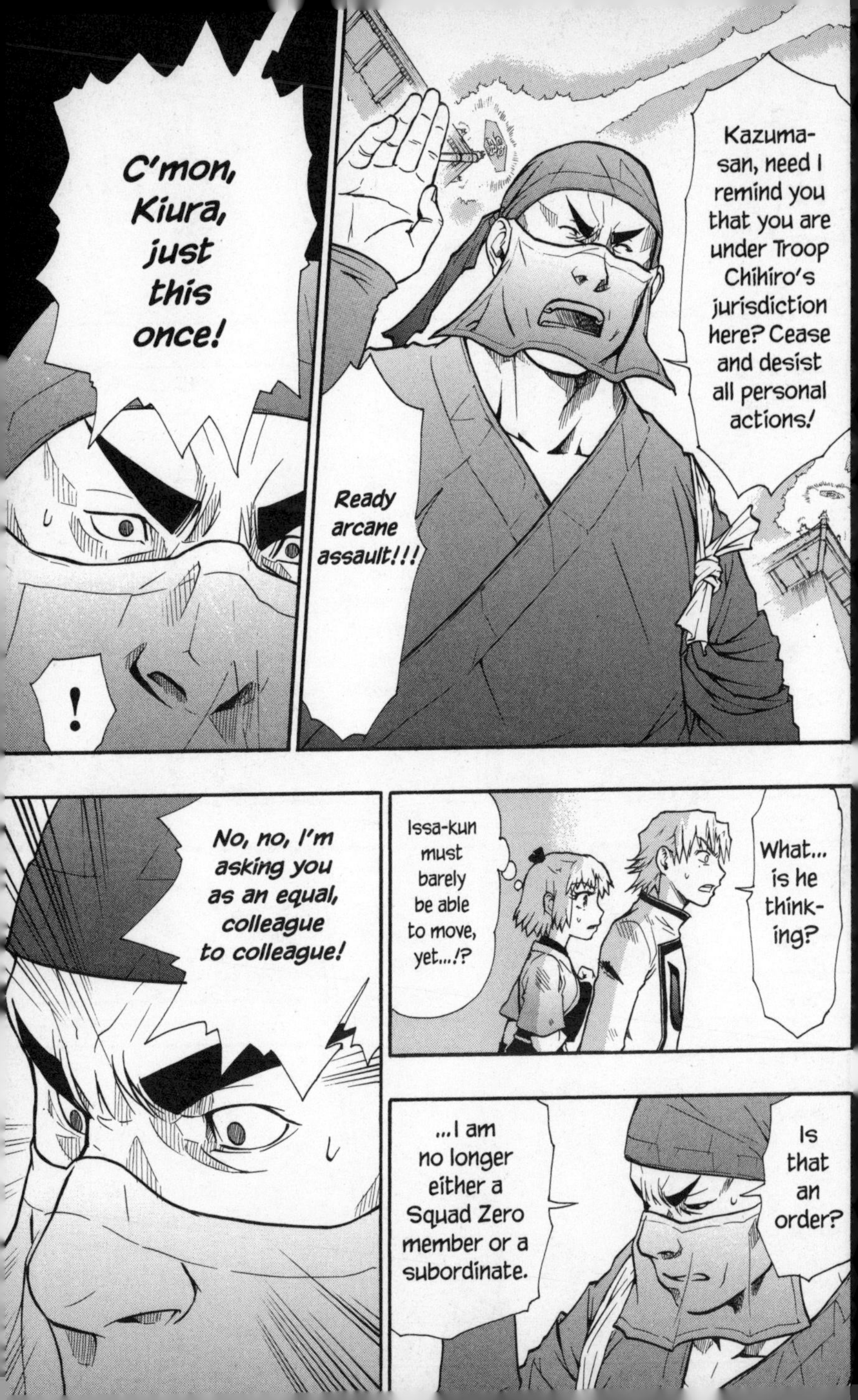
Kazuma-san, need I remind you that you are under Troop Chihiro's jurisdiction here? Cease and desist all personal actions!
Ready arcane assault!!!
C'mon, Kiura, just this once!
!
What... is he thinking?
Issa-kun must barely be able to move, yet...!?
Is that an order?
...I am no longer either a Squad Zero member or a subordinate.
No, no, I'm asking you as an equal, colleague to colleague!

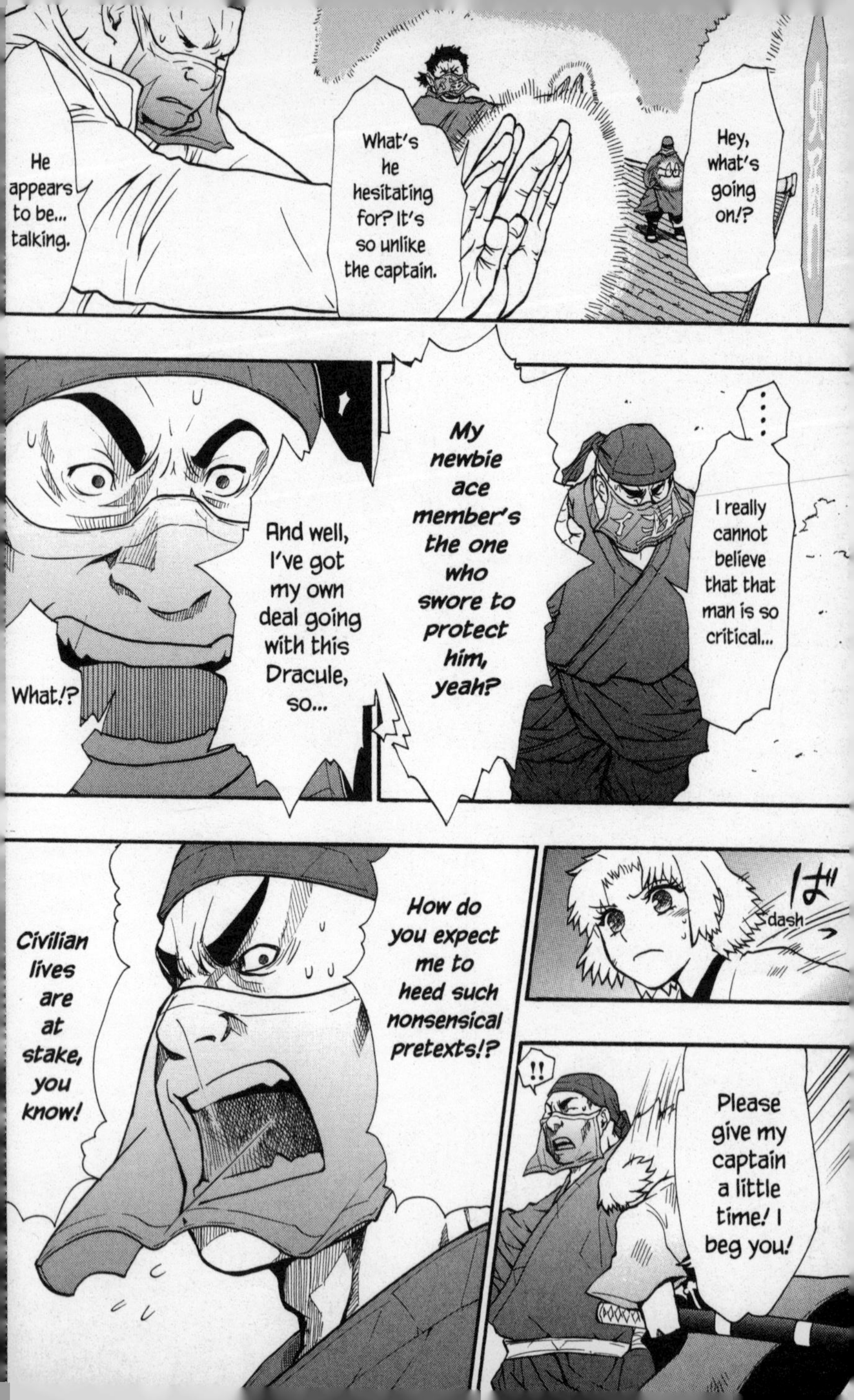
Hey, what's going on!?
What's he hesitating for? It's so unlike the captain.
He appears to be... talking.
....
I really cannot believe that that man is so critical...
My newbie ace member's the one who swore to protect him, yeah?
And well, I've got my own deal going with this Dracule, so...
What!?
ばっ
dash
!!
Please give my captain a little time! I beg you!
How do you expect me to heed such nonsensical pretexts!?
Civilian lives are at stake, you know!

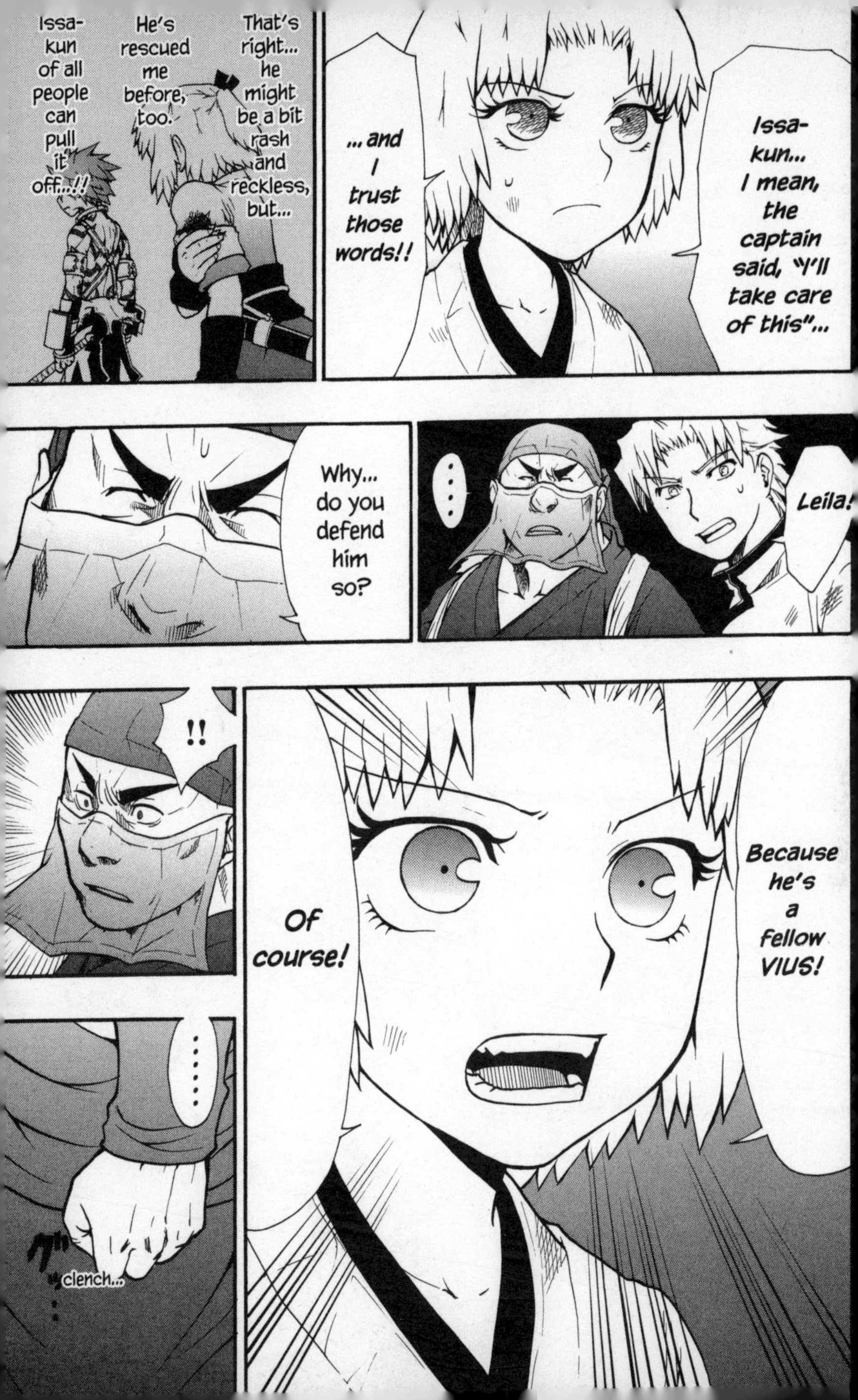
Issa-kun... I mean, the captain said, "I'll take care of this"...
...and I trust those words!!
That's right... he might be a bit rash and reckless, but...
He's rescued me before, too.
Issa-kun of all people can pull it off...!!
Leila!
...
Why... do you defend him so?
Because he's a fellow VIUS!
Of course!
!!
......
clench...

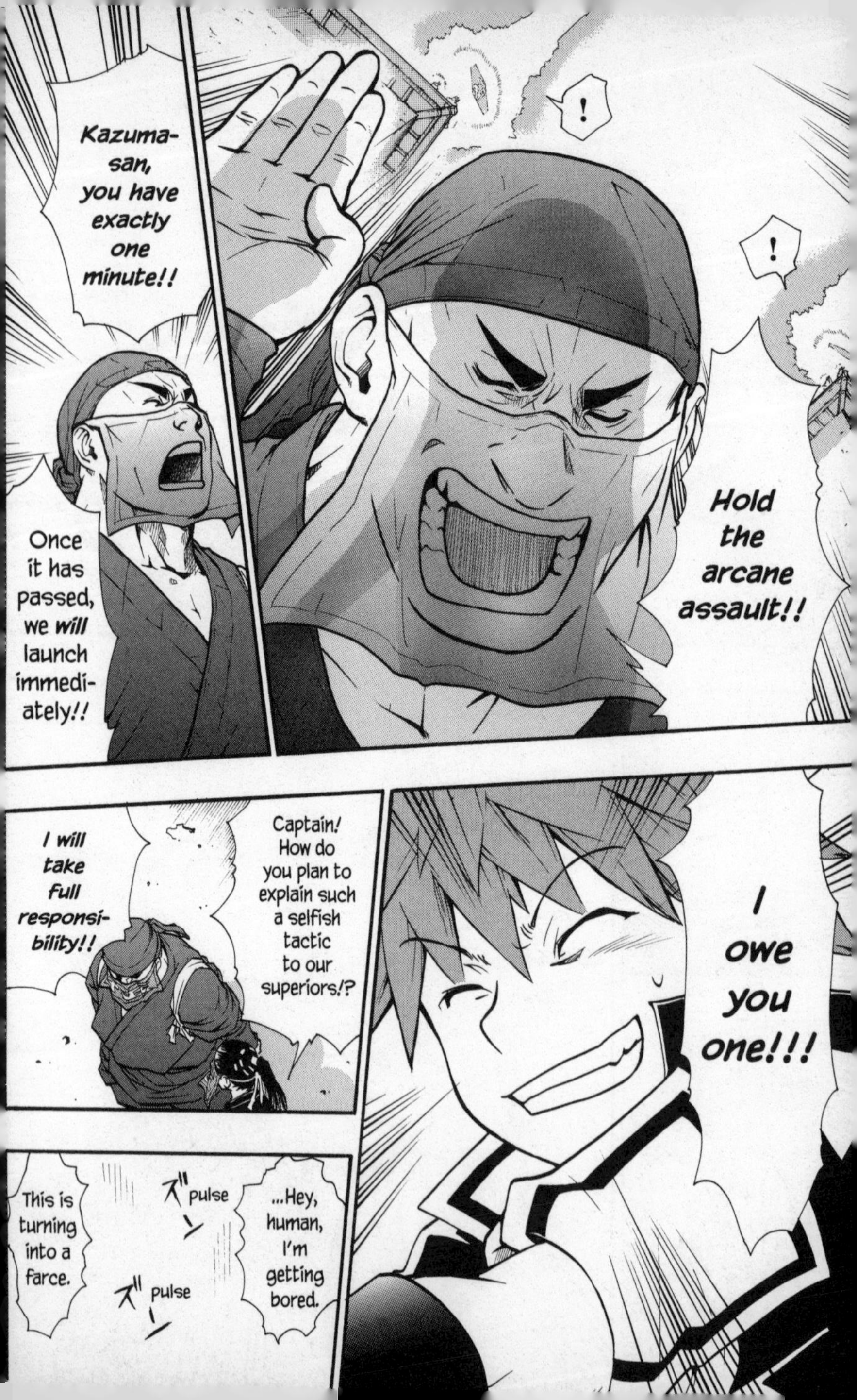
!
!
Hold the arcane assault!!
Kazuma-san, you have exactly one minute!!
Once it has passed, we will launch immediately!!
I owe you one!!!
Captain! How do you plan to explain such a selfish tactic to our superiors!?
I will take full responsibility!!
...Hey, human, I'm getting bored.
ズ pulse
ズ pulse
This is turning into a farce.

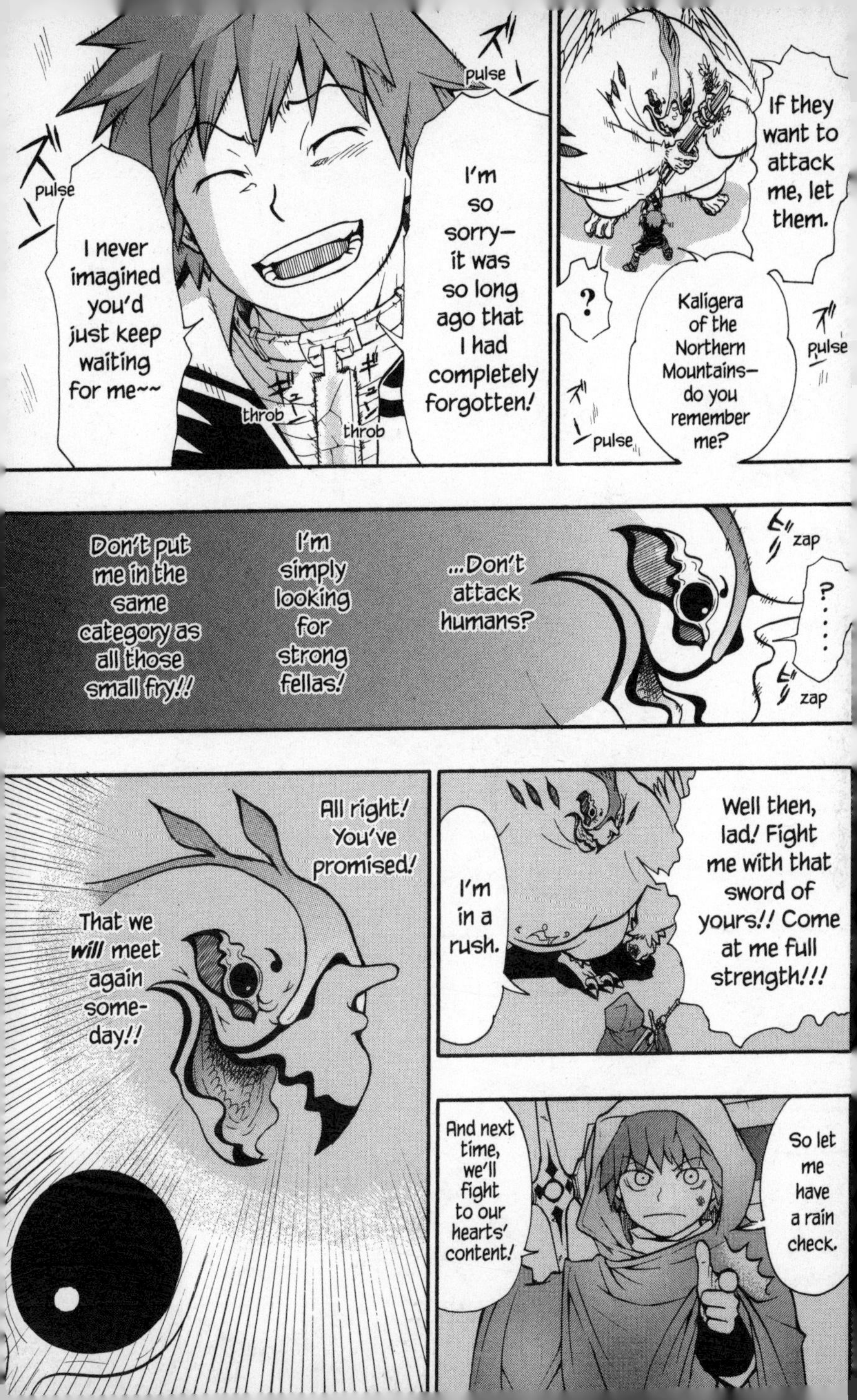

If they want to attack me, let them.
?
Kaligera of the Northern Mountains—do you remember me?
pulse
pulse
pulse
I'm so sorry—it was so long ago that I had completely forgotten!
throb
throb
pulse
I never imagined you'd just keep waiting for me~~
?......
zap
zap
...Don't attack humans?
I'm simply looking for strong fellas!
Don't put me in the same category as all those small fry!!
Well then, lad! Fight me with that sword of yours!! Come at me full strength!!!
I'm in a rush.
So let me have a rain check.
And next time, we'll fight to our hearts' content!
All right! You've promised!
That we *will* meet again someday!!

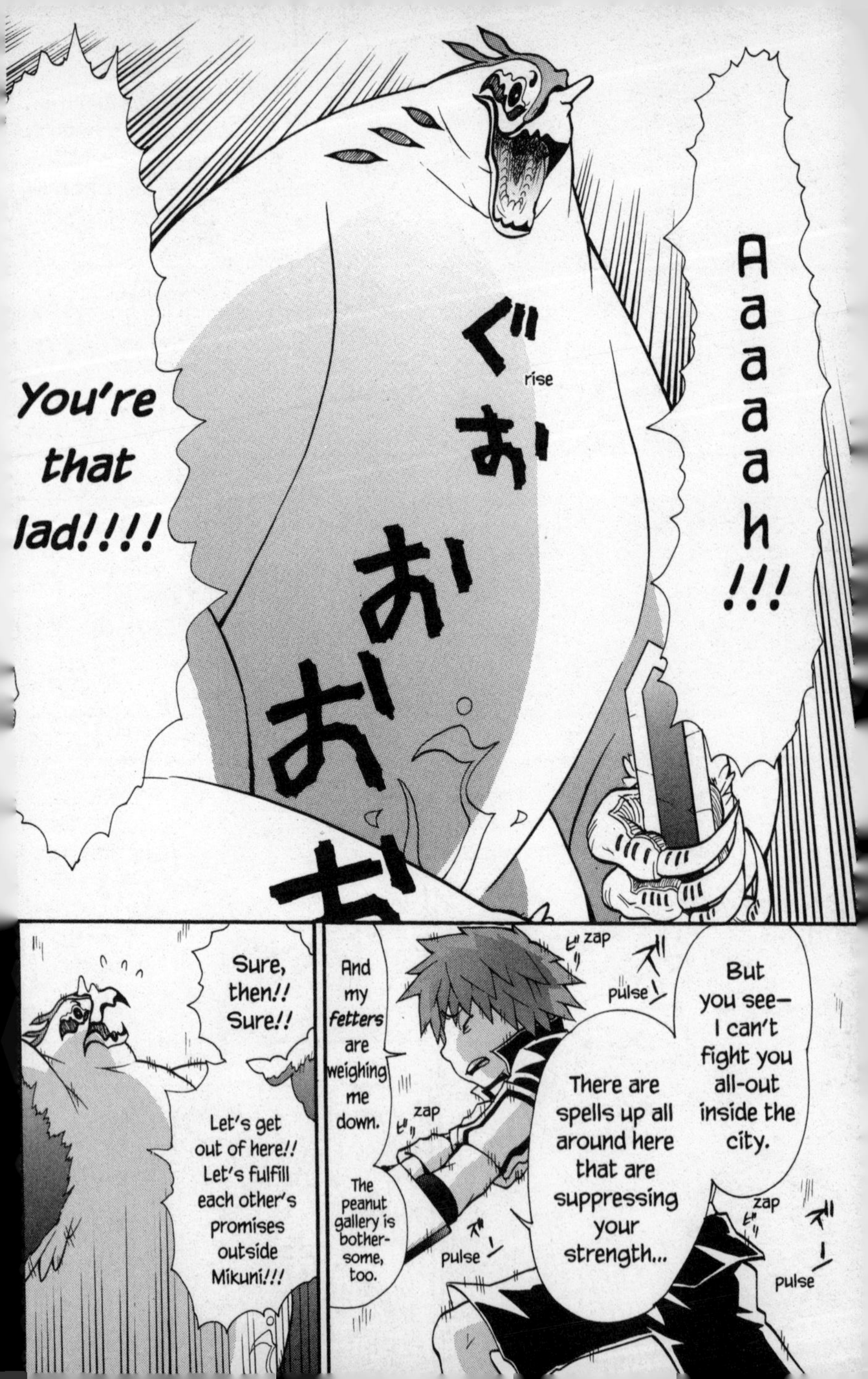
Aaaaah!!!
ぐおおお
rise
You're that lad!!!!
zap
pulse
But you see— I can't fight you all-out inside the city.
There are spells up all around here that are suppressing your strength...
zap
pulse
And my fetters are weighing me down.
zap
pulse
The peanut gallery is bothersome, too.
Sure, then!! Sure!!
Let's get out of here!! Let's fulfill each other's promises outside Mikuni!!!

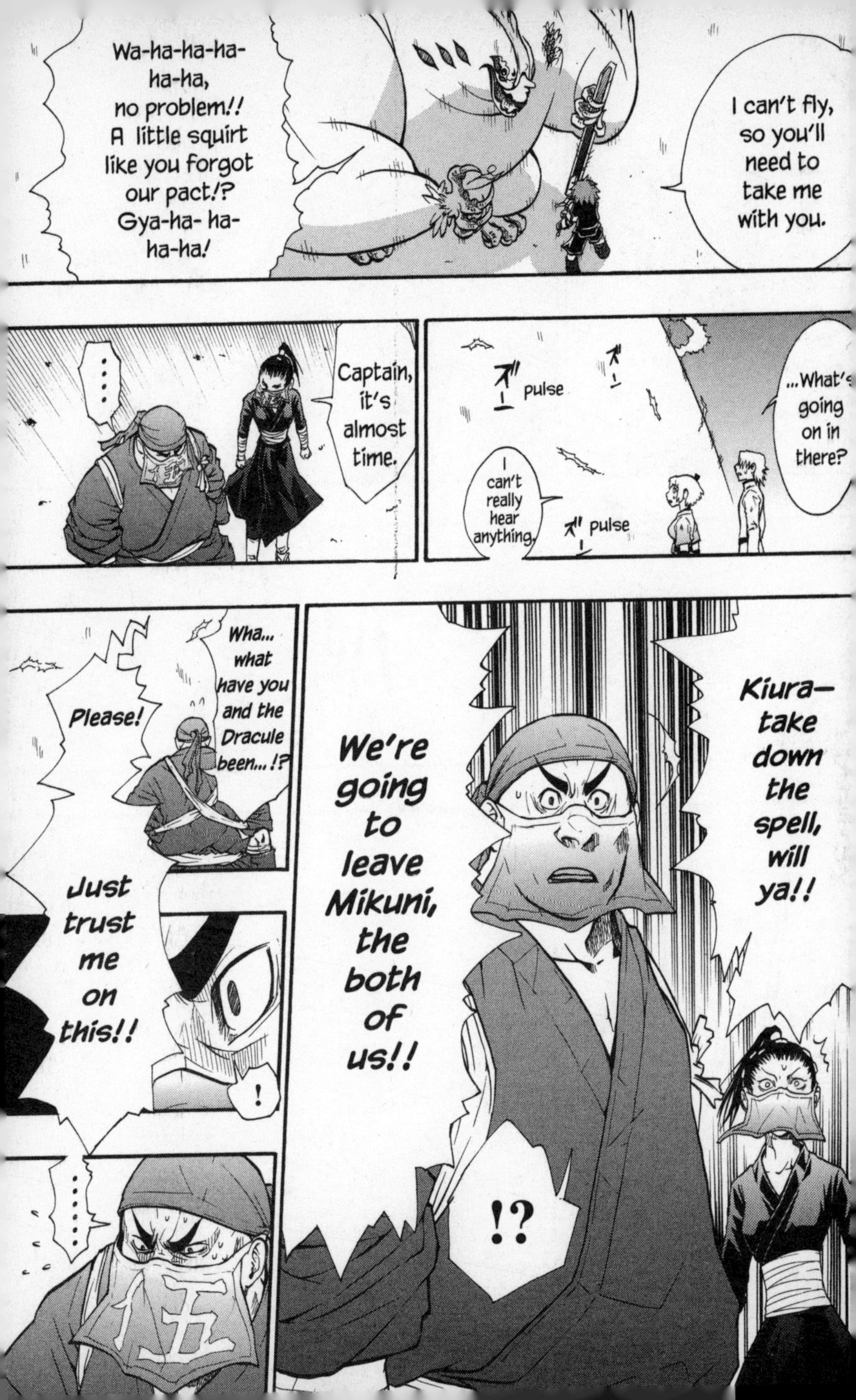
I can't fly, so you'll need to take me with you.
Wa-ha-ha-ha-ha-ha, no problem!! A little squirt like you forgot our pact!? Gya-ha-ha-ha-ha!
...What's going on in there?
pulse
I can't really hear anything.
pulse
Captain, it's almost time.
....
Kiura—take down the spell, will ya!!
We're going to leave Mikuni, the both of us!!
!?
Wha... what have you and the Dracule been...!?
Please!
Just trust me on this!!
!
......

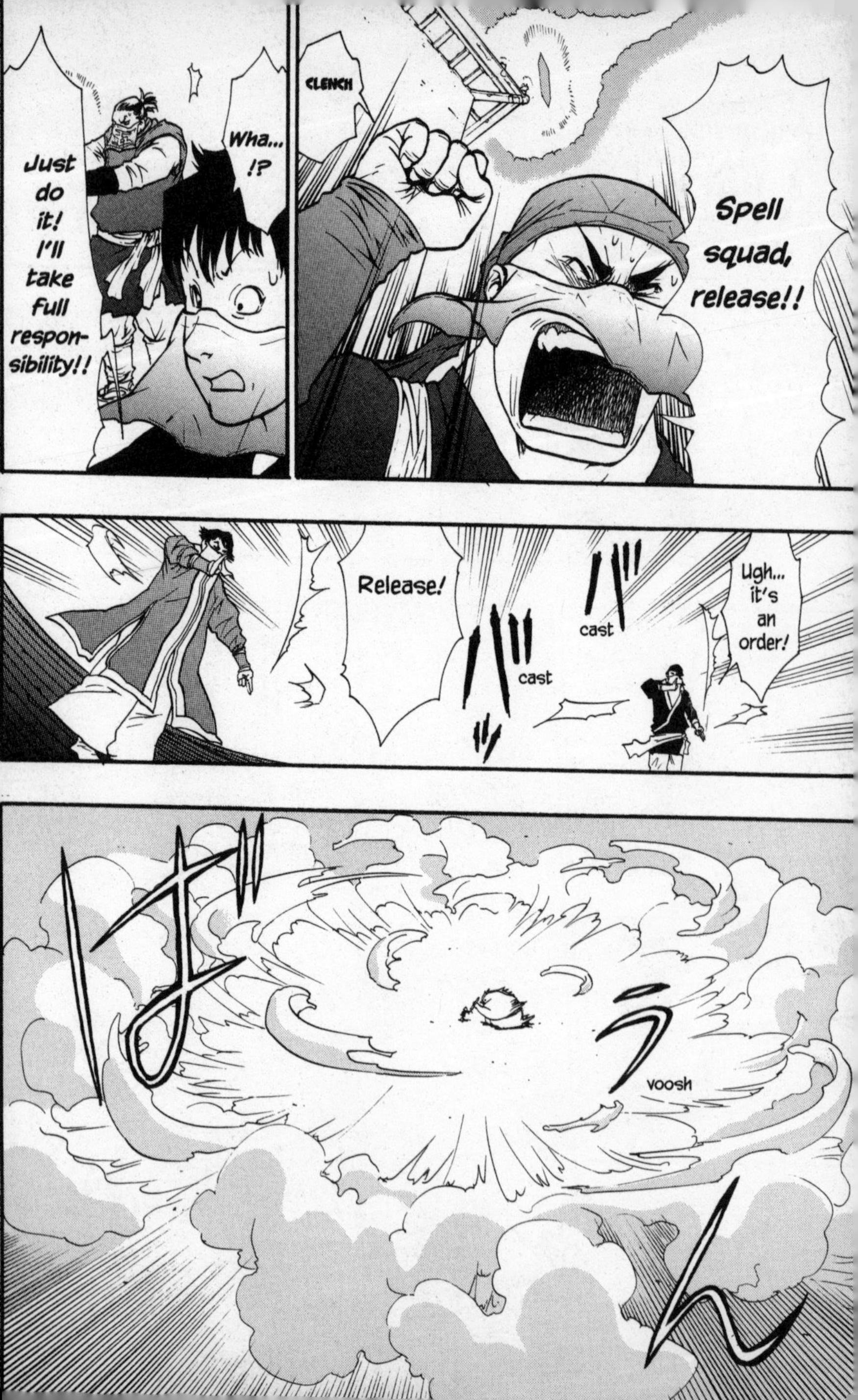
Spell squad, release!!
CLENCH
Wha... !?
Just do it! I'll take full respon-sibility!!
Ugh... it's an order!
cast
cast
Release!
voosh

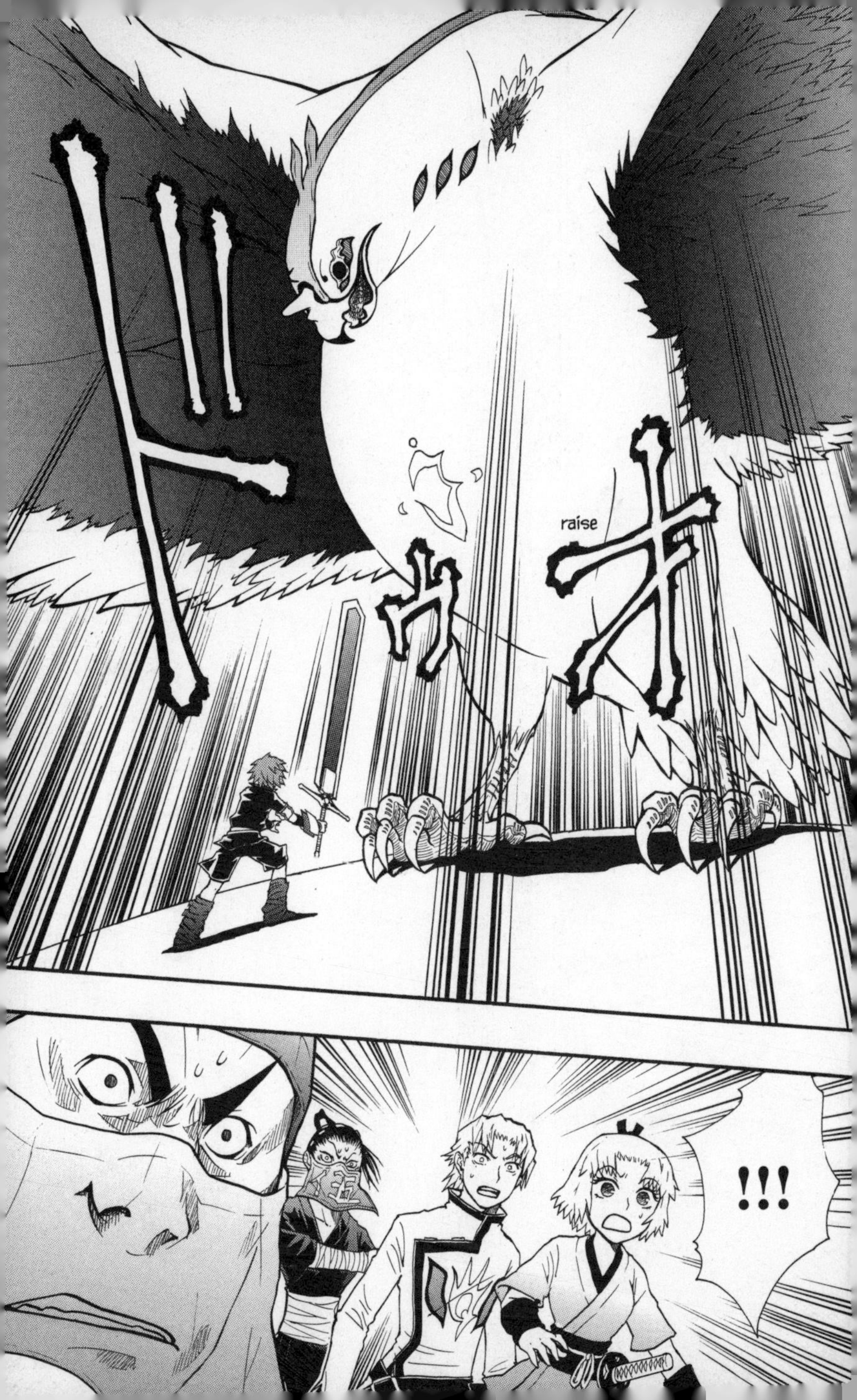
raise
!!!

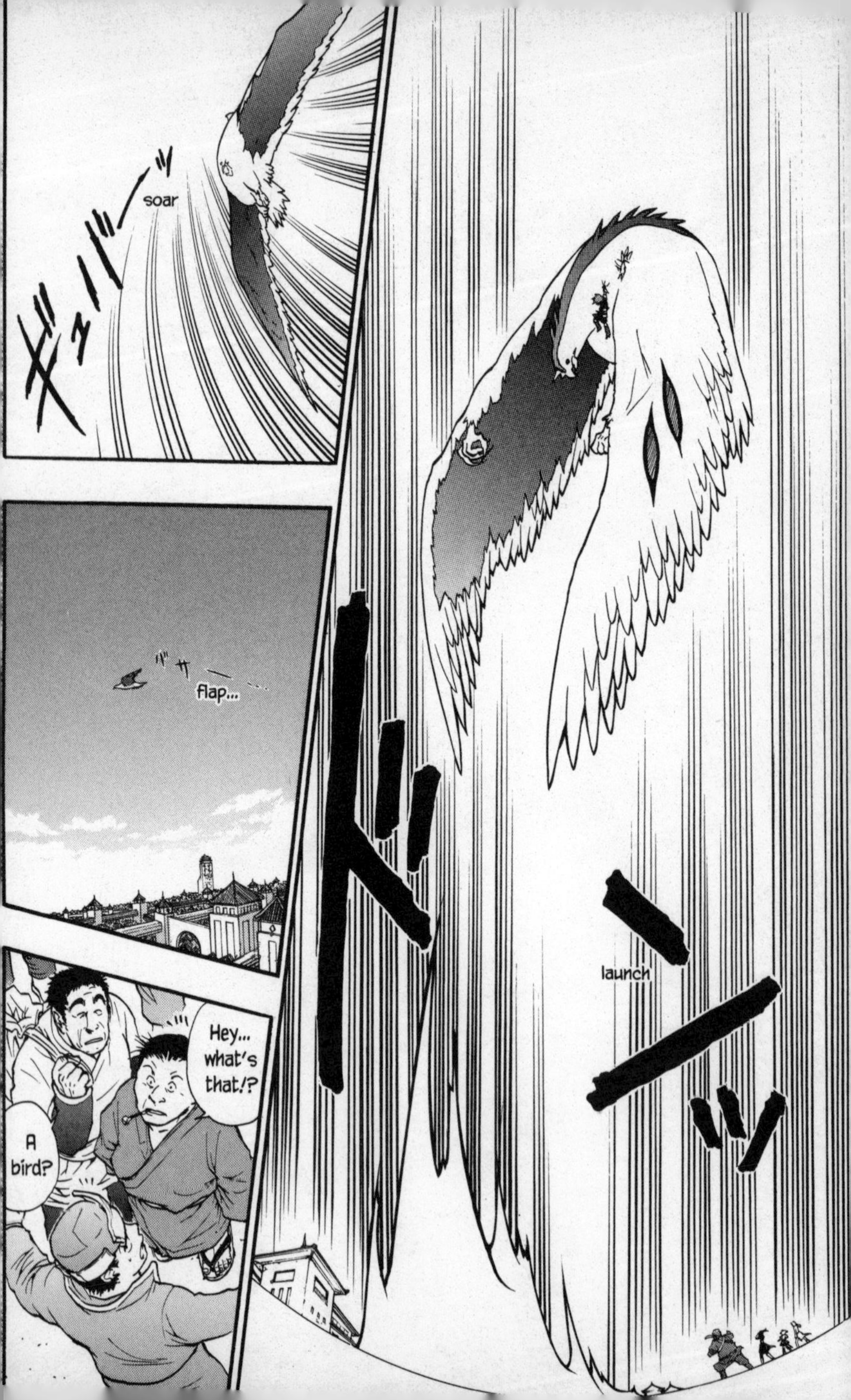
launch
soar
flap...
Hey... what's that!?
A bird?

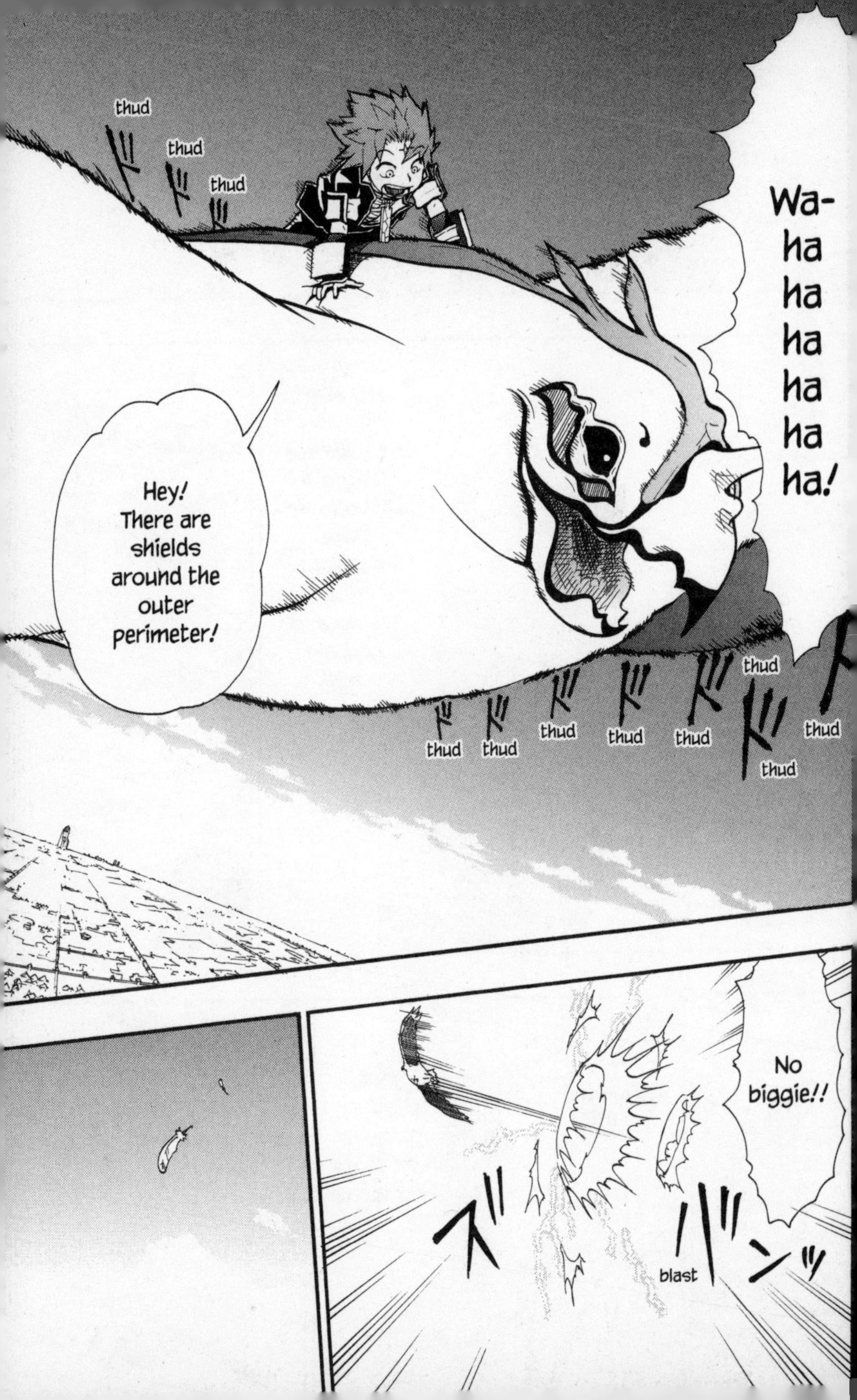
Wa-ha ha ha ha ha ha!
thud
thud
thud
Hey! There are shields around the outer perimeter!
thud
thud
thud
thud
thud
thud
thud
thud
No biggie!!
blast

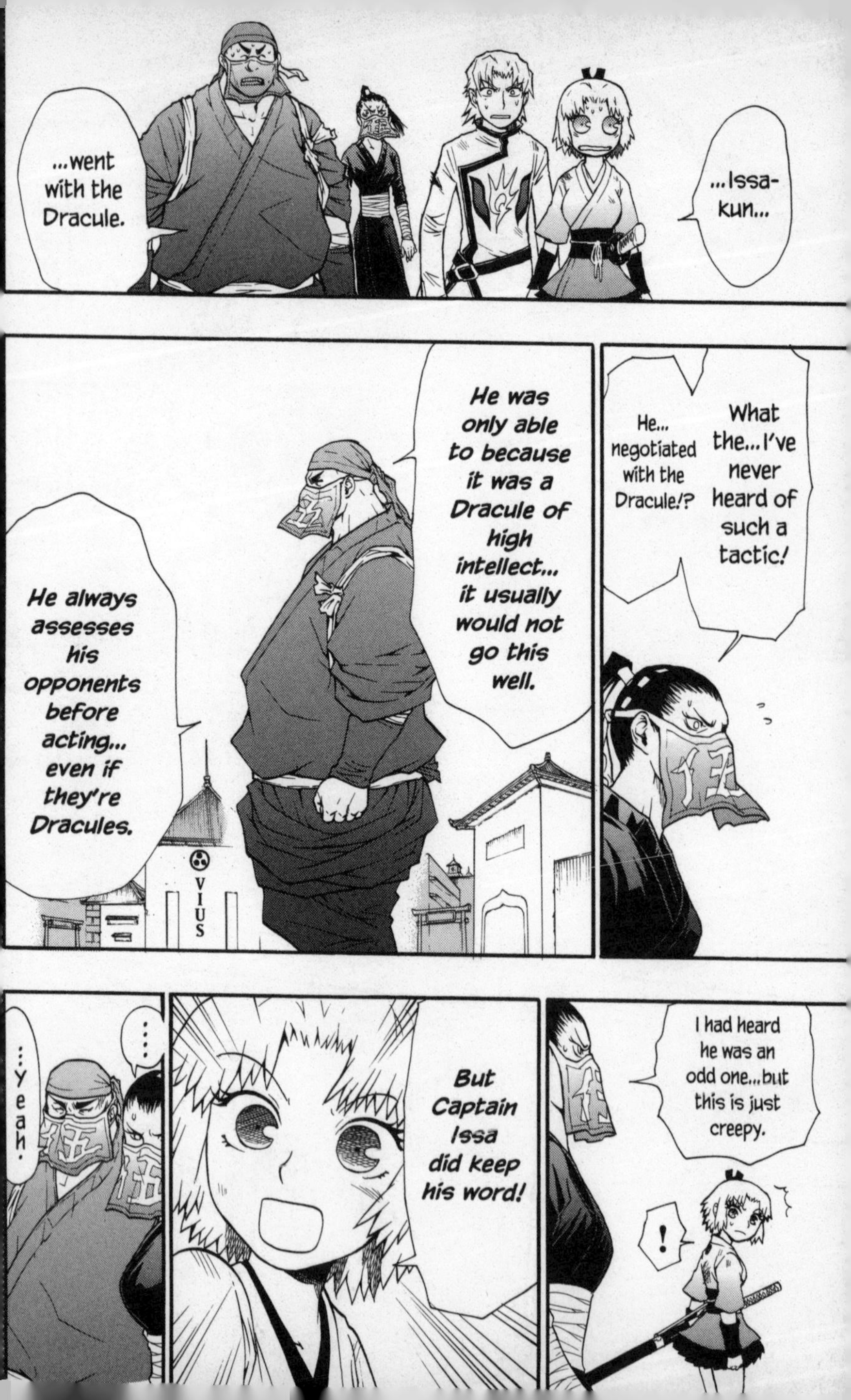
...Issa-kun...
...went with the Dracule.
What the...I've never heard of such a tactic!
He... negotiated with the Dracule!?
He was only able to because it was a Dracule of high intellect... it usually would not go this well.
He always assesses his opponents before acting... even if they're Dracules.
VIUS
I had heard he was an odd one...but this is just creepy.
!
But Captain Issa did keep his word!
....
...Yeah.

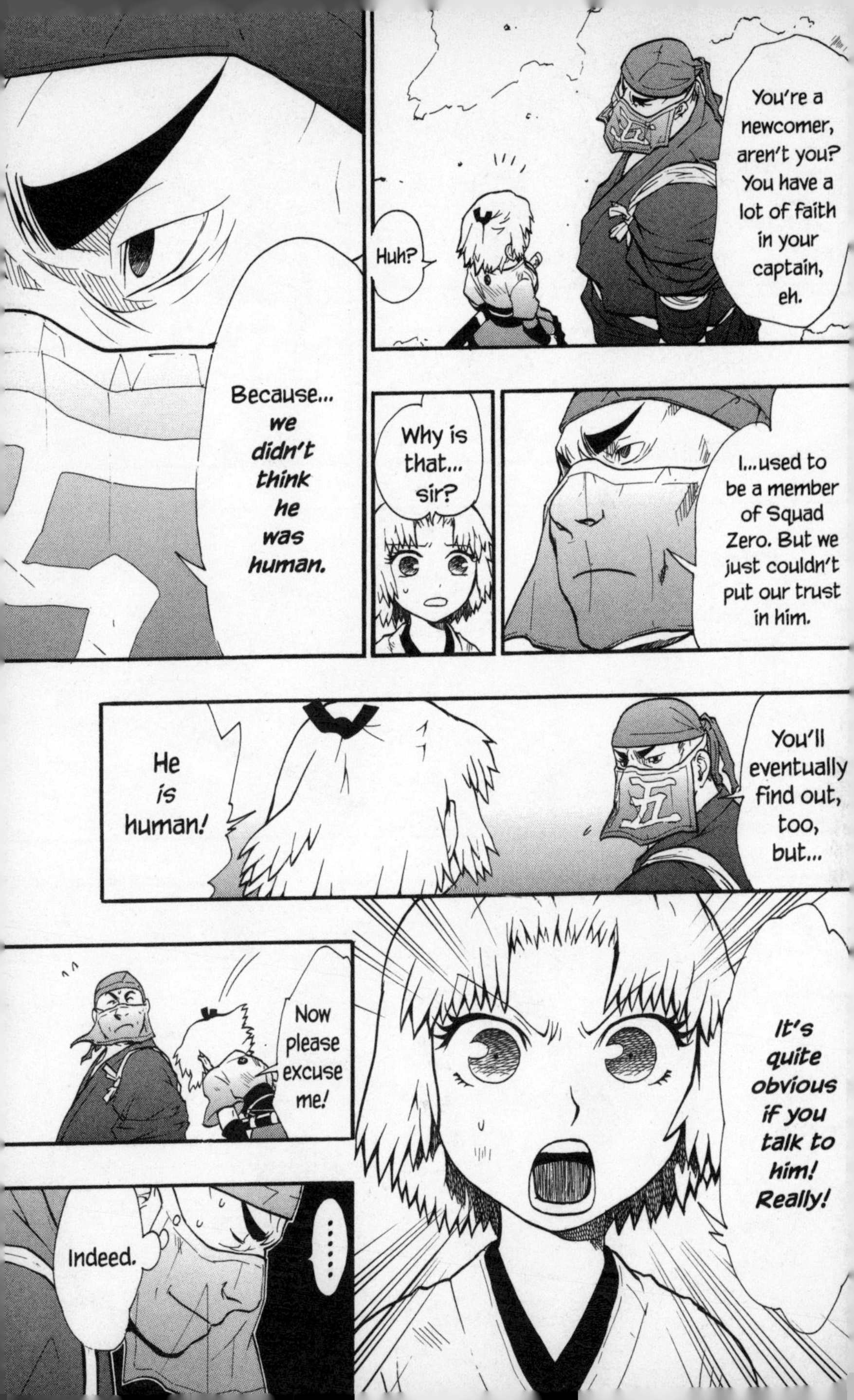
You're a newcomer, aren't you? You have a lot of faith in your captain, eh.
Huh?
I...used to be a member of Squad Zero. But we just couldn't put our trust in him.
Why is that... sir?
Because... we didn't think he was human.
You'll eventually find out, too, but...
He is human!
It's quite obvious if you talk to him! Really!
Now please excuse me!
......
Indeed.

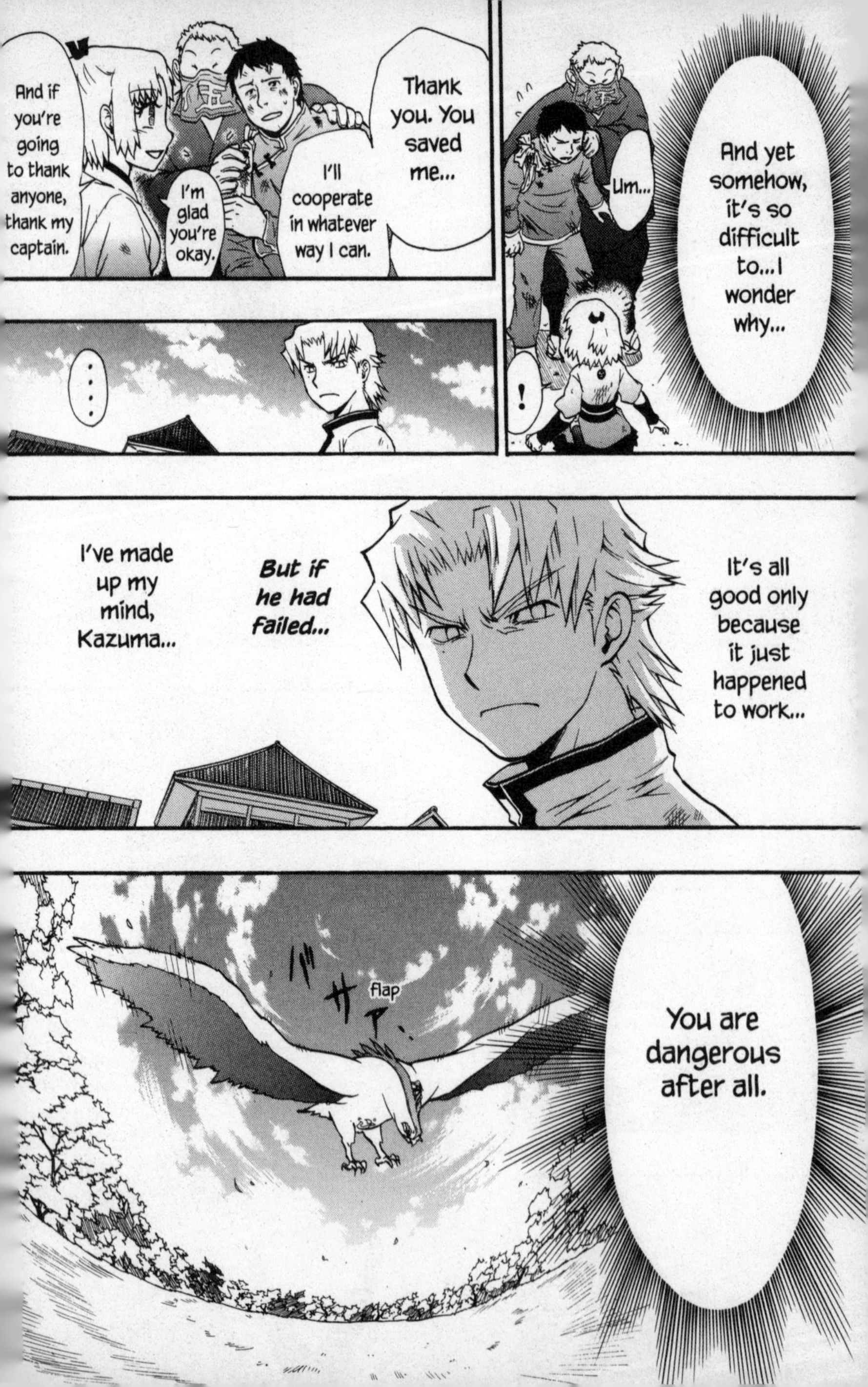
And yet somehow, it's so difficult to...I wonder why...
Um...
!
Thank you. You saved me...
I'll cooperate in whatever way I can.
I'm glad you're okay.
And if you're going to thank anyone, thank my captain.
...
It's all good only because it just happened to work...
But if he had failed...
I've made up my mind, Kazuma...
You are dangerous after all.
Flap

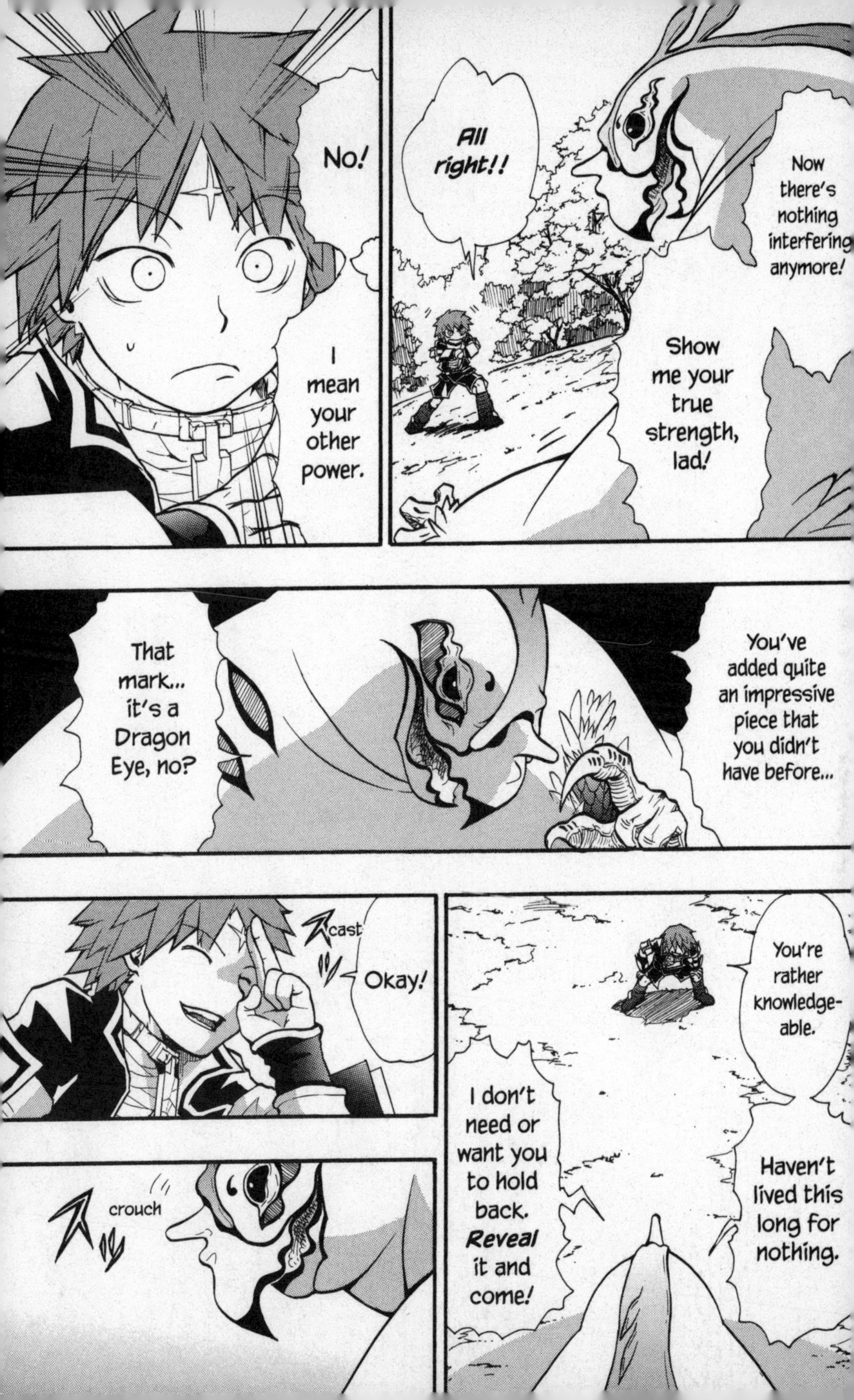
Now there's nothing interfering anymore!
Show me your true strength, lad!
All right!!
No!
I mean your other power.
You've added quite an impressive piece that you didn't have before...
That mark... it's a Dragon Eye, no?
You're rather knowledge-able.
Haven't lived this long for nothing.
I don't need or want you to hold back. Reveal it and come!
cast
Okay!
crouch

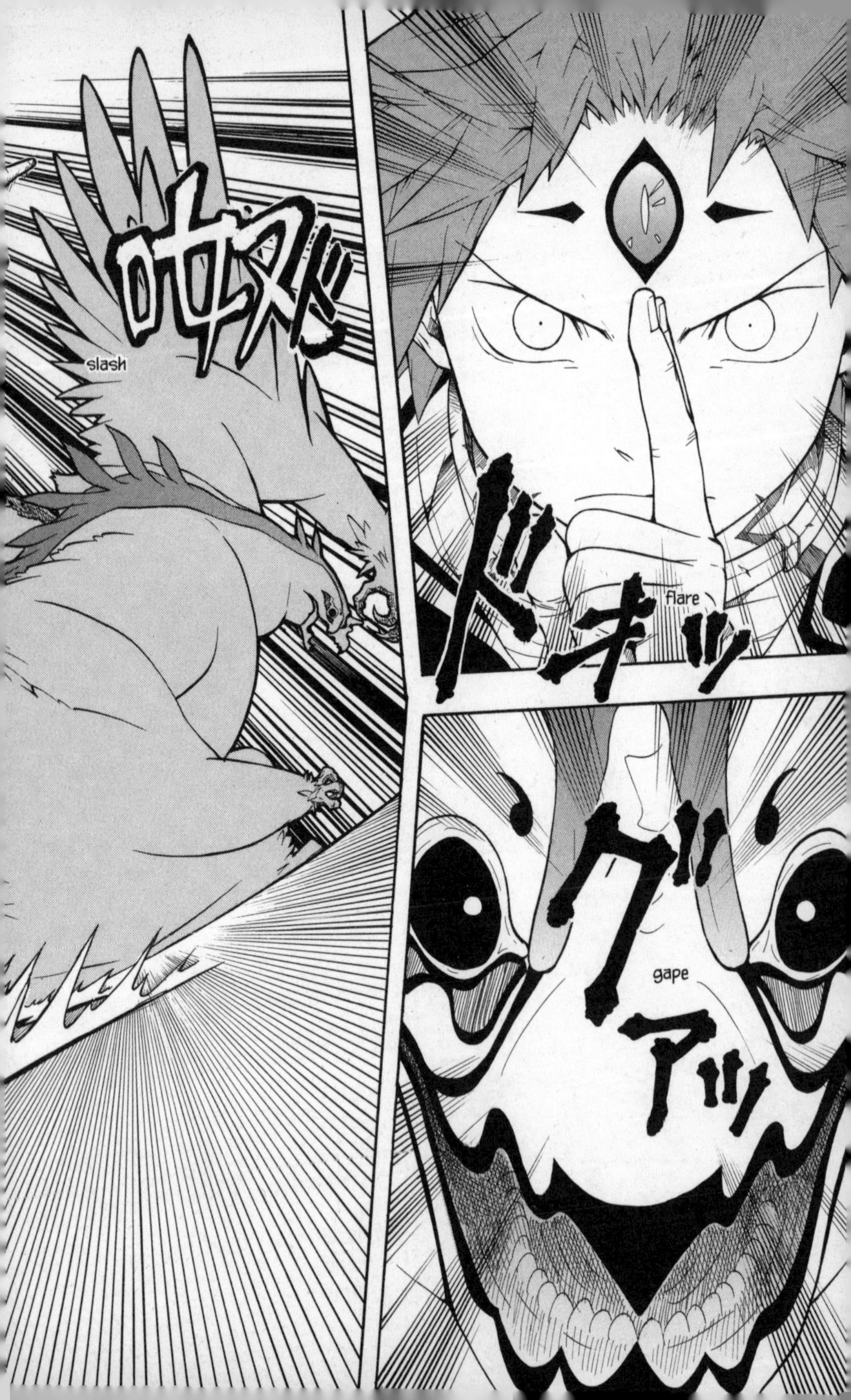
ドオッ
flare
グアッ
gape
slash

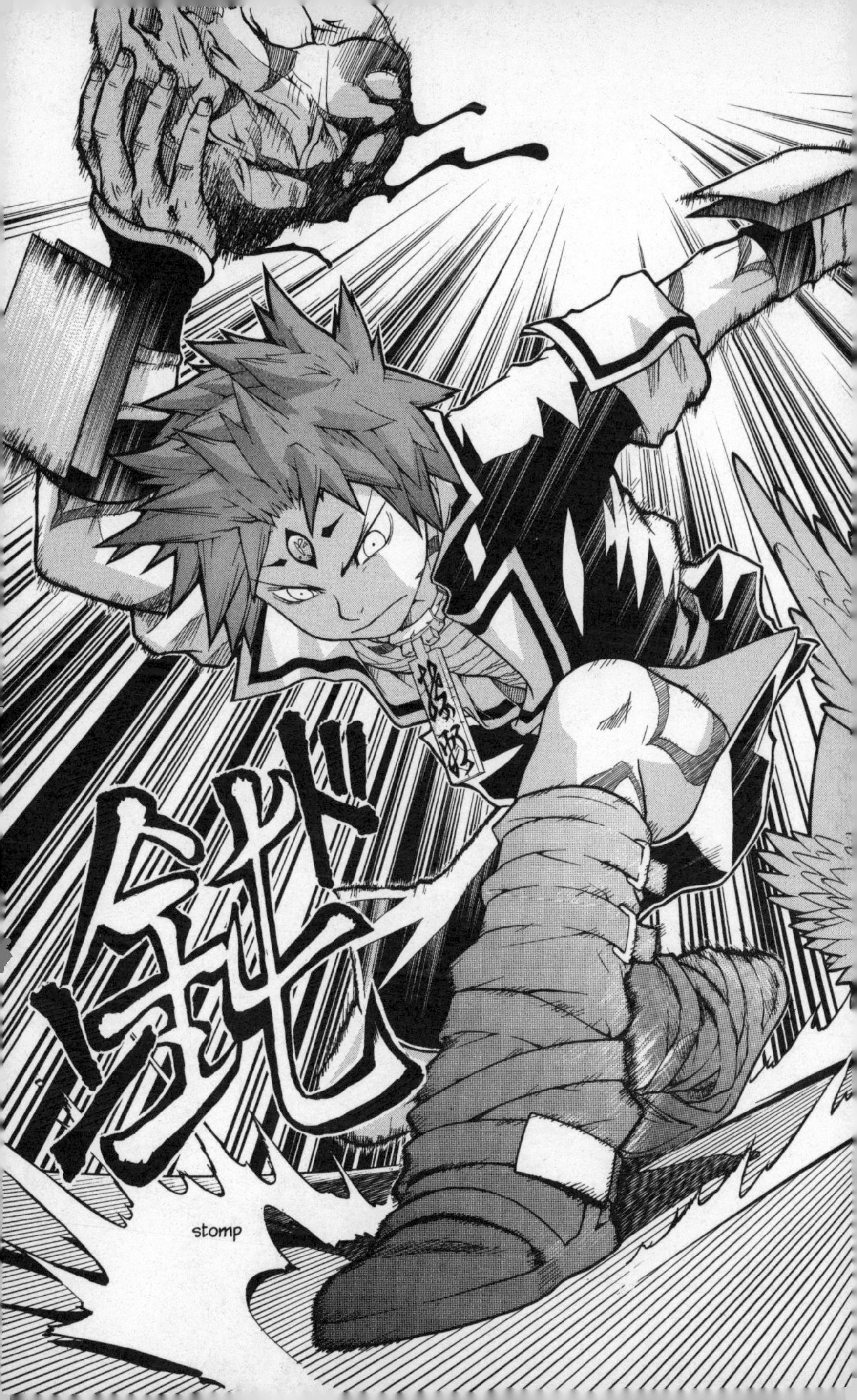
stomp

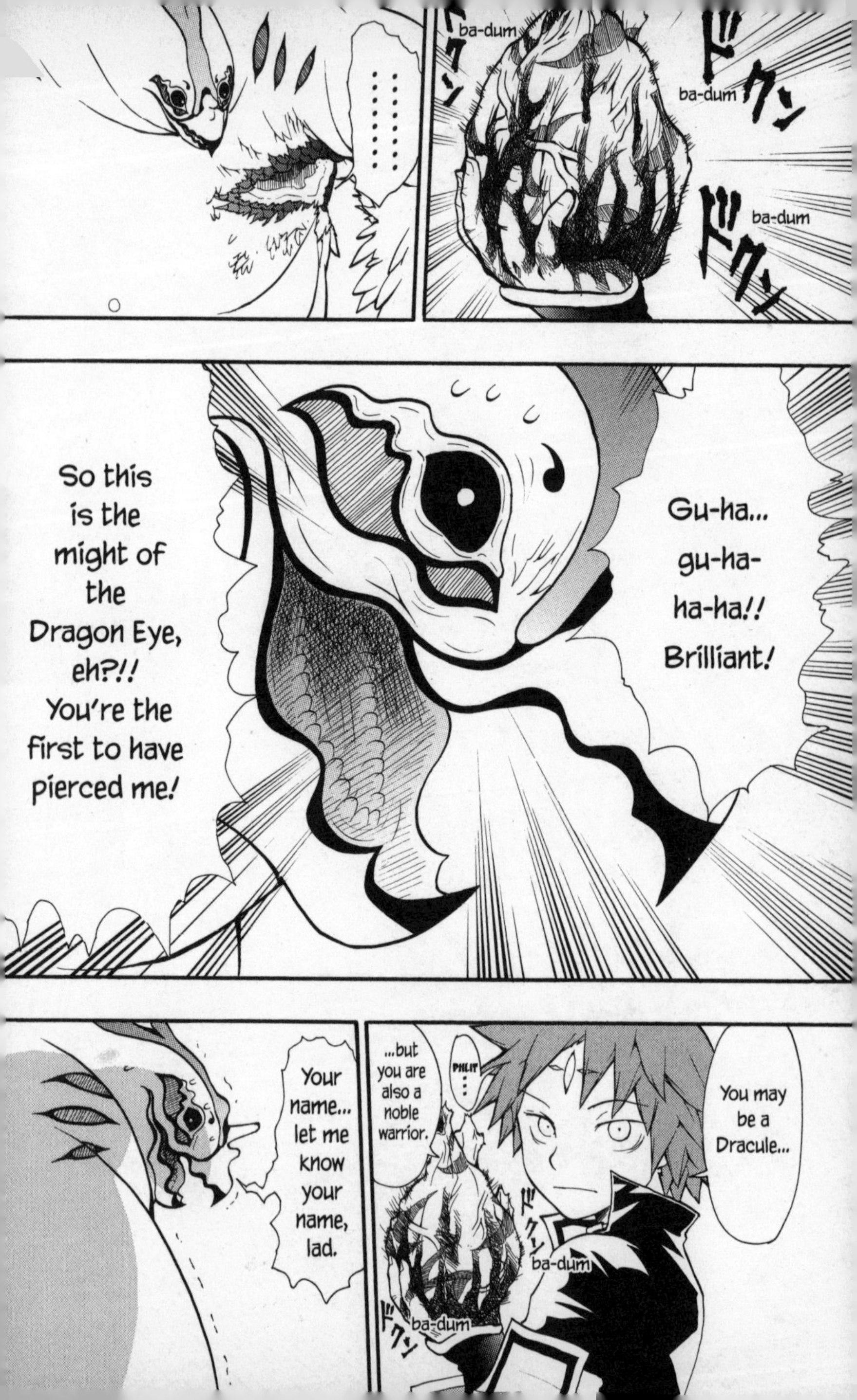
ba-dum
ba-dum
ba-dum
Gu-ha... gu-ha-ha-ha!! Brilliant!
So this is the might of the Dragon Eye, eh?!! You're the first to have pierced me!
You may be a Dracule...
PHLIT
...but you are also a noble warrior.
ba-dum
ba-dum
Your name... let me know your name, lad.

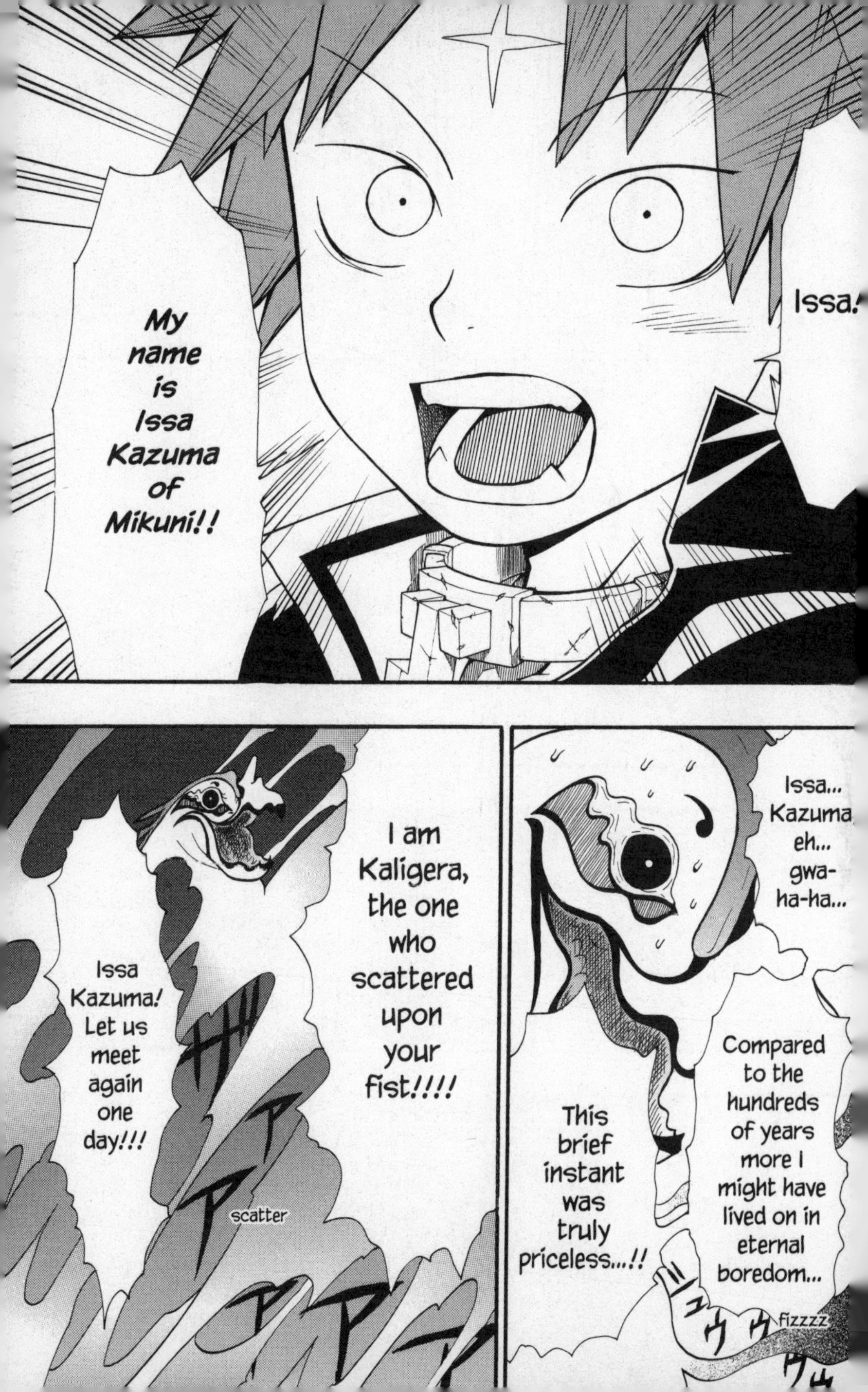
Issa!
My name is Issa Kazuma of Mikuni!!
Issa... Kazuma, eh... gwa-ha-ha...
Compared to the hundreds of years more I might have lived on in eternal boredom...
This brief instant was truly priceless...!!
fizzzz
I am Kaligera, the one who scattered upon your fist!!!!
Issa Kazuma! Let us meet again one day!!!
scatter

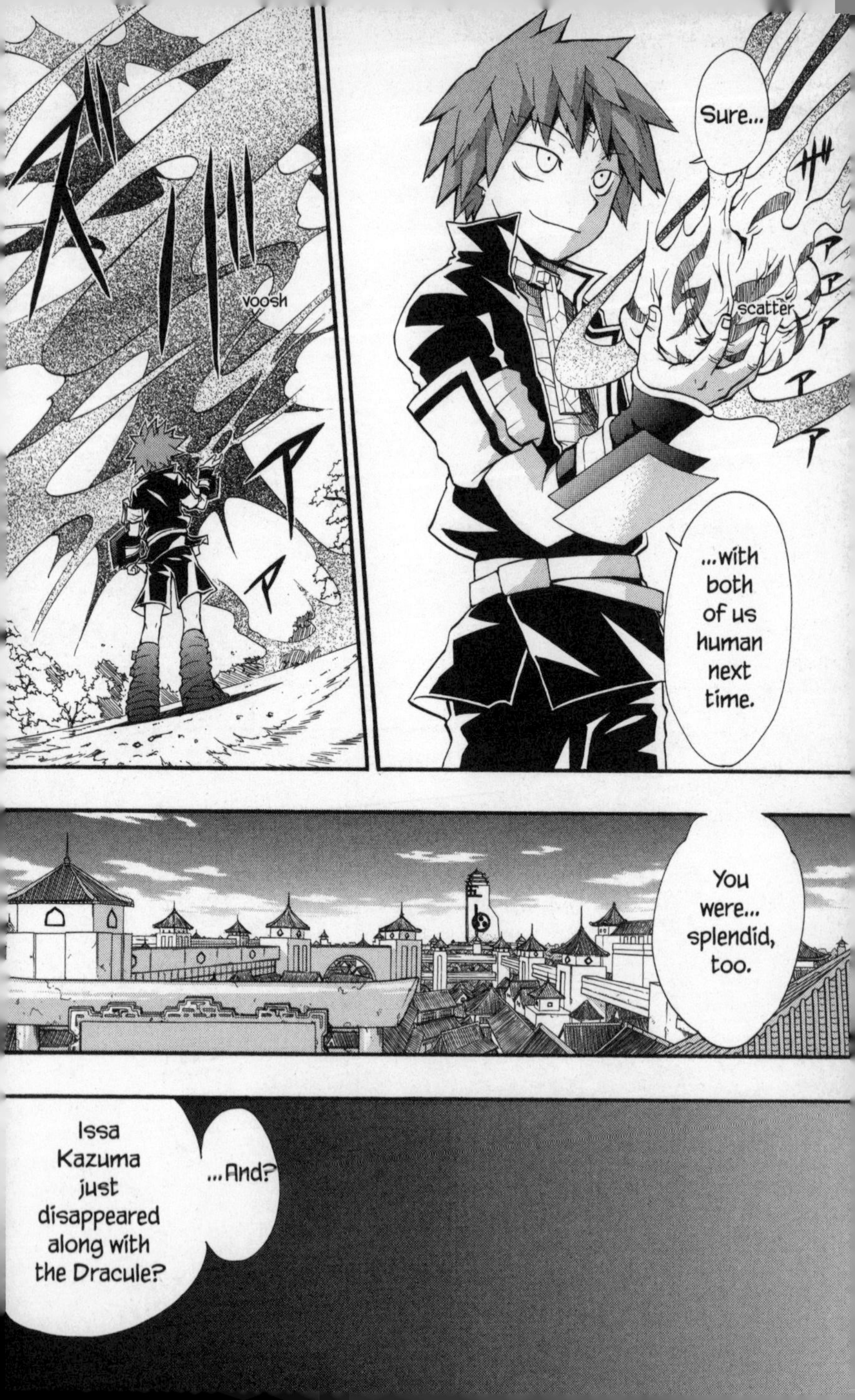
Sure...
scatter
...with both of us human next time.
voosh
You were... splendid, too.
...And?
Issa Kazuma just disappeared along with the Dracule?

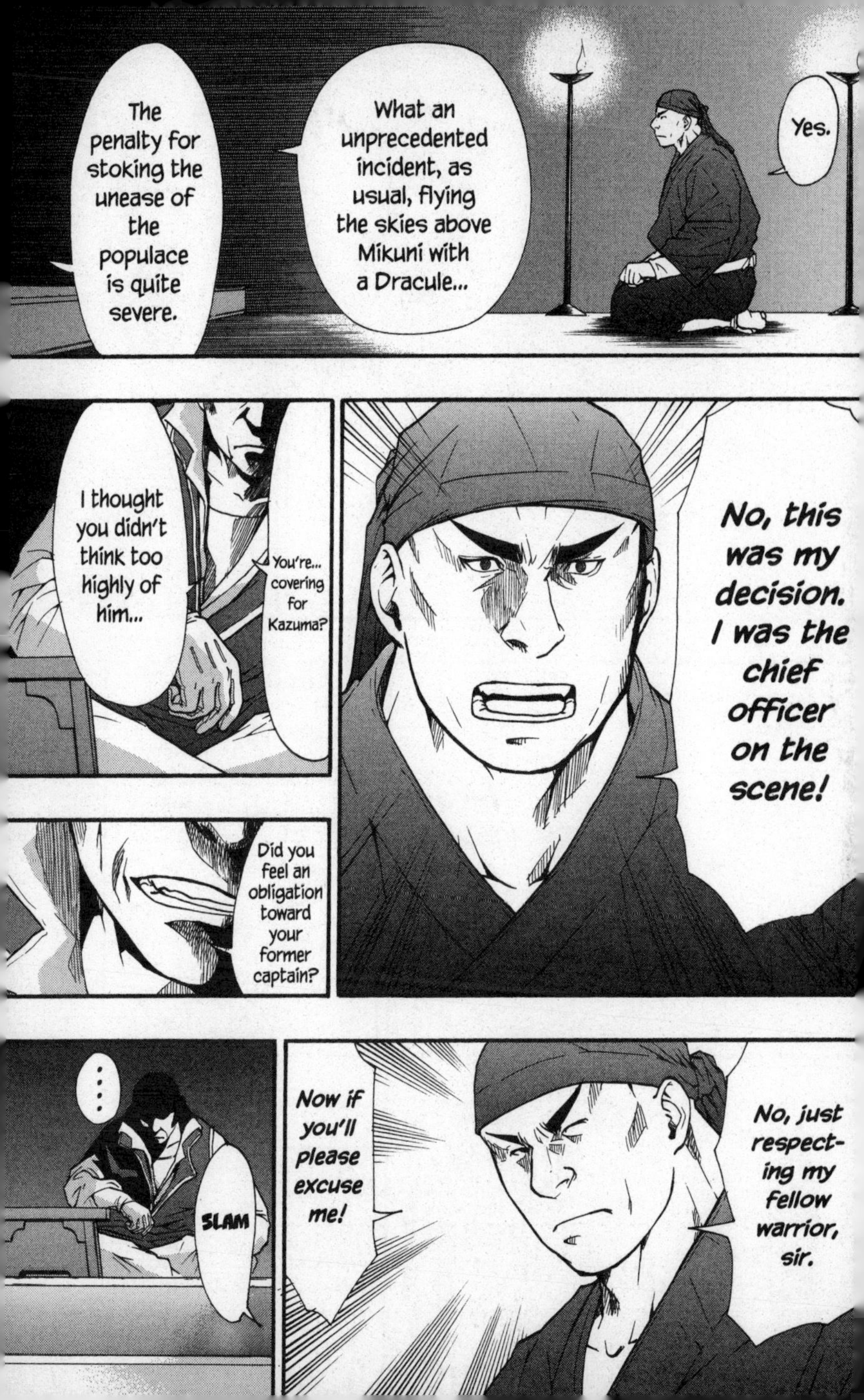
Yes.
What an unprecedented incident, as usual, flying the skies above Mikuni with a Dracule...
The penalty for stoking the unease of the populace is quite severe.
No, this was my decision. I was the chief officer on the scene!
You're... covering for Kazuma?
I thought you didn't think too highly of him...
Did you feel an obligation toward your former captain?
No, just respecting my fellow warrior, sir.
Now if you'll please excuse me!
....
SLAM

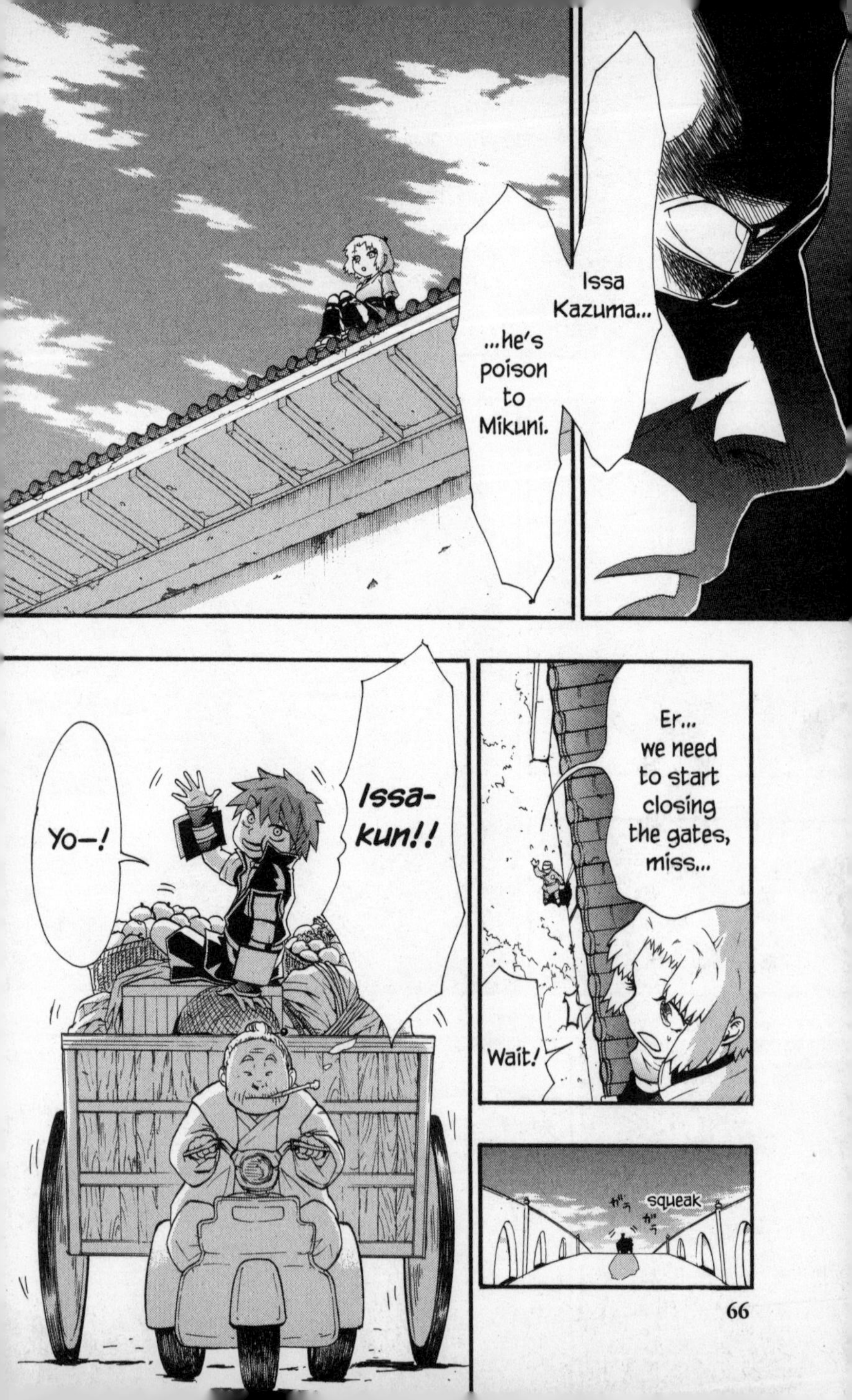
Issa Kazuma...
...he's poison to Mikuni.
Er... we need to start closing the gates, miss...
Wait!
squeak
Issa-kun!!
Yo—!

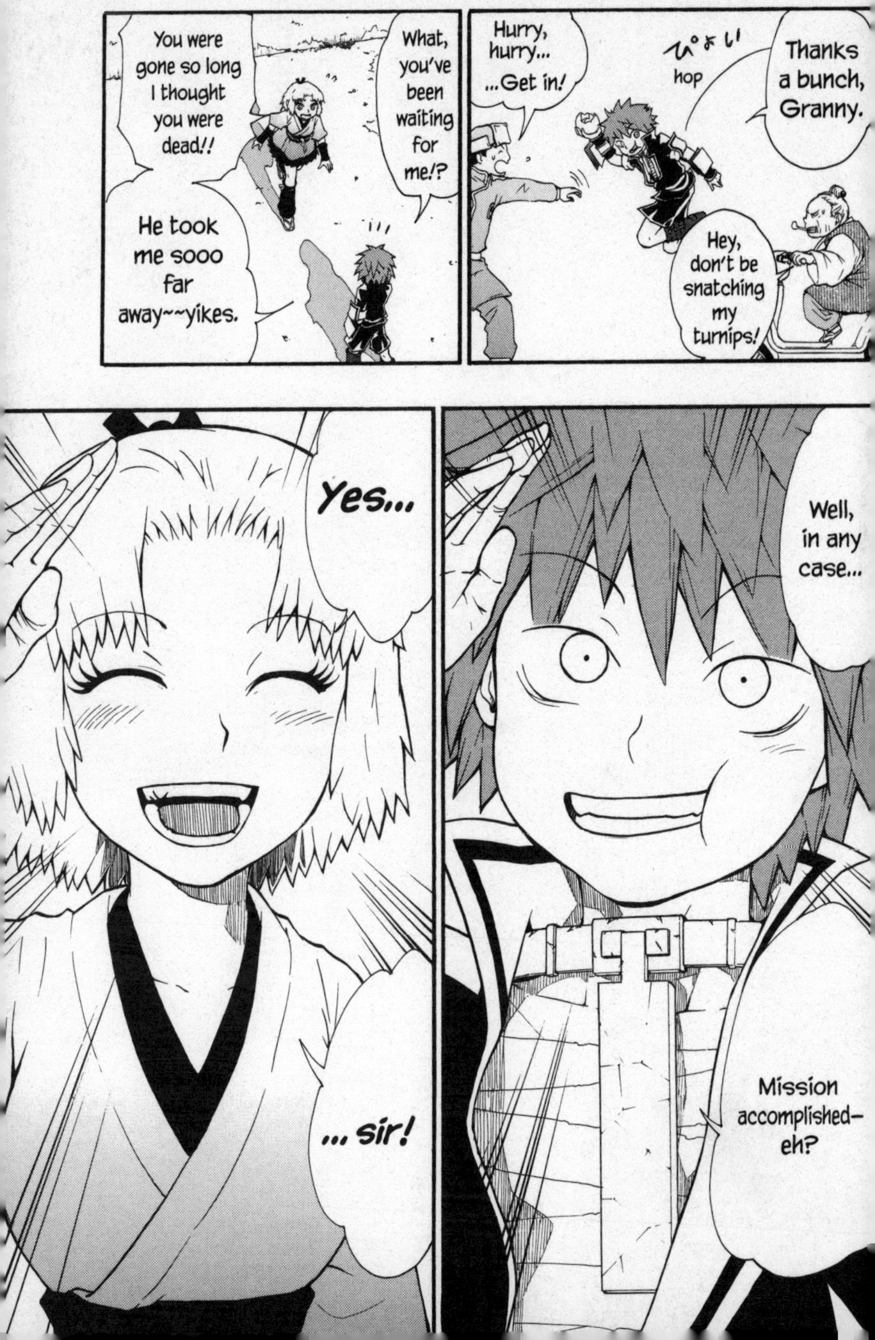
Thanks a bunch, Granny.
ぴょい
hop
Hurry, hurry... ...Get in!
Hey, don't be snatching my turnips!
What, you've been waiting for me!?
You were gone so long I thought you were dead!!
He took me sooo far away~~yikes.
Well, in any case...
Mission accomplished—eh?
Yes...
... sir!

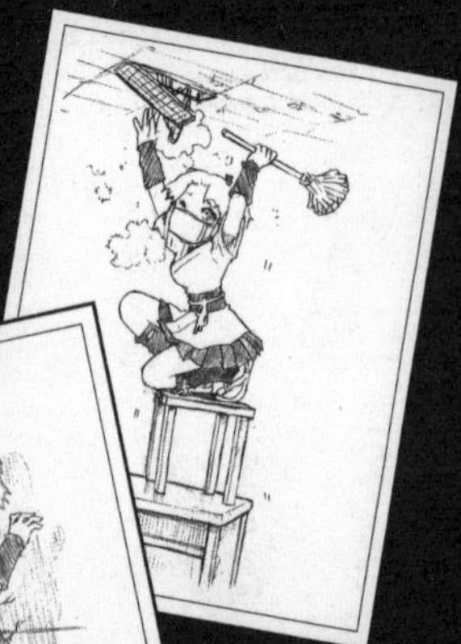

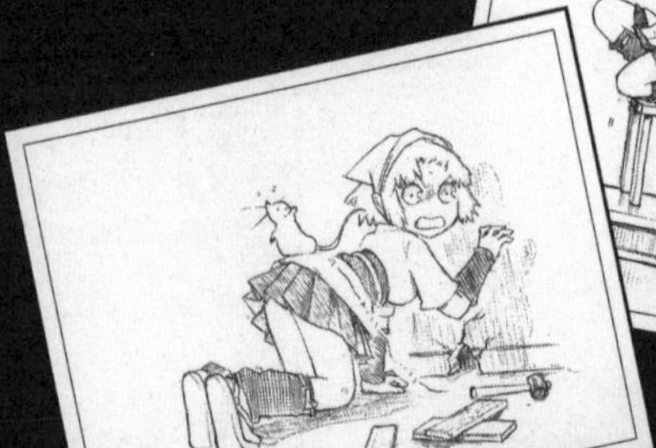

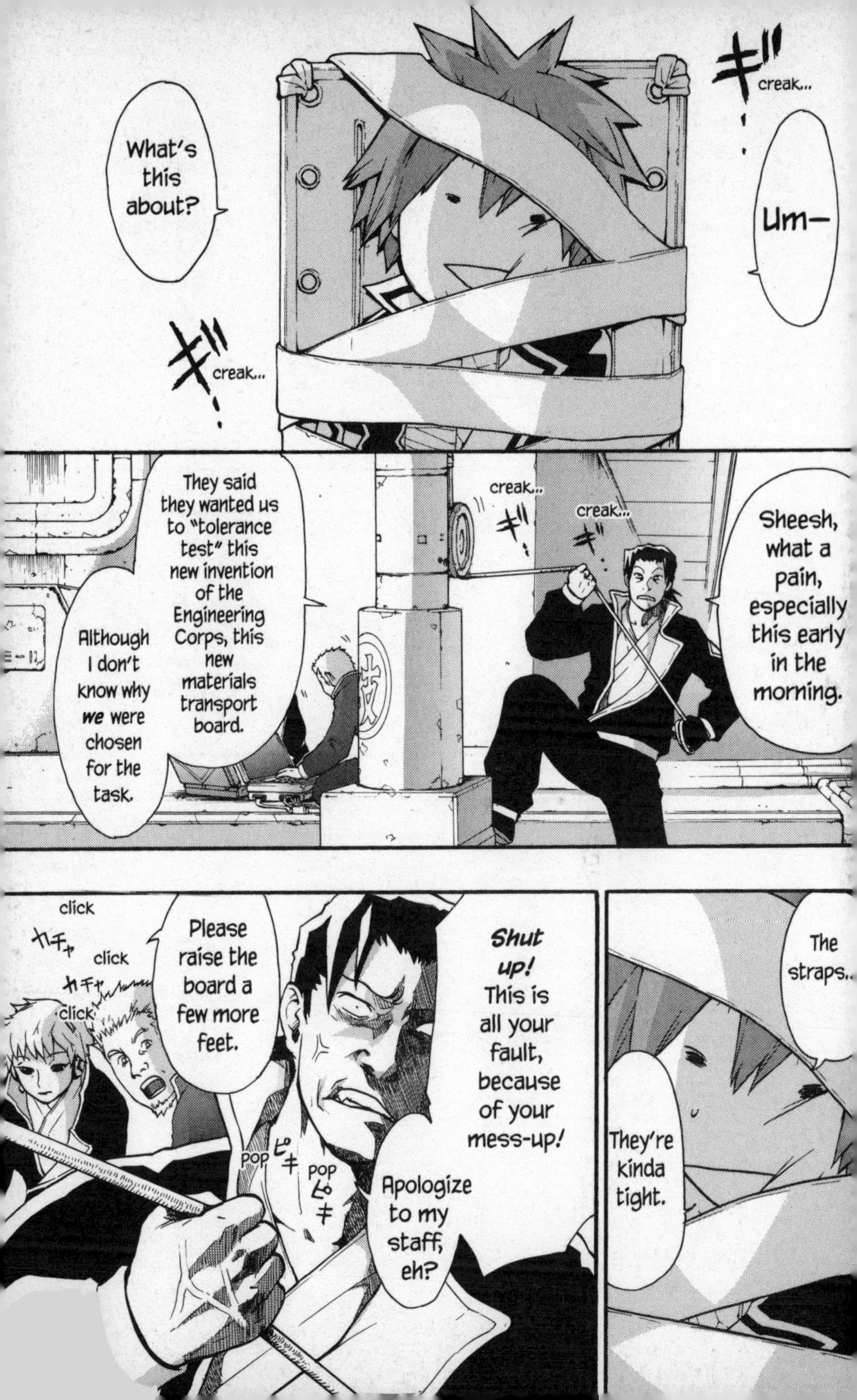

ギ
creak...
Um—
What's this about?
ギ
creak...
Sheesh, what a pain, especially this early in the morning.
creak...
ギ
creak...
ギ
They said they wanted us to "tolerance test" this new invention of the Engineering Corps, this new materials transport board.
Although I don't know why *we* were chosen for the task.
The straps..
They're kinda tight.
Shut up! This is all your fault, because of your mess-up!
Apologize to my staff, eh?
pop
ピキ
pop
ピキ
Please raise the board a few more feet.
click
カチャ
click
カチャ
click

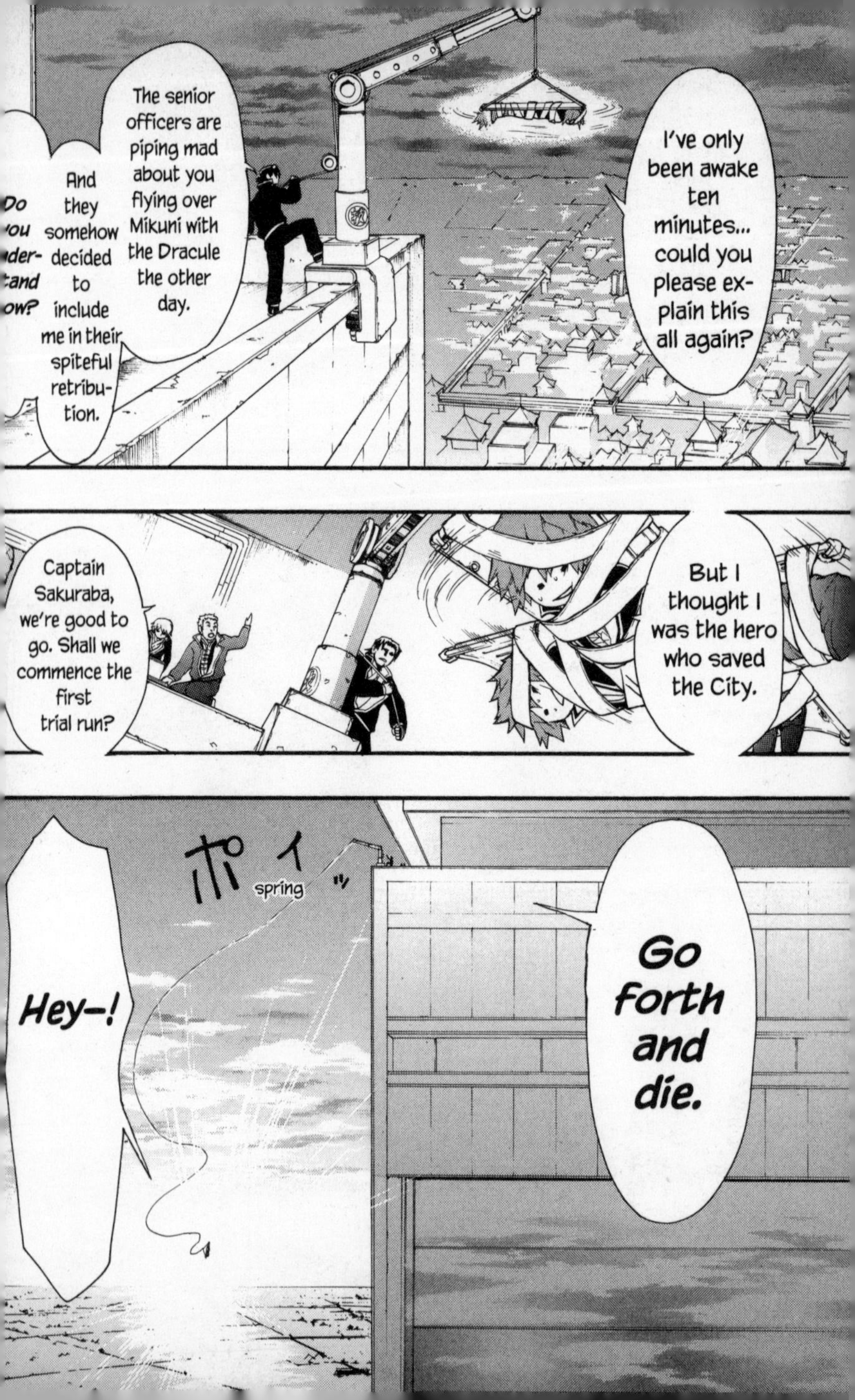

I've only been awake ten minutes... could you please explain this all again?
The senior officers are piping mad about you flying over Mikuni with the Dracule the other day.
And they somehow decided to include me in their spiteful retribution.
Do ou der- tand ow?
But I thought I was the hero who saved the City.
Captain Sakuraba, we're good to go. Shall we commence the first trial run?
Go forth and die.
ポイッ
spring
Hey—!

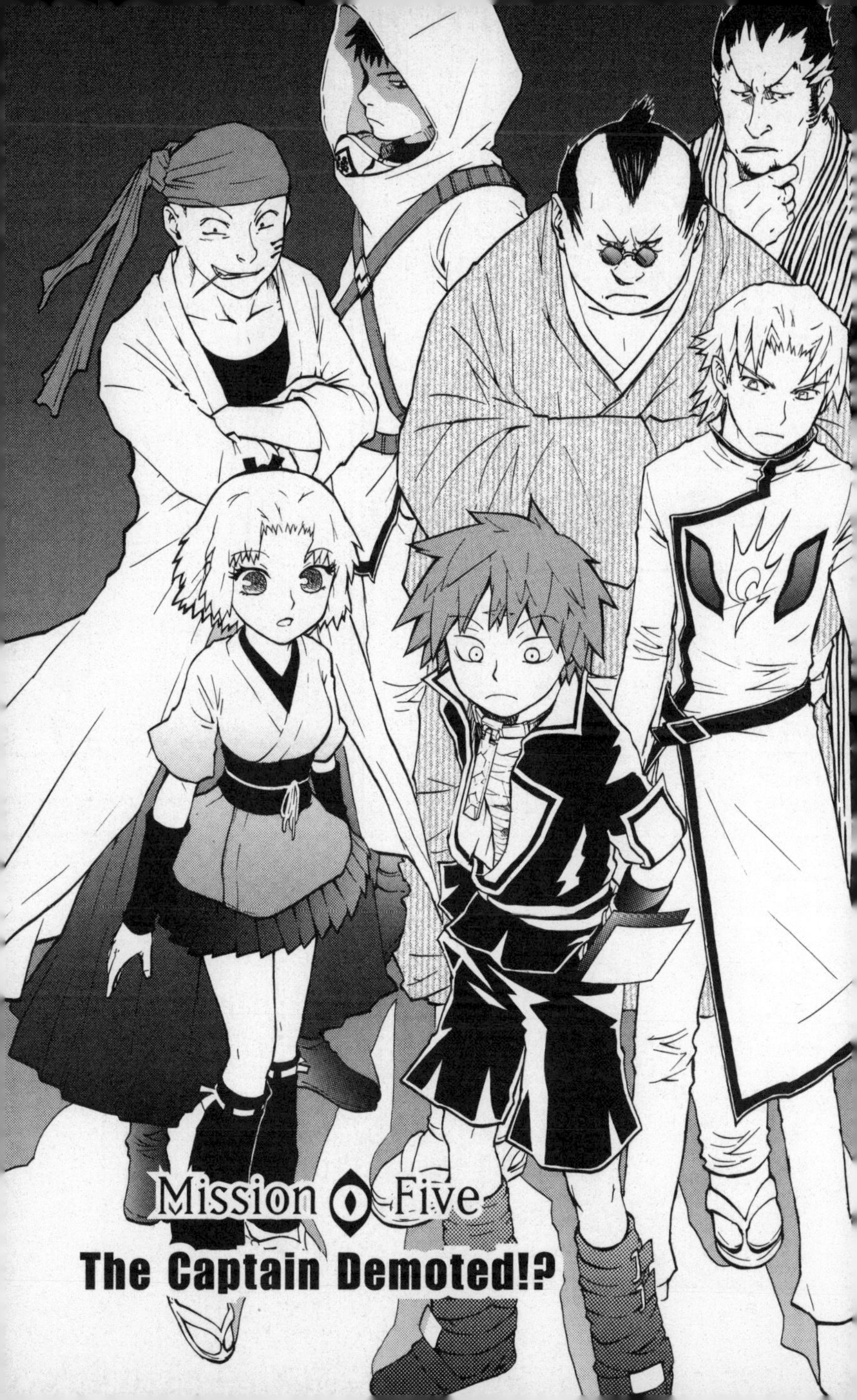
Mission Five
The Captain Demoted!?

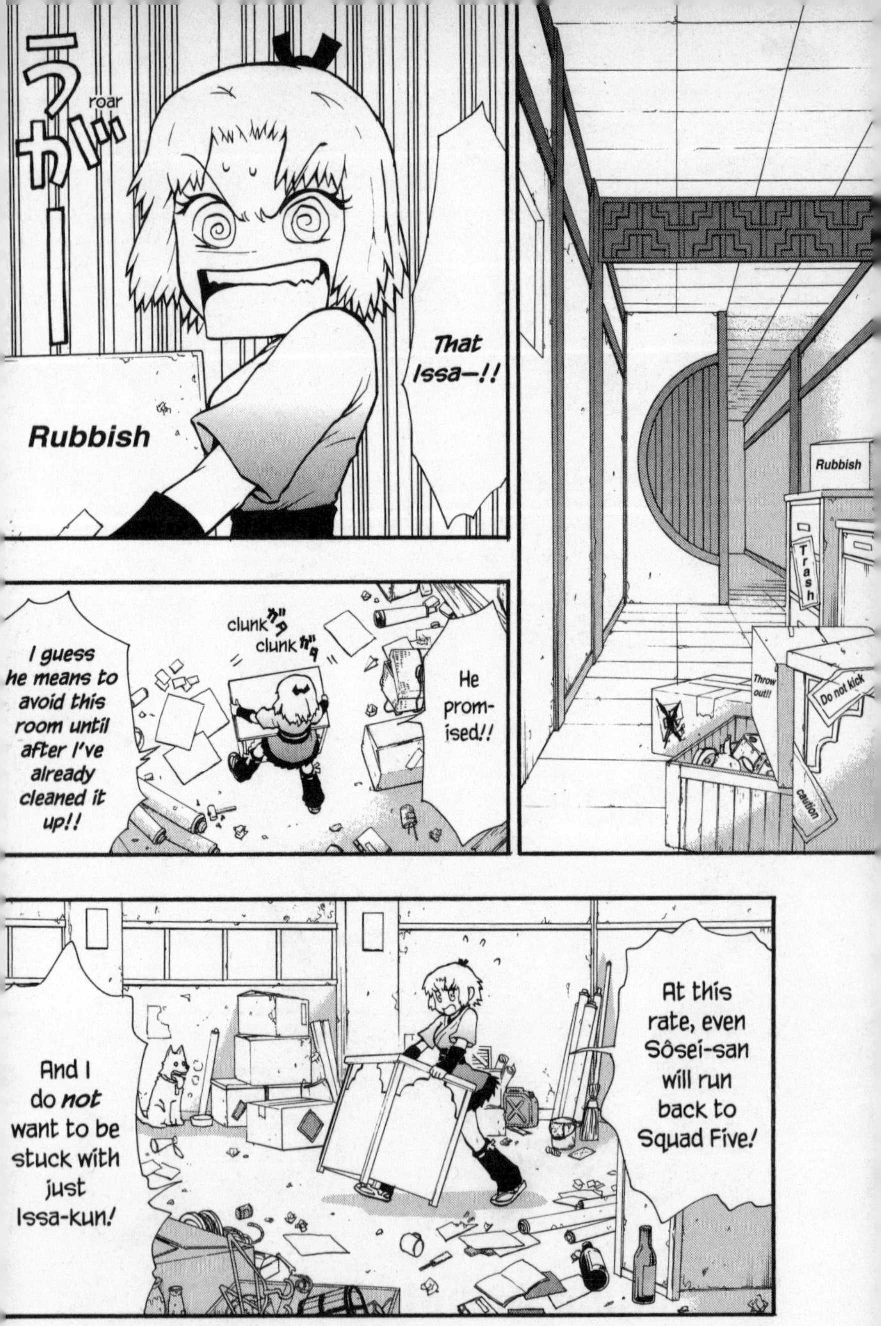
Rubbish
Trash
Throw out!!
Do not kick
caution
That Issa—!!
roar
Rubbish
He promised!!
clunk clunk
I guess he means to avoid this room until after I've already cleaned it up!!
At this rate, even Sôsei-san will run back to Squad Five!
And I do *not* want to be stuck with just Issa-kun!

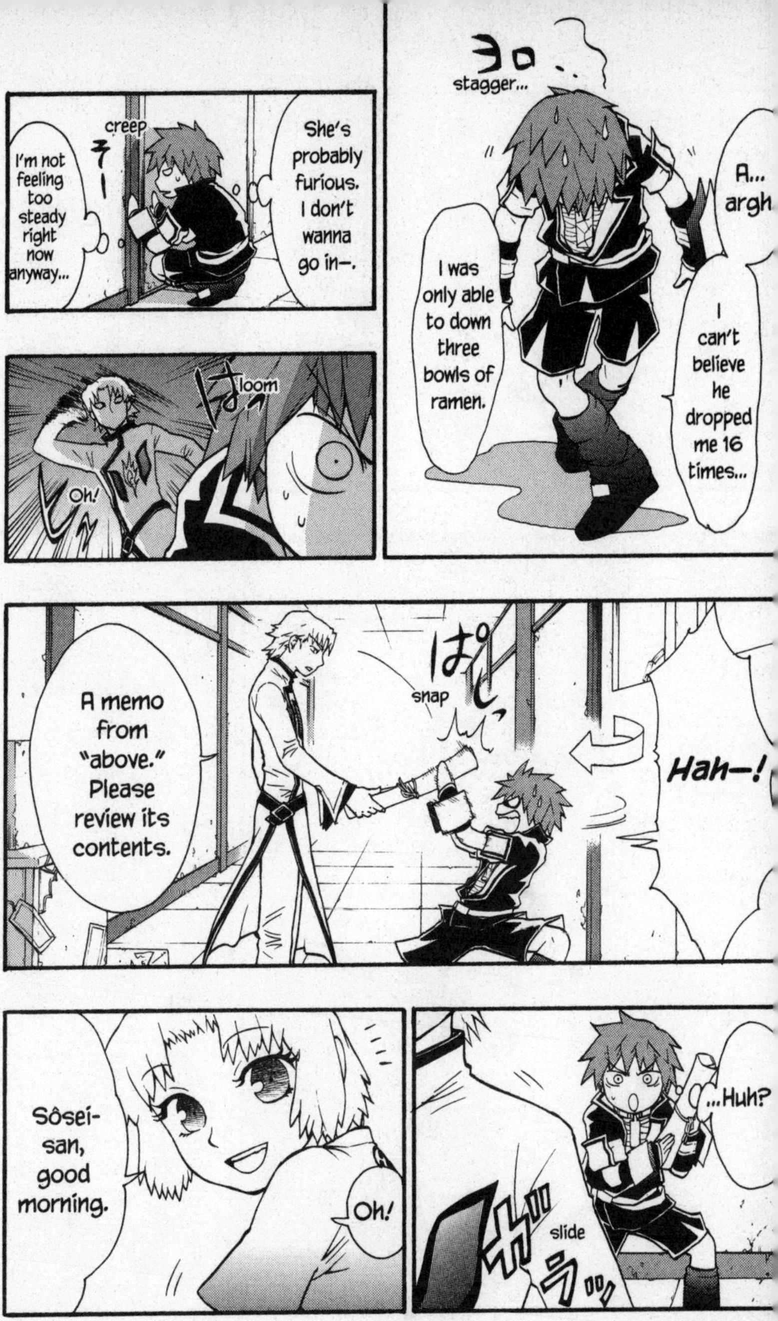
stagger...
A... argh
I can't believe he dropped me 16 times...
I was only able to down three bowls of ramen.
She's probably furious. I don't wanna go in–.
creep
I'm not feeling too steady right now anyway...
loom
Oh!
Hah–!
snap
A memo from "above." Please review its contents.
...Huh?
slide
Oh!
Sôsei-san, good morning.

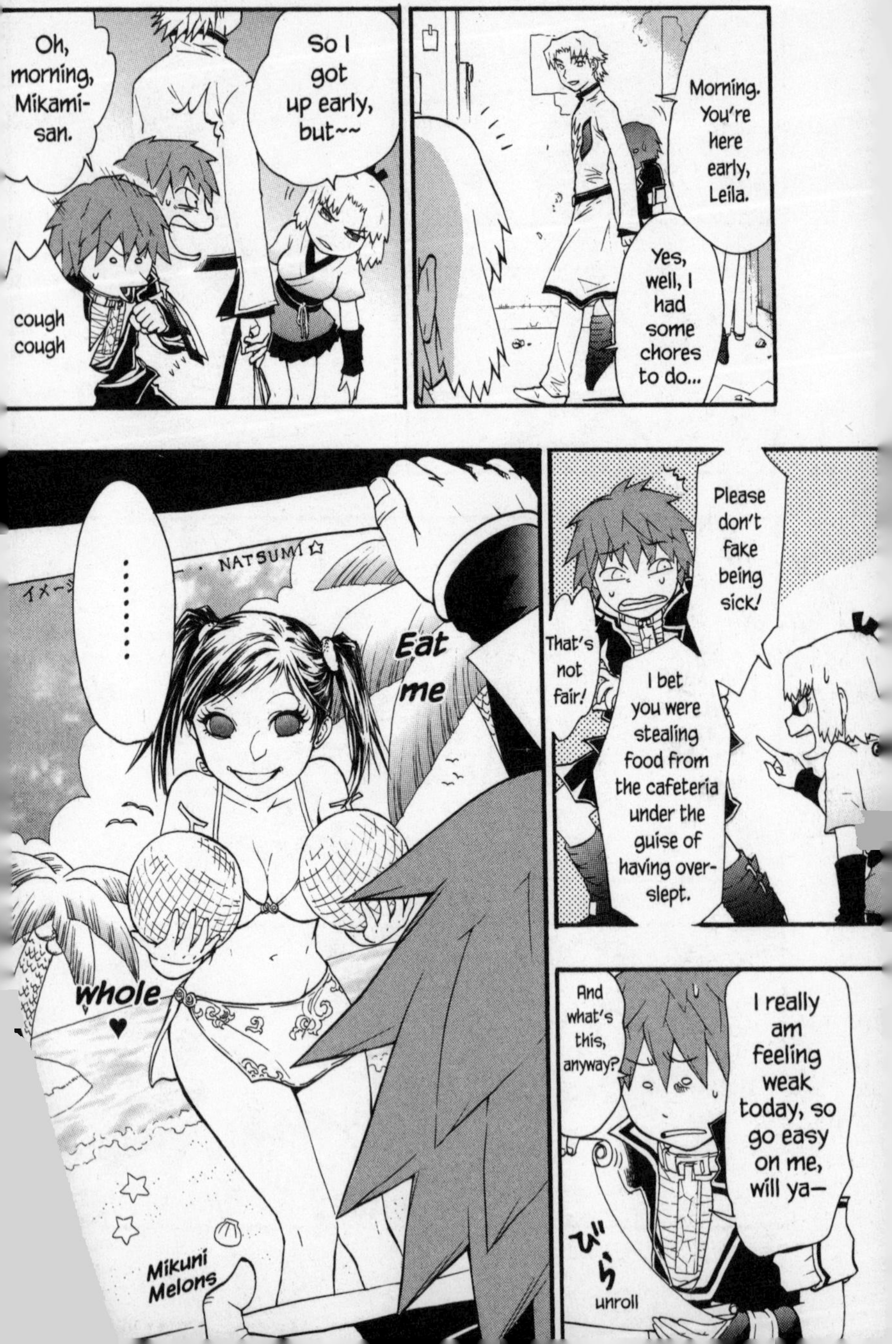

Morning. You're here early, Leila.
Yes, well, I had some chores to do...
So I got up early, but~~
Oh, morning, Mikami-san.
cough cough
Please don't fake being sick!
I bet you were stealing food from the cafeteria under the guise of having over-slept.
That's not fair!
I really am feeling weak today, so go easy on me, will ya—
And what's this, anyway?
びら
unroll
......
NATSUMI☆
イメージ
Eat me
whole ♥
Mikuni Melons

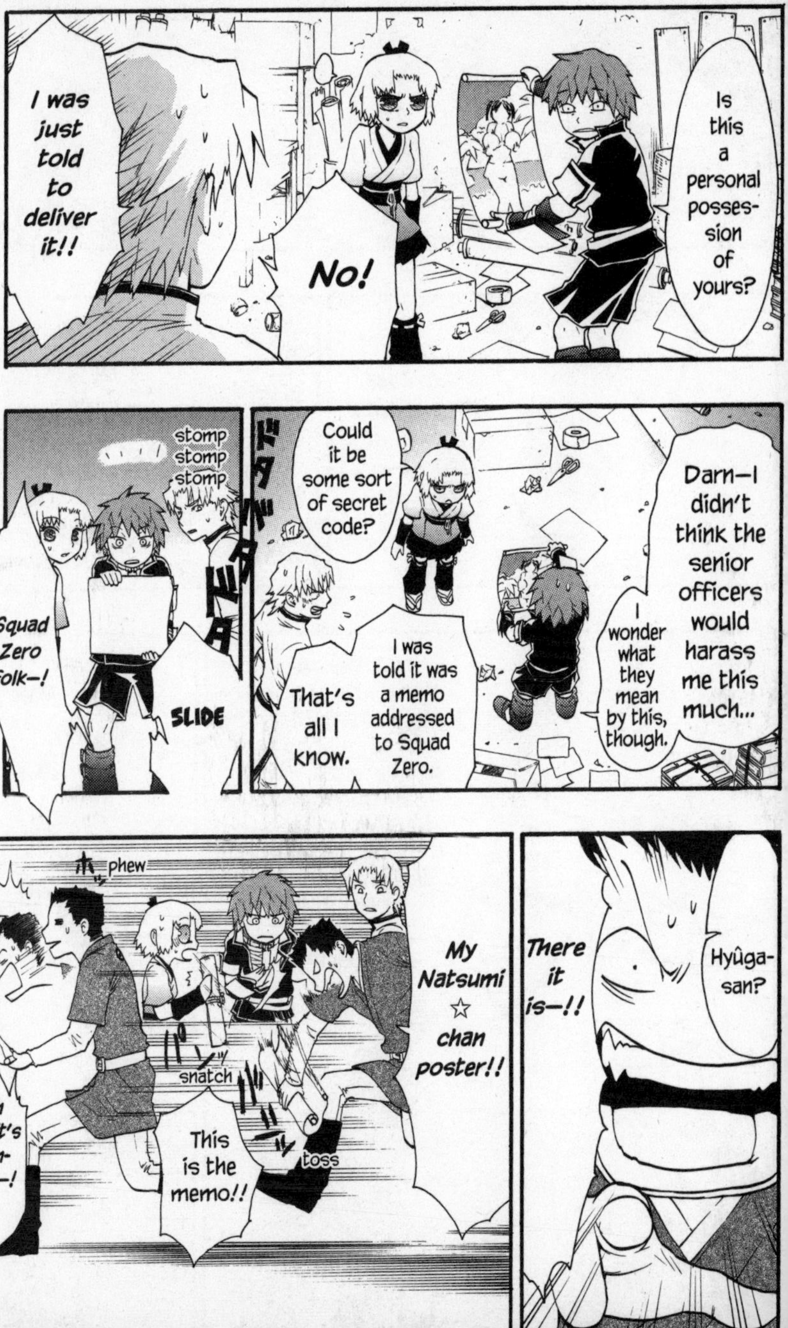
Is this a personal posses-sion of yours?
No!
I was just told to deliver it!!
Darn—I didn't think the senior officers would harass me this much...
I wonder what they mean by this, though.
Could it be some sort of secret code?
I was told it was a memo addressed to Squad Zero.
That's all I know.
stomp stomp stomp
......
Squad Zero folk—!
SLIDE
Hyûga-san?
There it is—!!
My Natsumi☆chan poster!!
phew
This is the memo!!
snatch
toss
Oh no—it's wrin-kled—!

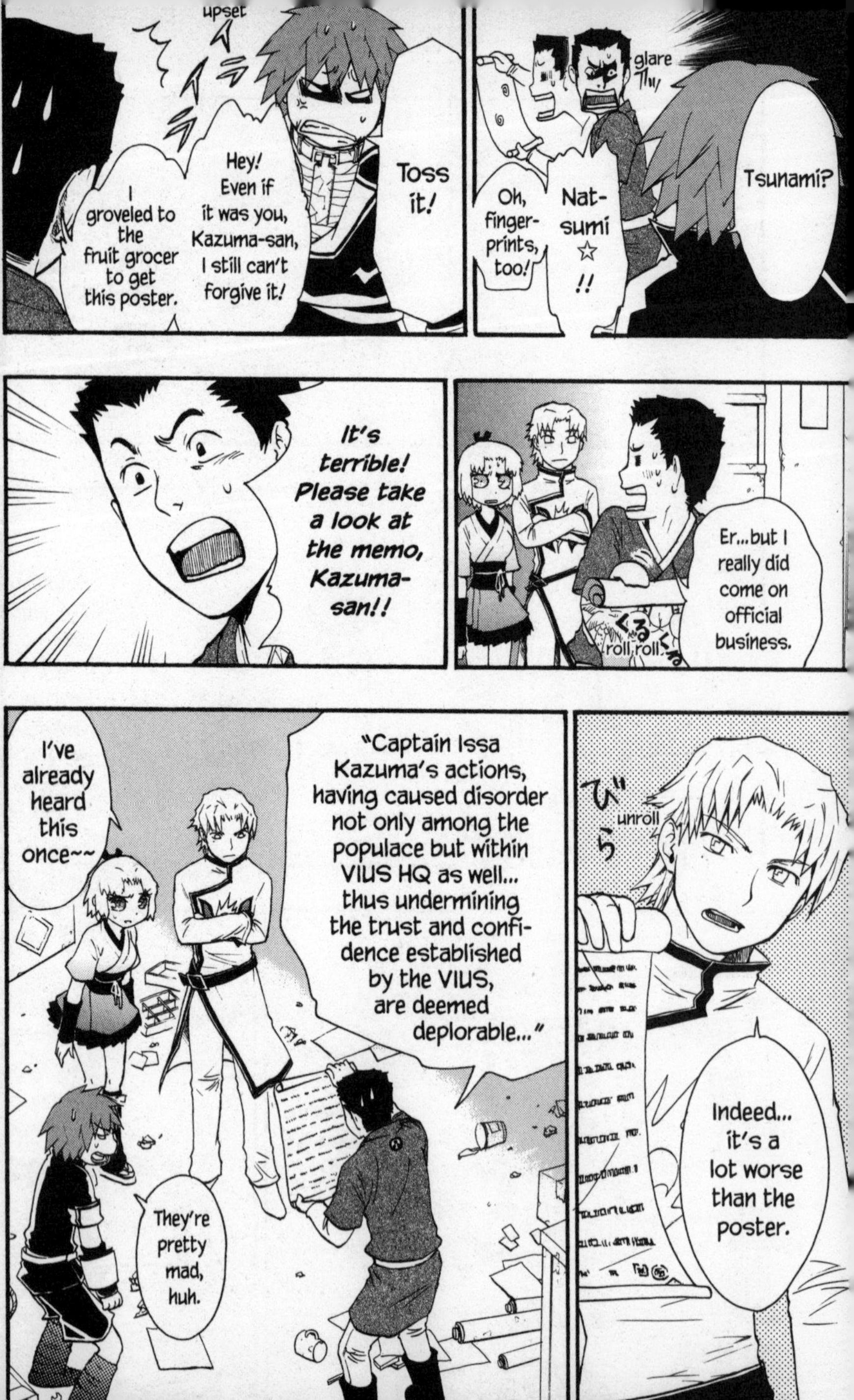
glare
Tsunami?
Nat-sumi ☆ !!
Oh, finger-prints, too!
upset
Toss it!
Hey! Even if it was you, Kazuma-san, I still can't forgive it!
I groveled to the fruit grocer to get this poster.
Er...but I really did come on official business.
roll roll
It's terrible! Please take a look at the memo, Kazuma-san!!
unroll
Indeed... it's a lot worse than the poster.
"Captain Issa Kazuma's actions, having caused disorder not only among the populace but within VIUS HQ as well... thus undermining the trust and confi-dence established by the VIUS, are deemed deplorable..."
I've already heard this once~~
They're pretty mad, huh.

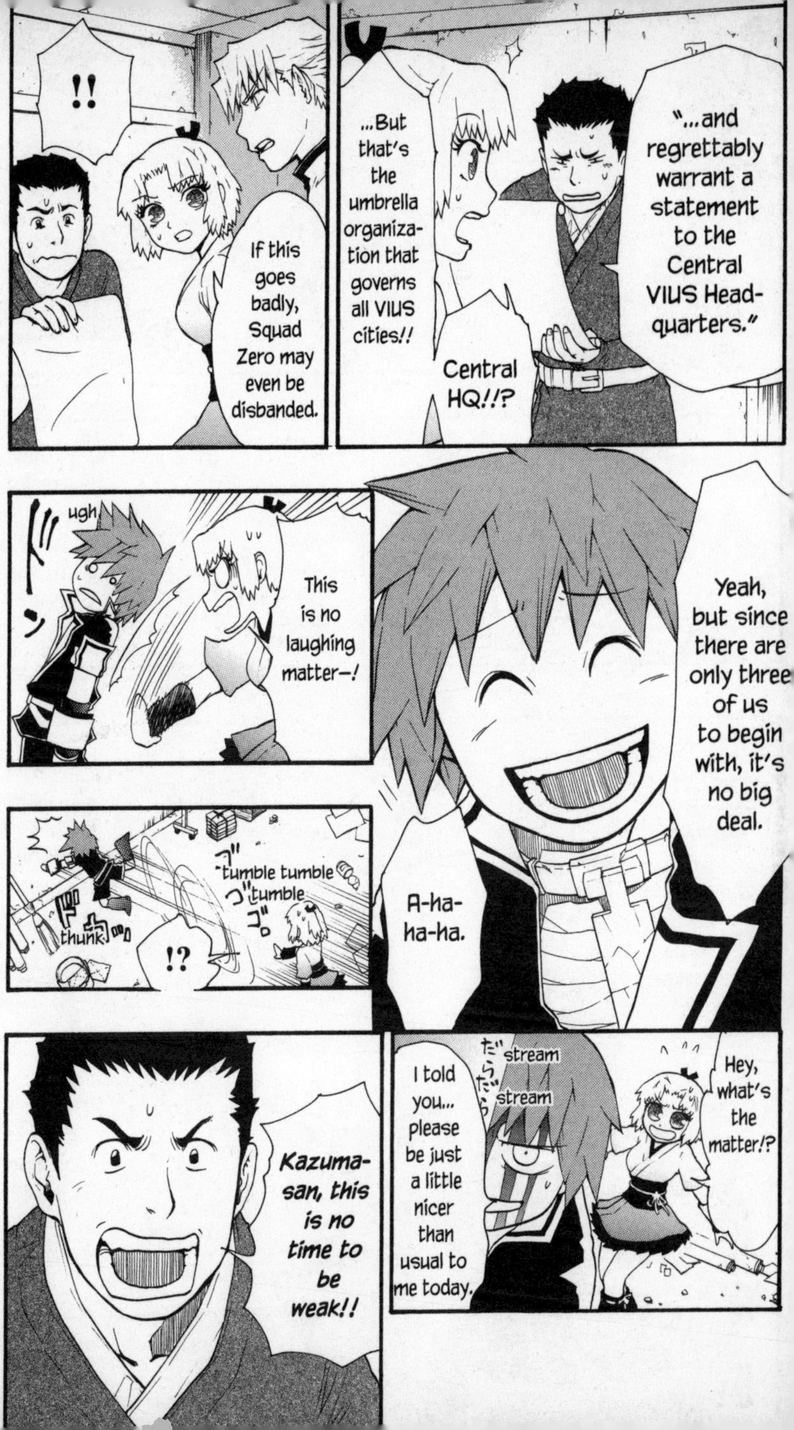
"...and regrettably warrant a statement to the Central VIUS Headquarters."
Central HQ!!?
...But that's the umbrella organization that governs all VIUS cities!!
!!
If this goes badly, Squad Zero may even be disbanded.
Yeah, but since there are only three of us to begin with, it's no big deal.
A-ha-ha-ha.
ugh
This is no laughing matter—!
tumble tumble
tumble
thunk
!?
Hey, what's the matter!?
stream
stream
I told you... please be just a little nicer than usual to me today.
Kazuma-san, this is no time to be weak!!

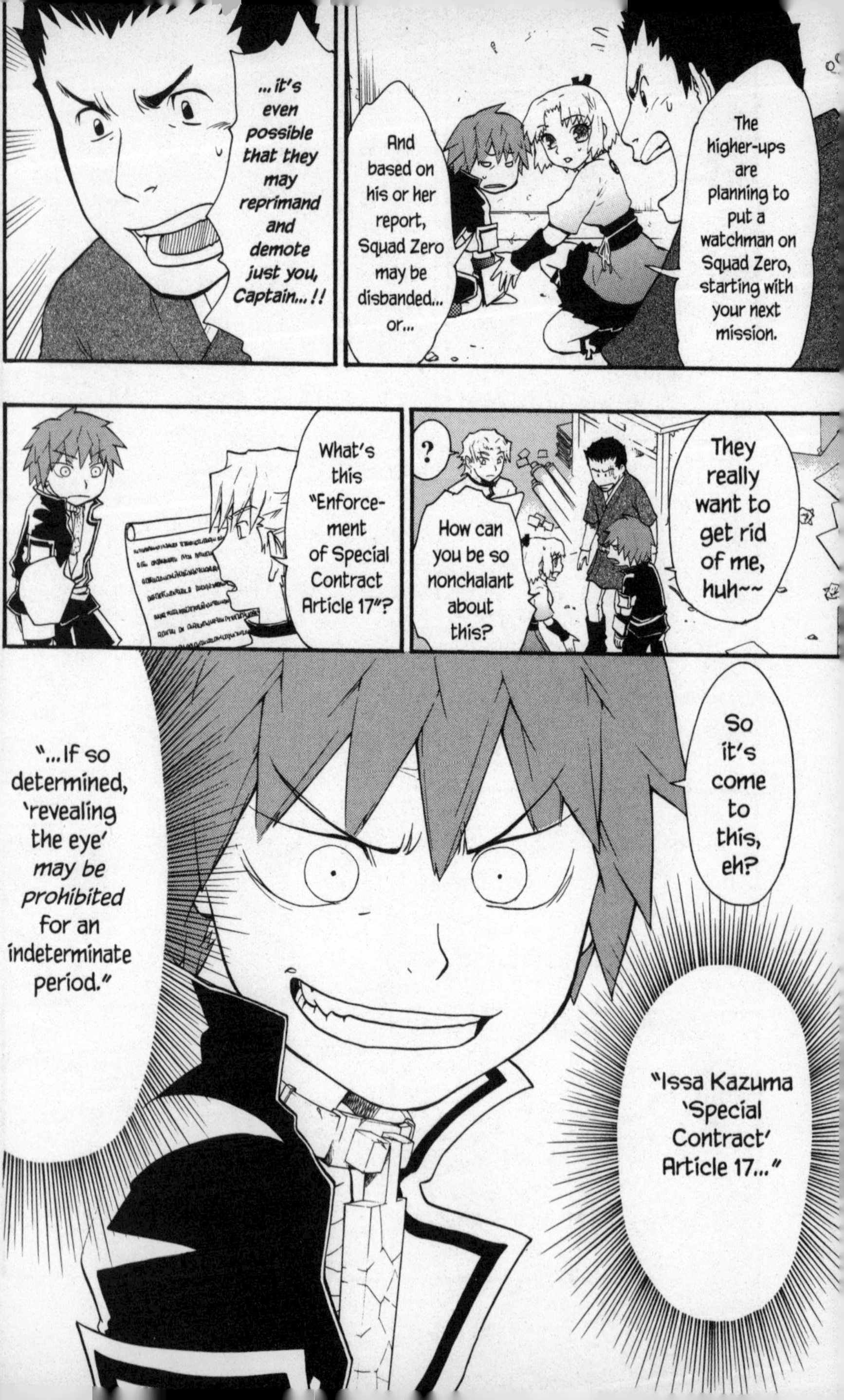
The higher-ups are planning to put a watchman on Squad Zero, starting with your next mission.
And based on his or her report, Squad Zero may be disbanded... or...
...it's even possible that they may reprimand and demote just you, Captain...!!
They really want to get rid of me, huh~~
?
How can you be so nonchalant about this?
What's this "Enforcement of Special Contract Article 17"?
So it's come to this, eh?
"Issa Kazuma 'Special Contract' Article 17..."
"...If so determined, 'revealing the eye' may be prohibited for an indeterminate period."

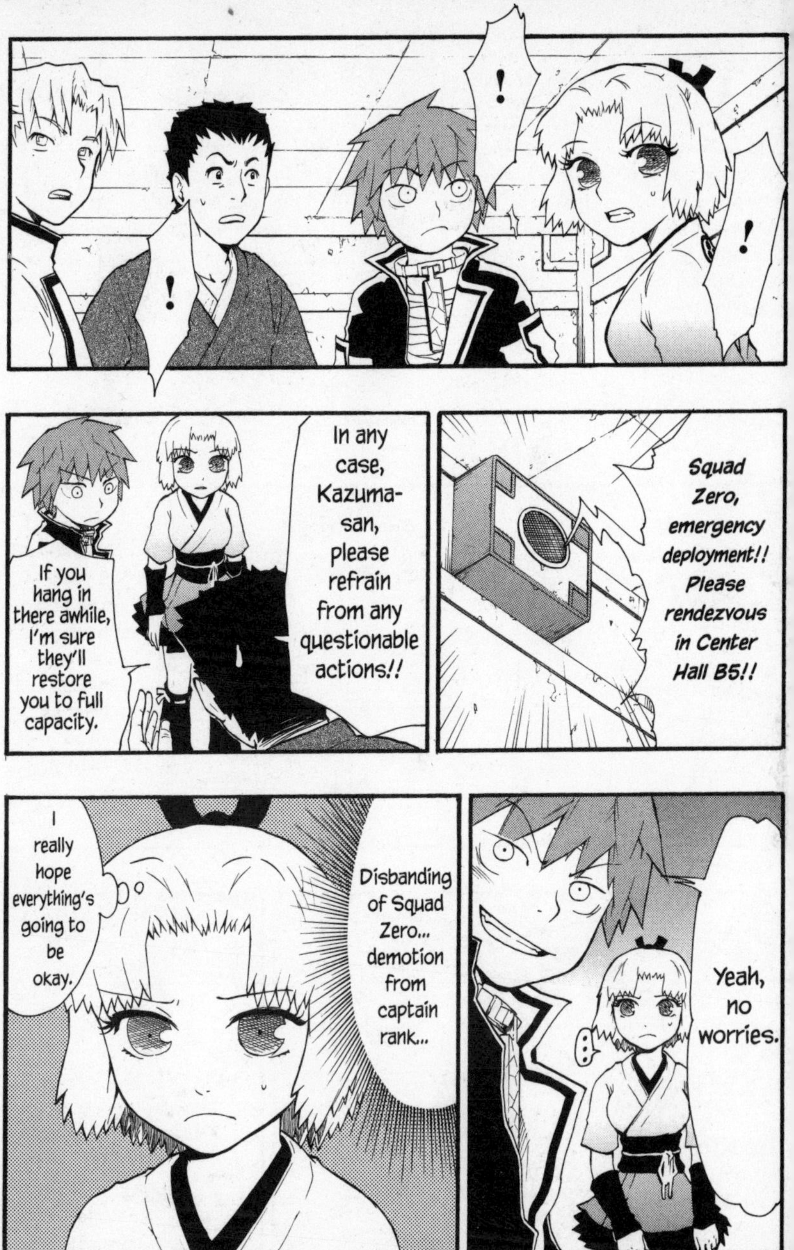

!
!
!
Squad Zero, emergency deployment!! Please rendezvous in Center Hall B5!!
In any case, Kazuma-san, please refrain from any questionable actions!!
If you hang in there awhile, I'm sure they'll restore you to full capacity.
Yeah, no worries.
...
Disbanding of Squad Zero... demotion from captain rank...
I really hope everything's going to be okay.

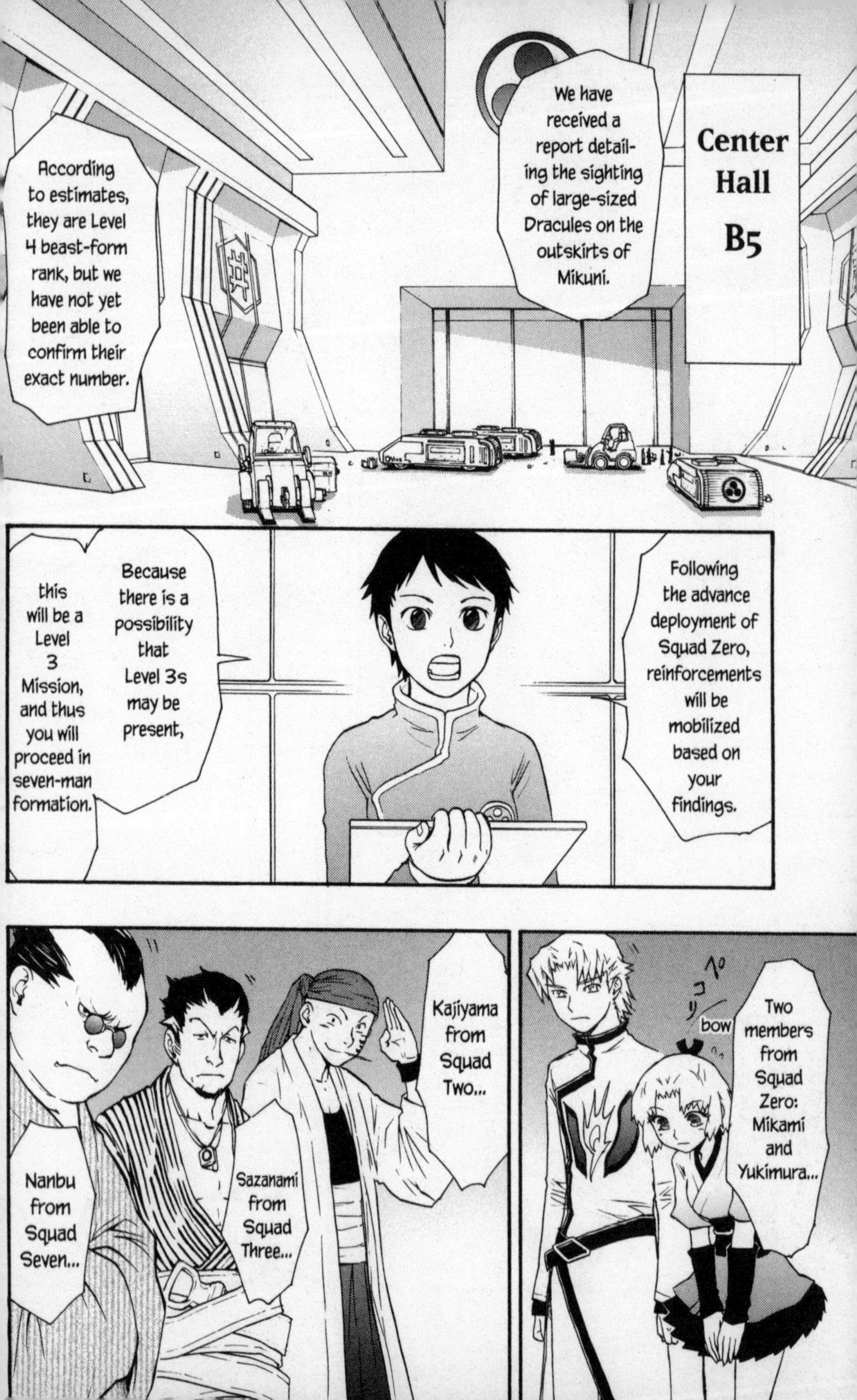

Center Hall B5
We have received a report detailing the sighting of large-sized Dracules on the outskirts of Mikuni.
According to estimates, they are Level 4 beast-form rank, but we have not yet been able to confirm their exact number.
Following the advance deployment of Squad Zero, reinforcements will be mobilized based on your findings.
Because there is a possibility that Level 3s may be present,
this will be a Level 3 Mission, and thus you will proceed in seven-man formation.
Two members from Squad Zero: Mikami and Yukimura...
bow
Kajiyama from Squad Two...
Sazanami from Squad Three...
Nanbu from Squad Seven...

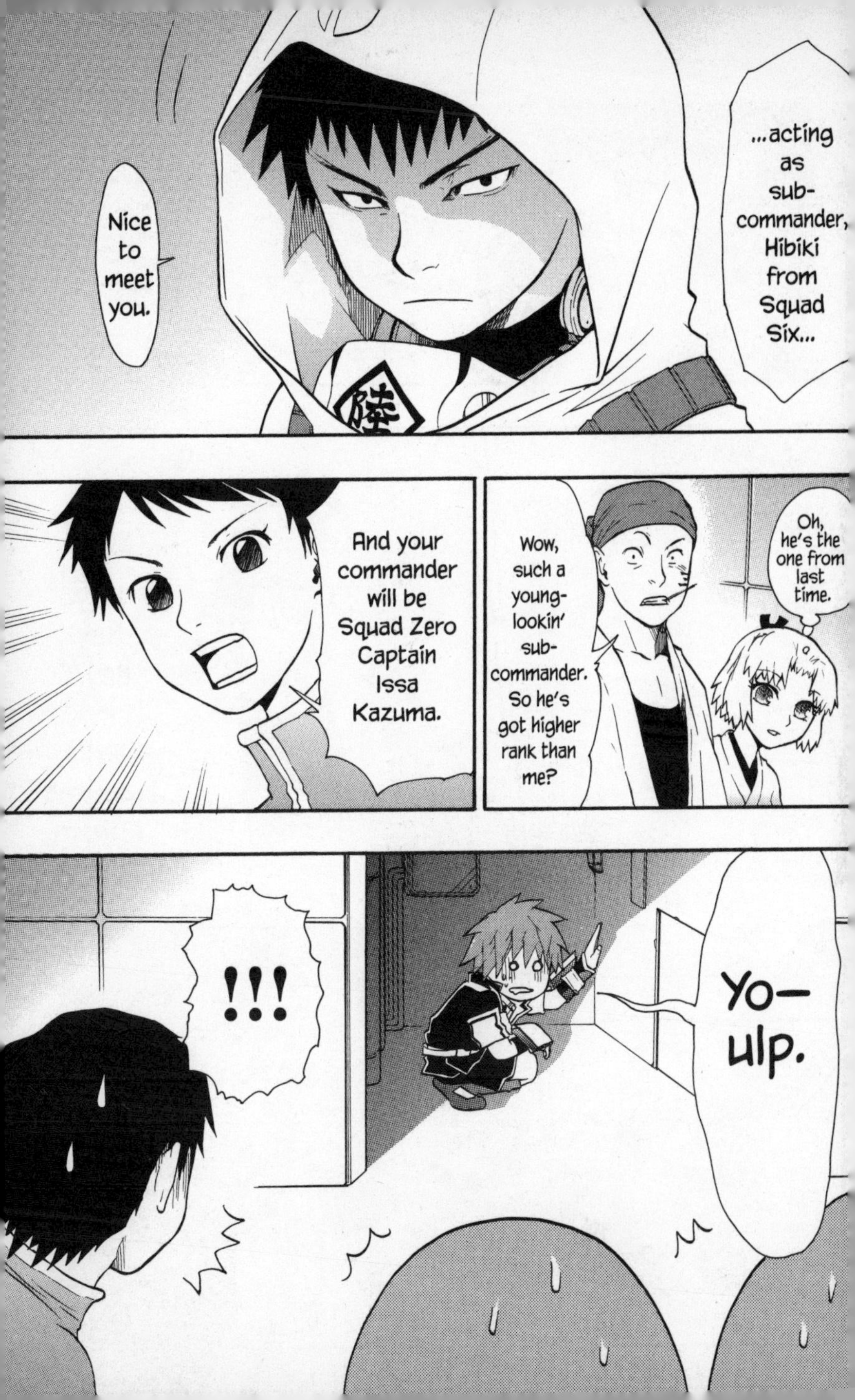
...acting as sub-commander, Hibiki from Squad Six...
Nice to meet you.
Oh, he's the one from last time.
Wow, such a young-lookin' sub-commander. So he's got higher rank than me?
And your commander will be Squad Zero Captain Issa Kazuma.
Yo— ulp.
!!!

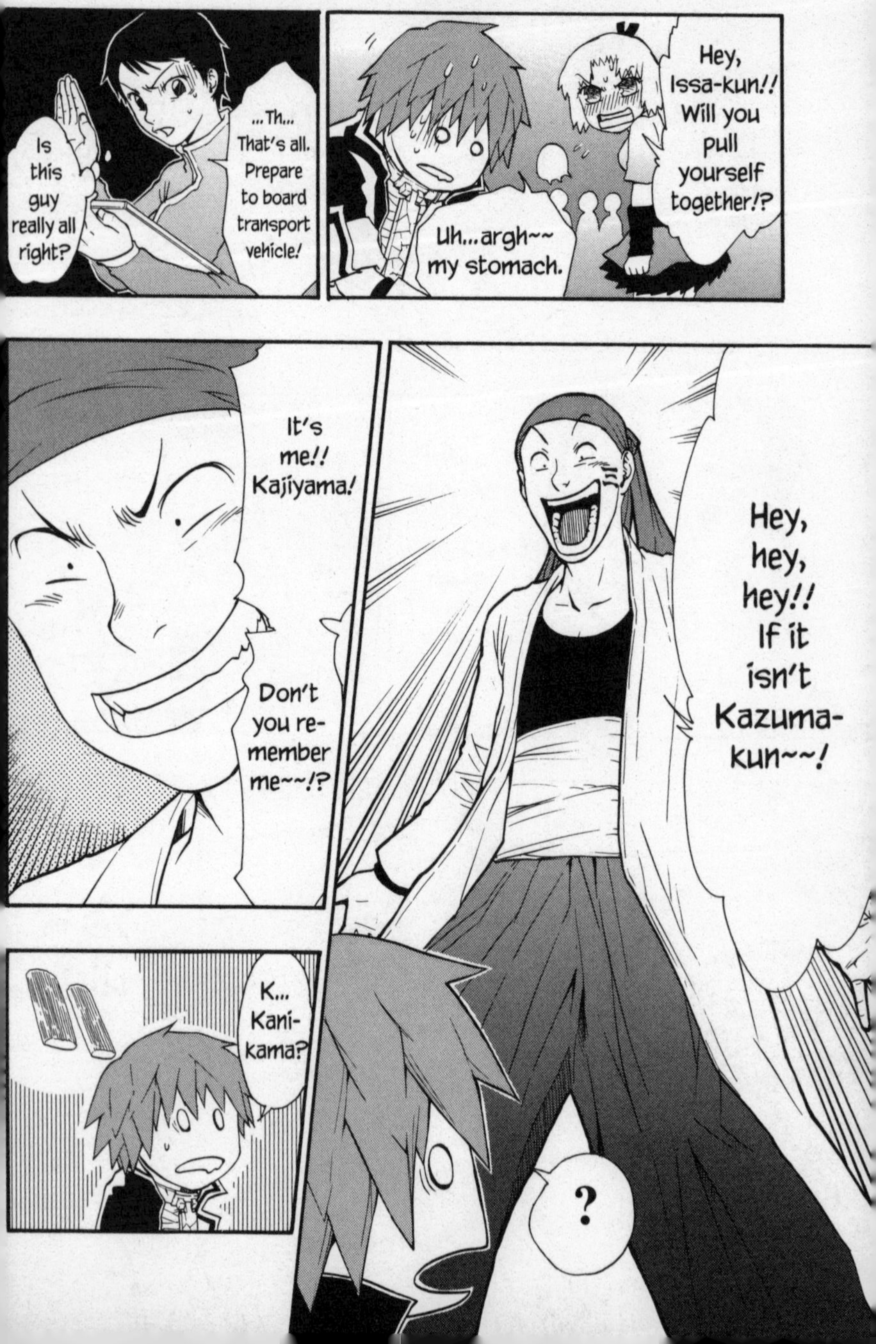
Hey, Issa-kun!! Will you pull yourself together!?
Uh...argh~~ my stomach.
...Th... That's all. Prepare to board transport vehicle!
Is this guy really all right?
Hey, hey, hey!! If it isn't Kazuma-kun~~!
?
It's me!! Kajiyama!
Don't you re-member me~~!?
K... Kani-kama?

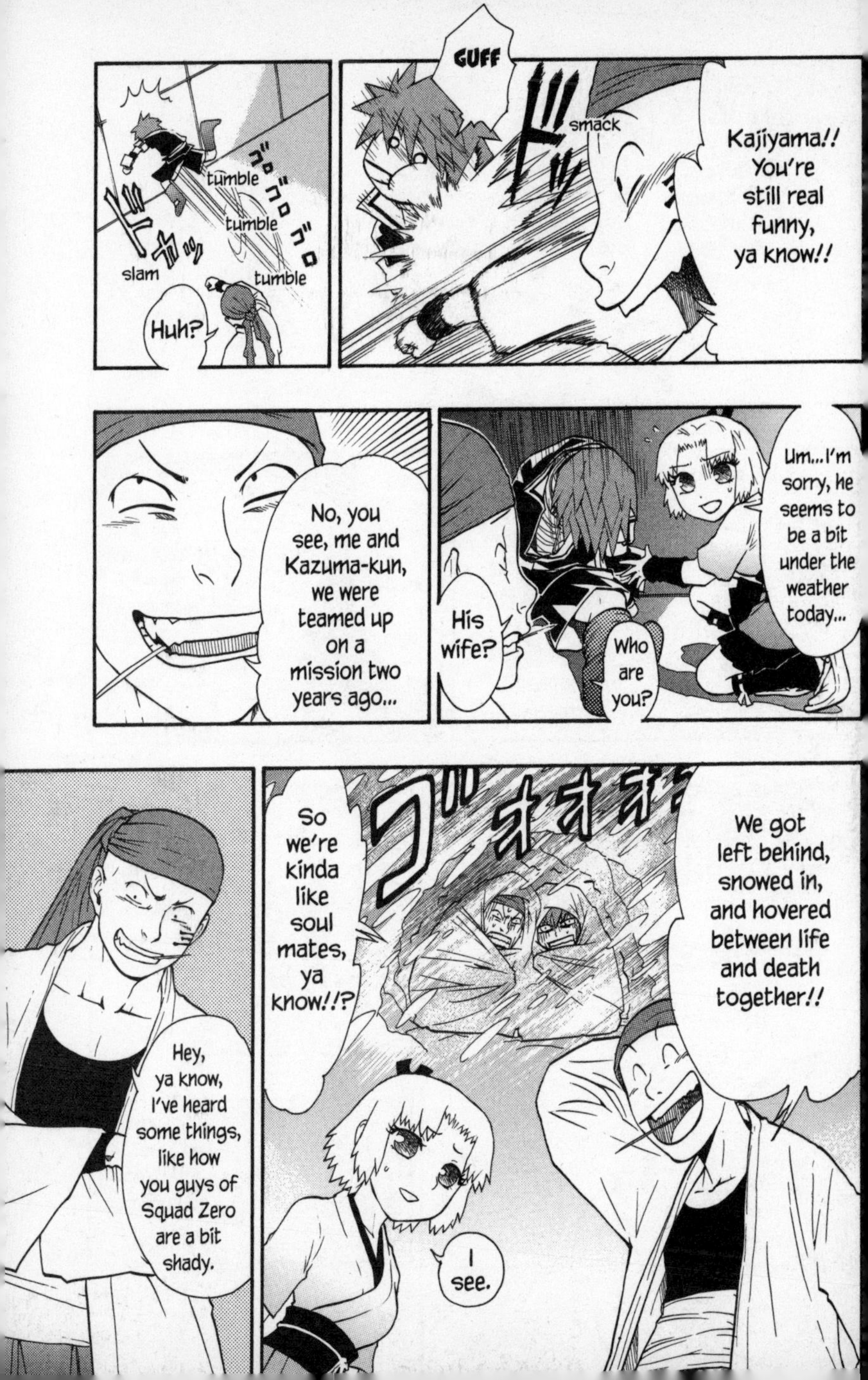
GUFF
smack
Kajiyama!! You're still real funny, ya know!!
tumble
tumble
slam
tumble
Huh?
Um...I'm sorry, he seems to be a bit under the weather today...
Who are you?
His wife?
No, you see, me and Kazuma-kun, we were teamed up on a mission two years ago...
We got left behind, snowed in, and hovered between life and death together!!
So we're kinda like soul mates, ya know!!?
I see.
Hey, ya know, I've heard some things, like how you guys of Squad Zero are a bit shady.

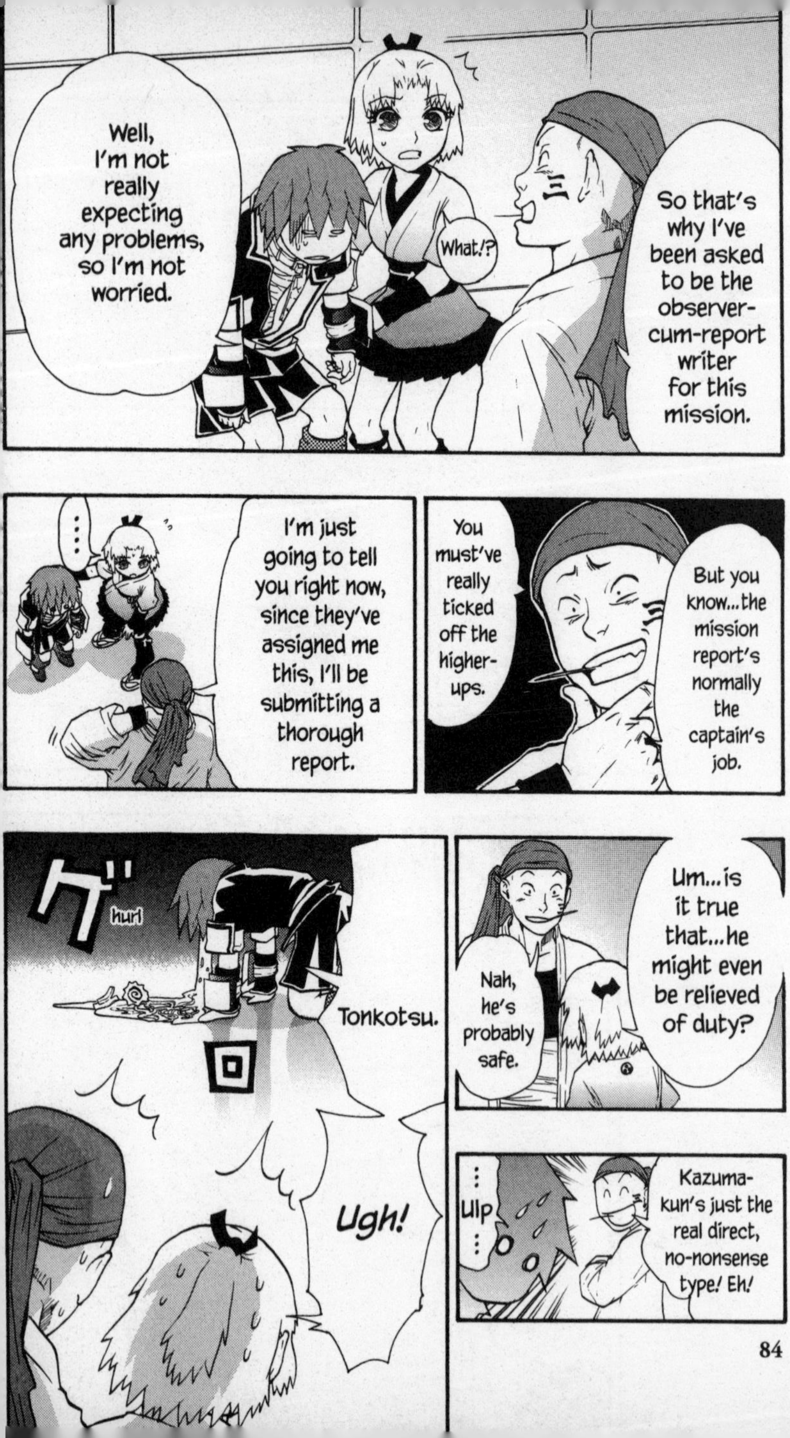

So that's why I've been asked to be the observer-cum-report writer for this mission.
What!?
Well, I'm not really expecting any problems, so I'm not worried.
But you know...the mission report's normally the captain's job.
You must've really ticked off the higher-ups.
I'm just going to tell you right now, since they've assigned me this, I'll be submitting a thorough report.
....
Um...is it true that...he might even be relieved of duty?
Nah, he's probably safe.
Kazuma-kun's just the real direct, no-nonsense type! Eh!
...Ulp...
ゲ
hurl
Tonkotsu.
Ugh!

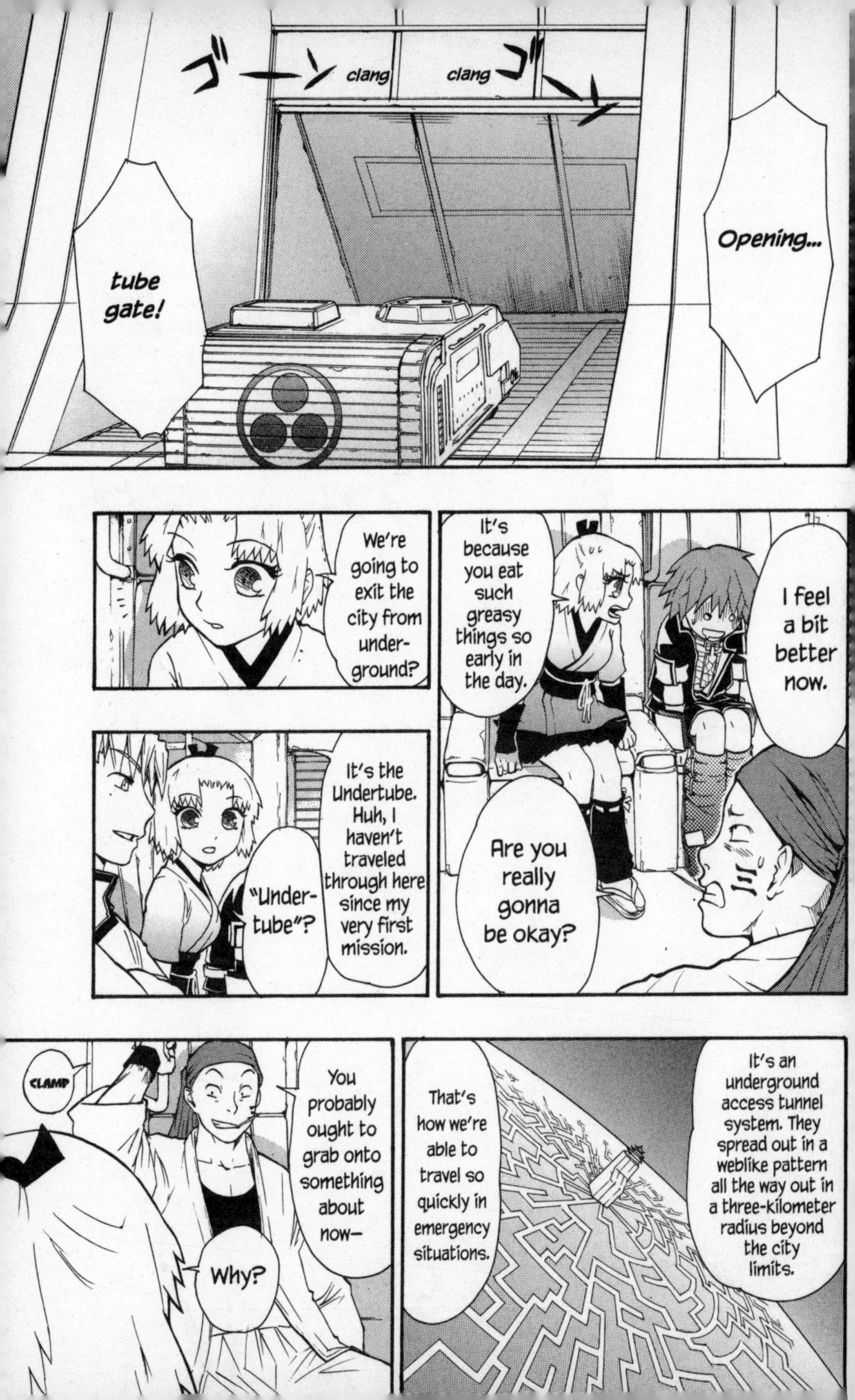
ゴーン
clang
clang
ゴーン
Opening...
tube gate!
I feel a bit better now.
It's because you eat such greasy things so early in the day.
Are you really gonna be okay?
We're going to exit the city from underground?
It's the Undertube. Huh, I haven't traveled through here since my very first mission.
"Under-tube"?
It's an underground access tunnel system. They spread out in a weblike pattern all the way out in a three-kilometer radius beyond the city limits.
That's how we're able to travel so quickly in emergency situations.
You probably ought to grab onto something about now—
Why?
CLAMP

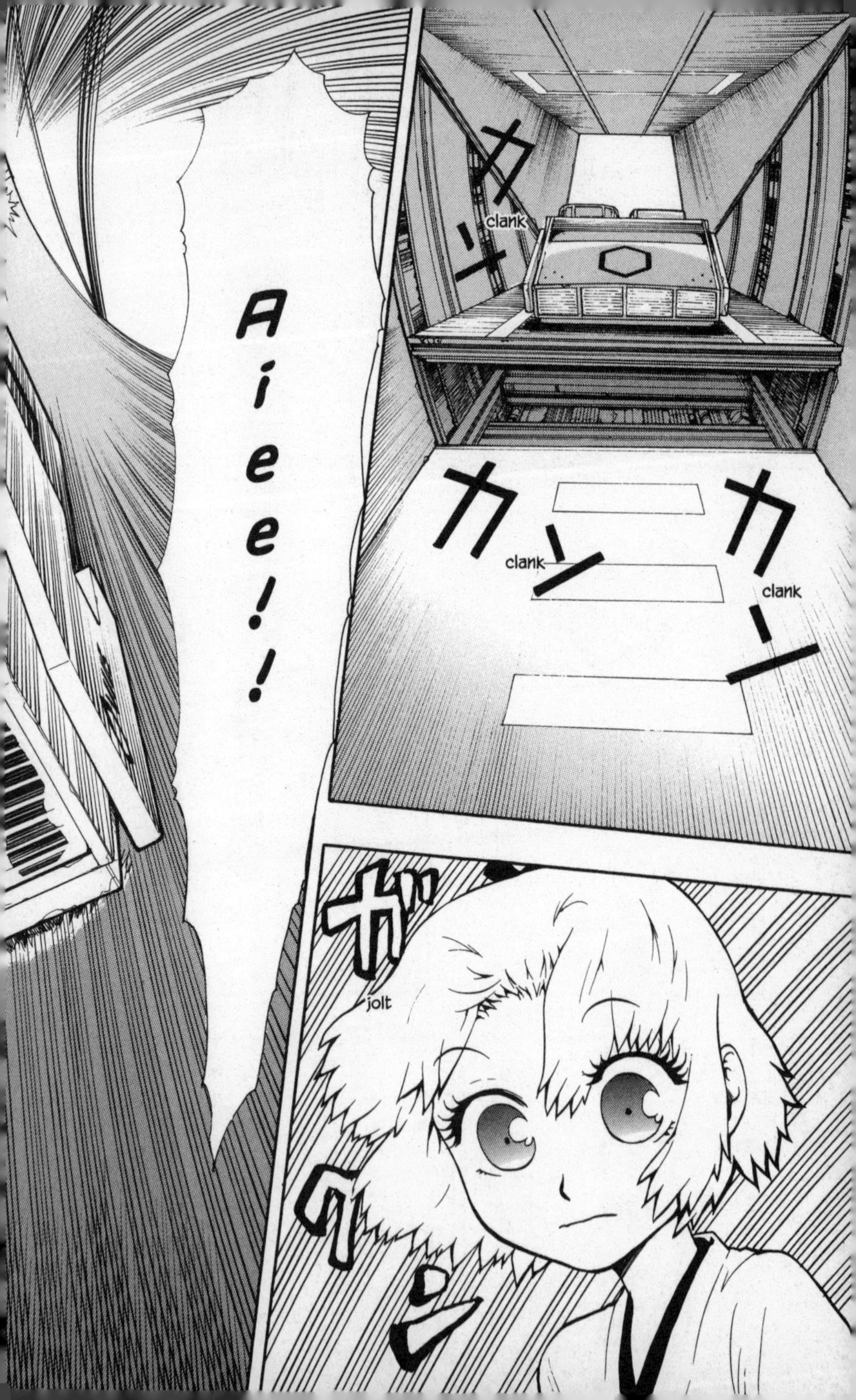
カチ
clank
カーン
clank
カン
clank
ガクン
jolt
Aieee!!

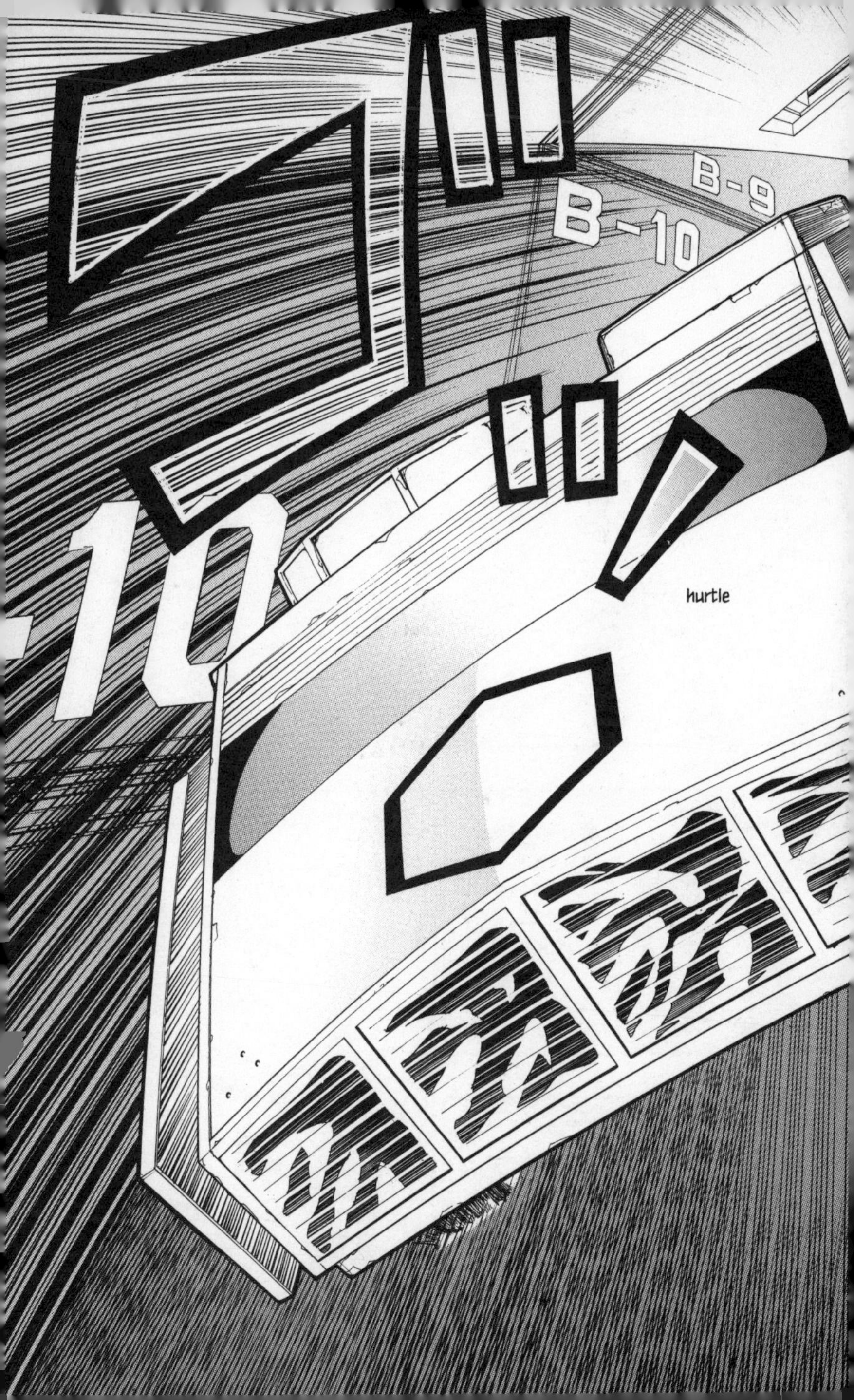
B-9
B-10
hurtle

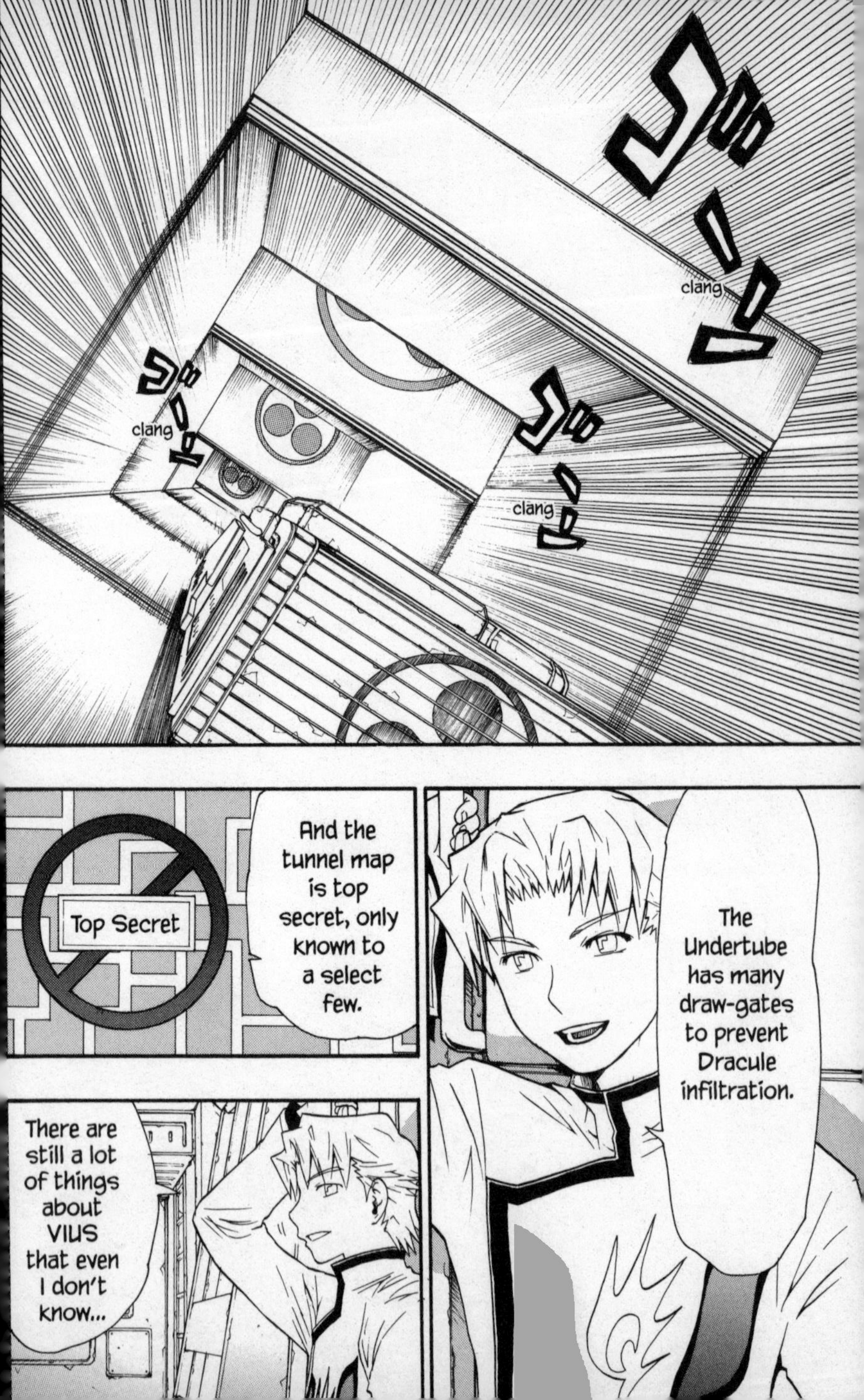
clang
clang
clang
The Undertube has many draw-gates to prevent Dracule infiltration.
And the tunnel map is top secret, only known to a select few.
Top Secret
There are still a lot of things about VIUS that even I don't know...

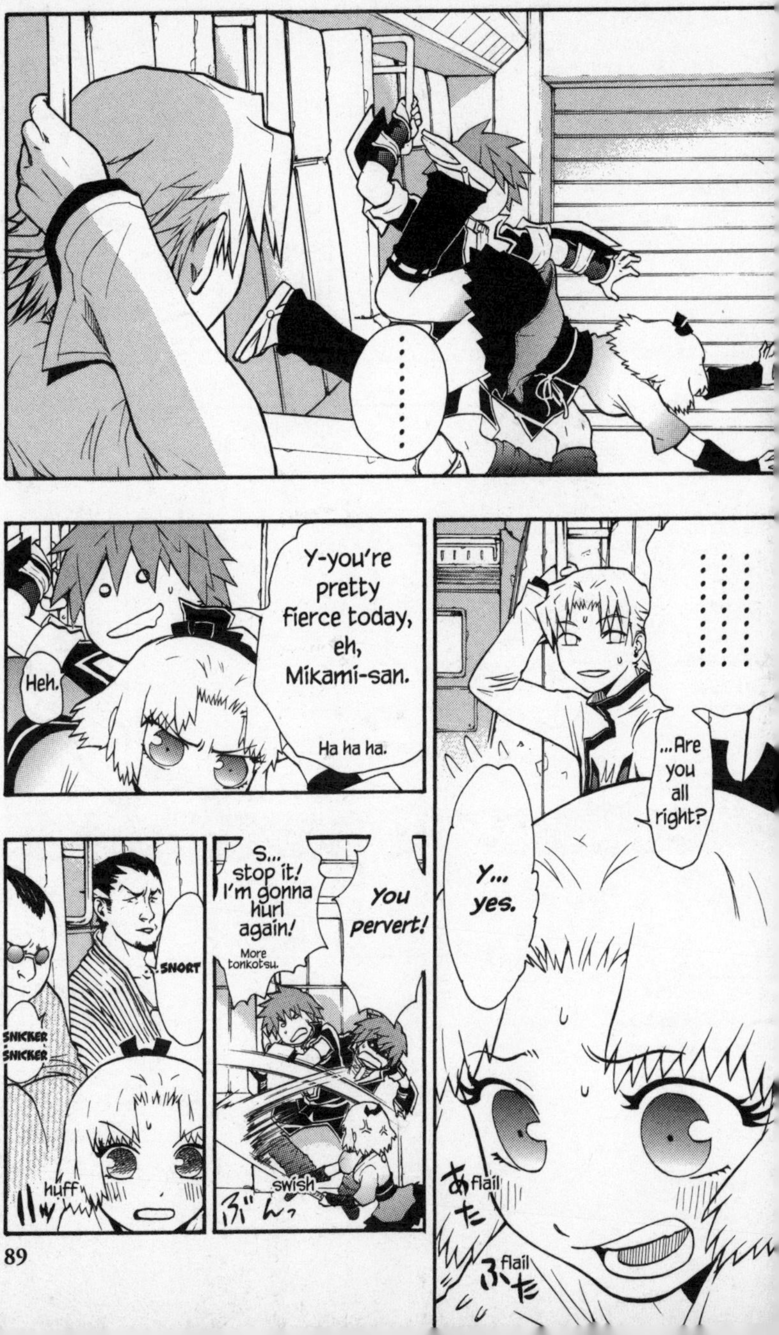
......
......
...Are you all right?
Y... yes.
あた flail
ふた flail
Y-you're pretty fierce today, eh, Mikami-san.
Ha ha ha.
Heh.
You pervert!
S... stop it! I'm gonna hurl again!
More tonkotsu.
swish
ぶんっ
...SNORT
SNICKER SNICKER
huff
ハッ

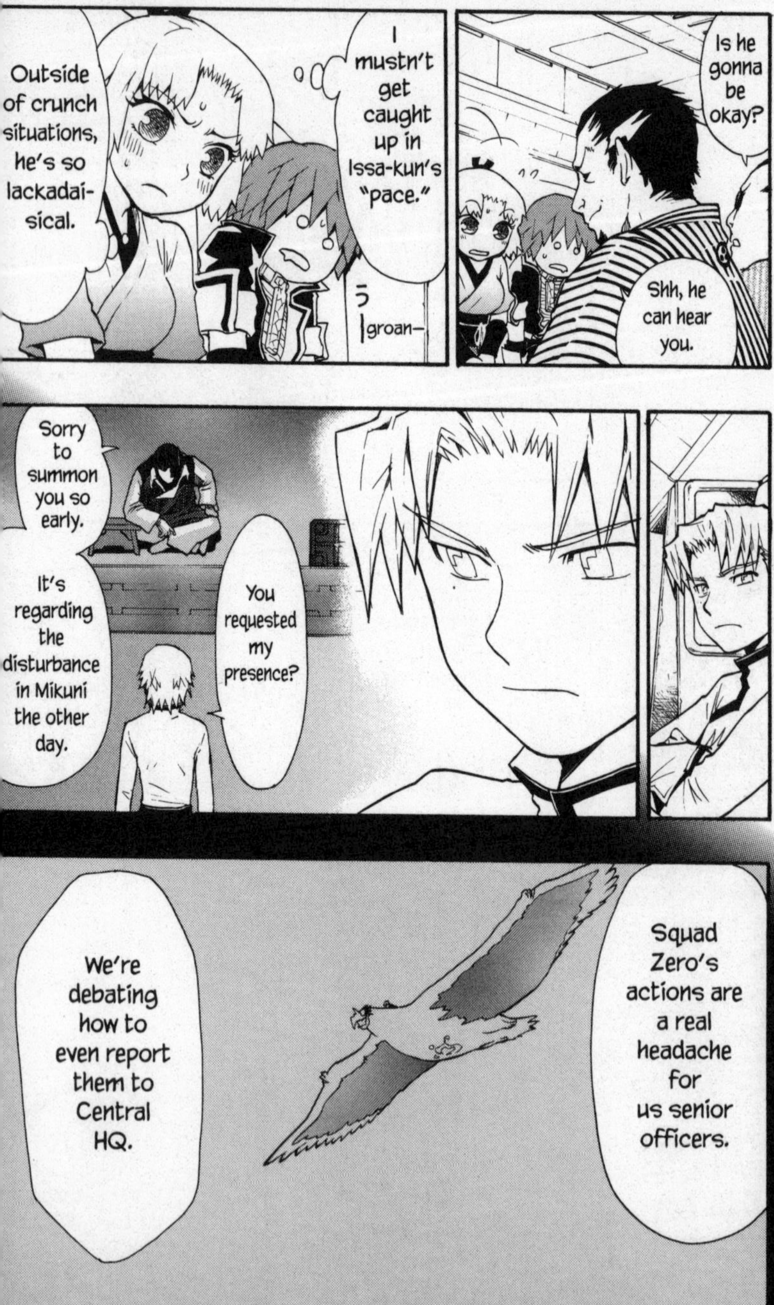
Is he gonna be okay?
Shh, he can hear you.
I mustn't get caught up in Issa-kun's "pace."
う
groan—
Outside of crunch situations, he's so lackadaisical.
You requested my presence?
Sorry to summon you so early.
It's regarding the disturbance in Mikuni the other day.
Squad Zero's actions are a real headache for us senior officers.
We're debating how to even report them to Central HQ.

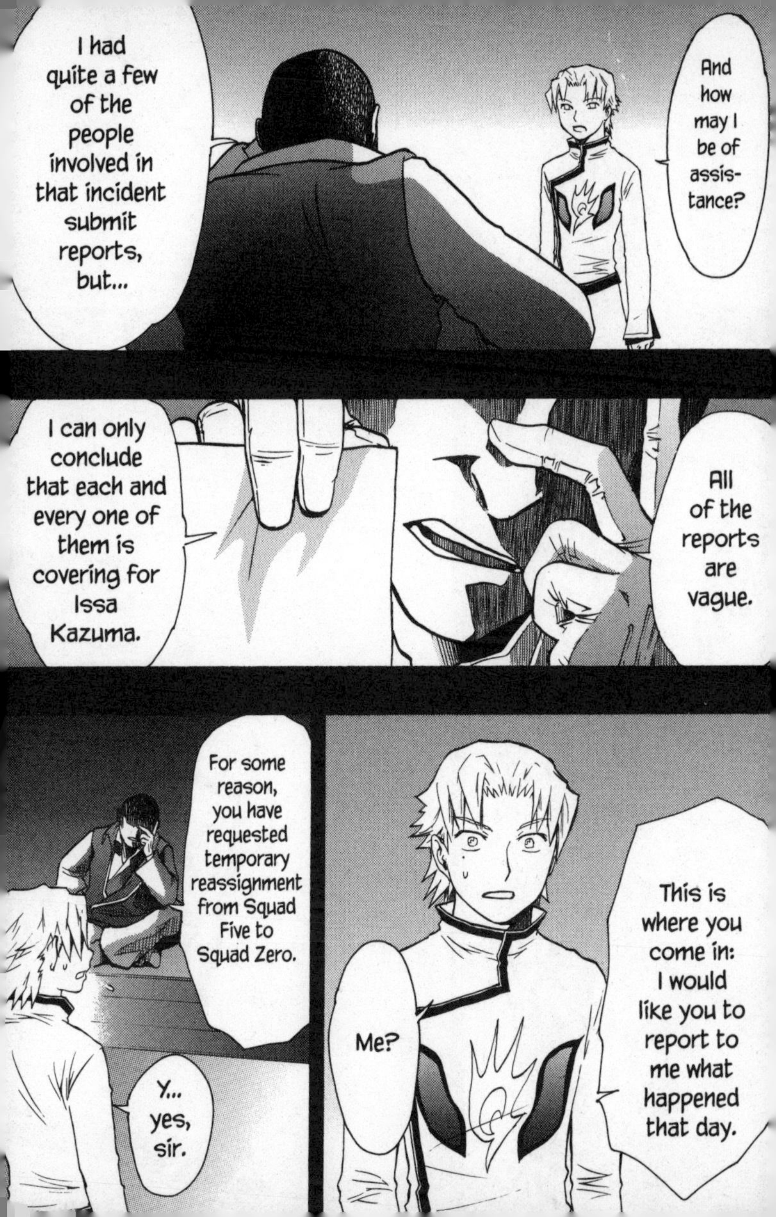
And how may I be of assistance?
I had quite a few of the people involved in that incident submit reports, but...
All of the reports are vague.
I can only conclude that each and every one of them is covering for Issa Kazuma.
This is where you come in: I would like you to report to me what happened that day.
Me?
For some reason, you have requested temporary reassignment from Squad Five to Squad Zero.
Y... yes, sir.

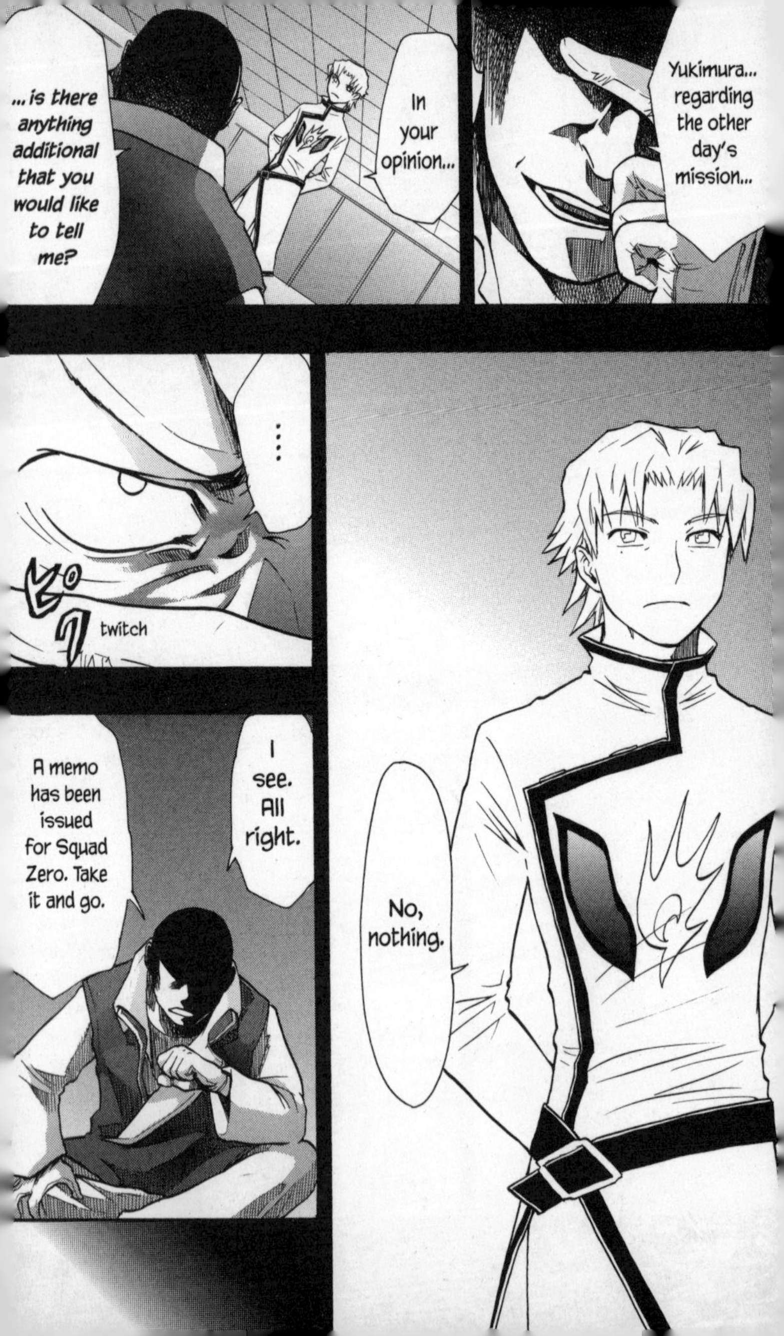
Yukimura... regarding the other day's mission...
In your opinion...
...is there anything additional that you would like to tell me?
No, nothing.
....
twitch
I see. All right.
A memo has been issued for Squad Zero. Take it and go.

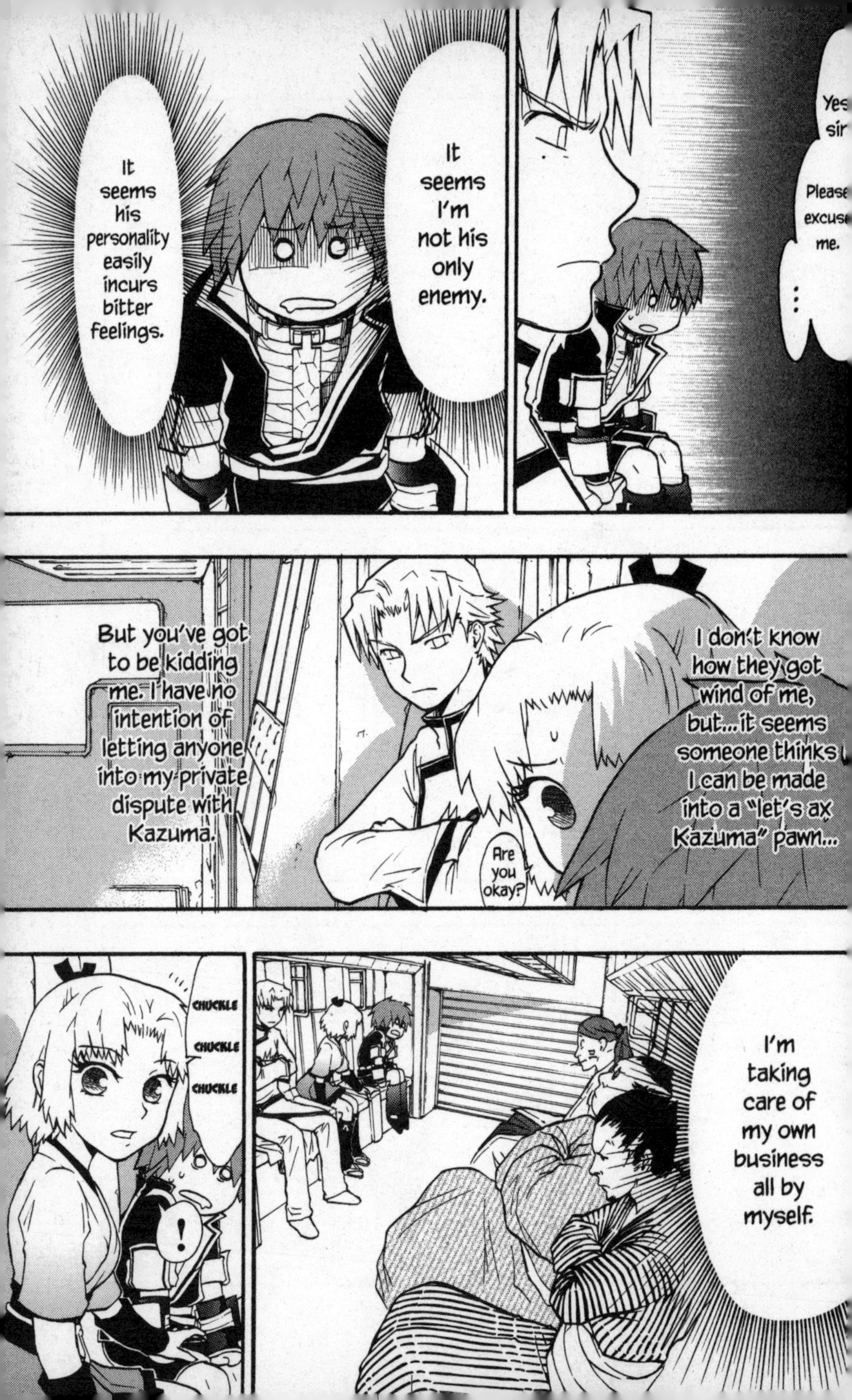
Yes sir
Please excus me.
...
It seems I'm not his only enemy.
It seems his personality easily incurs bitter feelings.
I don't know how they got wind of me, but...it seems someone thinks I can be made into a "let's ax Kazuma" pawn...
Are you okay?
But you've got to be kidding me. I have no intention of letting anyone into my private dispute with Kazuma.
I'm taking care of my own business all by myself.
CHUCKLE
CHUCKLE
CHUCKLE
!

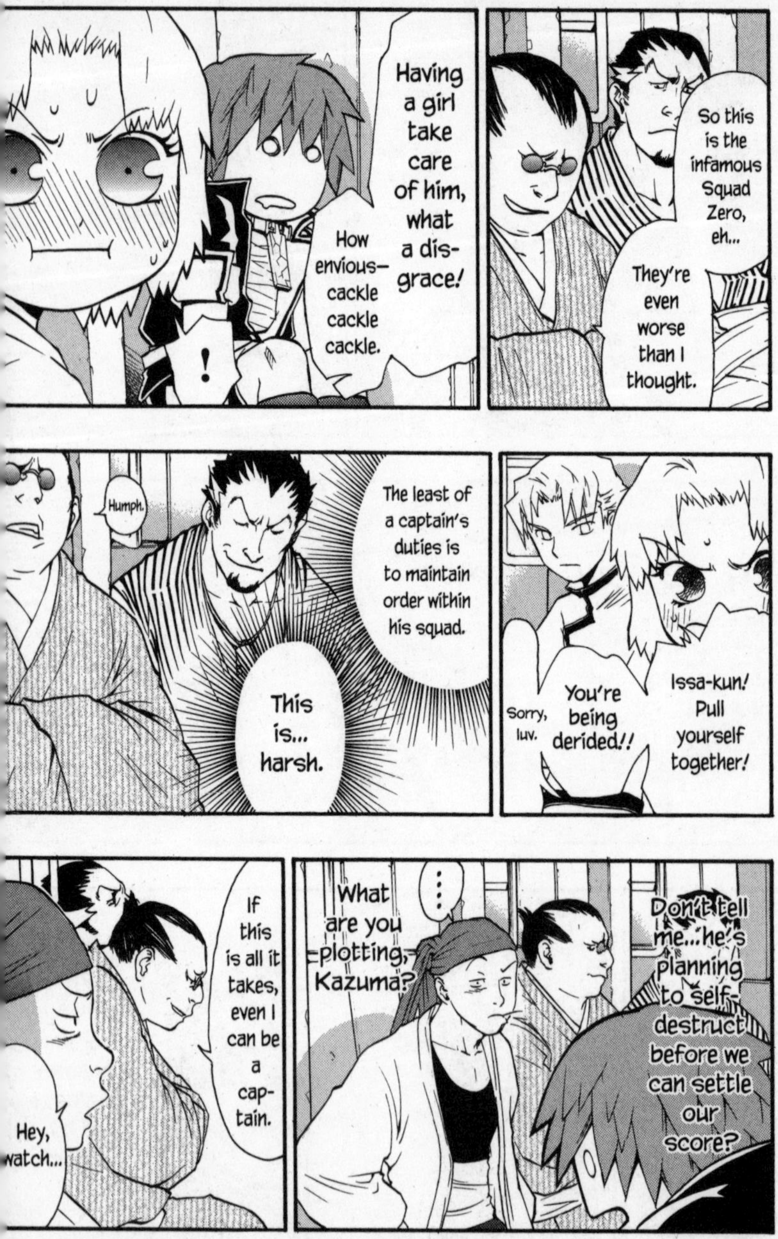
So this is the infamous Squad Zero, eh...
They're even worse than I thought.
Having a girl take care of him, what a disgrace!
How envious—cackle cackle cackle.
!
Issa-kun! Pull yourself together!
You're being derided!!
Sorry, luv.
The least of a captain's duties is to maintain order within his squad.
This is... harsh.
Humph.
Don't tell me...he's planning to self-destruct before we can settle our score?
...
What are you plotting, Kazuma?
If this is all it takes, even I can be a captain.
Hey, watch...

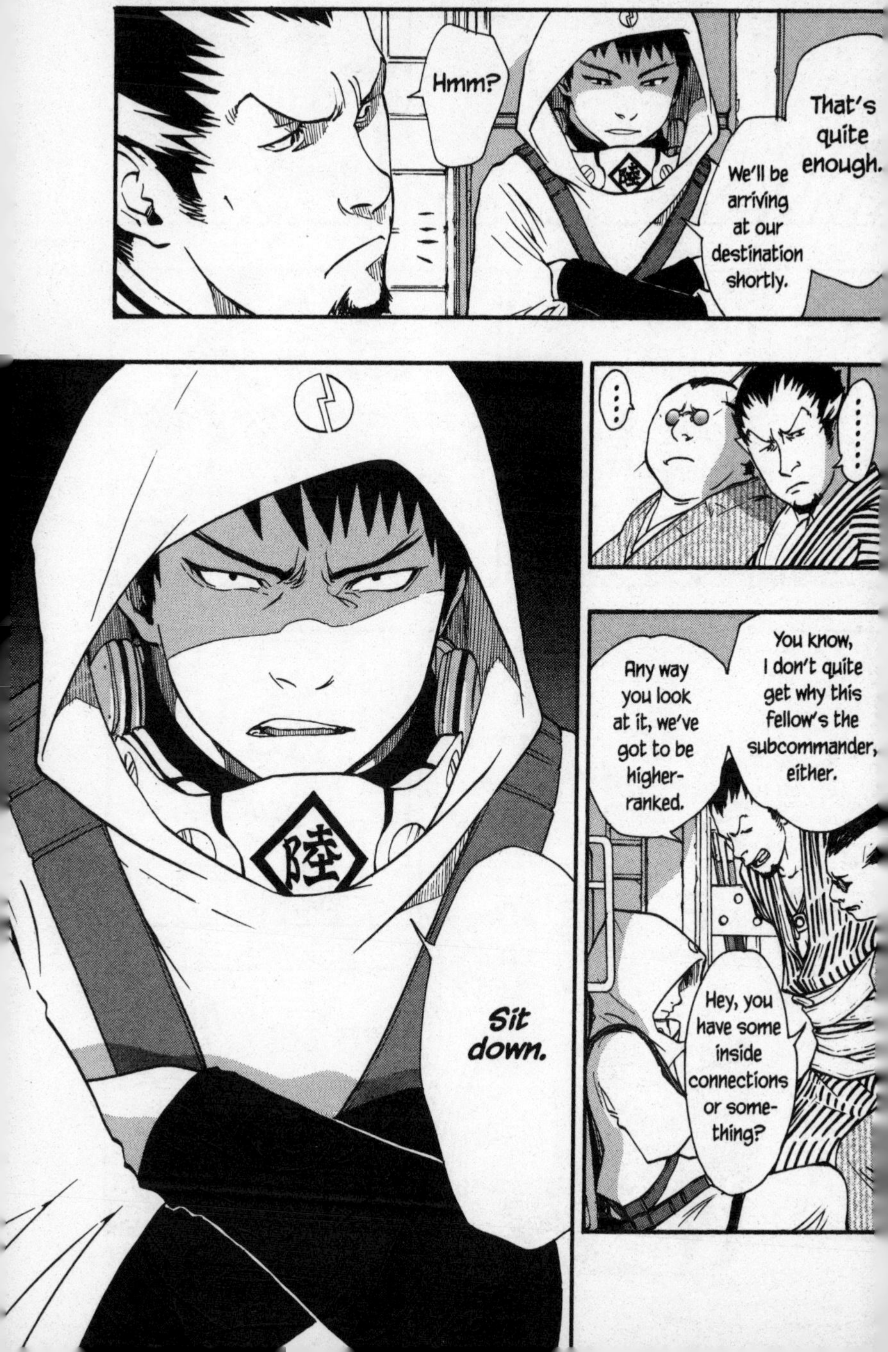
That's quite enough.
We'll be arriving at our destination shortly.
Hmm?
......
....
You know, I don't quite get why this fellow's the subcommander, either.
Any way you look at it, we've got to be higher-ranked.
Hey, you have some inside connections or something?
Sit down.

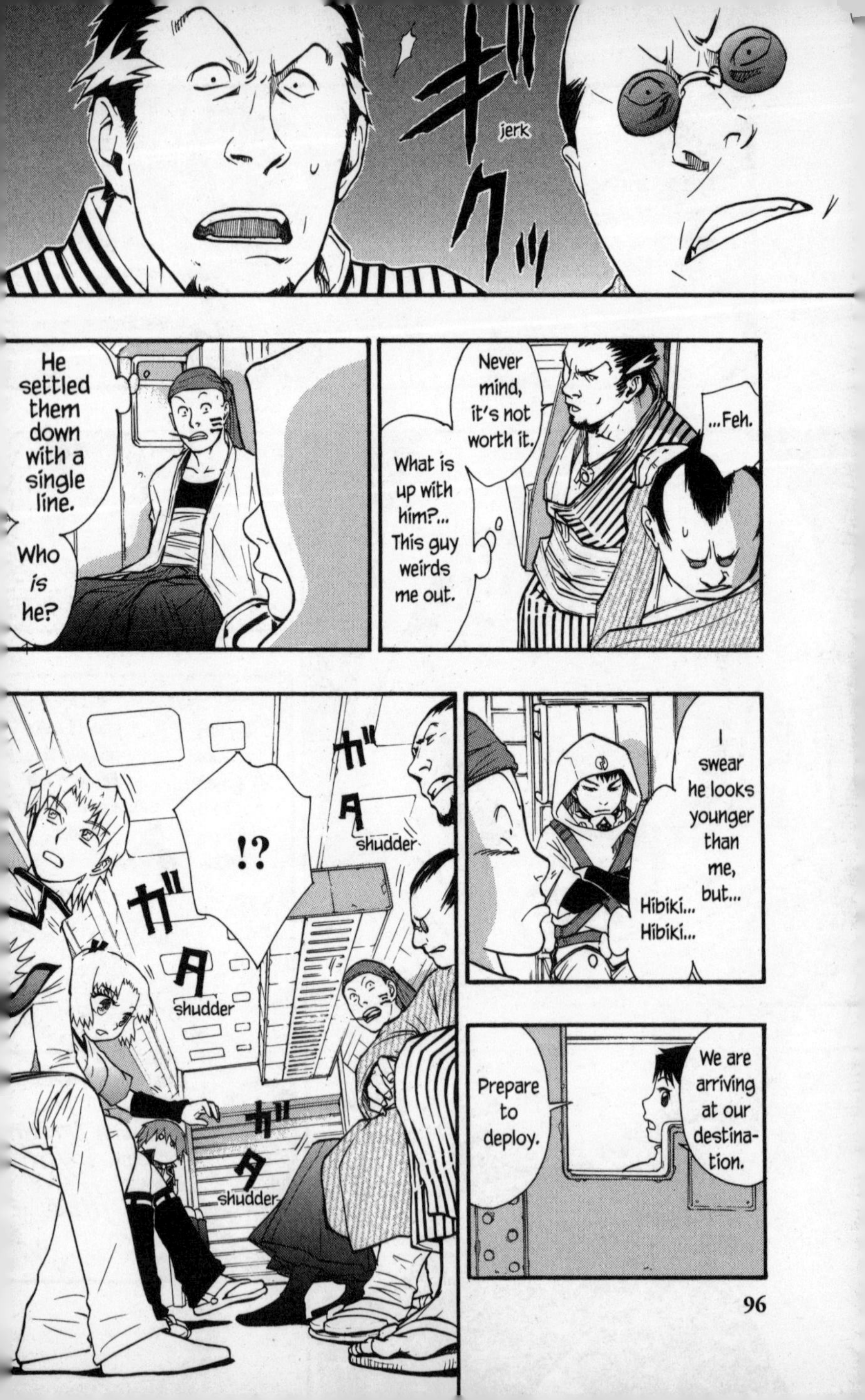
ギクッ
jerk
Never mind, it's not worth it.
...Feh.
What is up with him?... This guy weirds me out.
He settled them down with a single line.
Who is he?
I swear he looks younger than me, but...
Hibiki... Hibiki...
We are arriving at our destination.
Prepare to deploy.
ガタ
shudder
!?
ガタ
shudder
ガタ
shudder

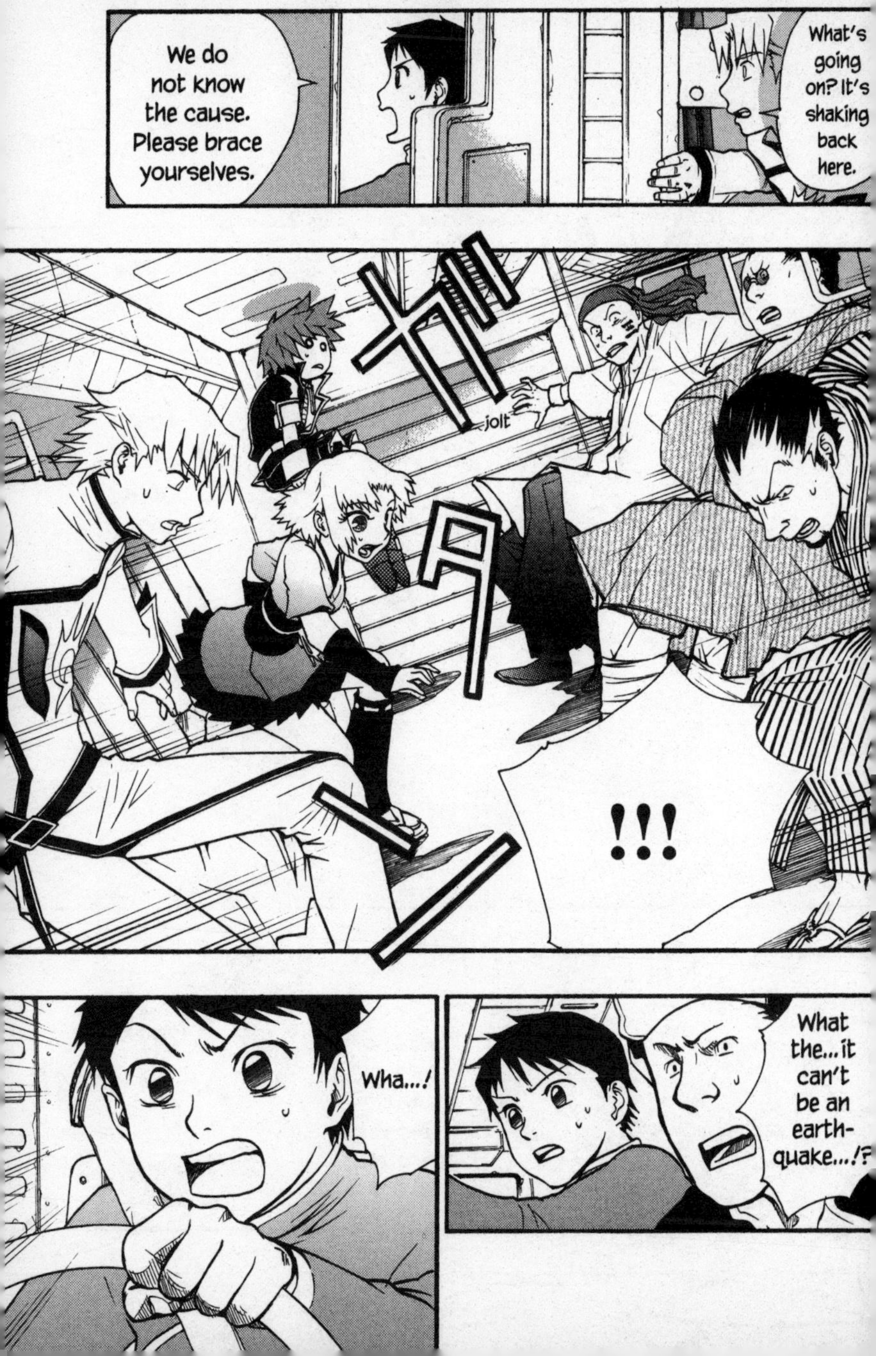
What's going on? It's shaking back here.
We do not know the cause. Please brace yourselves.
jolt
!!!
What the...it can't be an earthquake...!?
Wha...!

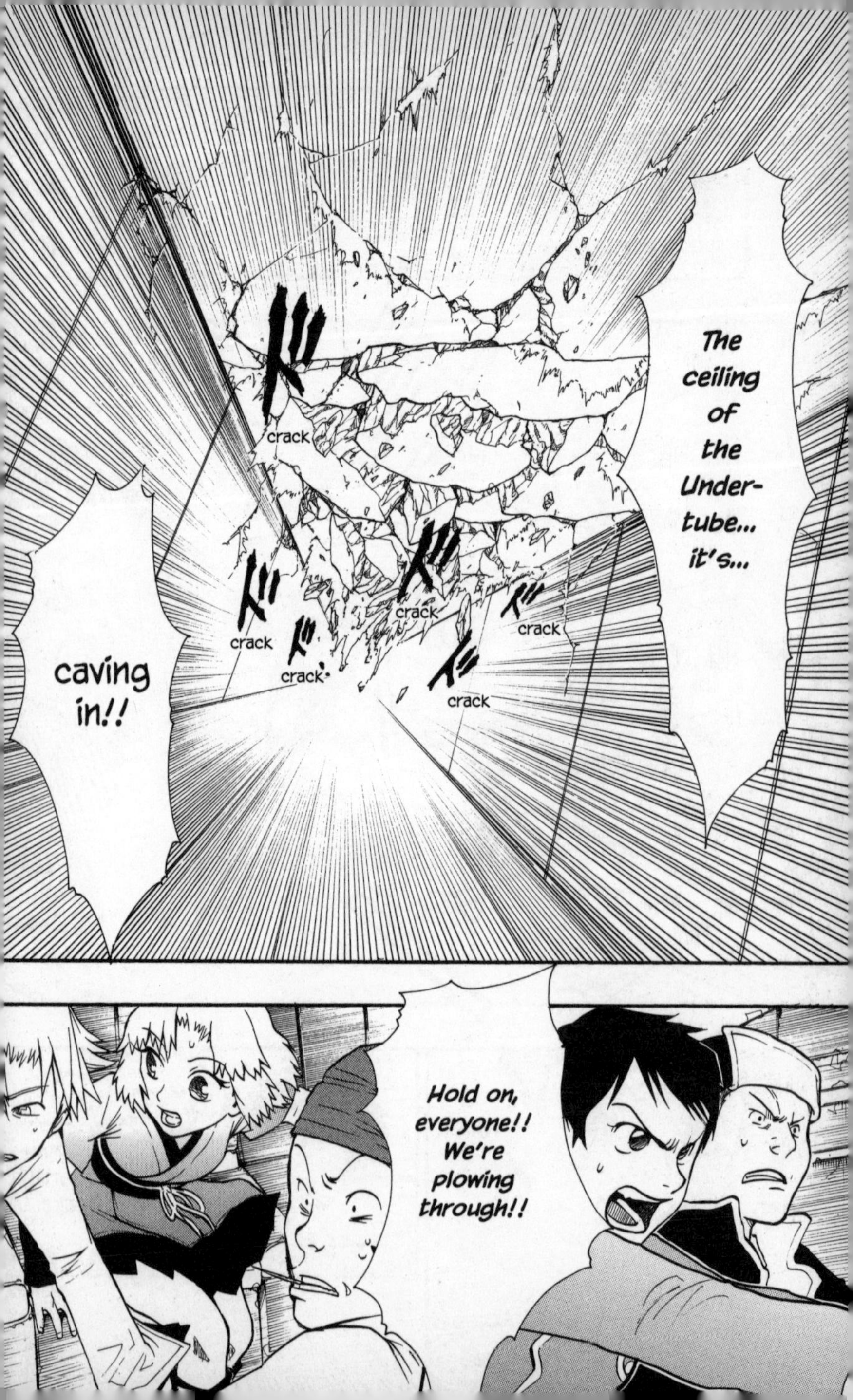
The ceiling of the Under-tube... it's...
crack
crack
crack
crack
crack
crack
caving in!!
Hold on, everyone!! We're plowing through!!

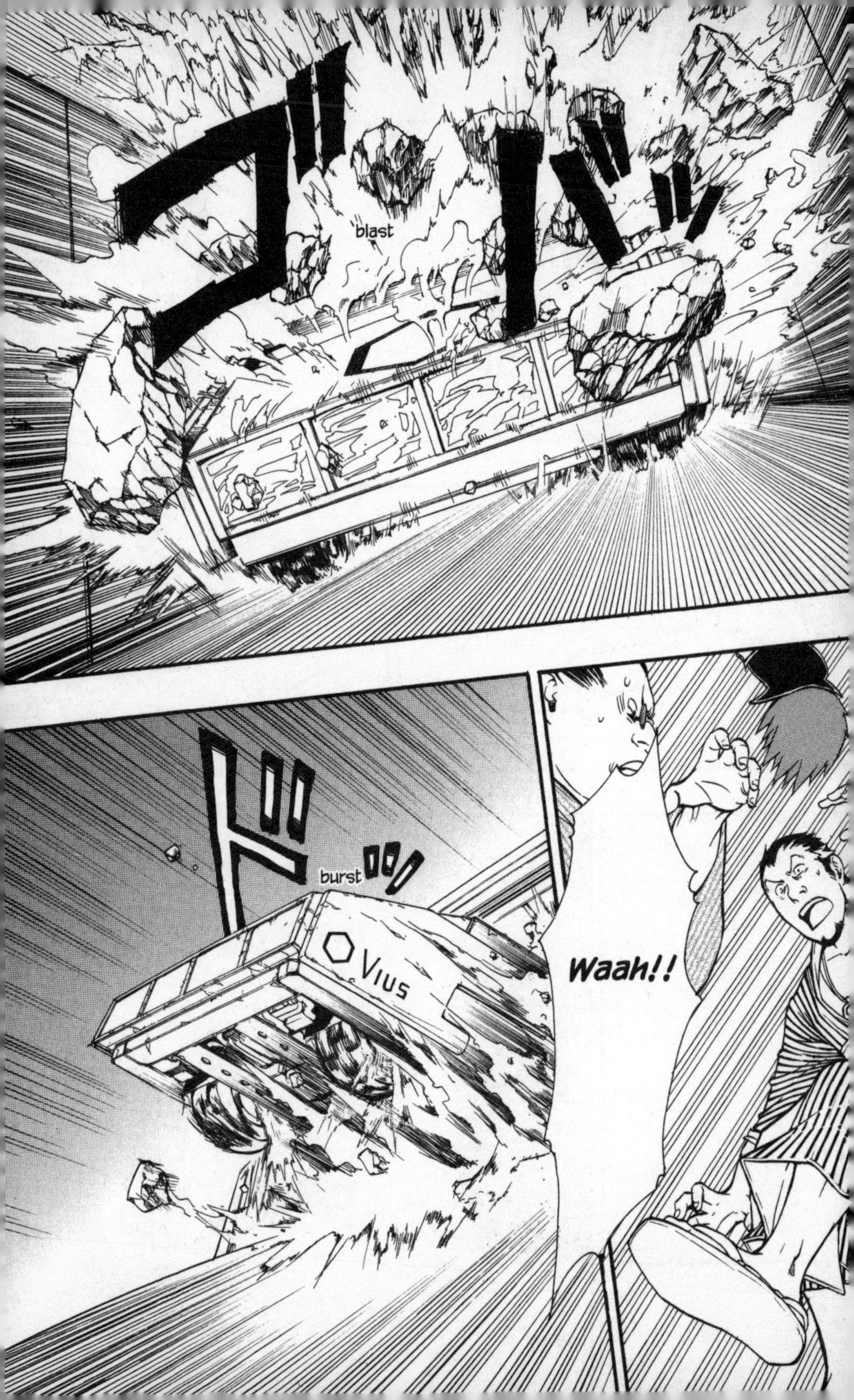
blast
burst
Vius
Waah!!

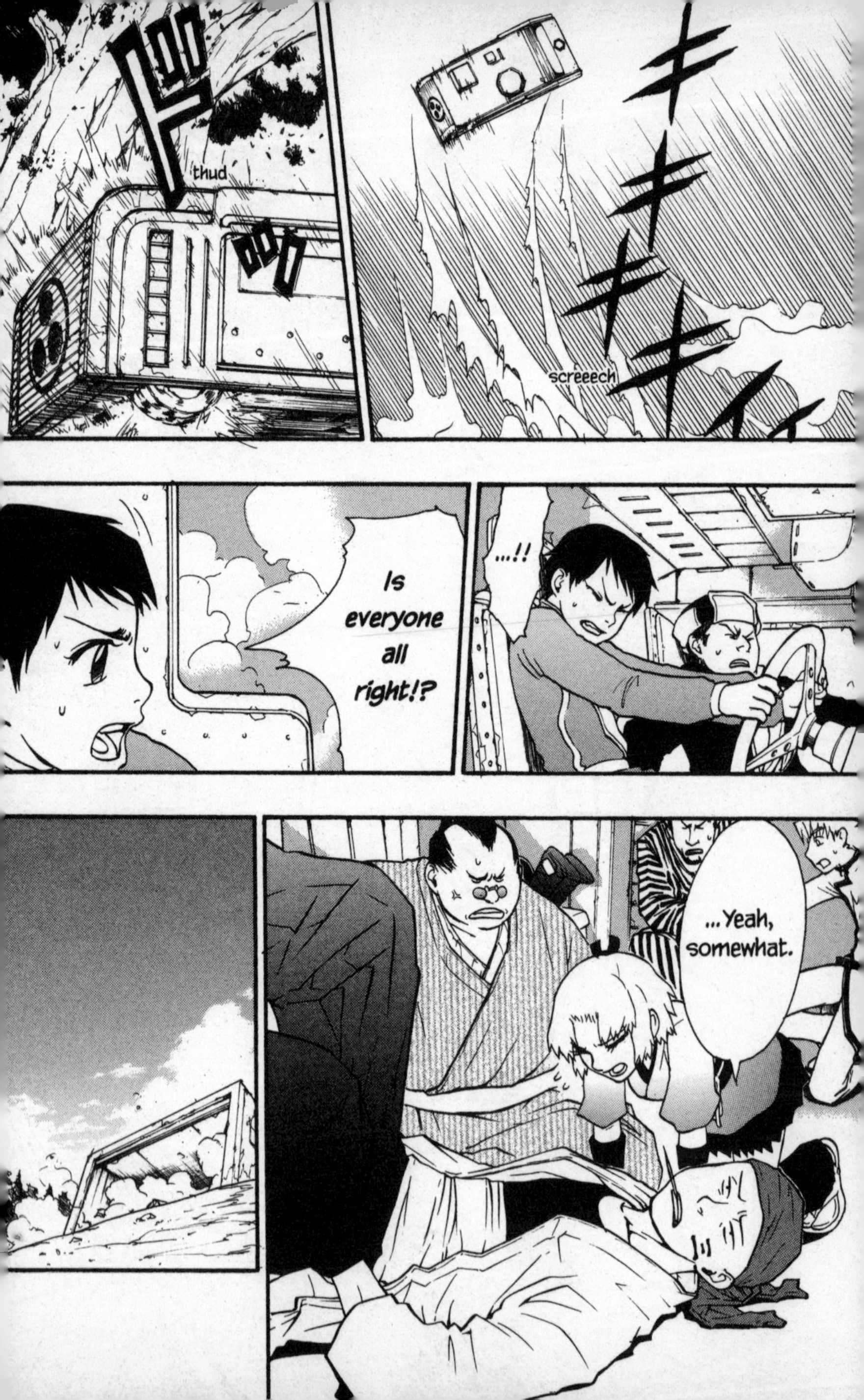
screeech
thud
...!!
Is everyone all right!?
...Yeah, somewhat.

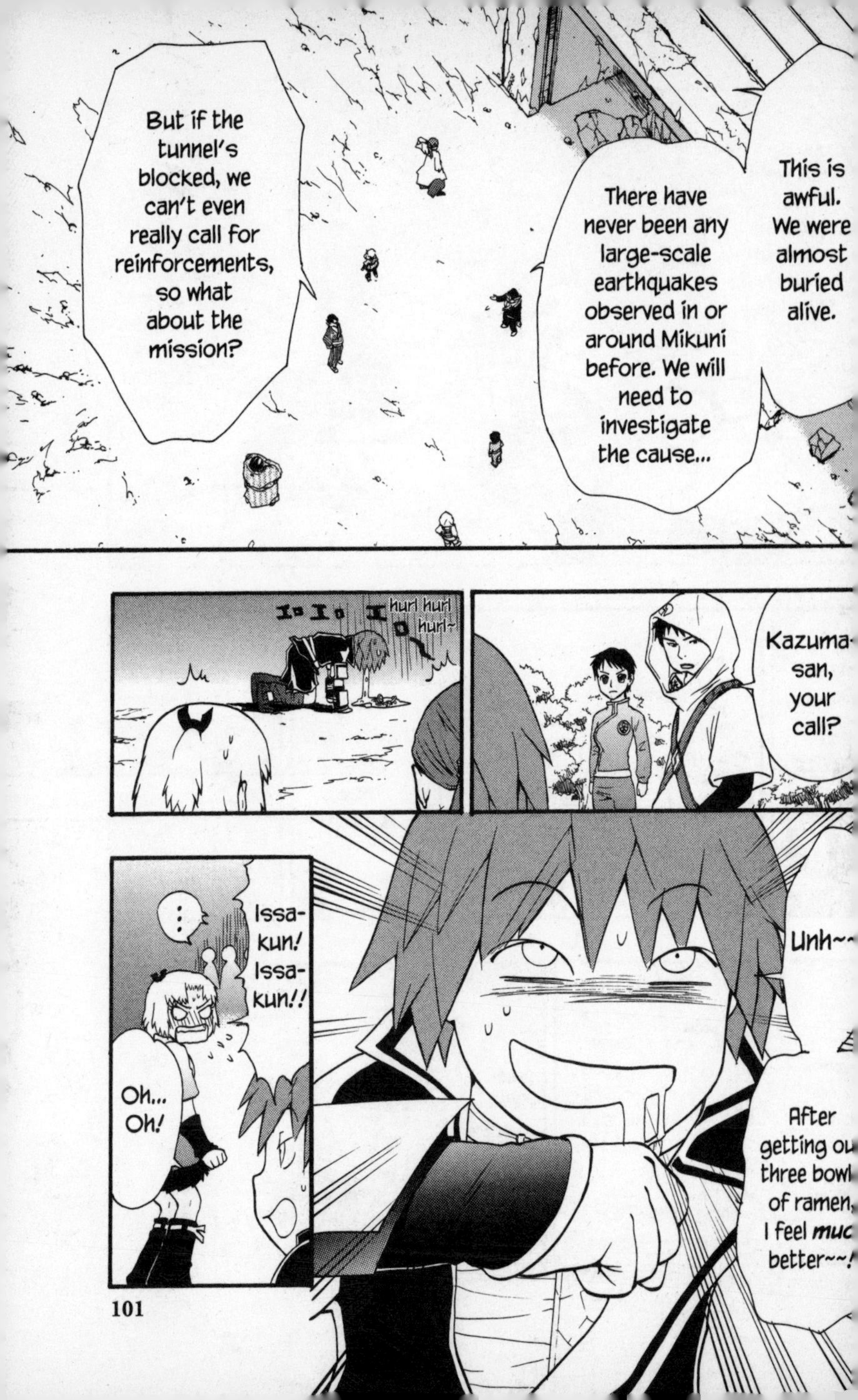
This is awful. We were almost buried alive.
There have never been any large-scale earthquakes observed in or around Mikuni before. We will need to investigate the cause...
But if the tunnel's blocked, we can't even really call for reinforcements, so what about the mission?
Kazuma-san, your call?
hurl hurl hurl~
Unh~~
After getting ou three bowl of ramen, I feel *muc* better~~!
Issa-kun! Issa-kun!!
...
Oh... Oh!

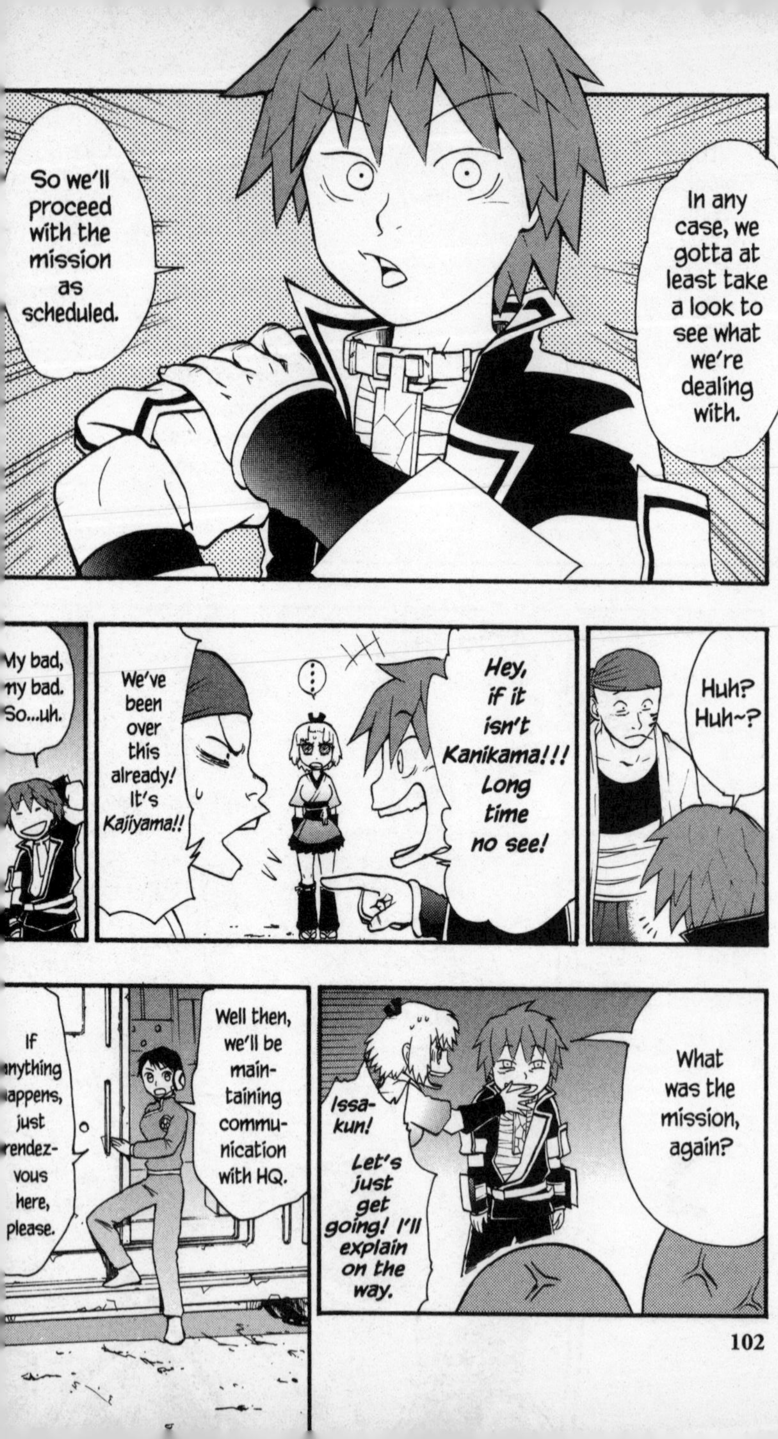
In any case, we gotta at least take a look to see what we're dealing with.
So we'll proceed with the mission as scheduled.
Huh? Huh~?
Hey, if it isn't Kanikama!!! Long time no see!
...
We've been over this already! It's Kajiyama!!
My bad, my bad. So...uh.
What was the mission, again?
Issa-kun!
Let's just get going! I'll explain on the way.
Well then, we'll be maintaining communication with HQ.
If anything happens, just rendez-vous here, please.

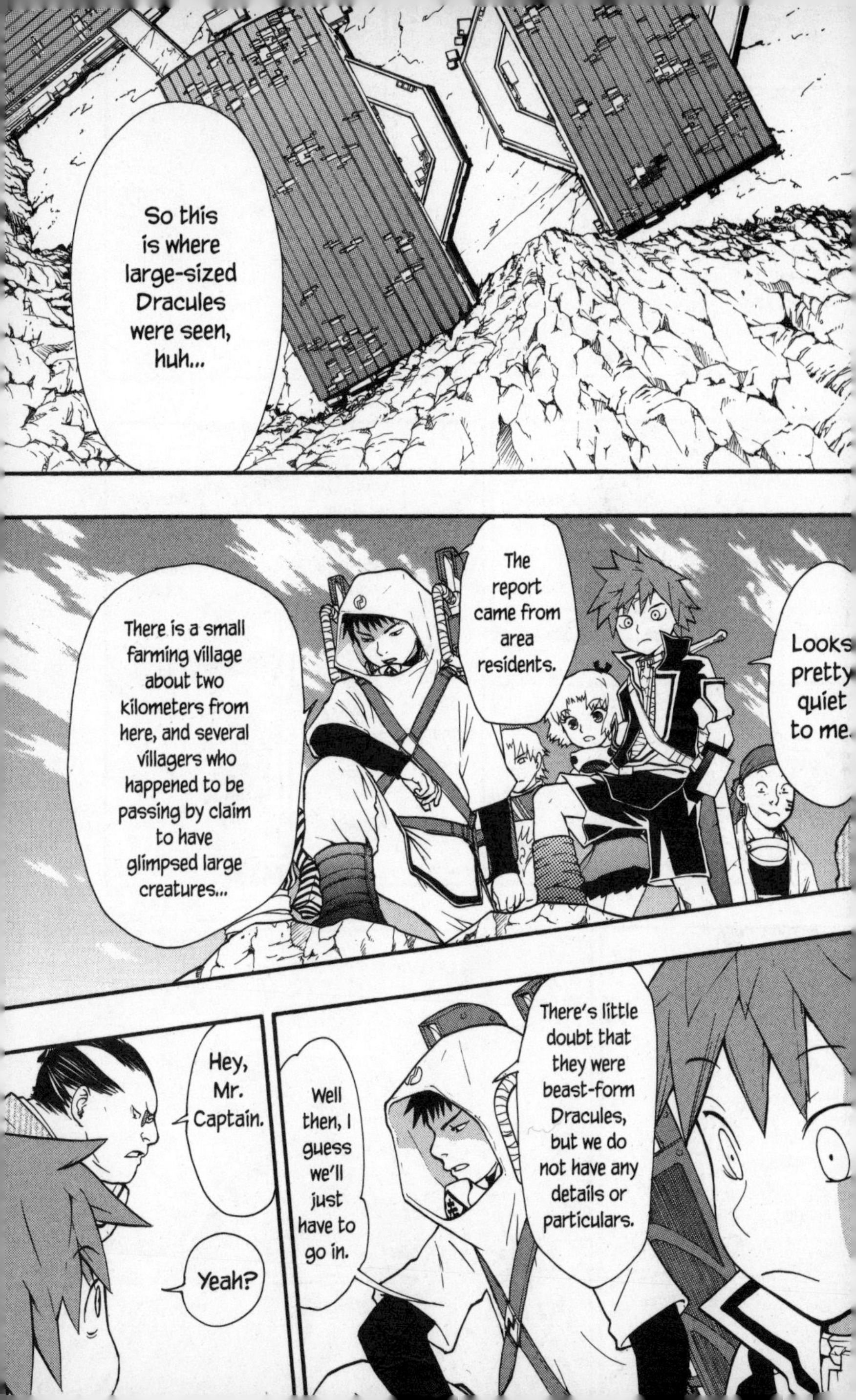
So this is where large-sized Dracules were seen, huh...
Looks pretty quiet to me.
The report came from area residents.
There is a small farming village about two kilometers from here, and several villagers who happened to be passing by claim to have glimpsed large creatures...
There's little doubt that they were beast-form Dracules, but we do not have any details or particulars.
Well then, I guess we'll just have to go in.
Hey, Mr. Captain.
Yeah?

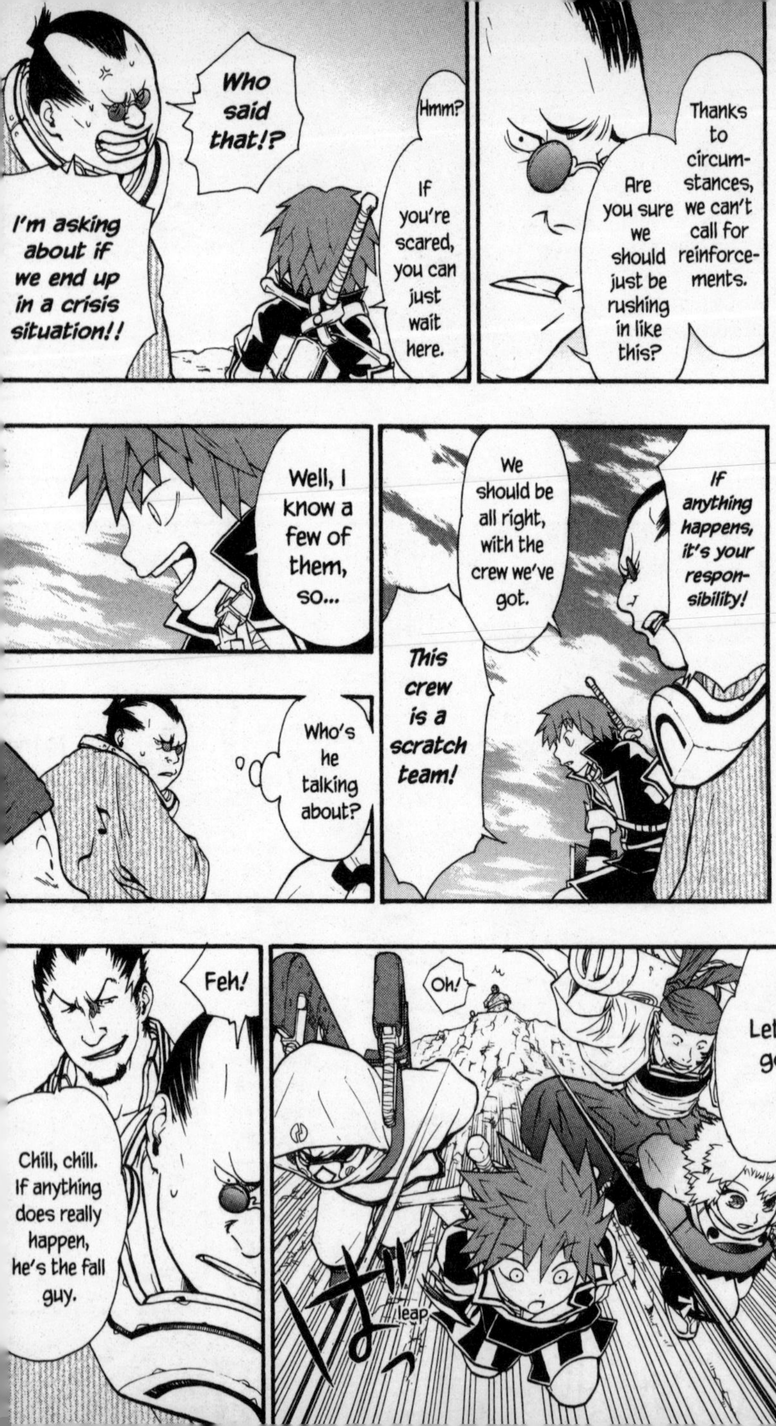

Thanks to circumstances, we can't call for reinforcements.
Are you sure we should just be rushing in like this?
Hmm?
If you're scared, you can just wait here.
Who said that!?
I'm asking about if we end up in a crisis situation!!
If anything happens, it's your responsibility!
We should be all right, with the crew we've got.
This crew is a scratch team!
Well, I know a few of them, so...
Who's he talking about?
Let's go.
Oh!
leap
Feh!
Chill, chill. If anything does really happen, he's the fall guy.

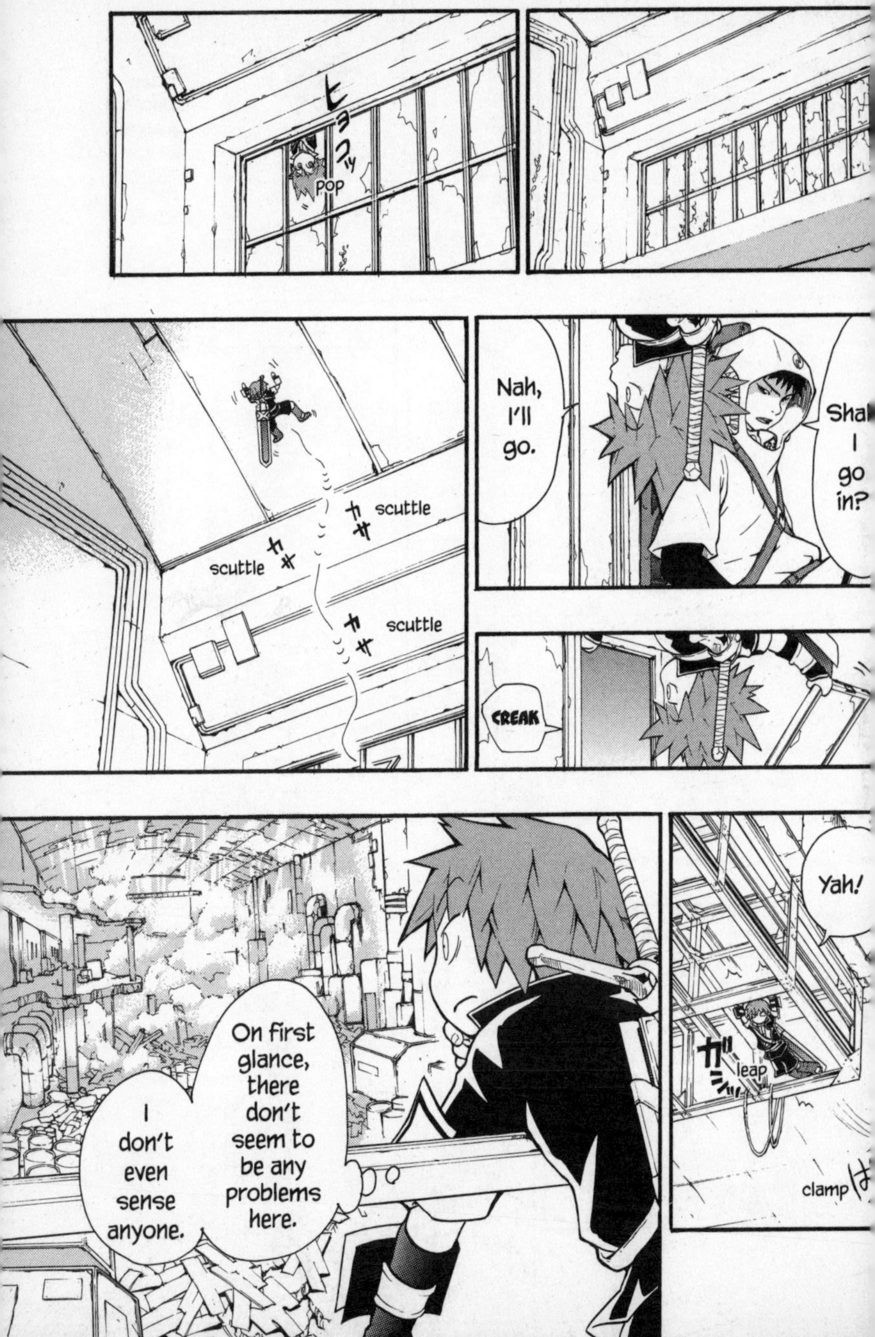
ヒョコッ
POP
Sha
I go in?
Nah, I'll go.
CREAK
カサ
scuttle
カサ
scuttle
カサ
scuttle
Yah!
ガシッ
leap
clamp
On first glance, there don't seem to be any problems here.
I don't even sense anyone.

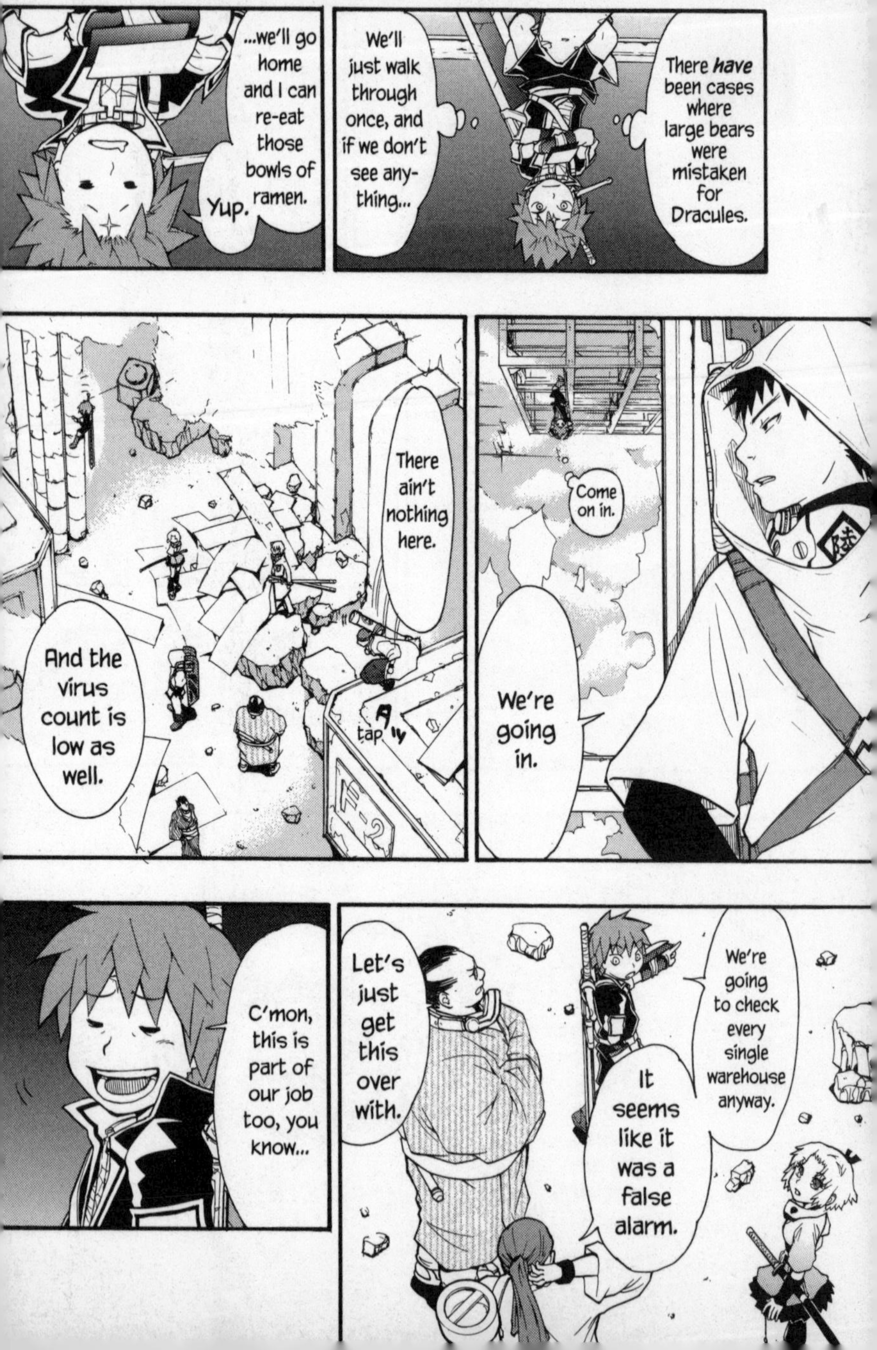
There *have* been cases where large bears were mistaken for Dracules.
We'll just walk through once, and if we don't see anything...
...we'll go home and I can re-eat those bowls of ramen.
Yup.
Come on in.
We're going in.
There ain't nothing here.
tap tap
And the virus count is low as well.
We're going to check every single warehouse anyway.
It seems like it was a false alarm.
Let's just get this over with.
C'mon, this is part of our job too, you know...

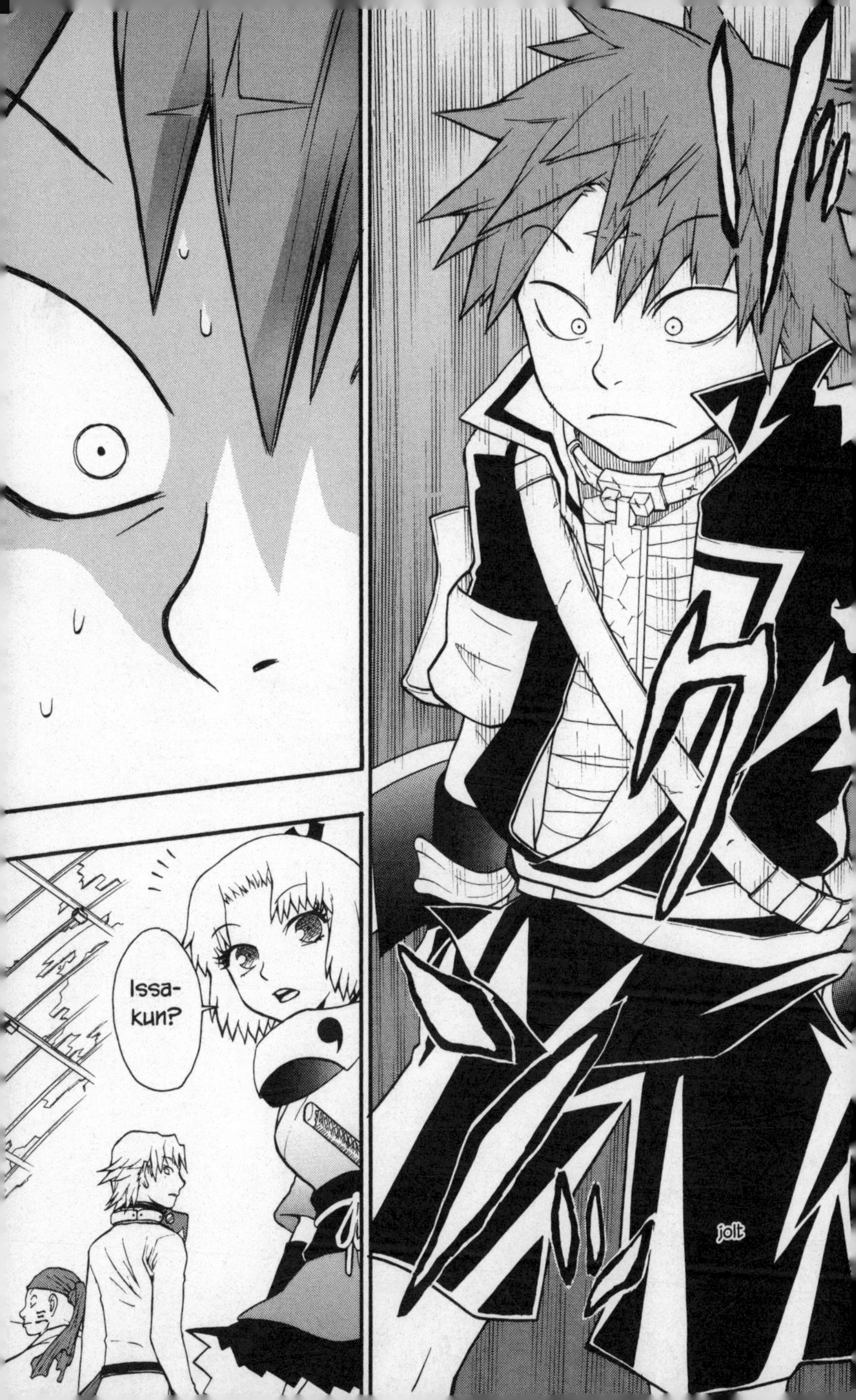
jolt
Issa-kun?

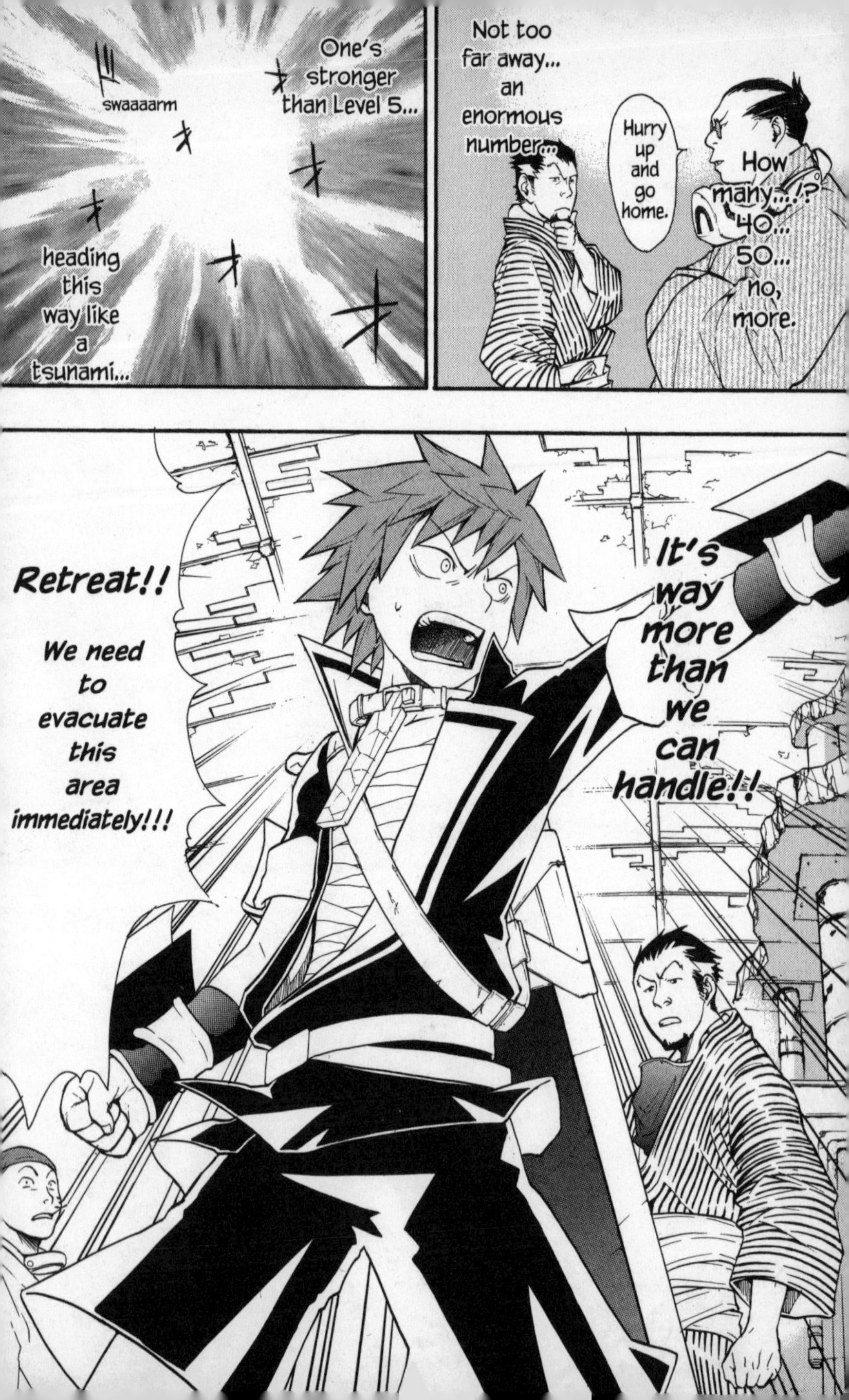
Not too far away... an enormous number...
How many...!? 40... 50... no, more.
Hurry up and go home.
One's stronger than Level 5...
swaaaarm
heading this way like a tsunami...
It's way more than we can handle!!
Retreat!!
We need to evacuate this area immediately!!!

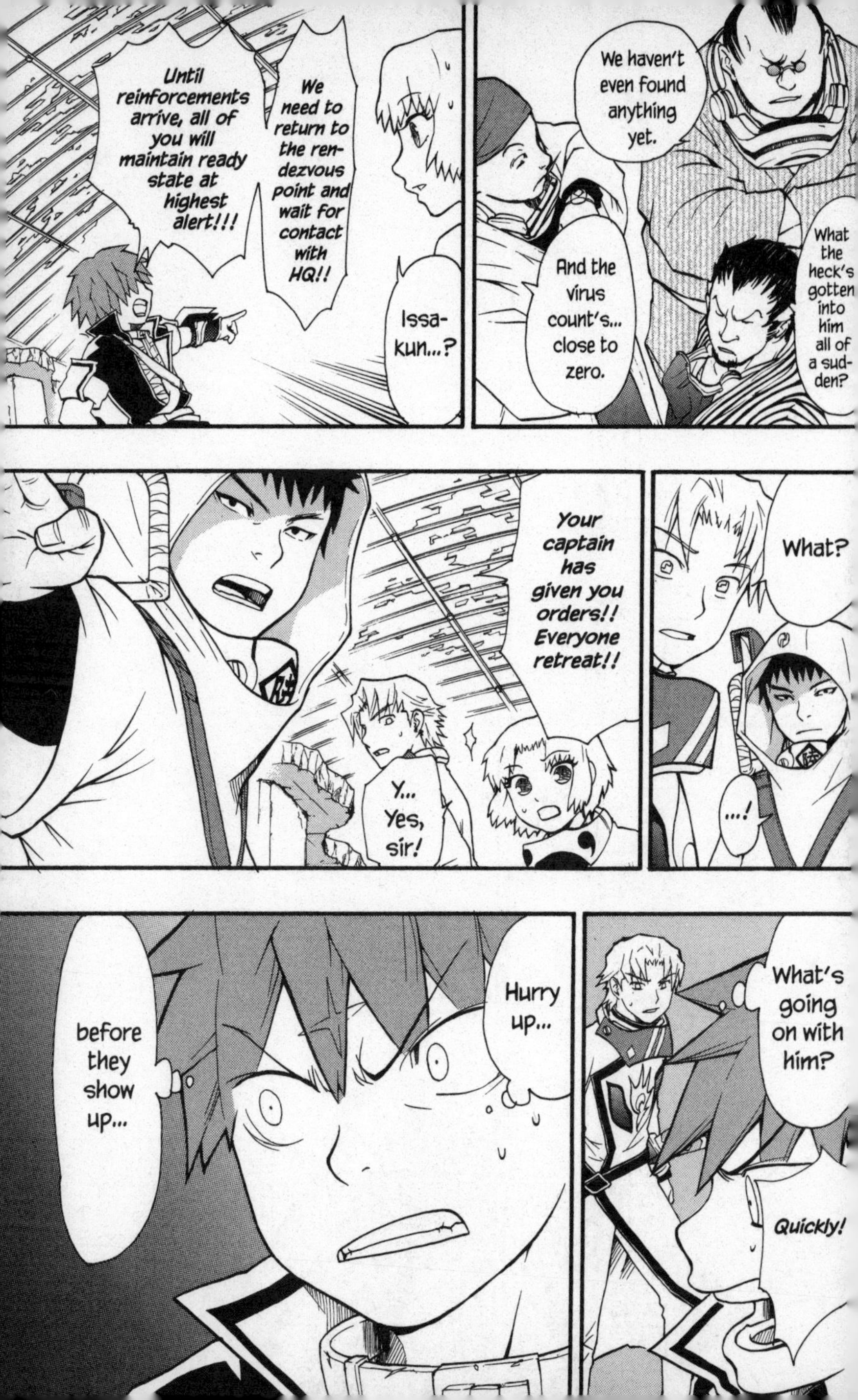
We haven't even found anything yet.
What the heck's gotten into him all of a sudden?
And the virus count's... close to zero.
We need to return to the rendezvous point and wait for contact with HQ!!
Until reinforcements arrive, all of you will maintain ready state at highest alert!!!
Issa-kun...?
What?
...!
Your captain has given you orders!! Everyone retreat!!
Y... Yes, sir!
What's going on with him?
Quickly!
Hurry up...
before they show up...

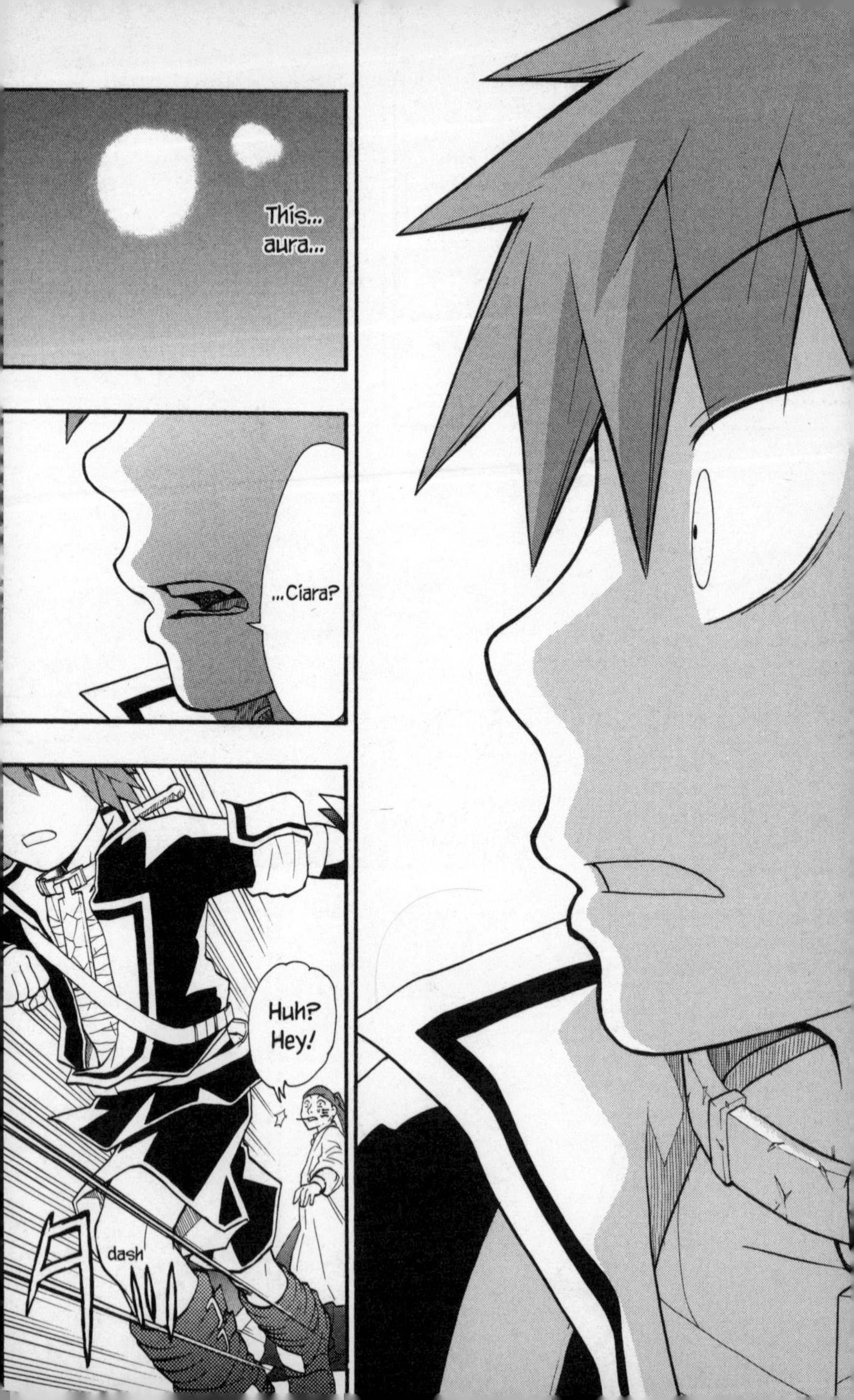
This... aura...
...Ciara?
Huh? Hey!
dash

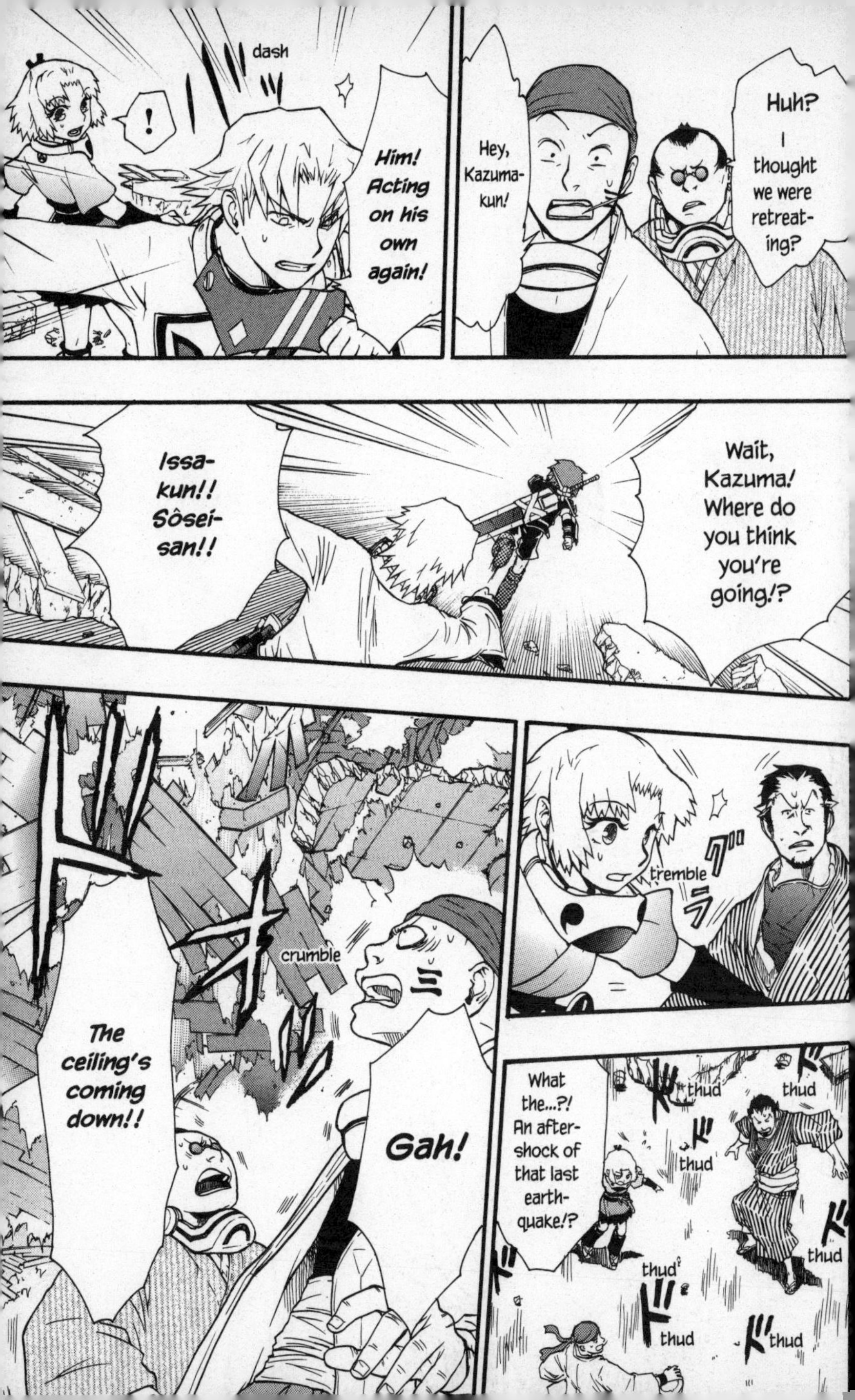
Huh? I thought we were retreating?
Hey, Kazuma-kun!
dash
Him! Acting on his own again!
!
Wait, Kazuma! Where do you think you're going!?
Issa-kun!! Sôsei-san!!
tremble
thud
thud
What the...?! An aftershock of that last earthquake!?
thud
thud
thud
thud
thud
crumble
The ceiling's coming down!!
Gah!

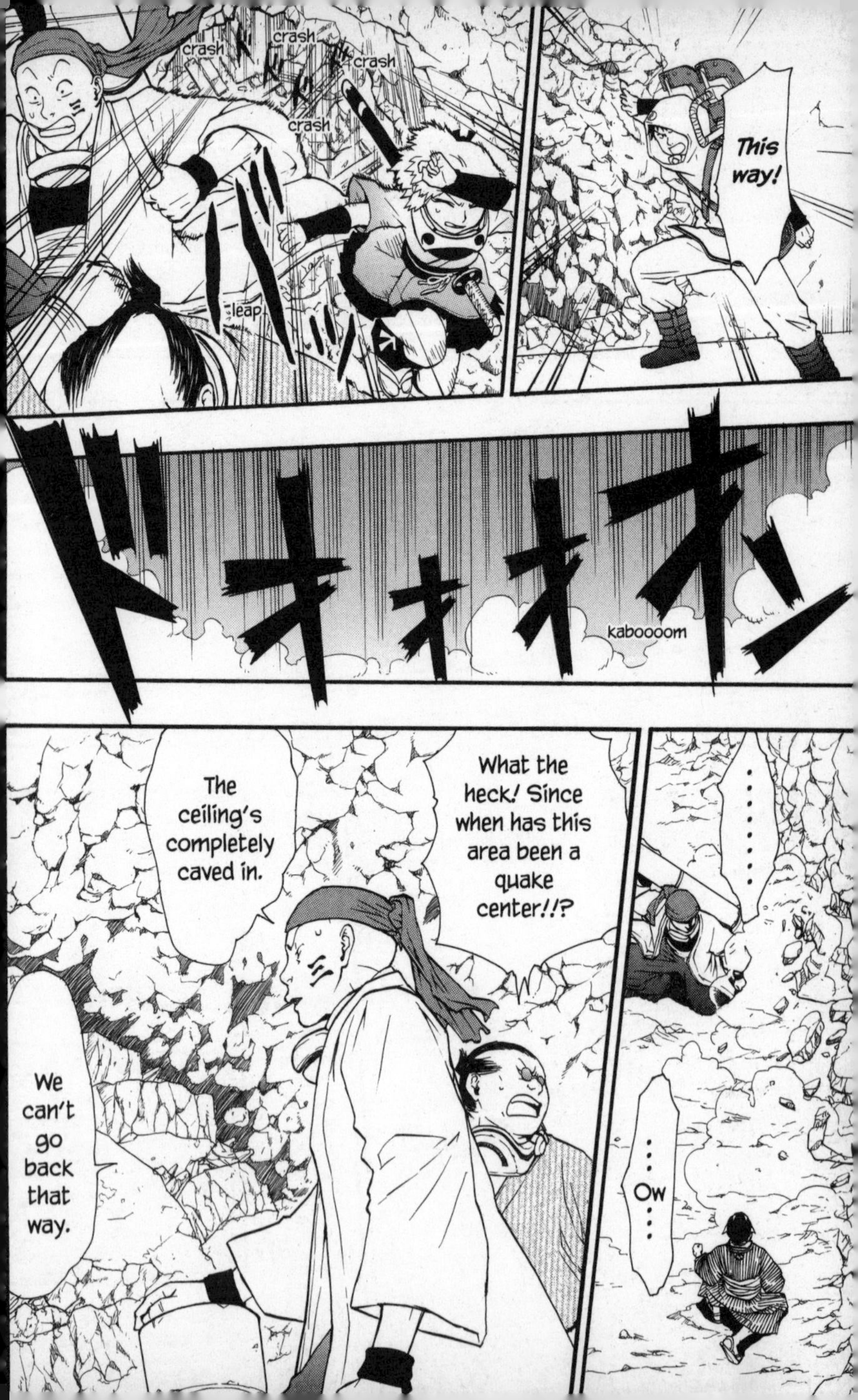
This way!
crash
crash
crash
crash
leap
kaboooom
......
...Ow...
What the heck! Since when has this area been a quake center!!?
The ceiling's completely caved in.
We can't go back that way.

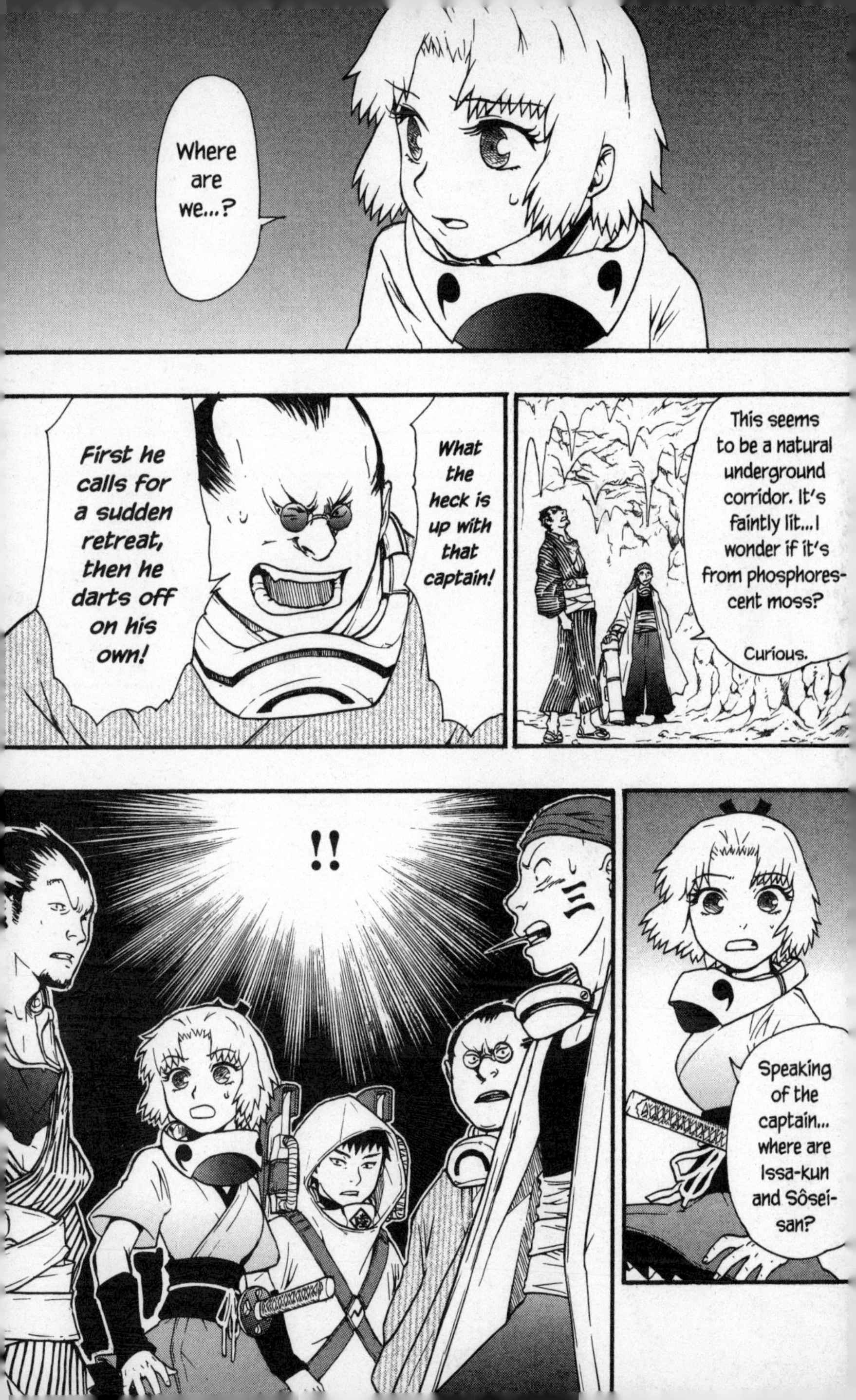
Where are we...?
This seems to be a natural underground corridor. It's faintly lit...I wonder if it's from phosphores-cent moss?
Curious.
What the heck is up with that captain!
First he calls for a sudden retreat, then he darts off on his own!
Speaking of the captain... where are Issa-kun and Sôsei-san?
!!

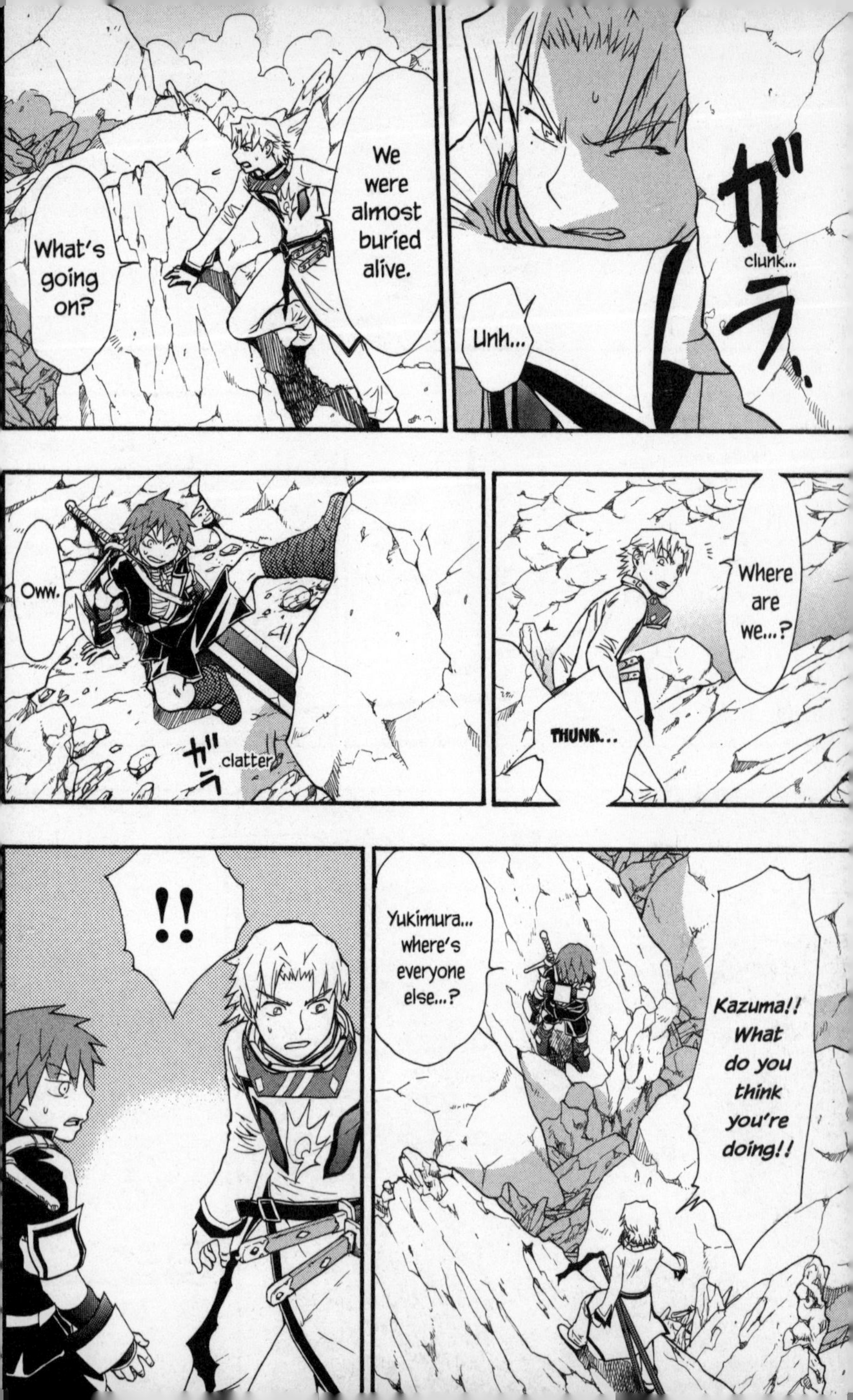
ガラ
clunk...
Unh...
We were almost buried alive.
What's going on?
Where are we...?
THUNK...
Oww.
ガラ
clatter
Yukimura... where's everyone else...?
Kazuma!! What do you think you're doing!!
!!

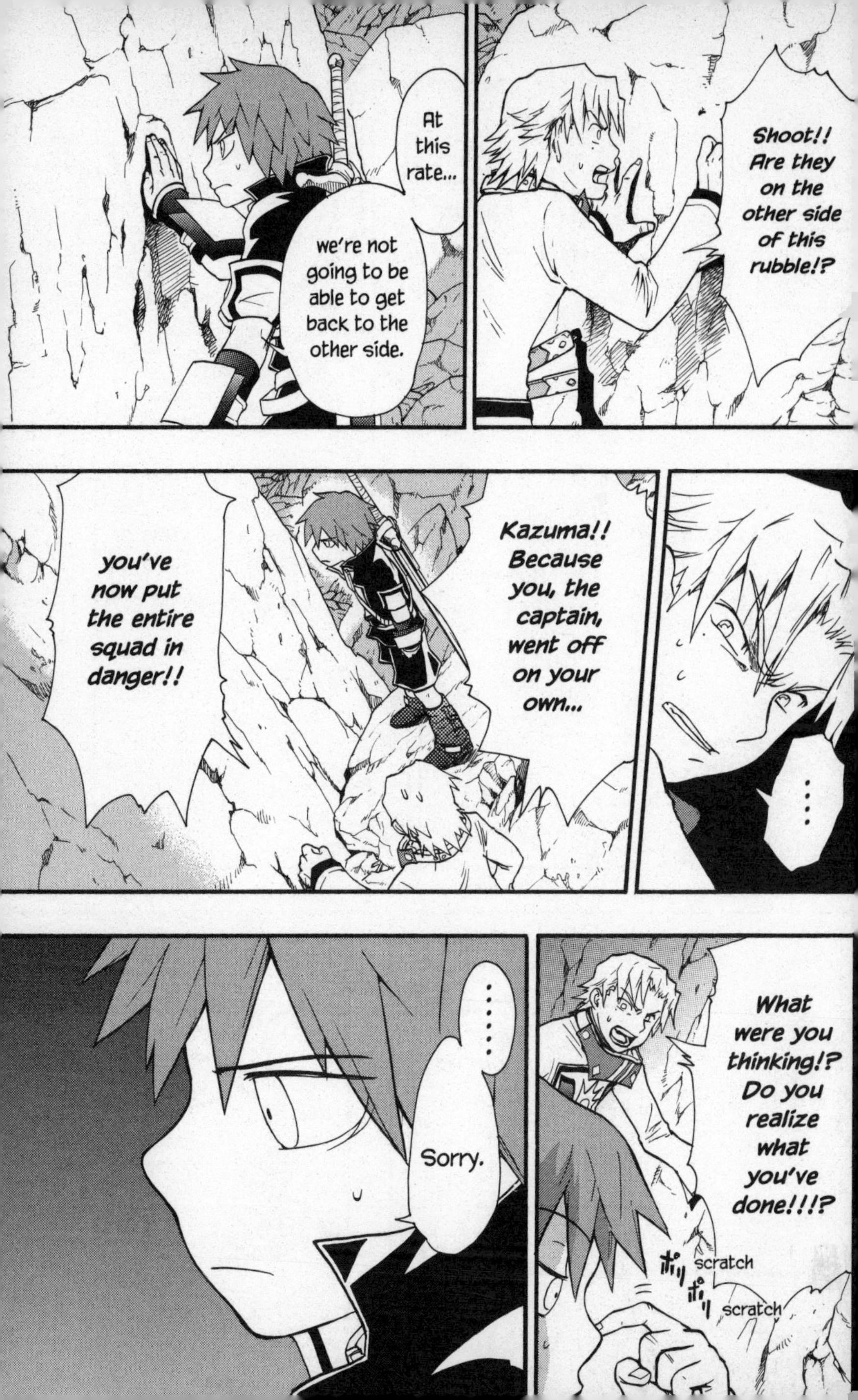
Shoot!! Are they on the other side of this rubble!?
At this rate...
we're not going to be able to get back to the other side.
....
Kazuma!! Because you, the captain, went off on your own...
you've now put the entire squad in danger!!
What were you thinking!? Do you realize what you've done!!!?
ポリ scratch
ポリ scratch
......
Sorry.

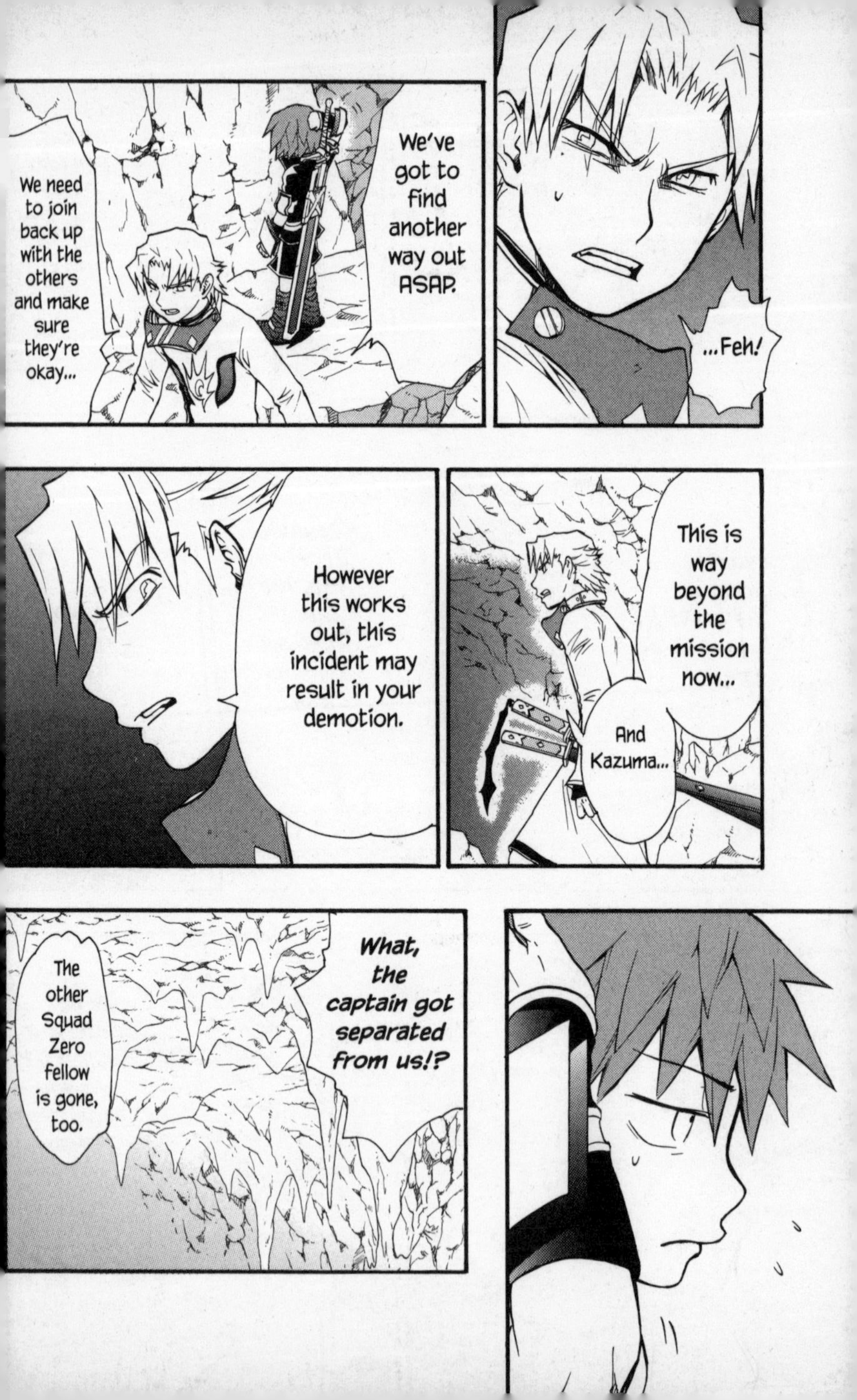
...Feh!
We've got to find another way out ASAP.
We need to join back up with the others and make sure they're okay...
This is way beyond the mission now...
And Kazuma...
However this works out, this incident may result in your demotion.
What, the captain got separated from us!?
The other Squad Zero fellow is gone, too.

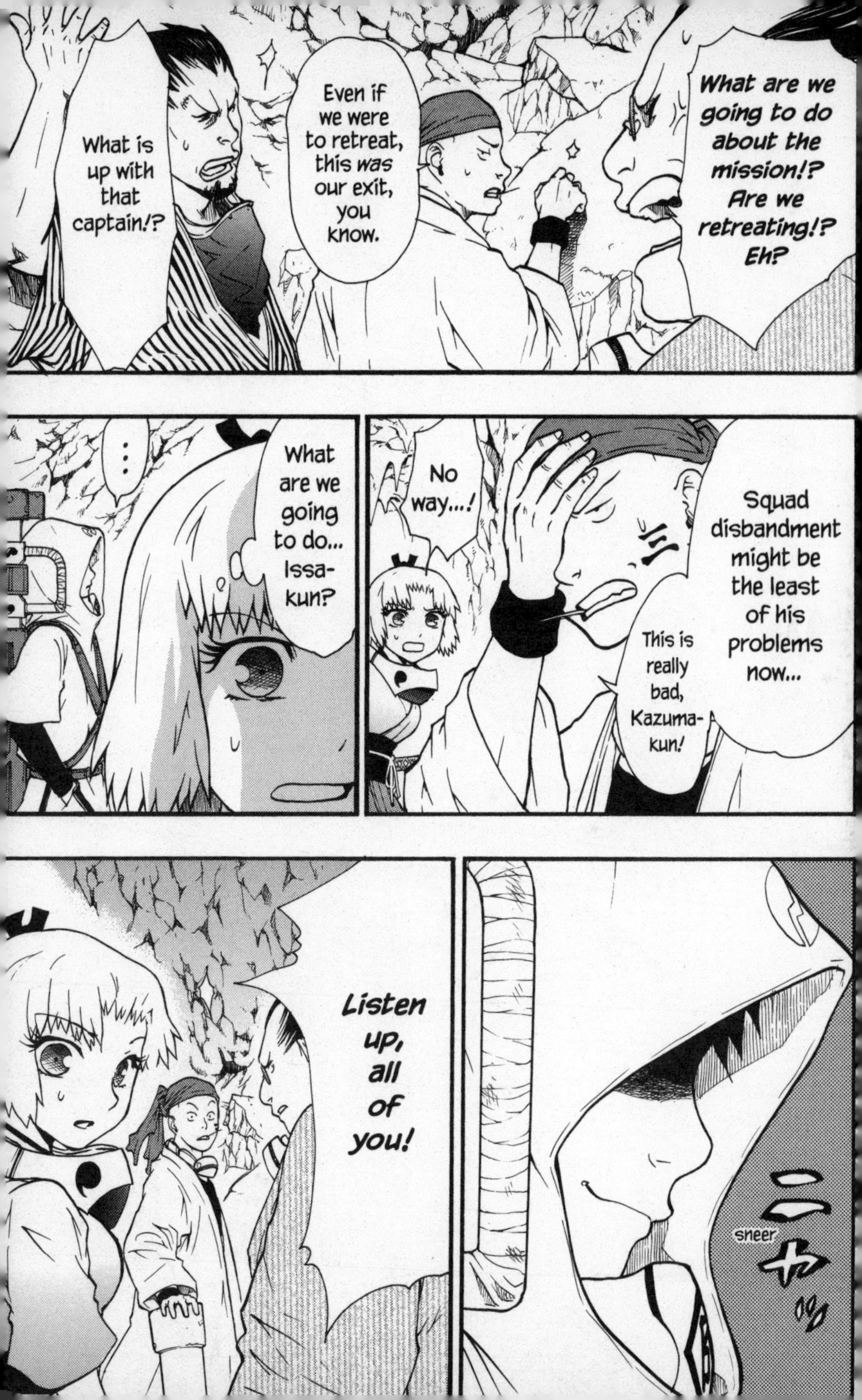
What are we going to do about the mission!? Are we retreating!? Eh?
Even if we were to retreat, this *was* our exit, you know.
What is up with that captain!?
Squad disbandment might be the least of his problems now...
This is really bad, Kazuma-kun!
No way...!
What are we going to do... Issa-kun?
...
sneer
Listen up, all of you!

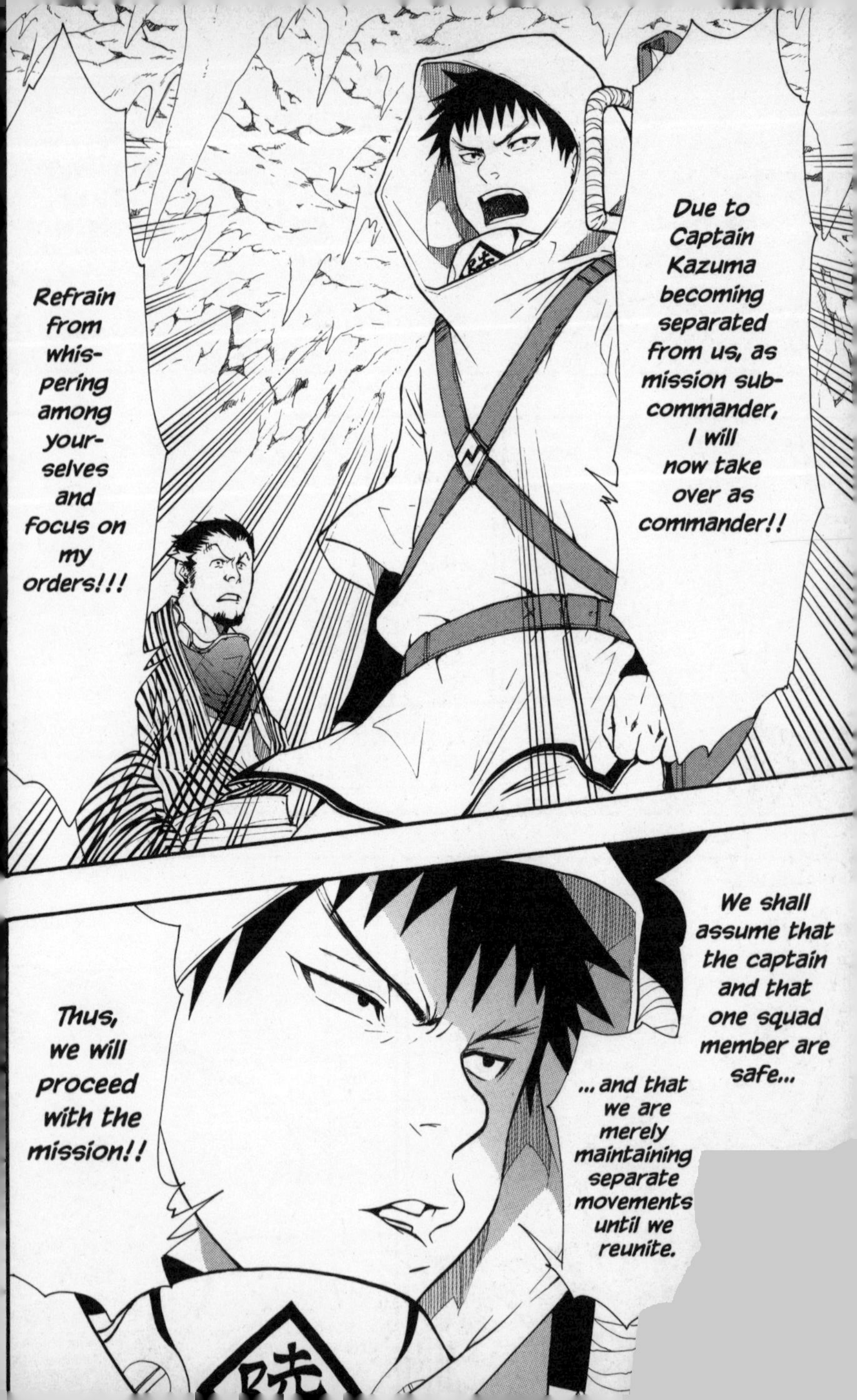
Due to Captain Kazuma becoming separated from us, as mission sub-commander, I will now take over as commander!!
Refrain from whis-pering among your-selves and focus on my orders!!!
We shall assume that the captain and that one squad member are safe...
...and that we are merely maintaining separate movements until we reunite.
Thus, we will proceed with the mission!!

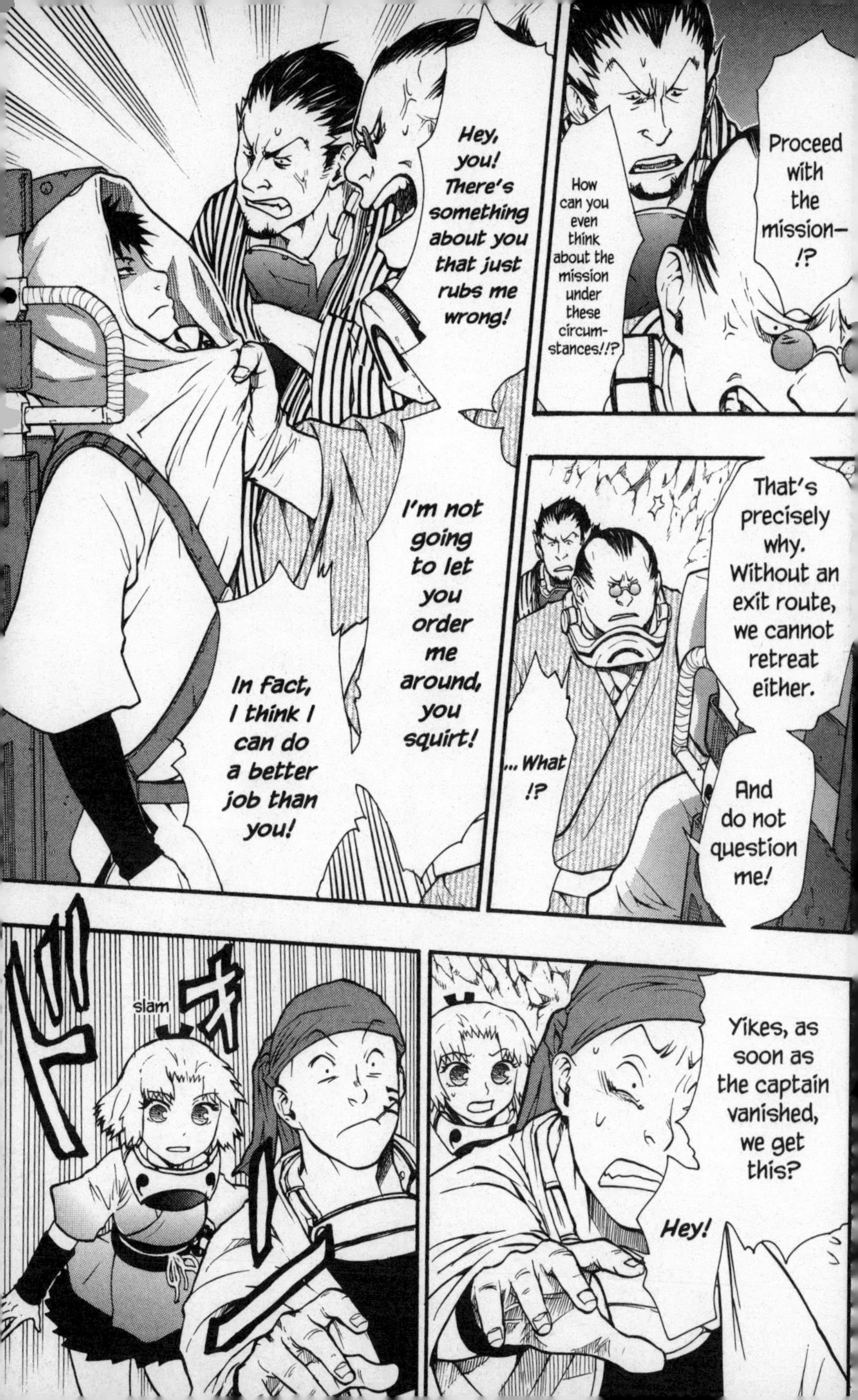
Proceed with the mission—!?
How can you even think about the mission under these circum-stances!!?
That's precisely why. Without an exit route, we cannot retreat either.
And do not question me!
...What !?
Hey, you! There's something about you that just rubs me wrong!
I'm not going to let you order me around, you squirt!
In fact, I think I can do a better job than you!
Yikes, as soon as the captain vanished, we get this?
Hey!
slam

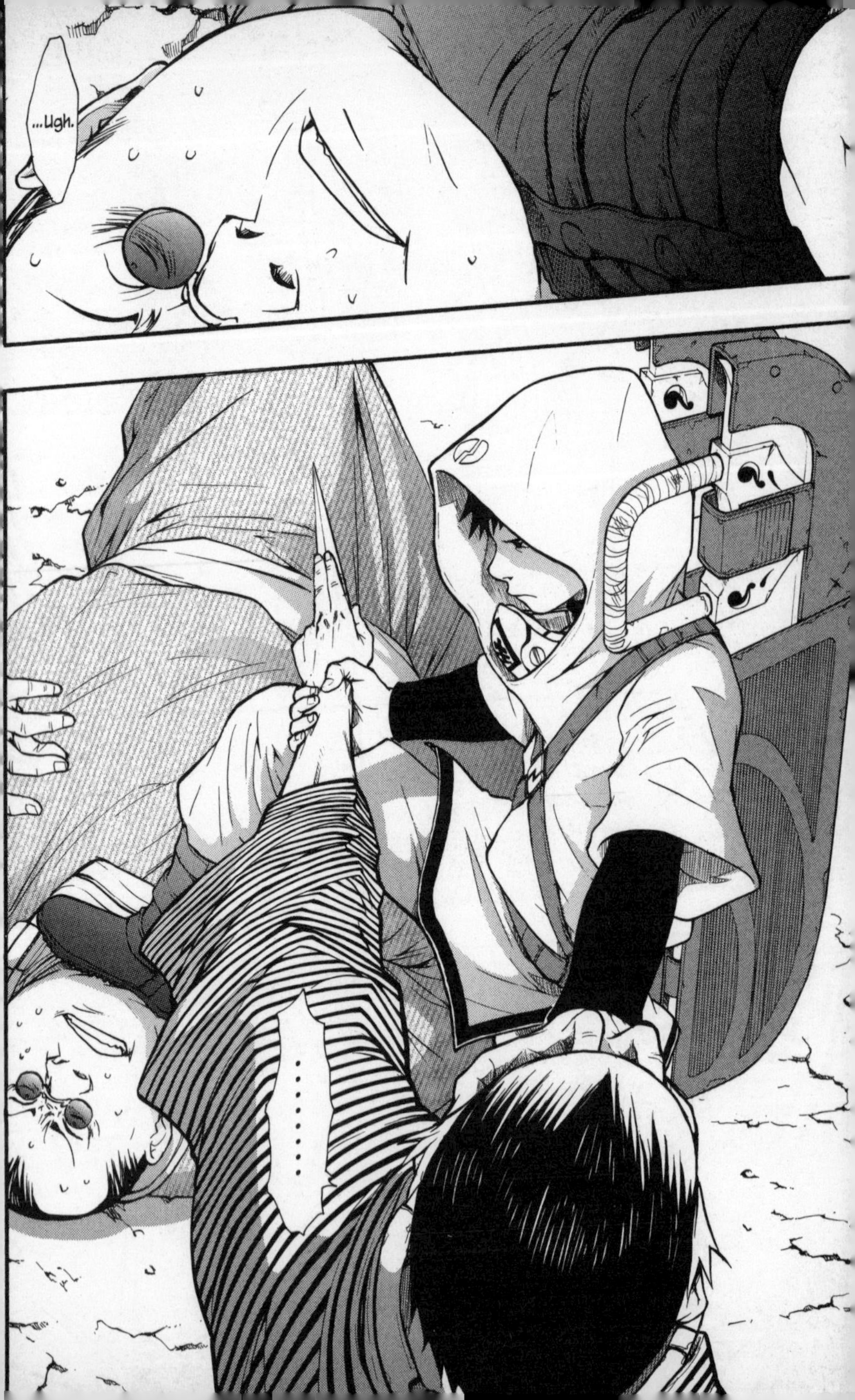
...Ugh.
......

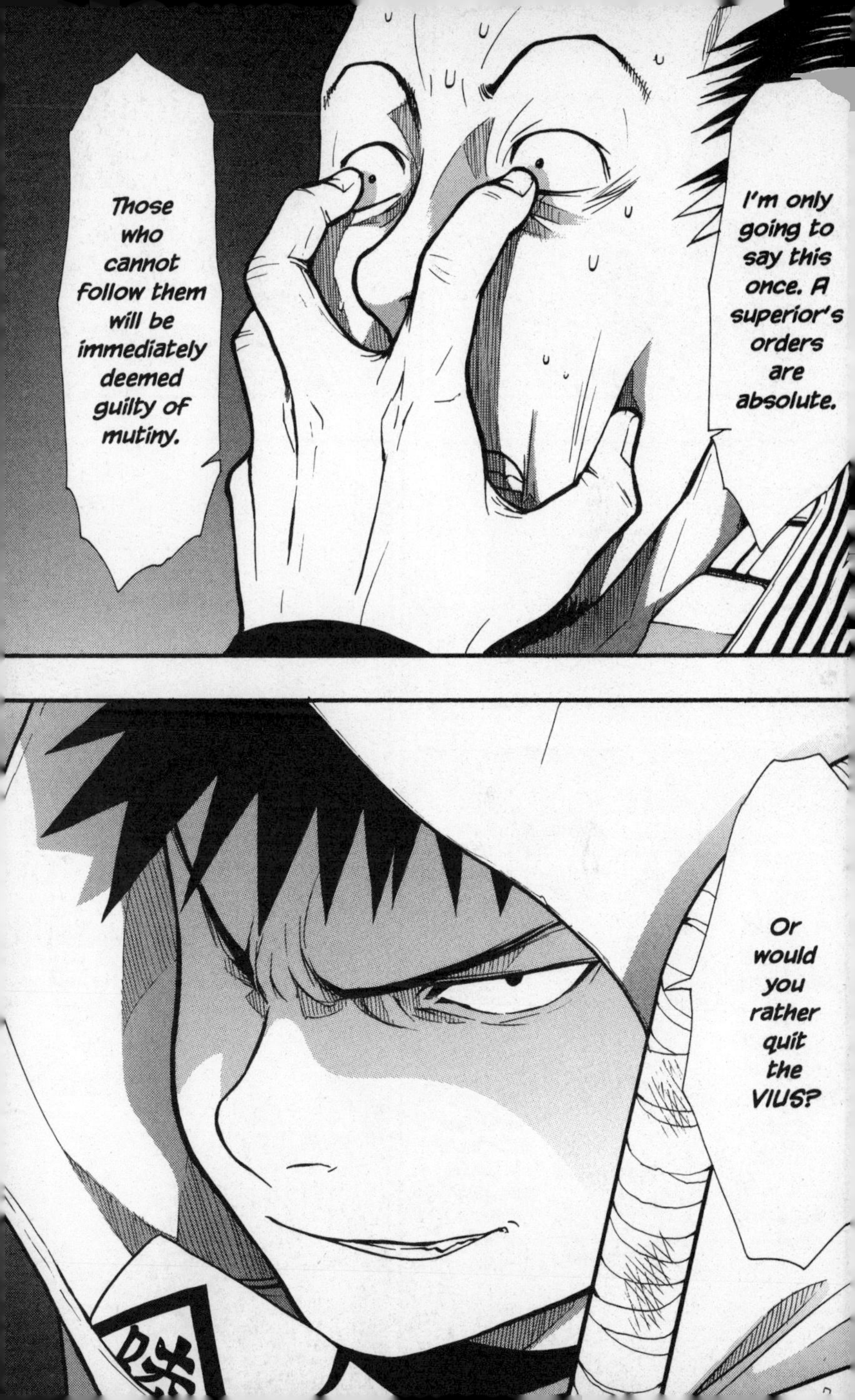
I'm only going to say this once. A superior's orders are absolute.
Those who cannot follow them will be immediately deemed guilty of mutiny.
Or would you rather quit the VIUS?

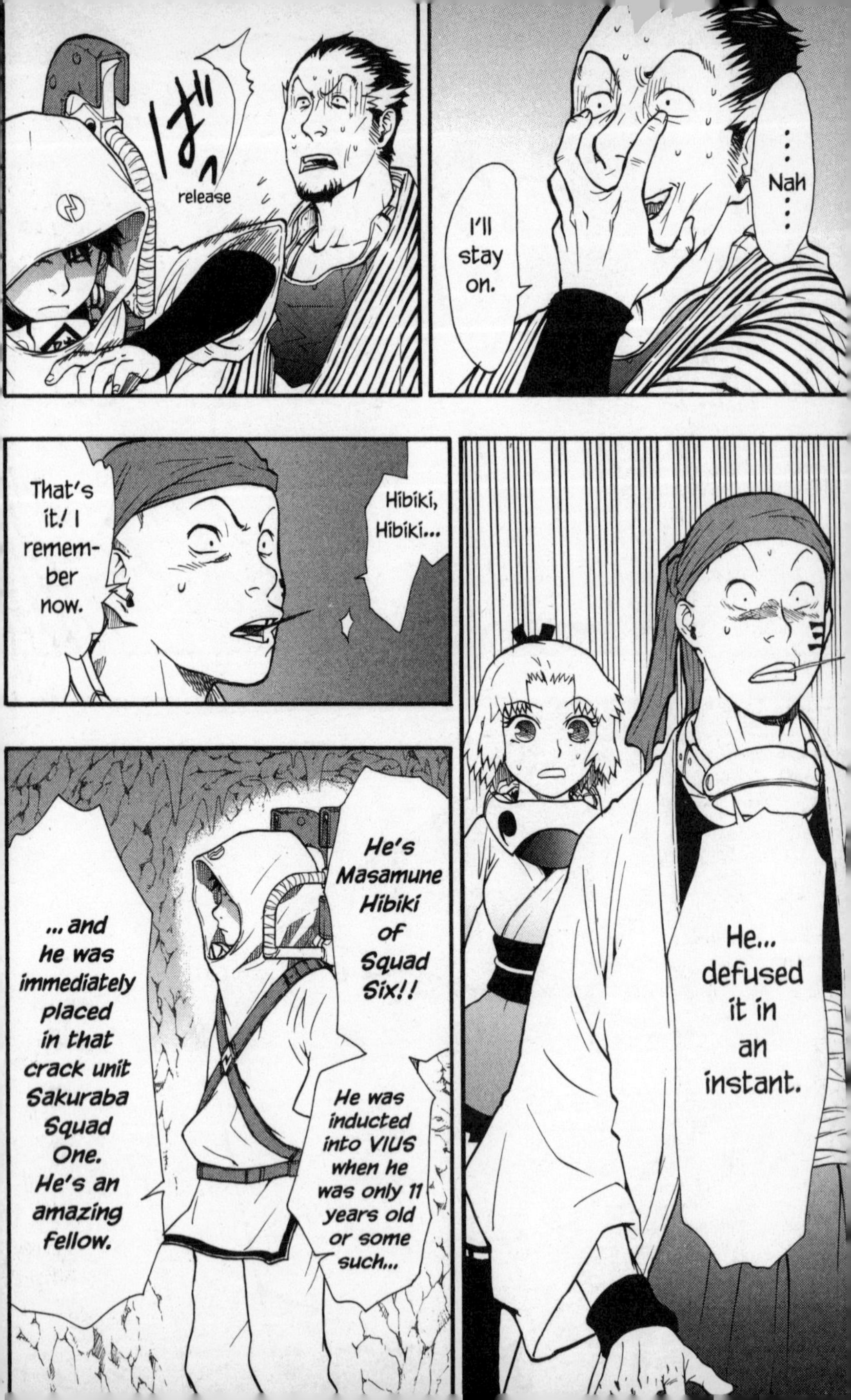
...Nah...
I'll stay on.
ぱ
release
He... defused it in an instant.
Hibiki, Hibiki...
That's it! I remember now.
He's Masamune Hibiki of Squad Six!!
He was inducted into VIUS when he was only 11 years old or some such...
...and he was immediately placed in that crack unit Sakuraba Squad One. He's an amazing fellow.

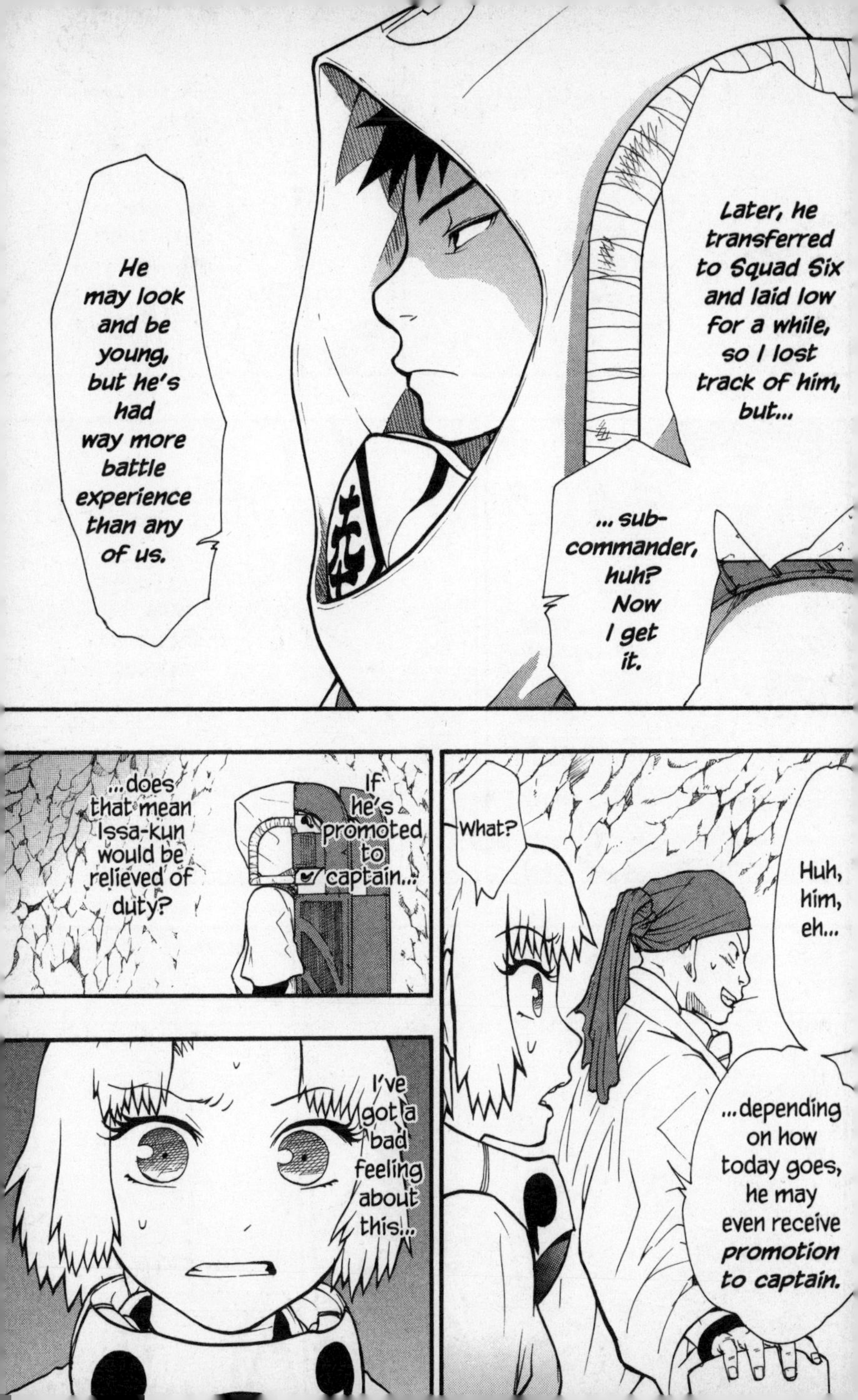
Later, he transferred to Squad Six and laid low for a while, so I lost track of him, but...
...sub-commander, huh? Now I get it.
He may look and be young, but he's had way more battle experience than any of us.
Huh, him, eh...
...depending on how today goes, he may even receive promotion to captain.
What?
If he's promoted to captain...
...does that mean Issa-kun would be relieved of duty?
I've got a bad feeling about this...

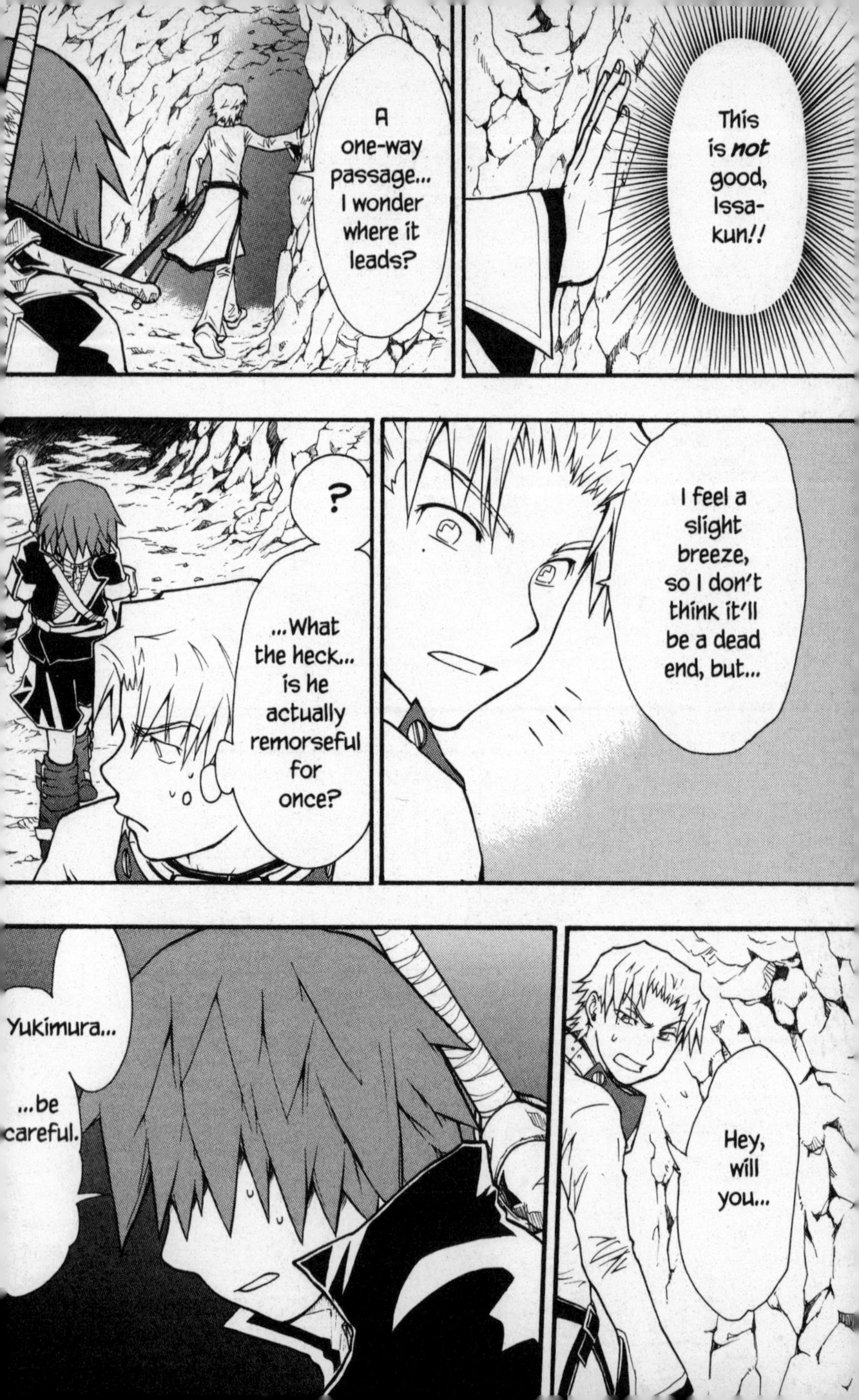
This is ***not*** good, Issa-kun!!
A one-way passage... I wonder where it leads?
I feel a slight breeze, so I don't think it'll be a dead end, but...
?
...What the heck... is he actually remorseful for once?
Hey, will you...
Yukimura...
...be careful.

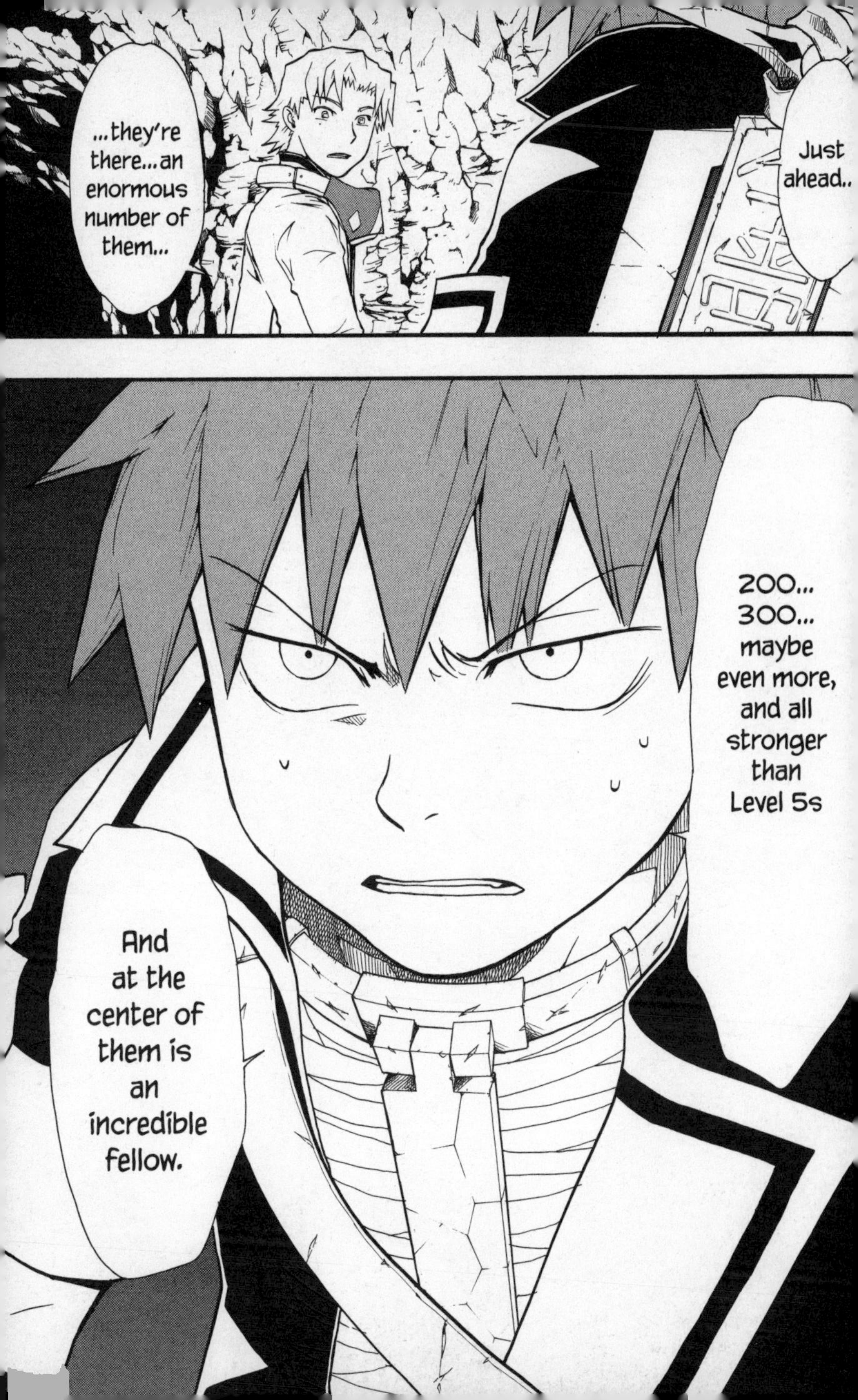
Just ahead..
...they're there...an enormous number of them...
200... 300... maybe even more, and all stronger than Level 5s
And at the center of them is an incredible fellow.

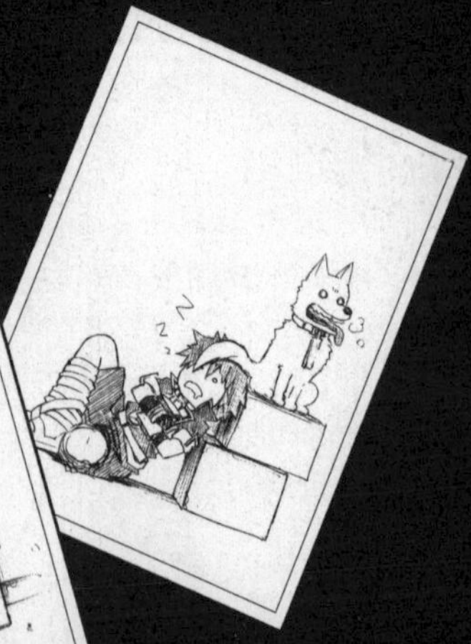

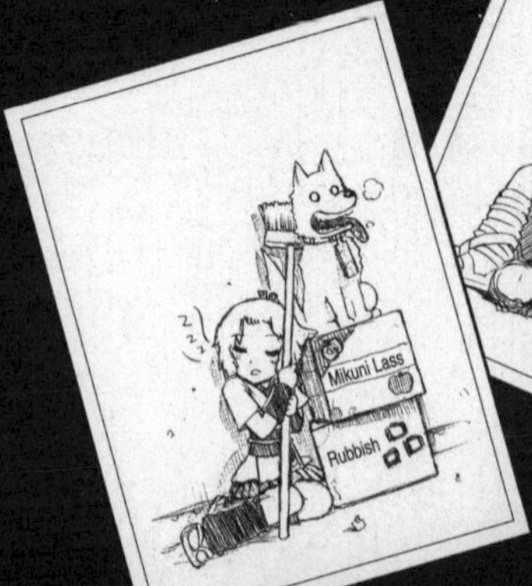
Mikuni Lass
Rubbish

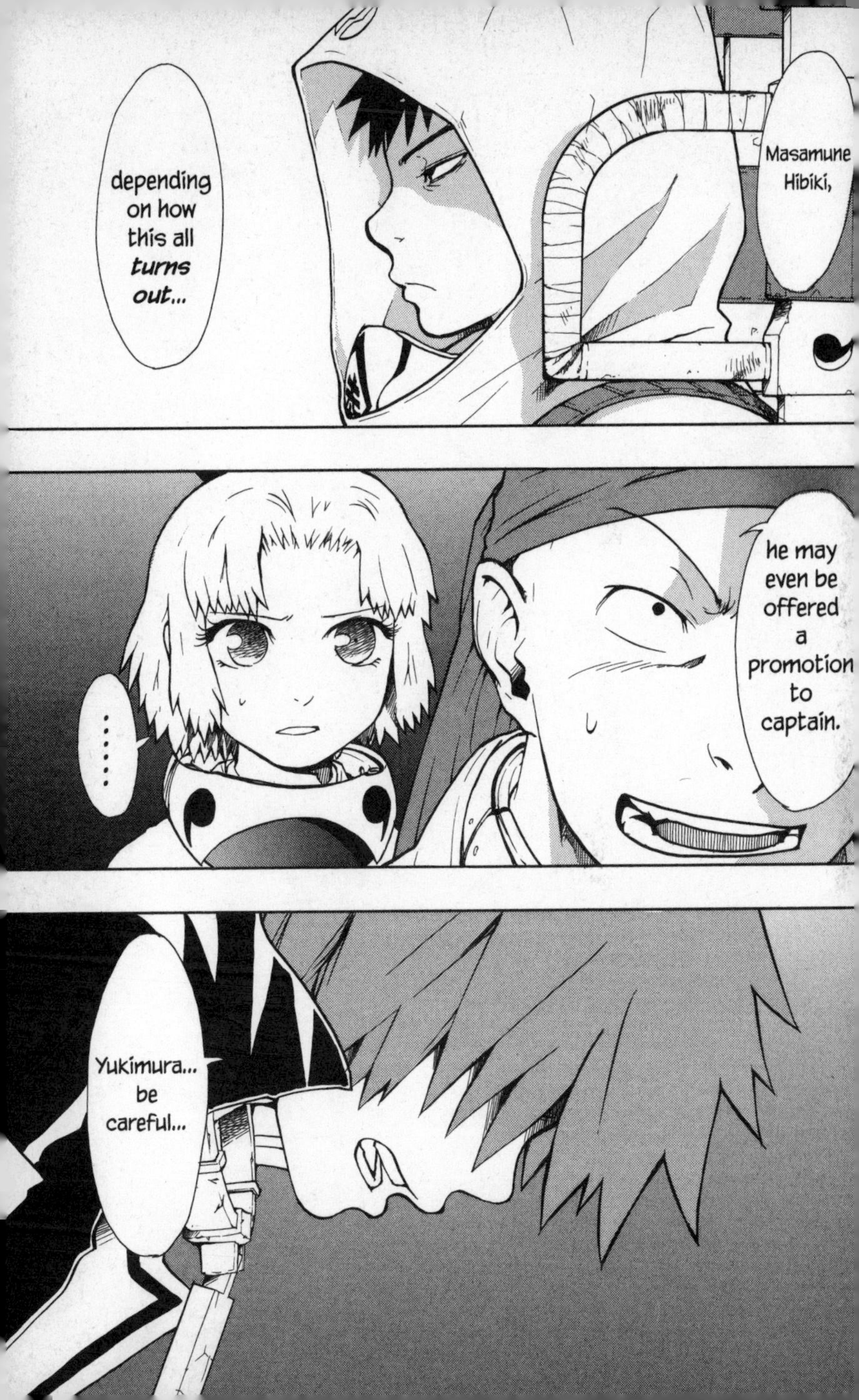
Masamune Hibiki,
depending on how this all *turns out*...
he may even be offered a promotion to captain.
......
Yukimura... be careful...

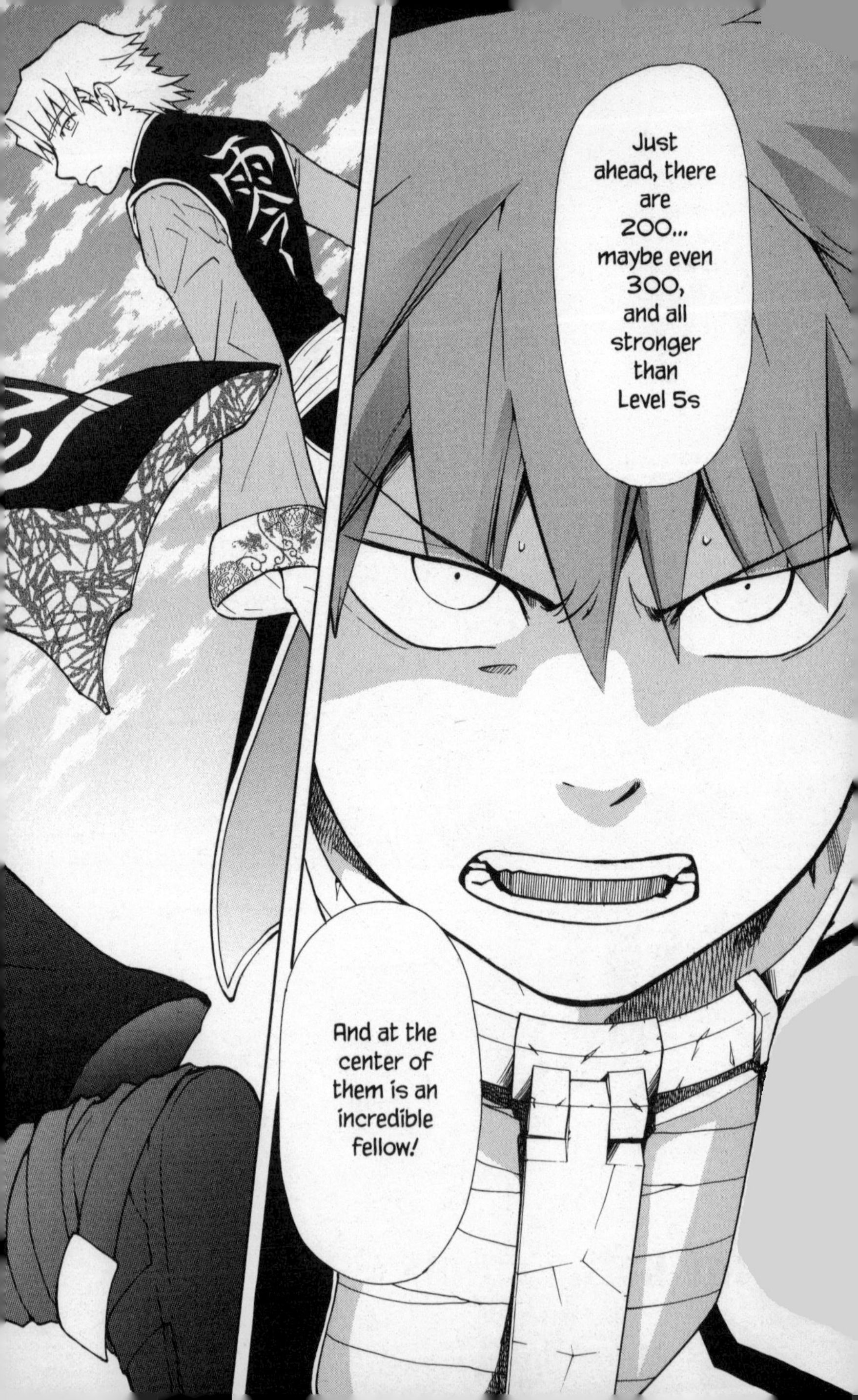
Just ahead, there are 200... maybe even 300, and all stronger than Level 5s
And at the center of them is an incredible fellow!

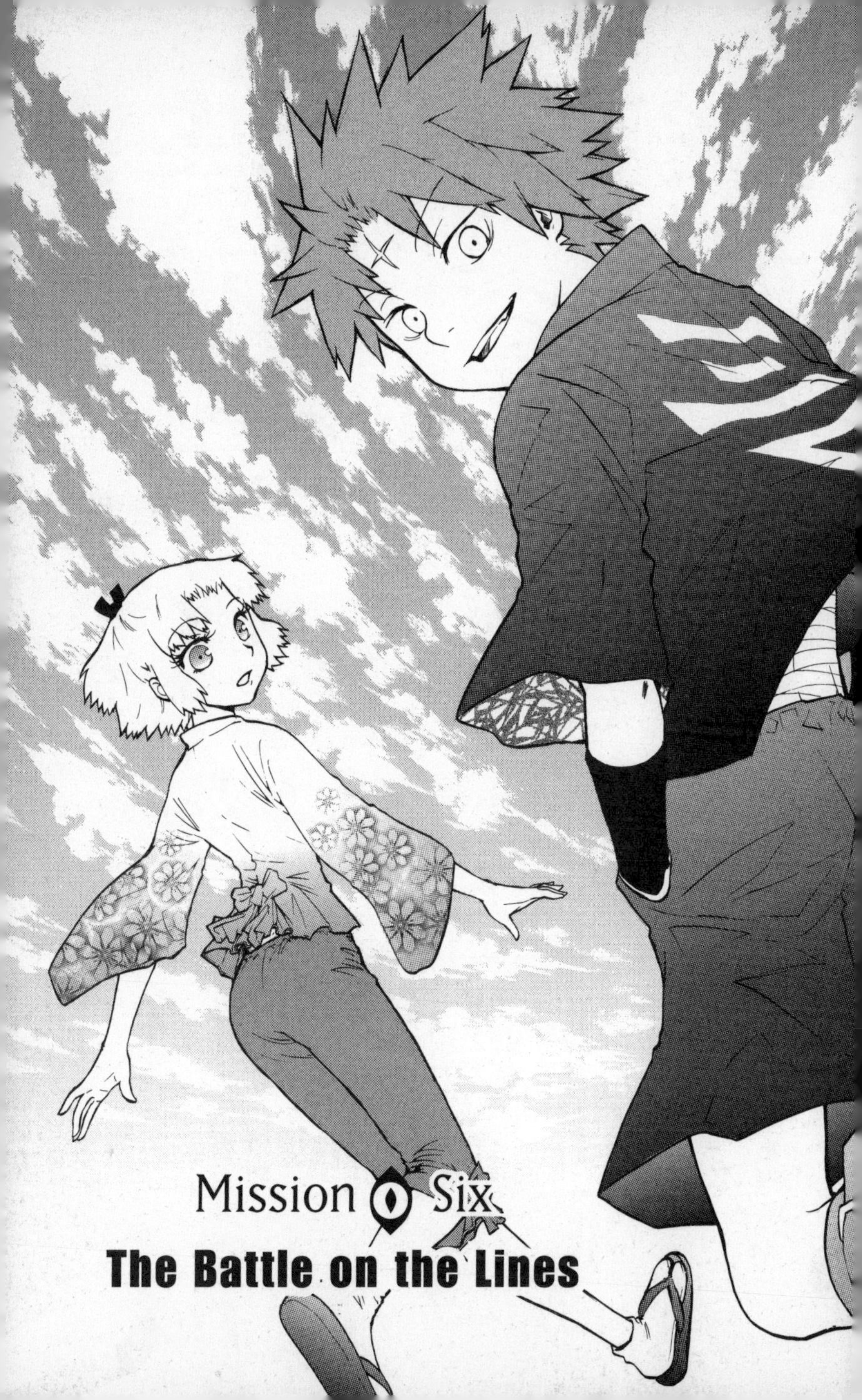
Mission Six
The Battle on the Lines

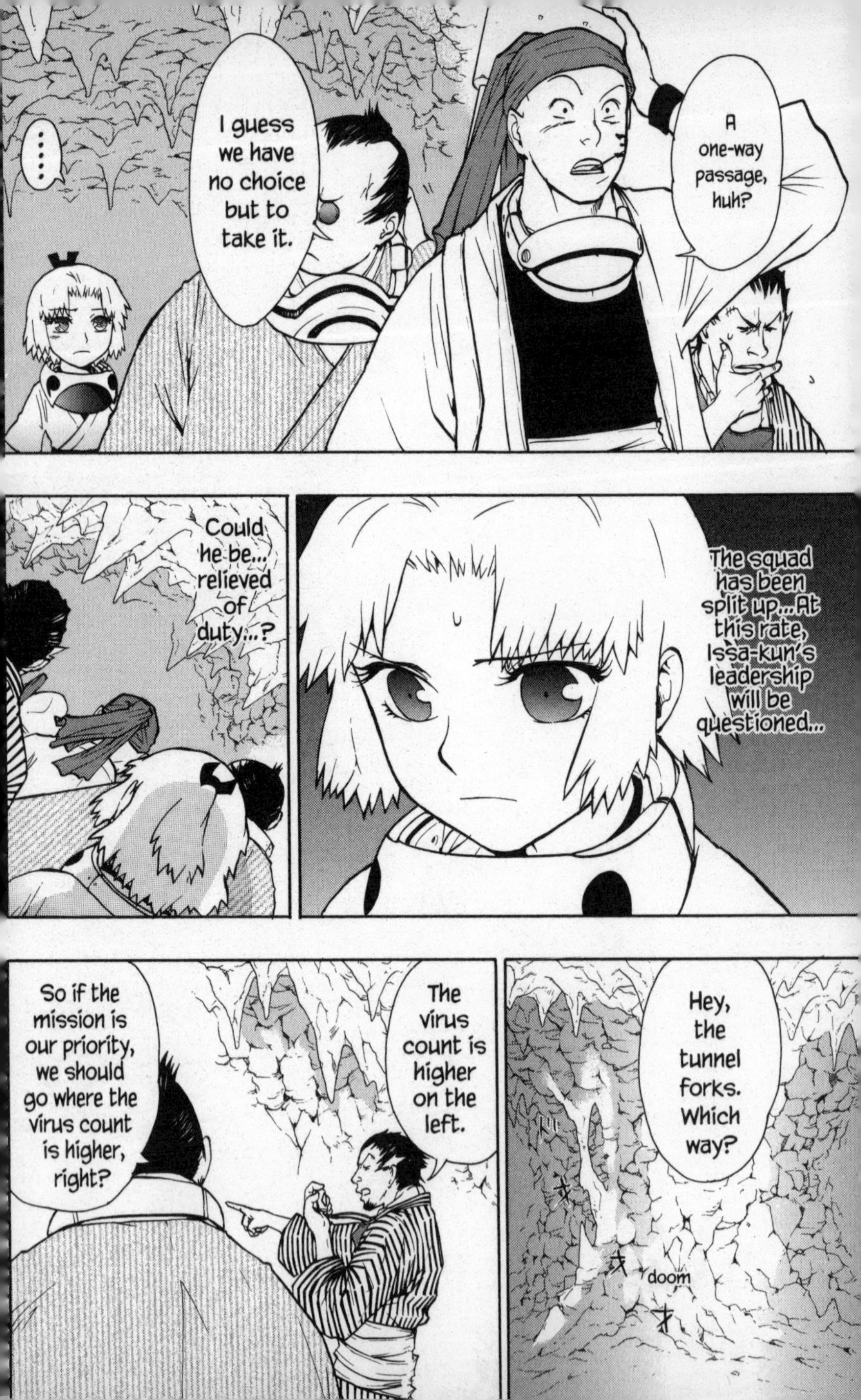
A one-way passage, huh?
I guess we have no choice but to take it.
......
The squad has been split up...At this rate, Issa-kun's leadership will be questioned...
Could he be... relieved of duty...?
Hey, the tunnel forks. Which way?
doom
The virus count is higher on the left.
So if the mission is our priority, we should go where the virus count is higher, right?

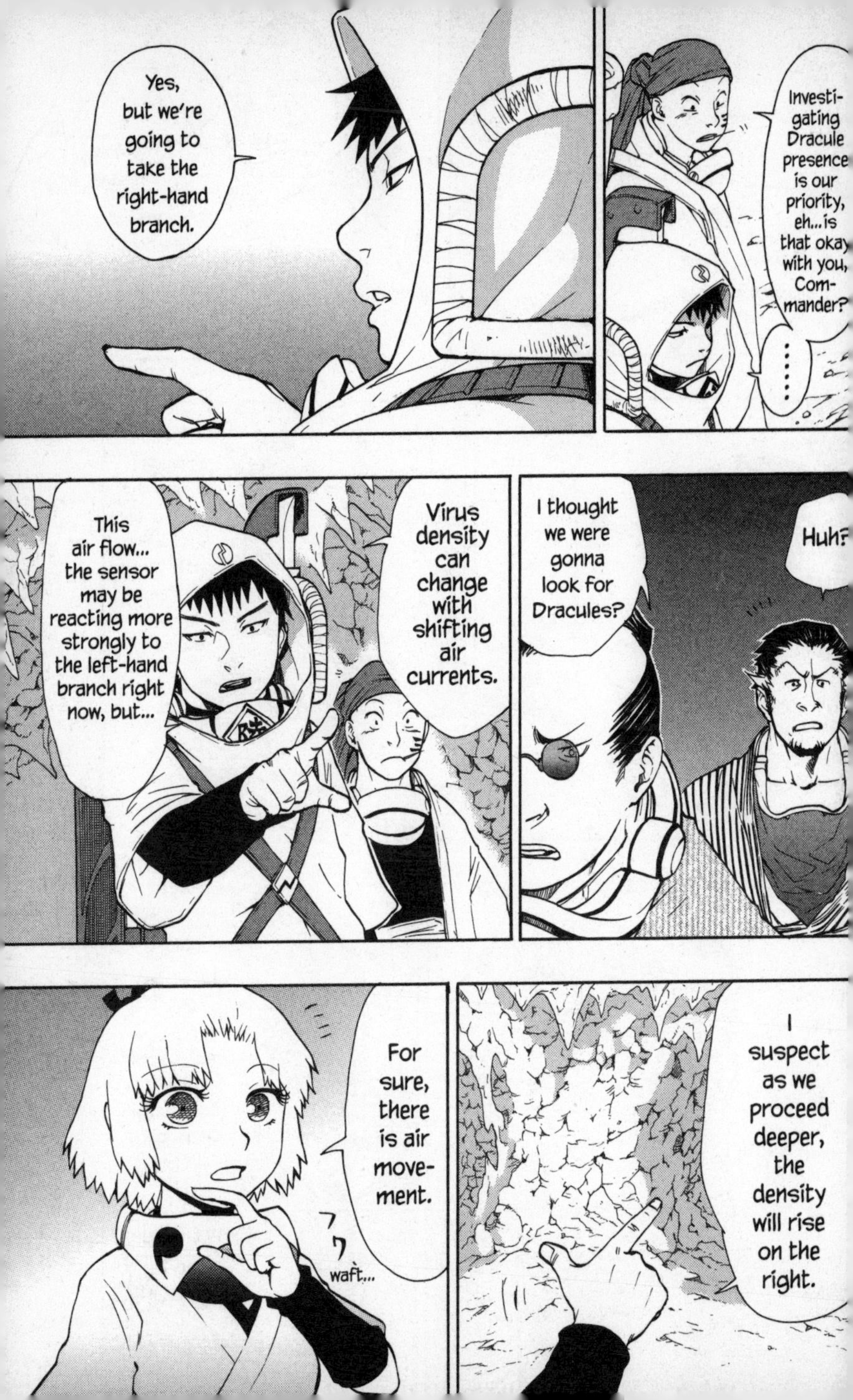
Investigating Dracule presence is our priority, eh...is that okay with you, Commander?
......
Yes, but we're going to take the right-hand branch.
Huh?
I thought we were gonna look for Dracules?
Virus density can change with shifting air currents.
This air flow... the sensor may be reacting more strongly to the left-hand branch right now, but...
I suspect as we proceed deeper, the density will rise on the right.
For sure, there is air movement.
waft...

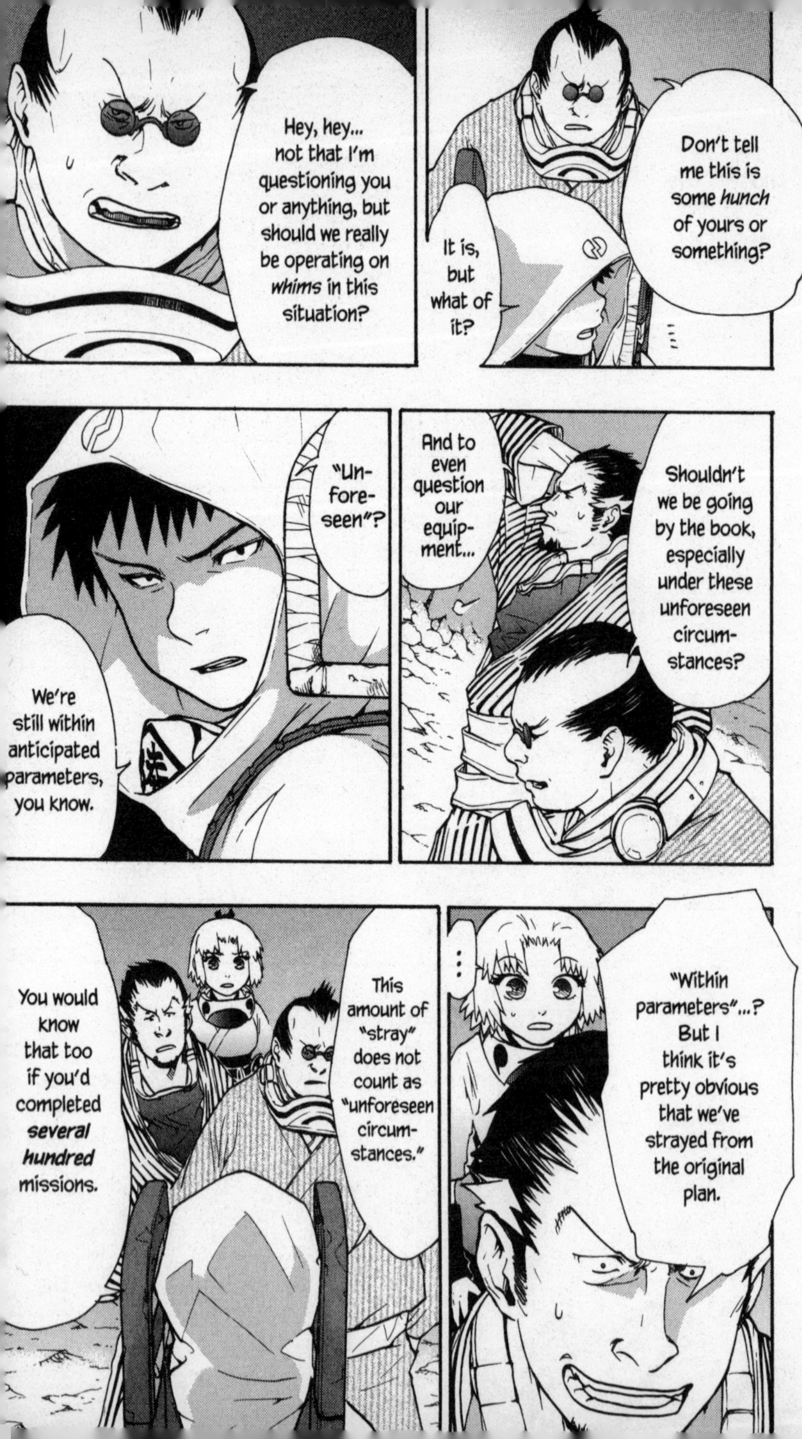

Don't tell me this is some *hunch* of yours or something?
It is, but what of it?
Hey, hey... not that I'm questioning you or anything, but should we really be operating on *whims* in this situation?
Shouldn't we be going by the book, especially under these unforeseen circumstances?
And to even question our equipment...
"Unforeseen"?
We're still within anticipated parameters, you know.
"Within parameters"...? But I think it's pretty obvious that we've strayed from the original plan.
...
This amount of "stray" does not count as "unforeseen circumstances."
You would know that too if you'd completed ***several hundred*** missions.

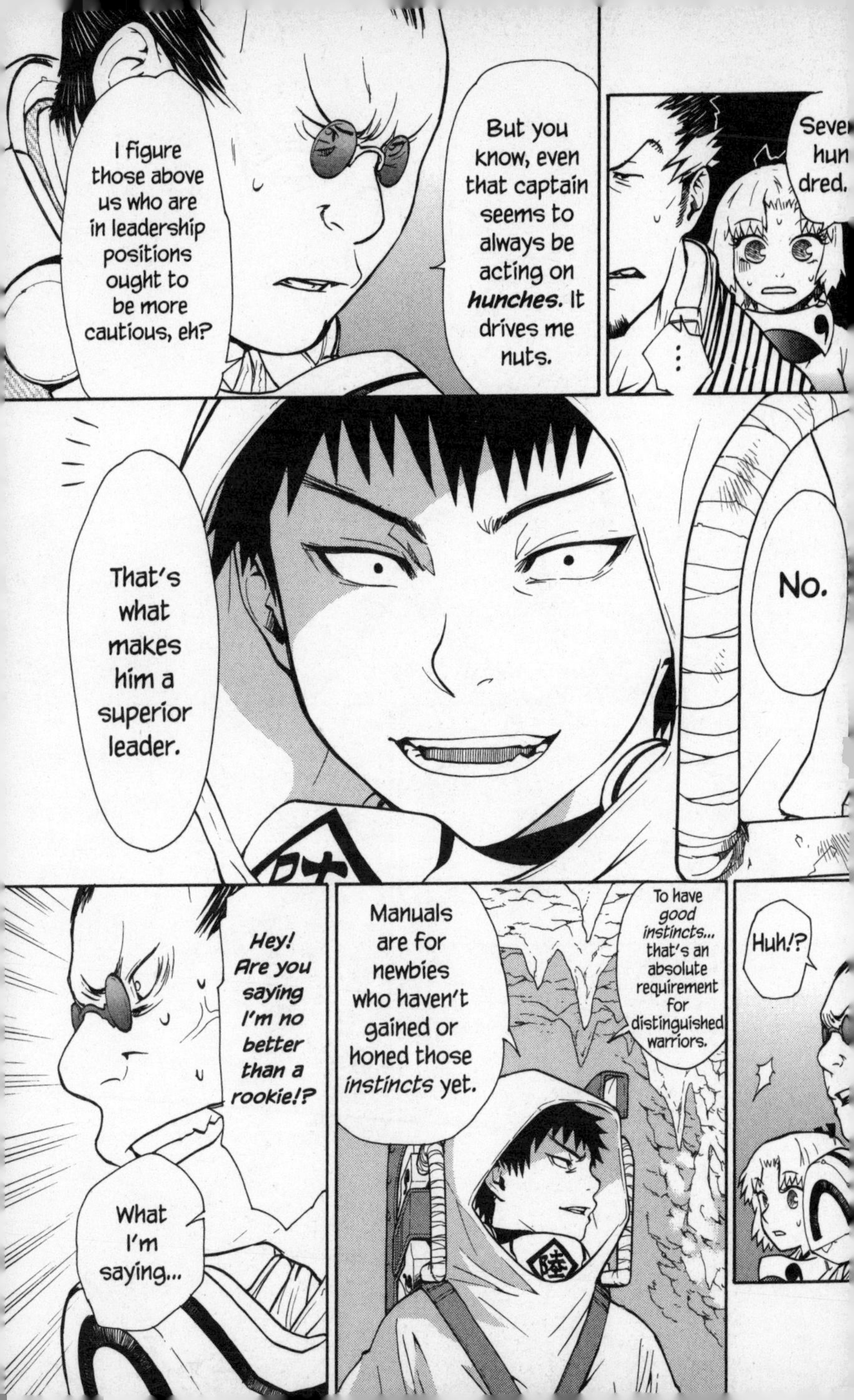
Seve hun dred.
...
But you know, even that captain seems to always be acting on *hunches.* It drives me nuts.
I figure those above us who are in leadership positions ought to be more cautious, eh?
No.
That's what makes him a superior leader.
Huh!?
To have *good instincts*... that's an absolute requirement for distinguished warriors.
Manuals are for newbies who haven't gained or honed those *instincts* yet.
Hey! Are you saying I'm no better than a rookie!?
What I'm saying...

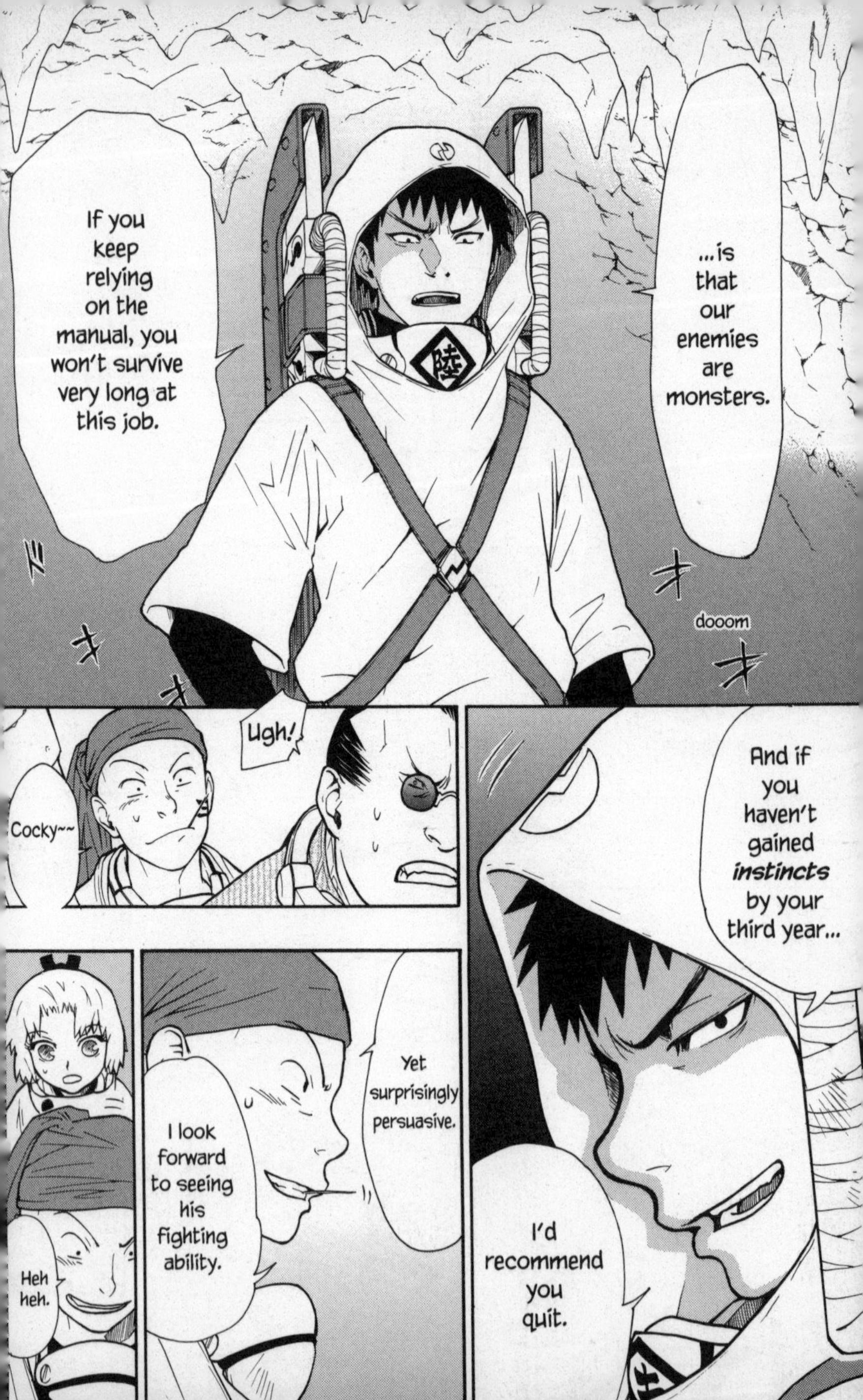

...is that our enemies are monsters.
If you keep relying on the manual, you won't survive very long at this job.
dooom
And if you haven't gained ***instincts*** by your third year...
I'd recommend you quit.
Ugh!
Cocky~~
Yet surprisingly persuasive.
I look forward to seeing his fighting ability.
Heh heh.

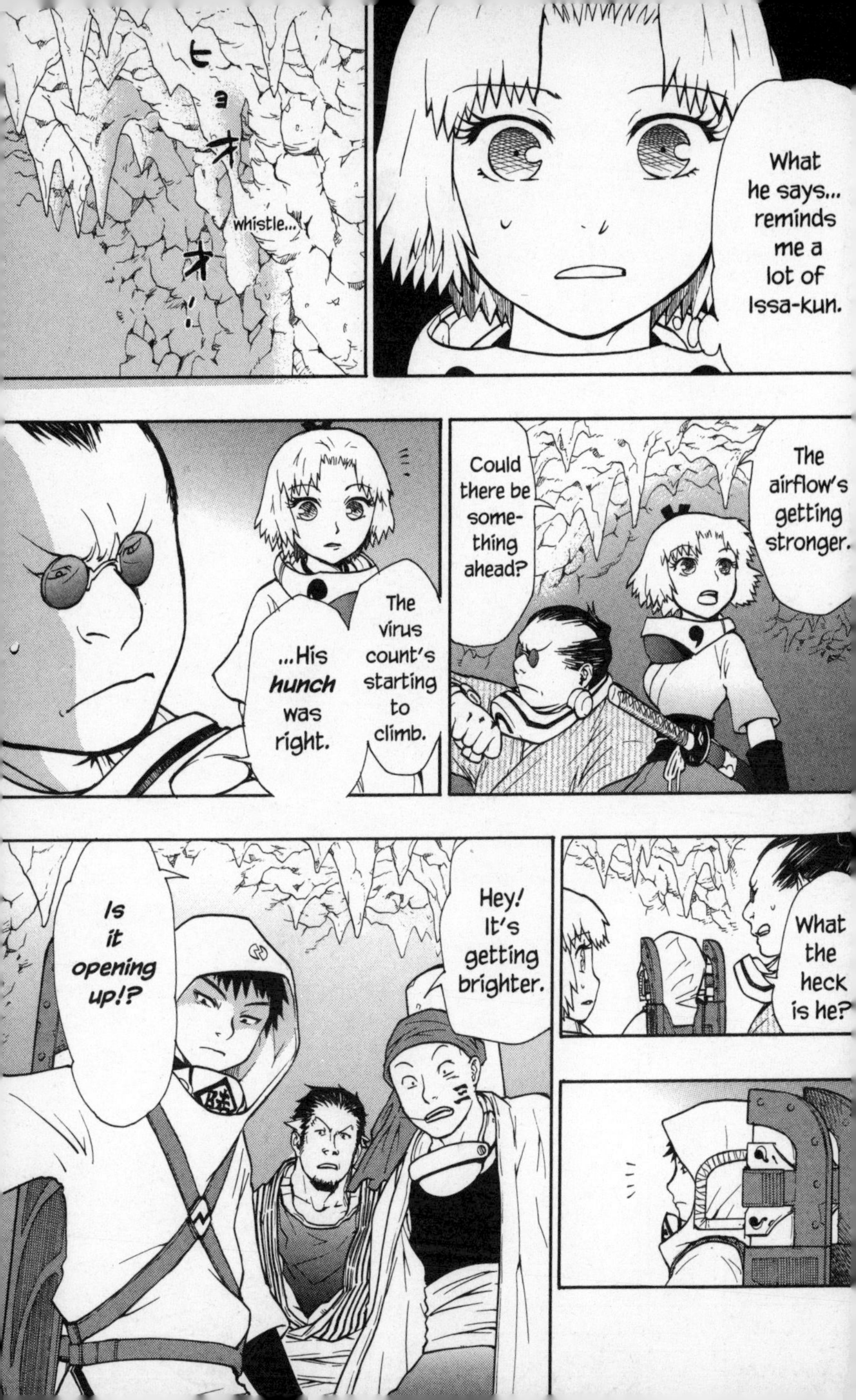

What he says... reminds me a lot of Issa-kun.
ヒョオオ!
whistle...
The airflow's getting stronger.
Could there be some-thing ahead?
The virus count's starting to climb.
...His **hunch** was right.
What the heck is he?
Hey! It's getting brighter.
Is it opening up!?

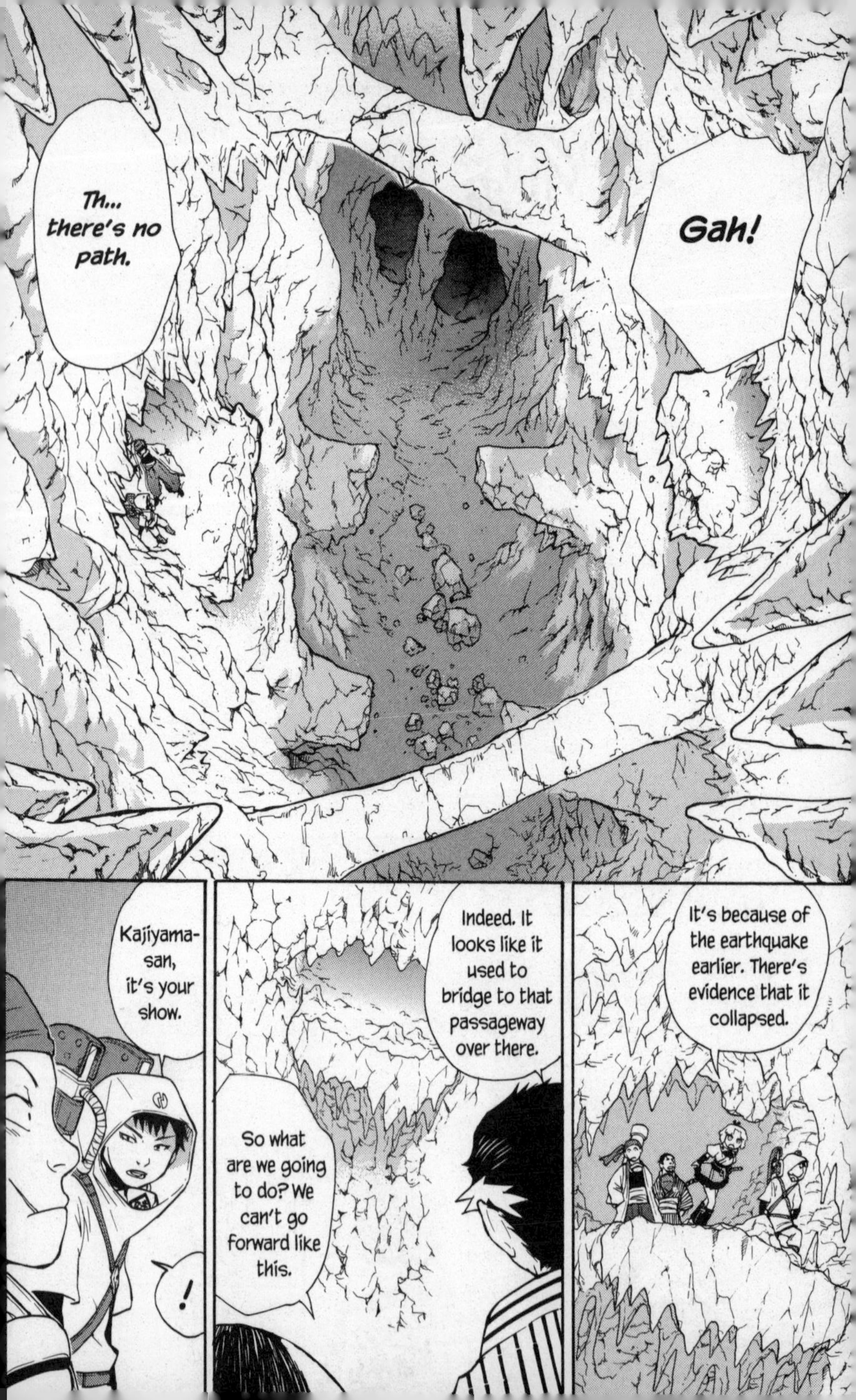
Gah!
Th... there's no path.
It's because of the earthquake earlier. There's evidence that it collapsed.
Indeed. It looks like it used to bridge to that passageway over there.
So what are we going to do? We can't go forward like this.
Kajiyama-san, it's your show.
!

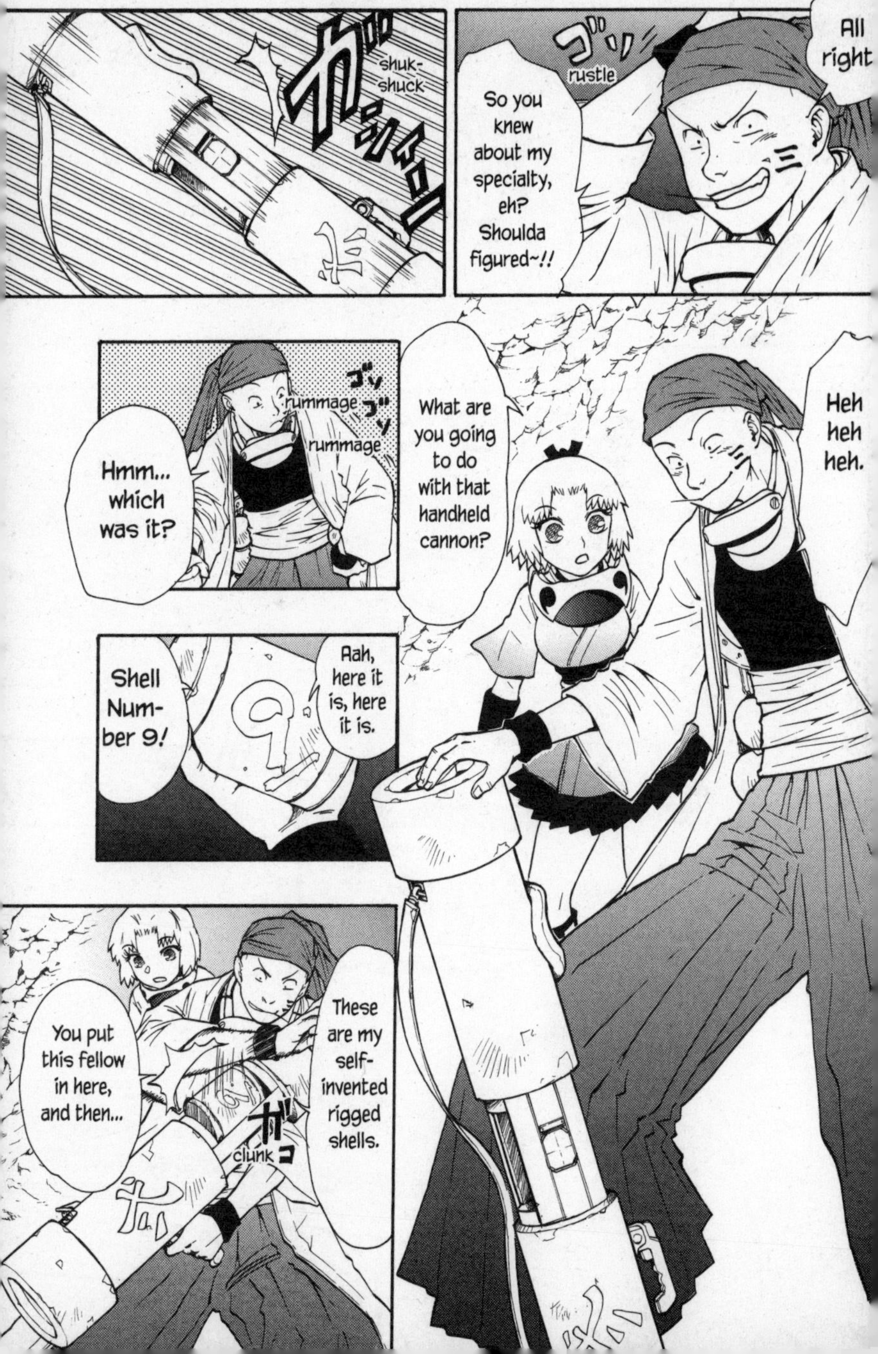
All right
rustle
So you knew about my specialty, eh? Shoulda figured~!!
shuk-shuck
Heh heh heh.
What are you going to do with that handheld cannon?
rummage
rummage
Hmm... which was it?
Aah, here it is, here it is.
Shell Number 9!
These are my self-invented rigged shells.
You put this fellow in here, and then...
clunk

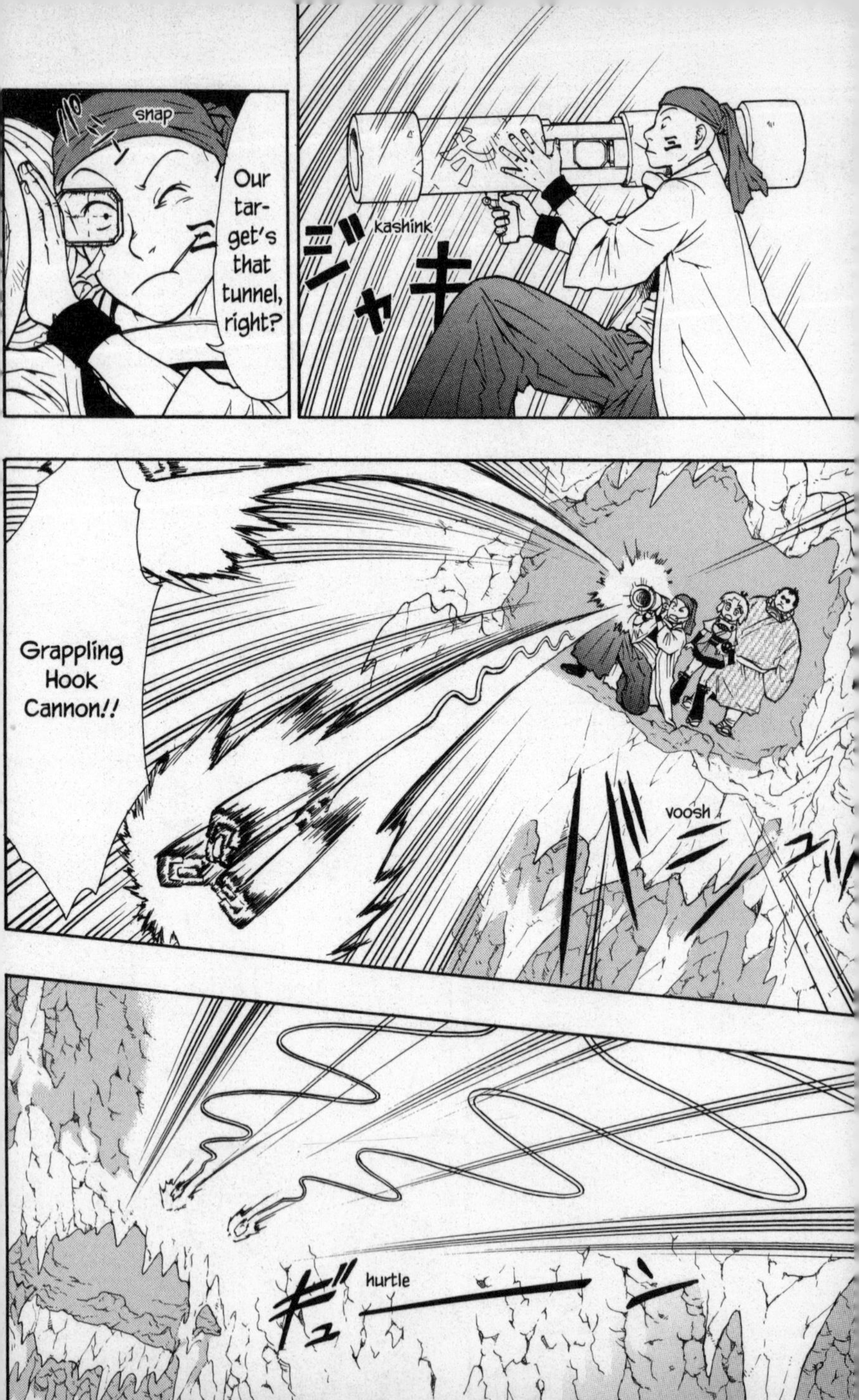
kashink
snap
Our tar-get's that tunnel, right?
Grappling Hook Cannon!!
voosh
hurtle

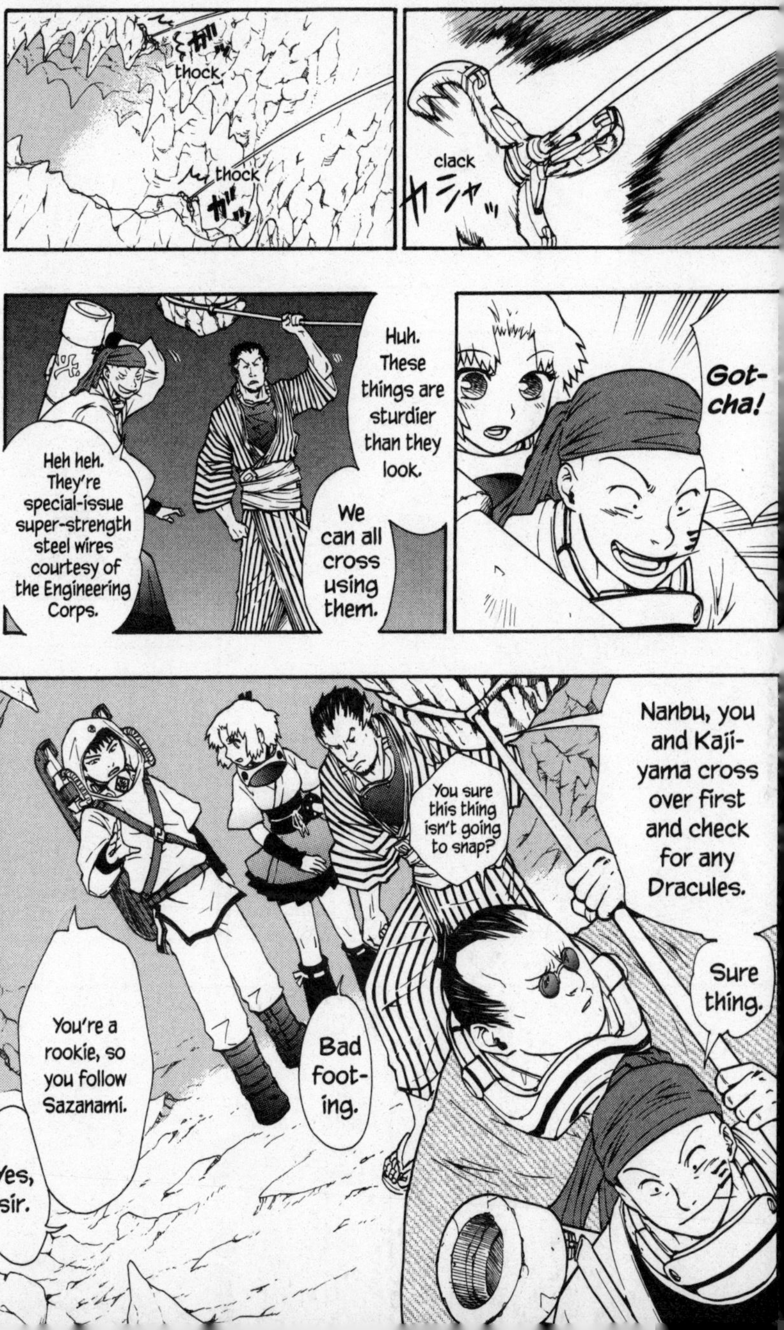
clack
thock
thock
Got-cha!
Huh. These things are sturdier than they look.
We can all cross using them.
Heh heh. They're special-issue super-strength steel wires courtesy of the Engineering Corps.
Nanbu, you and Kaji-yama cross over first and check for any Dracules.
Sure thing.
You sure this thing isn't going to snap?
Bad foot-ing.
You're a rookie, so you follow Sazanami.
Yes, sir.

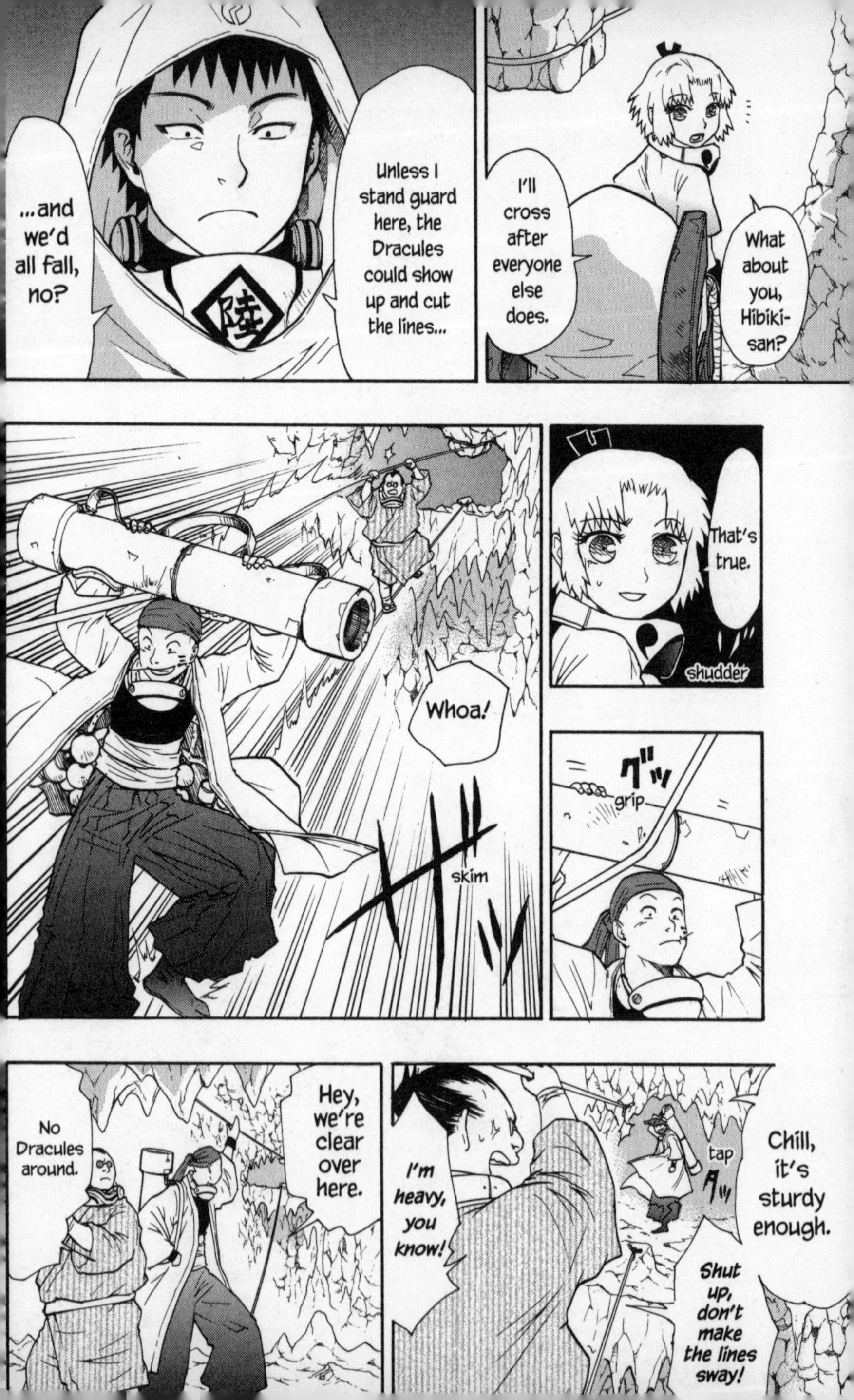

What about you, Hibiki-san?
I'll cross after everyone else does.
Unless I stand guard here, the Dracules could show up and cut the lines...
...and we'd all fall, no?
That's true.
shudder
grip
Whoa!
skim
Chill, it's sturdy enough.
tap
I'm heavy, you know!
Shut up, don't make the lines sway!
Hey, we're clear over here.
No Dracules around.

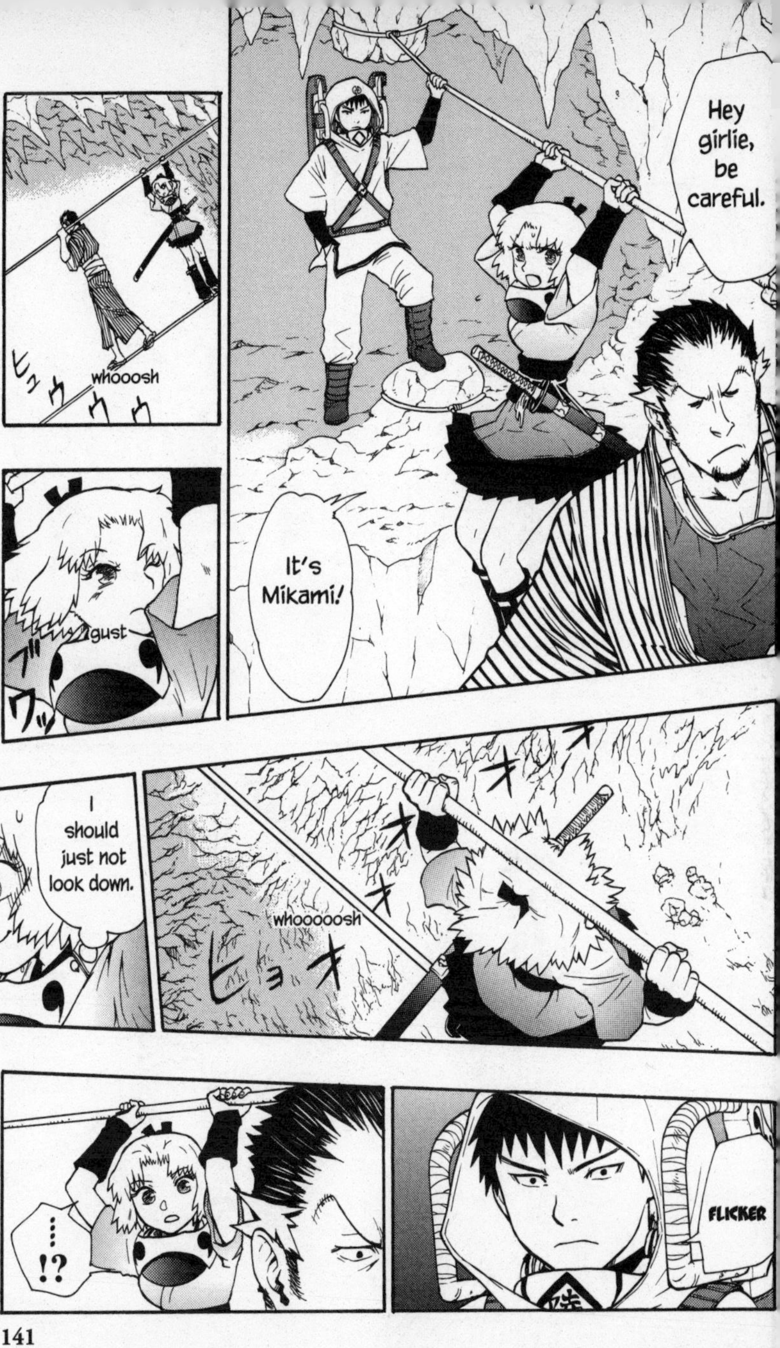
Hey girlie, be careful.
It's Mikami!
whooosh
ヒュウウウ
gust
ブワッ
whoooosh
ヒョオ
I should just not look down.
FLICKER
....!?

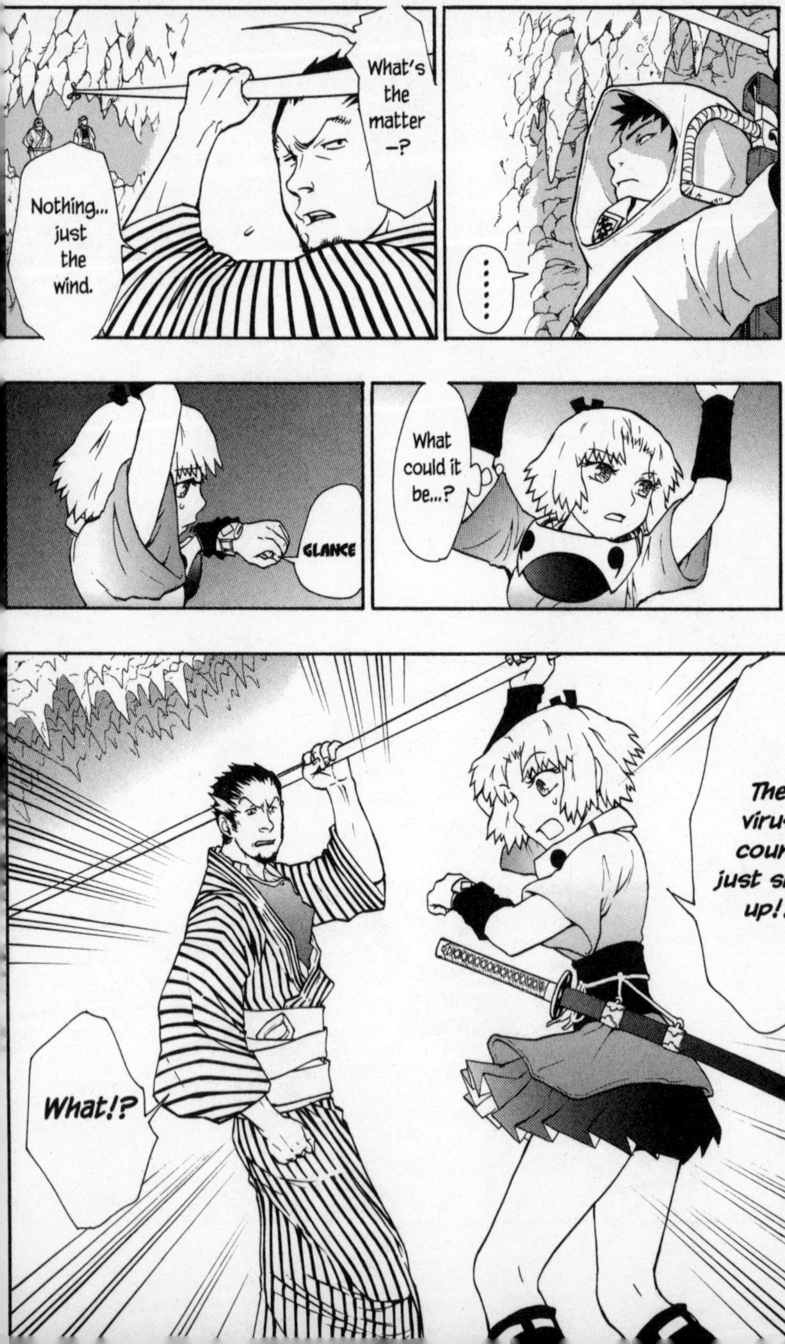
......
What's the matter—?
Nothing... just the wind.
What could it be...?
GLANCE
The virus count just shot up!!
What!?

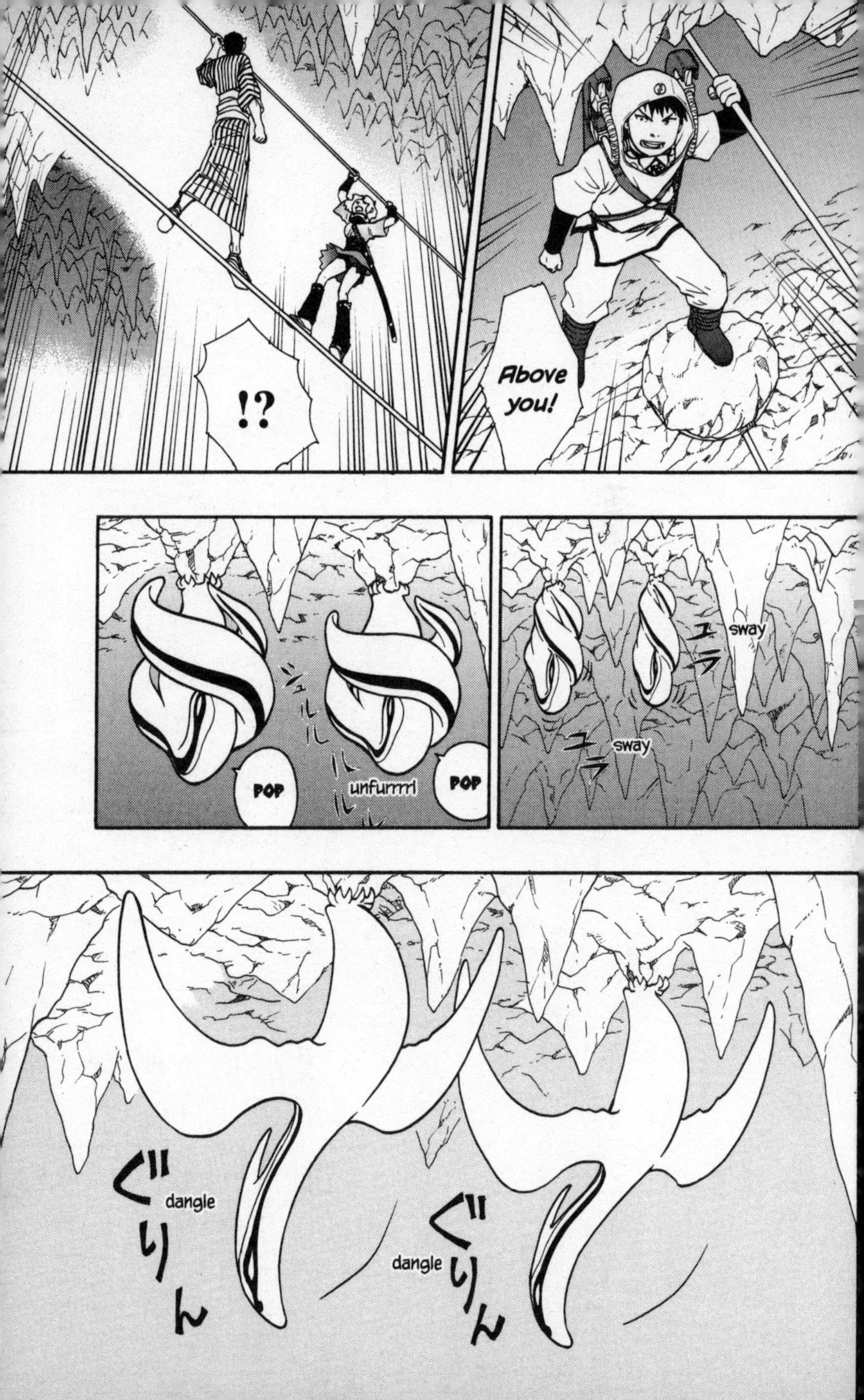
Above you!
!?
ユラ
sway
ユラ
sway
POP
unfurrrl
POP
ぐりん
dangle
ぐりん
dangle

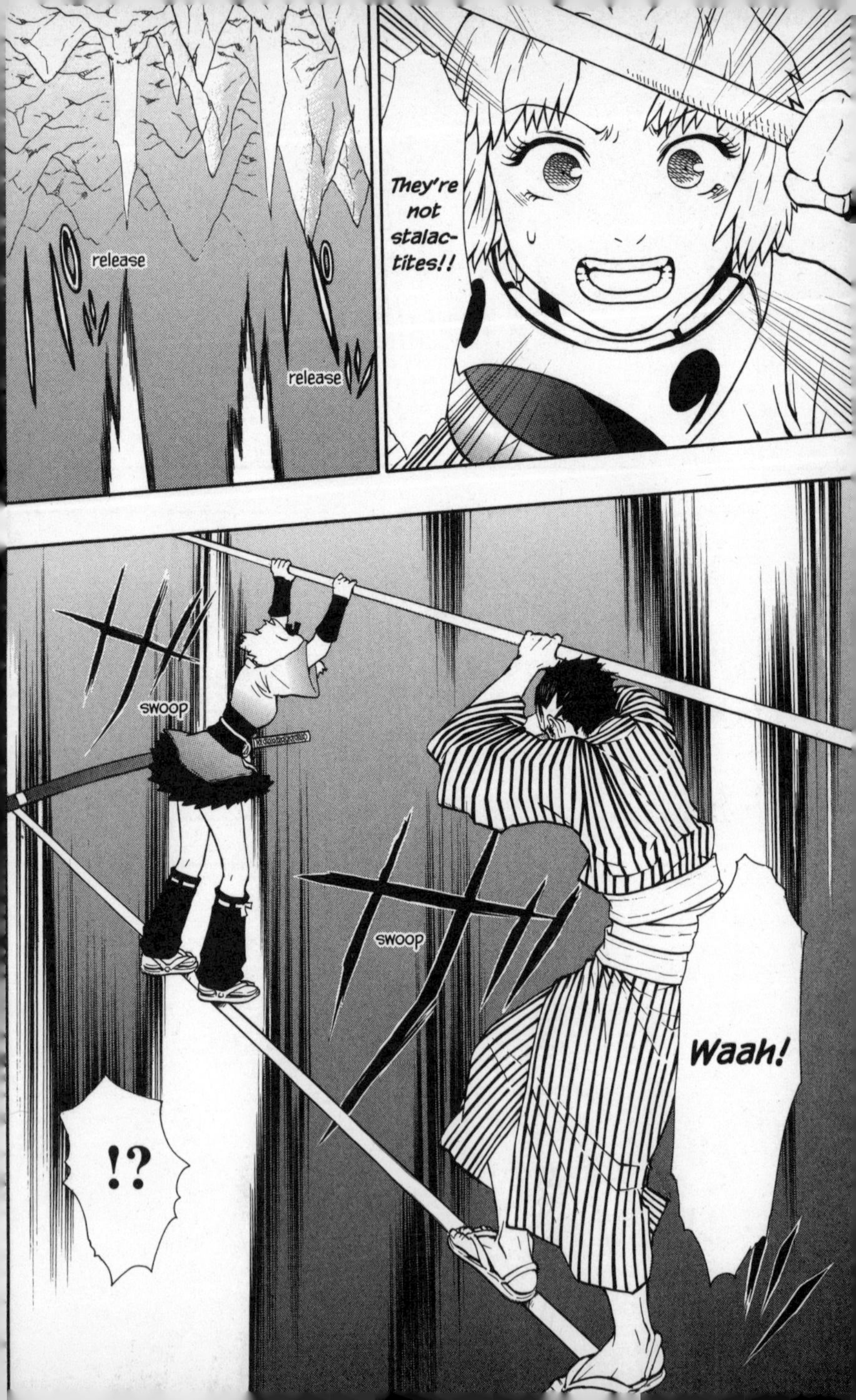
They're not stalac-tites!!
release
release
swoop
swoop
Waah!
!?

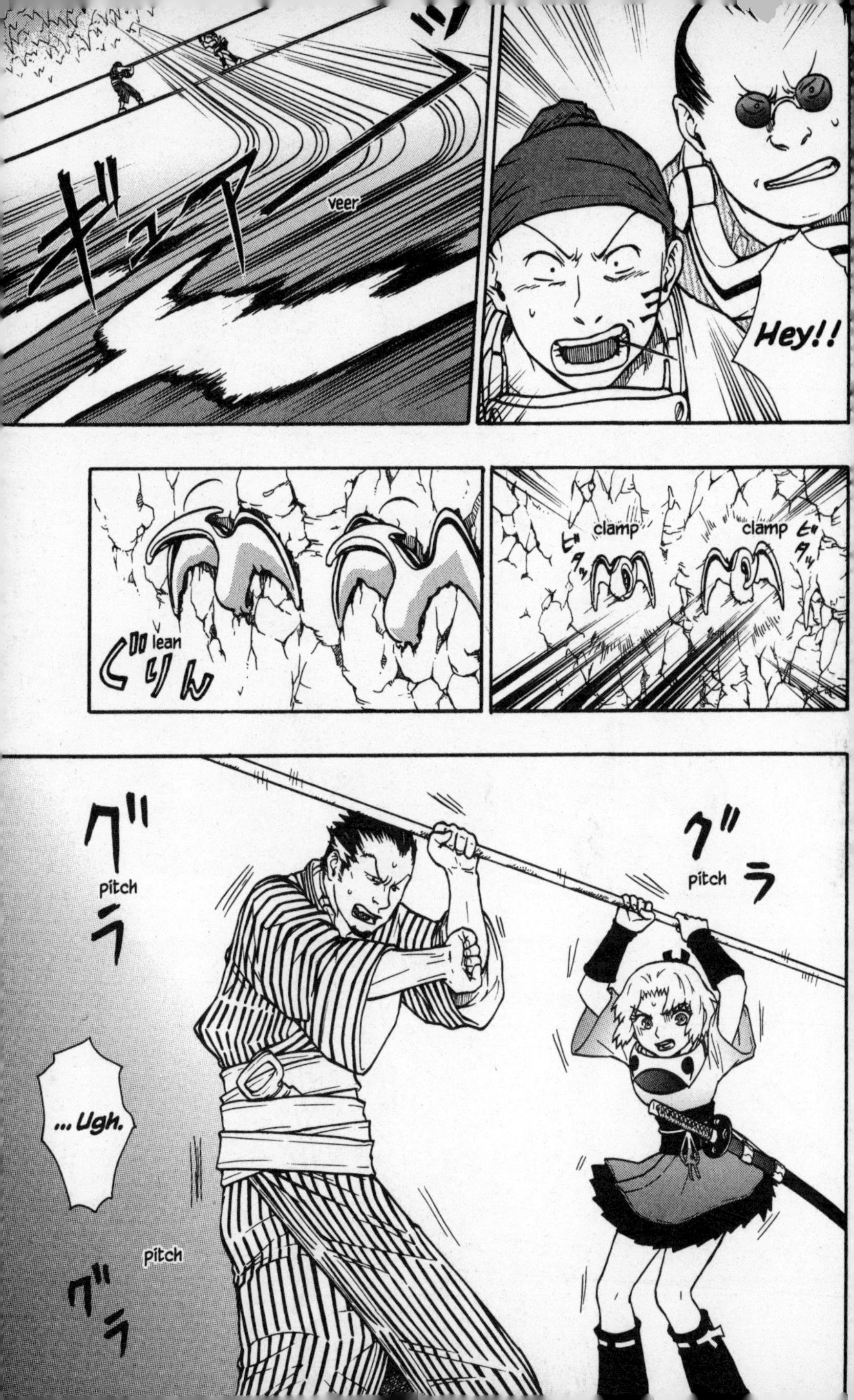

Hey!!
ギュア
veer
ビタッ
clamp
ビタッ
clamp
ぐりん
lean
グラ
pitch
グラ
pitch
...Ugh.
グラ
pitch

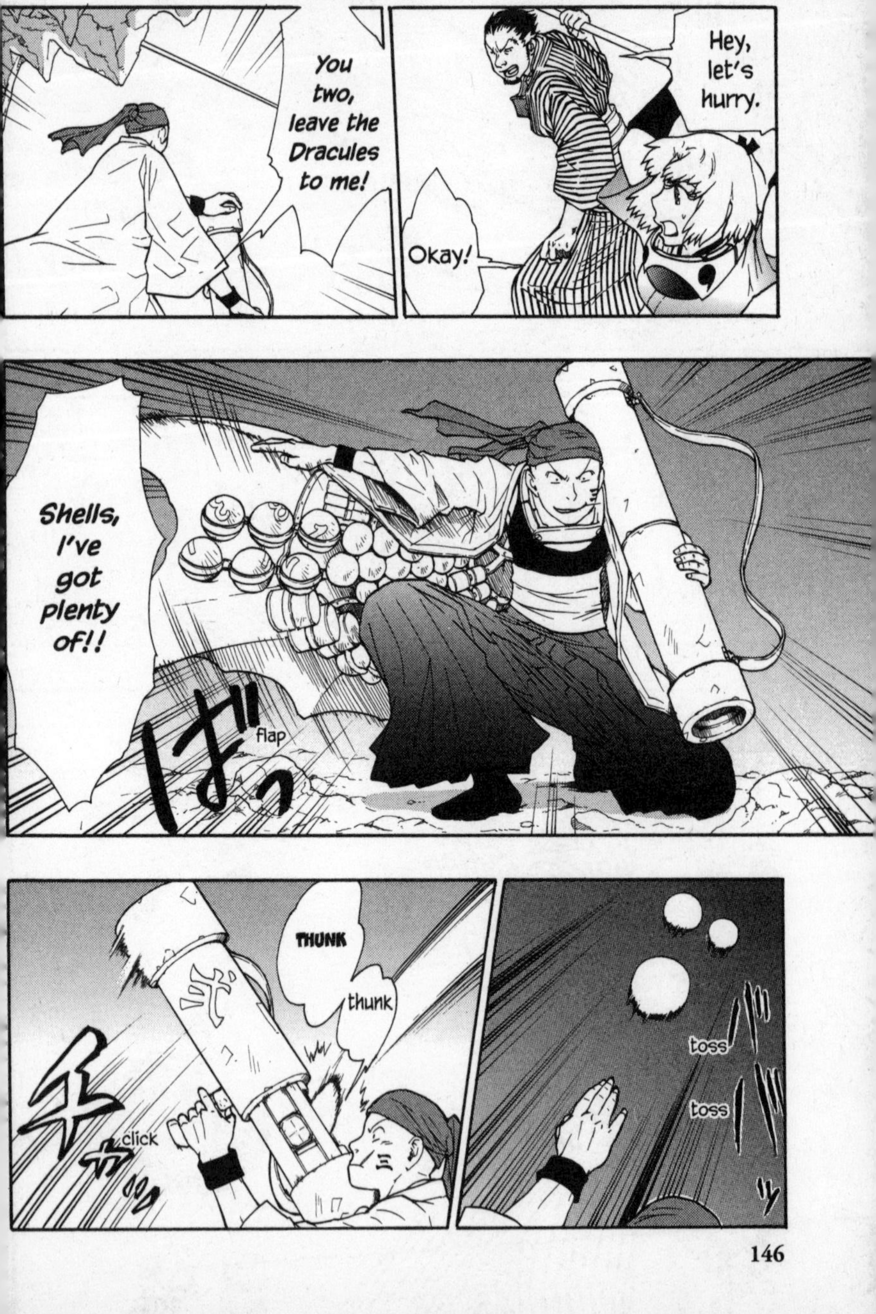
Hey, let's hurry.
Okay!
You two, leave the Dracules to me!
Shells, I've got plenty of!!
flap
toss
toss
THUNK
thunk
click

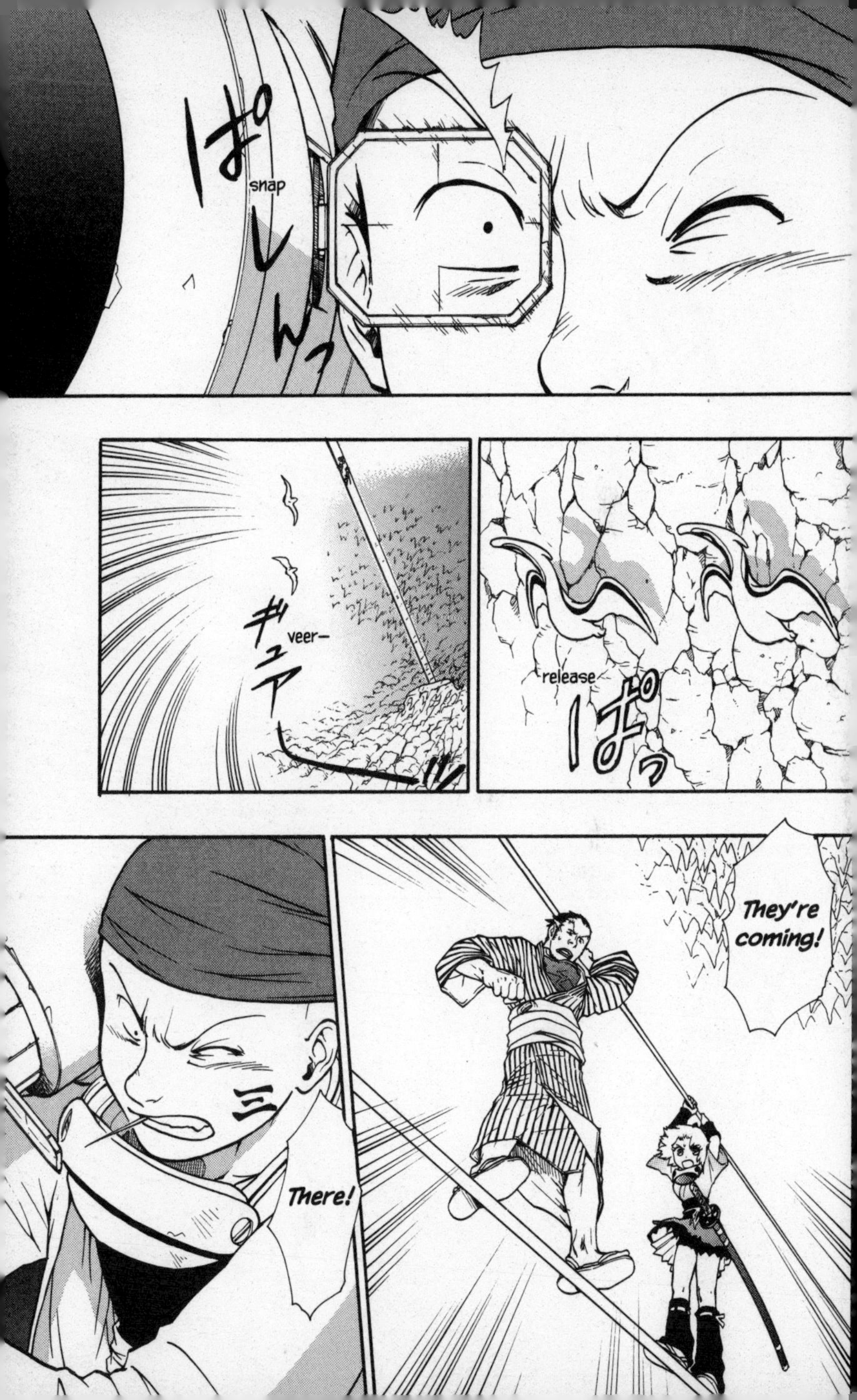
ぱしんっ
snap
ぽっ
release
ギュアーッ
veer–
They're coming!
There!

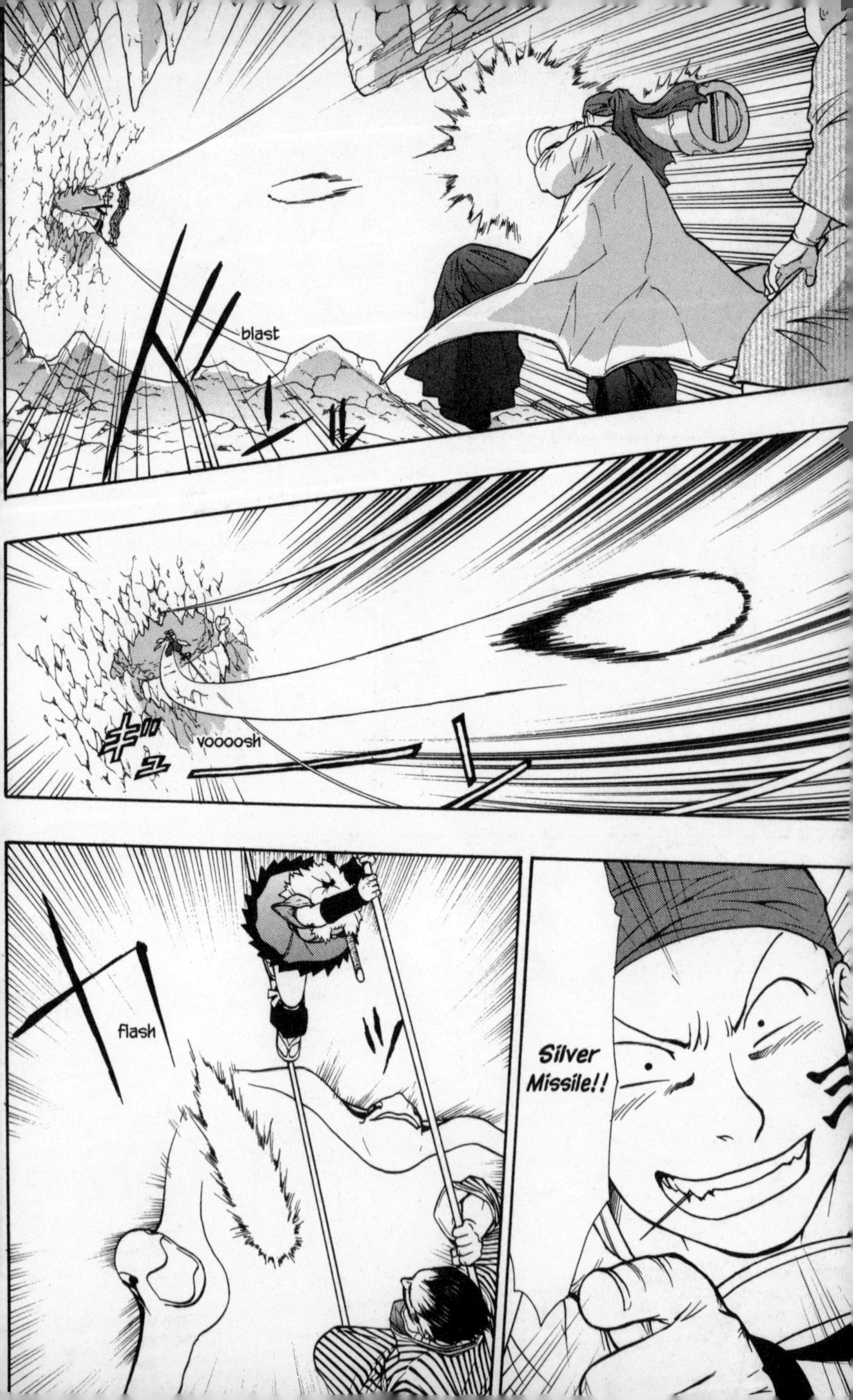
blast
voooosh
Silver Missile!!
flash

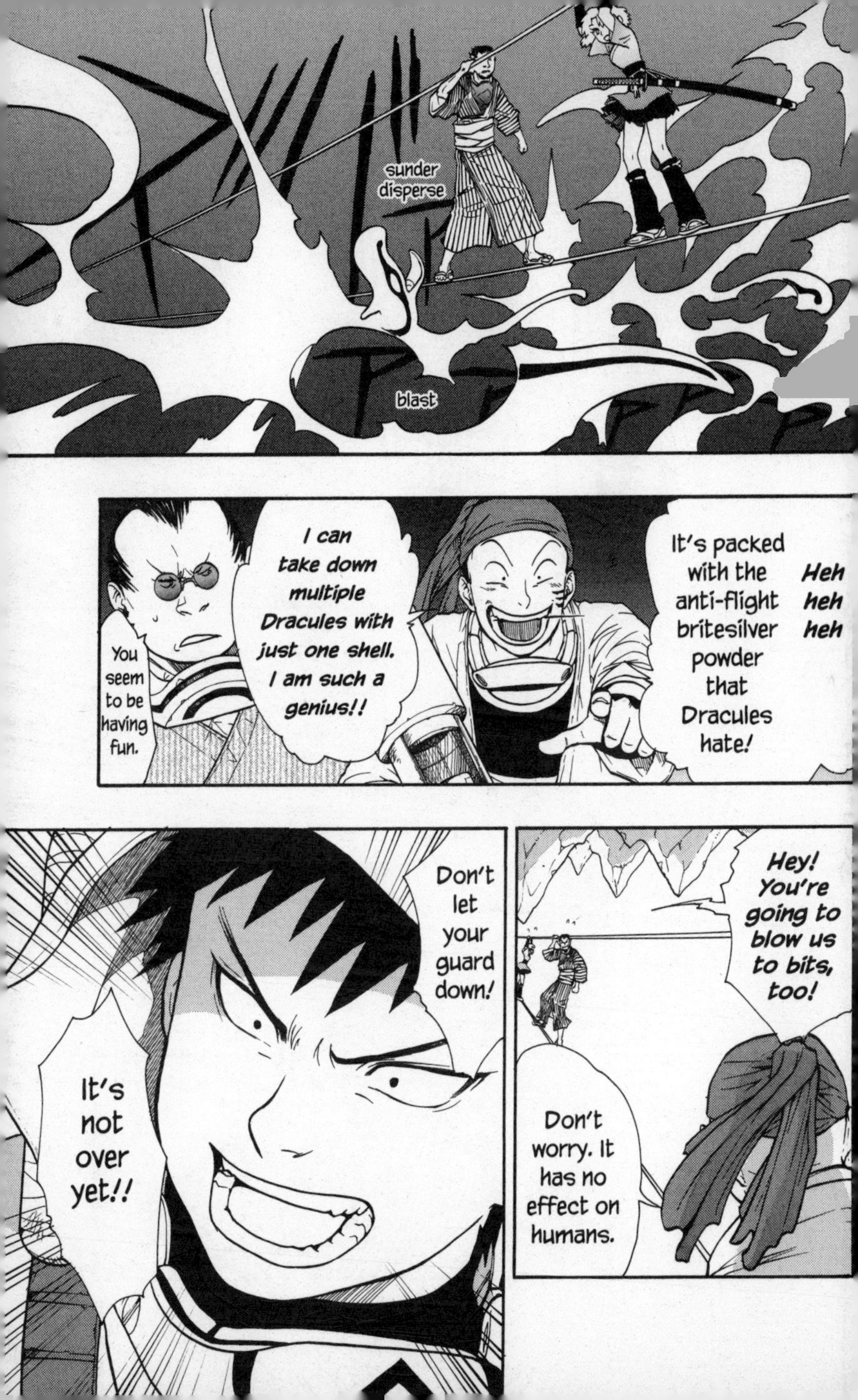
sunder
disperse
blast
Heh heh heh
It's packed with the anti-flight britesilver powder that Dracules hate!
I can take down multiple Dracules with just one shell. I am such a genius!!
You seem to be having fun.
Hey! You're going to blow us to bits, too!
Don't worry. It has no effect on humans.
Don't let your guard down!
It's not over yet!!

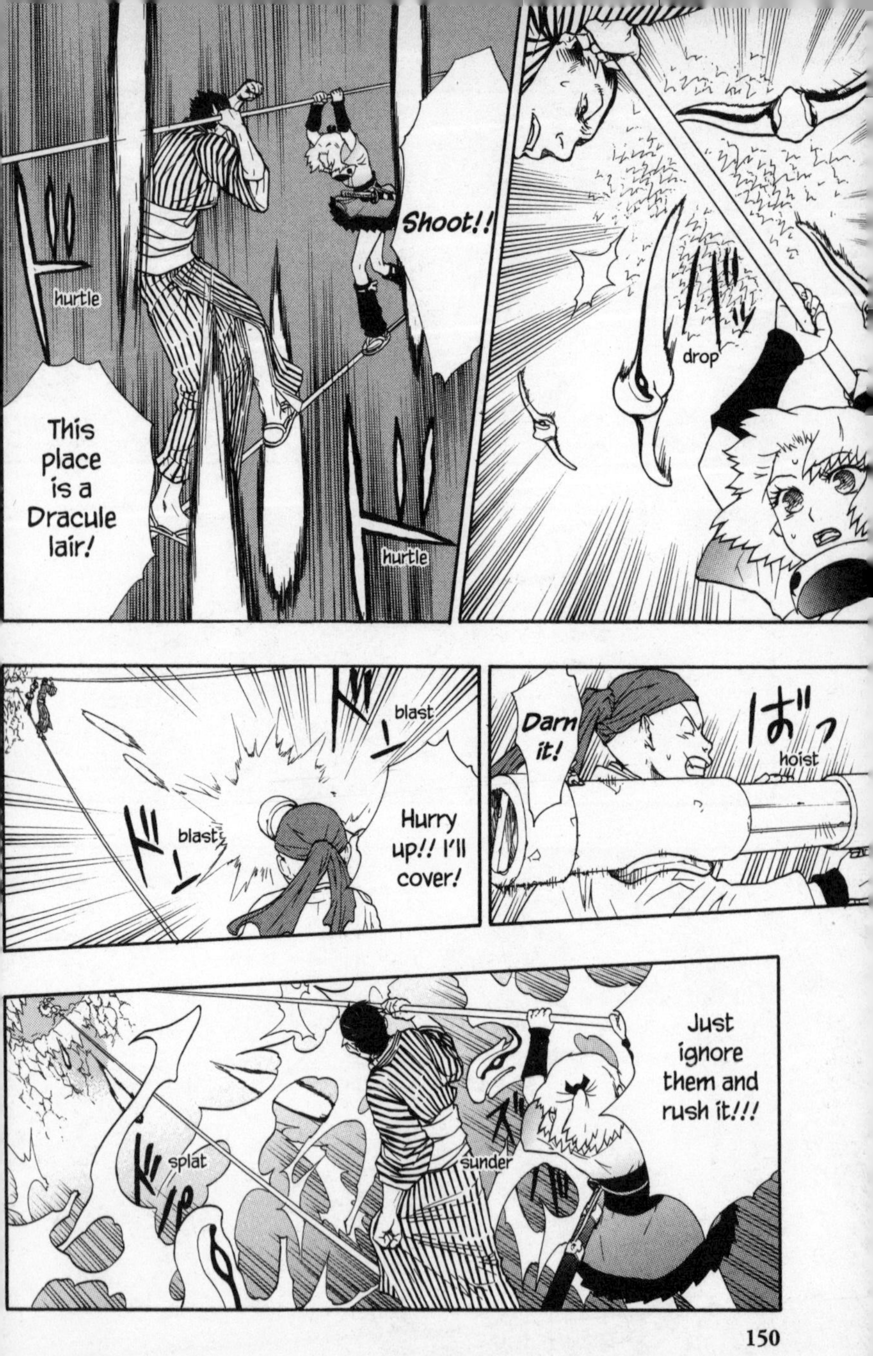
drop
Shoot!!
hurtle
This place is a Dracule lair!
hurtle
Darn it!
ばっ
hoist
blast
Hurry up!! I'll cover!
blast
Just ignore them and rush it!!!
sunder
splat

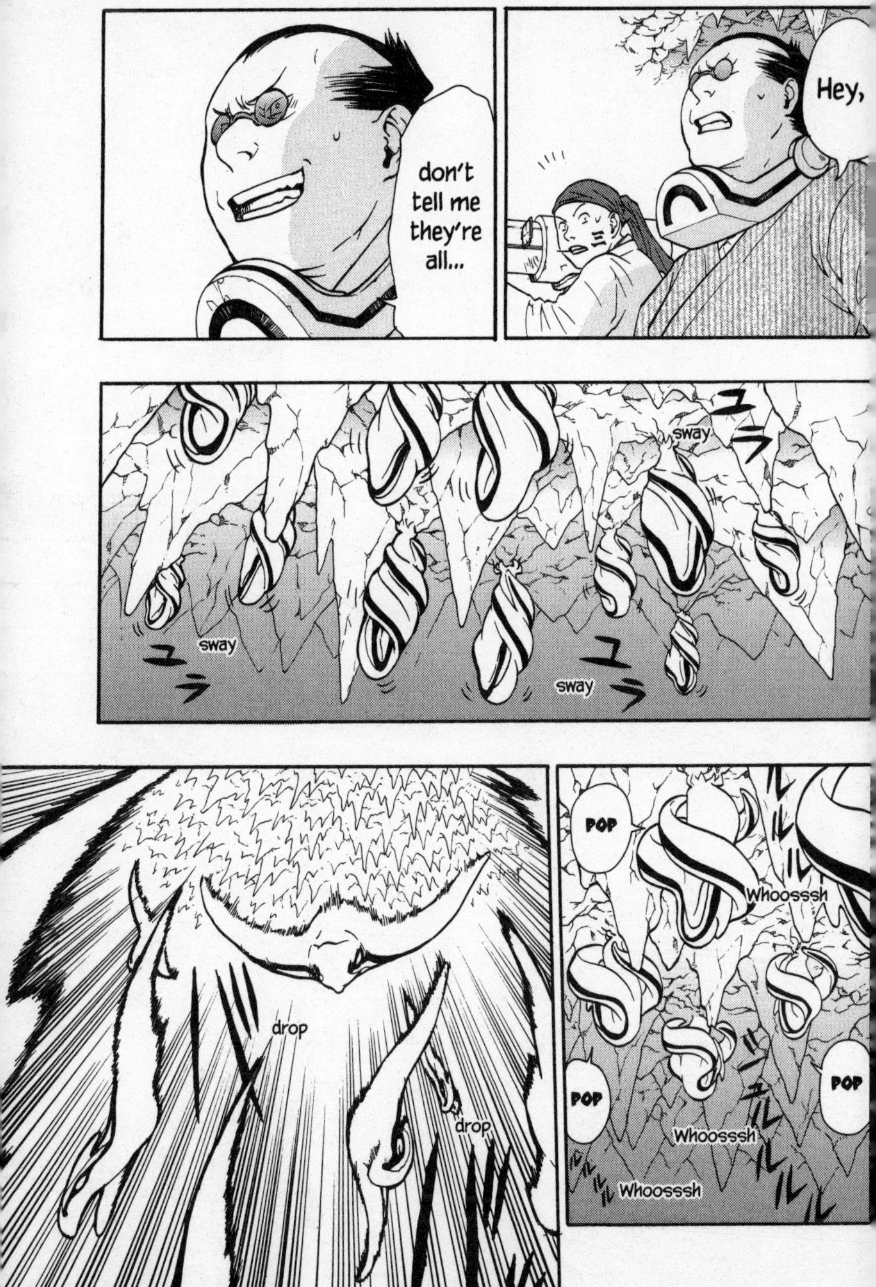

Hey,
don't tell me they're all...
sway
sway
sway
POP
Whoosssh
POP
POP
Whoosssh
Whoosssh
drop
drop

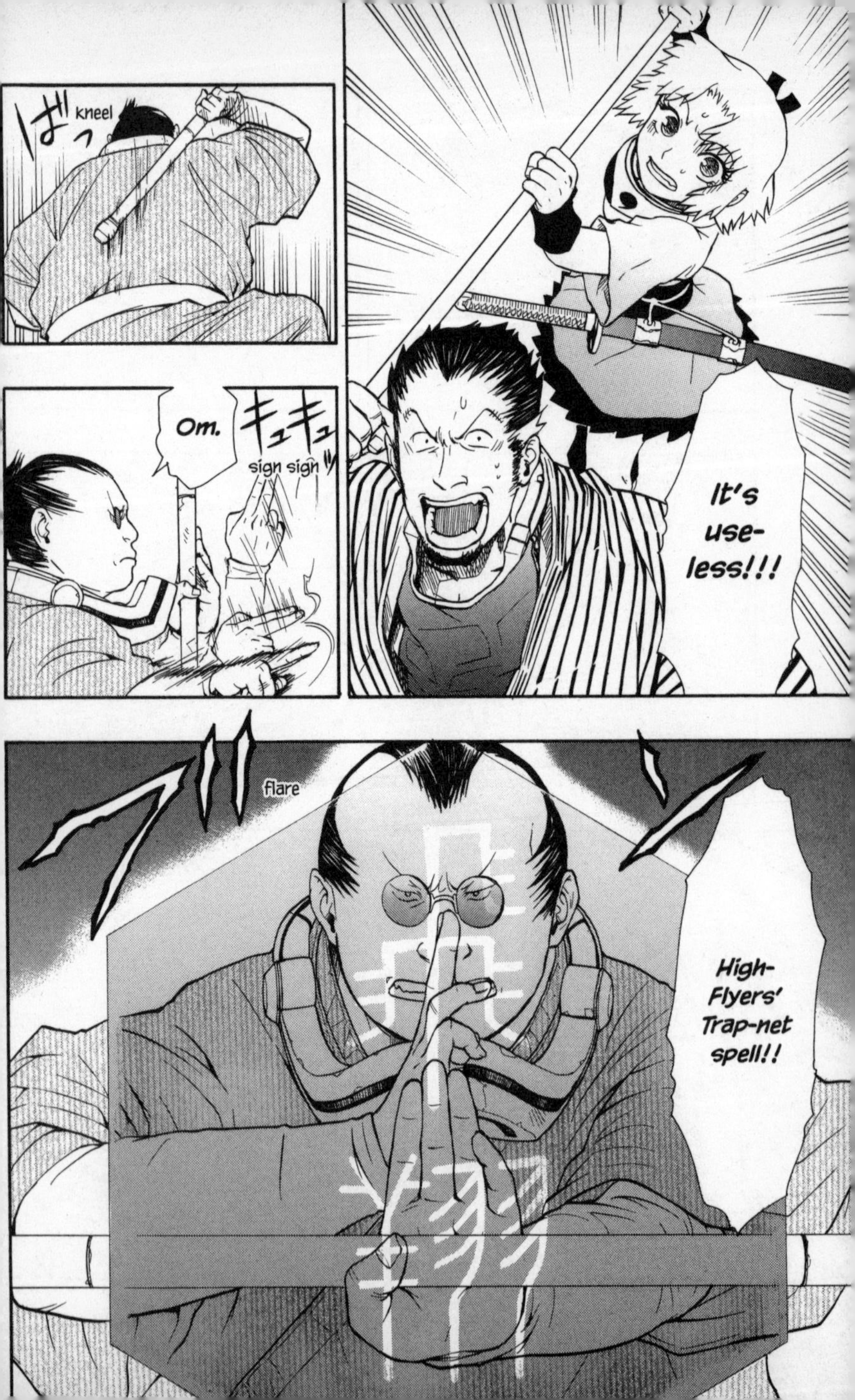
It's use-less!!!
ばっ
kneel
Om.
キュキュ
sign sign
flare
High-Flyers' Trap-net spell!!

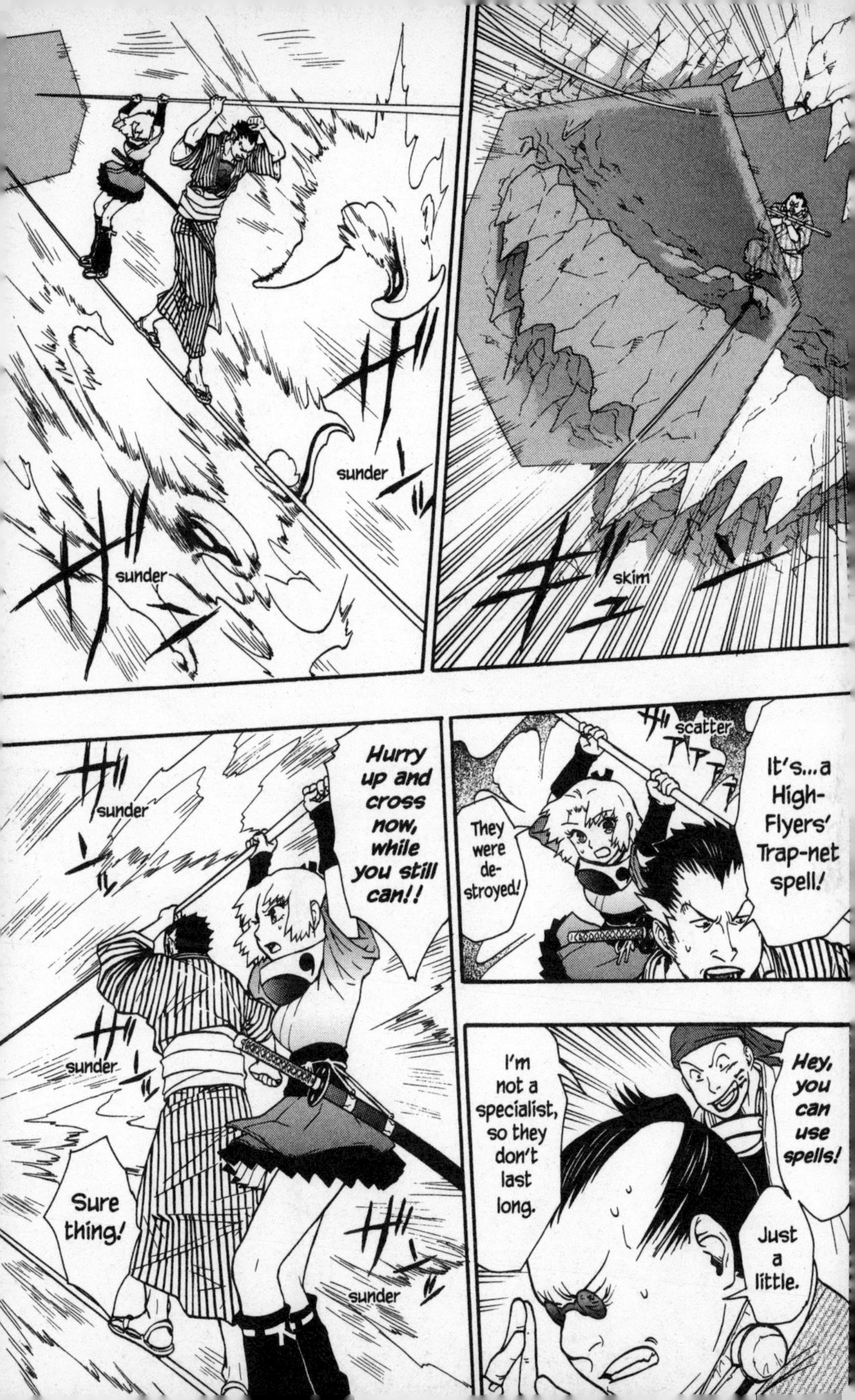
skim
sunder
sunder
scatter
It's...a High-Flyers' Trap-net spell!
They were de-stroyed!
Hey, you can use spells!
Just a little.
I'm not a specialist, so they don't last long.
Hurry up and cross now, while you still can!!
sunder
Sure thing!
sunder
sunder

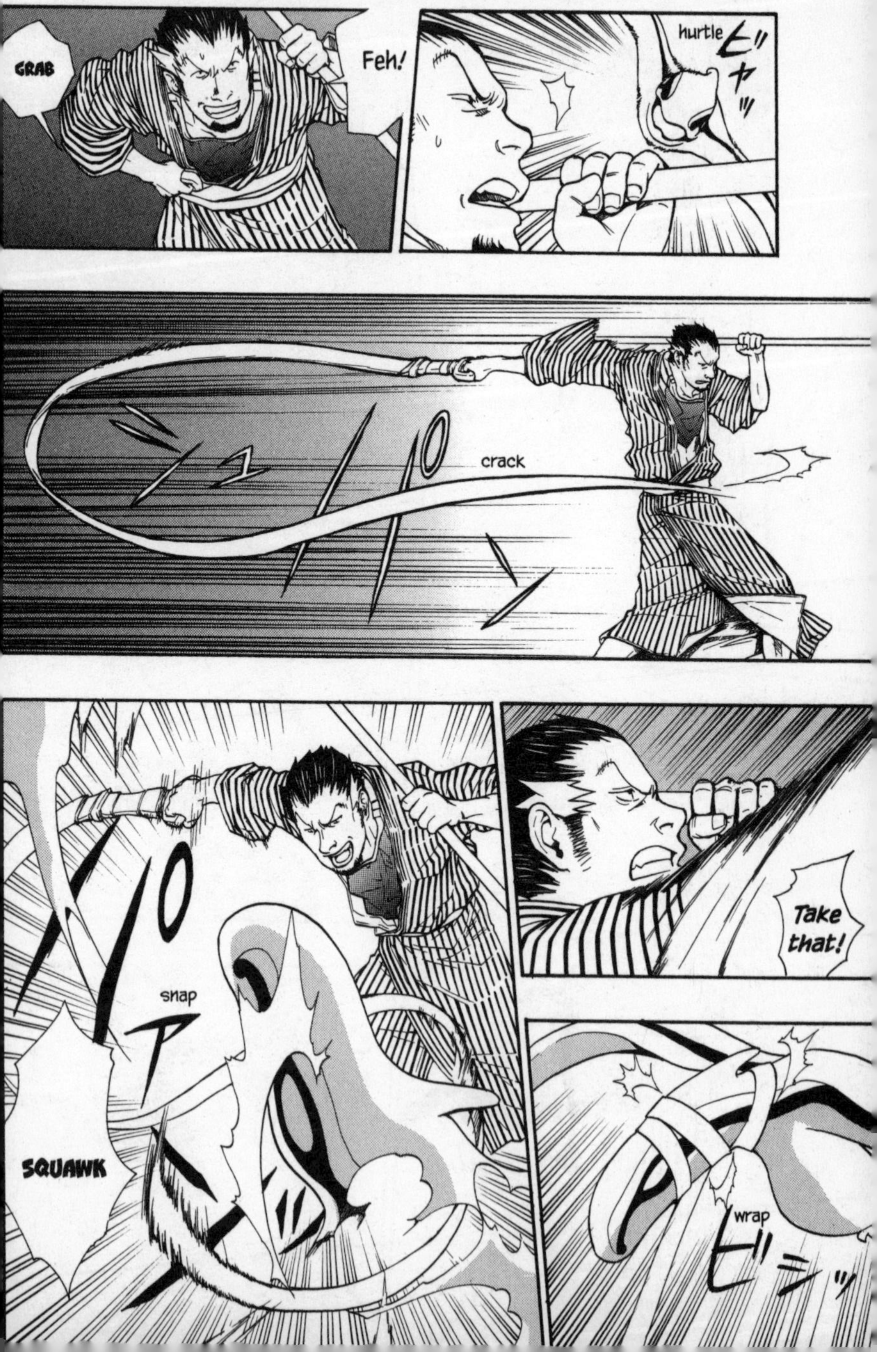
hurtle
Feh!
GRAB
crack
Take that!
wrap
snap
SQUAWK

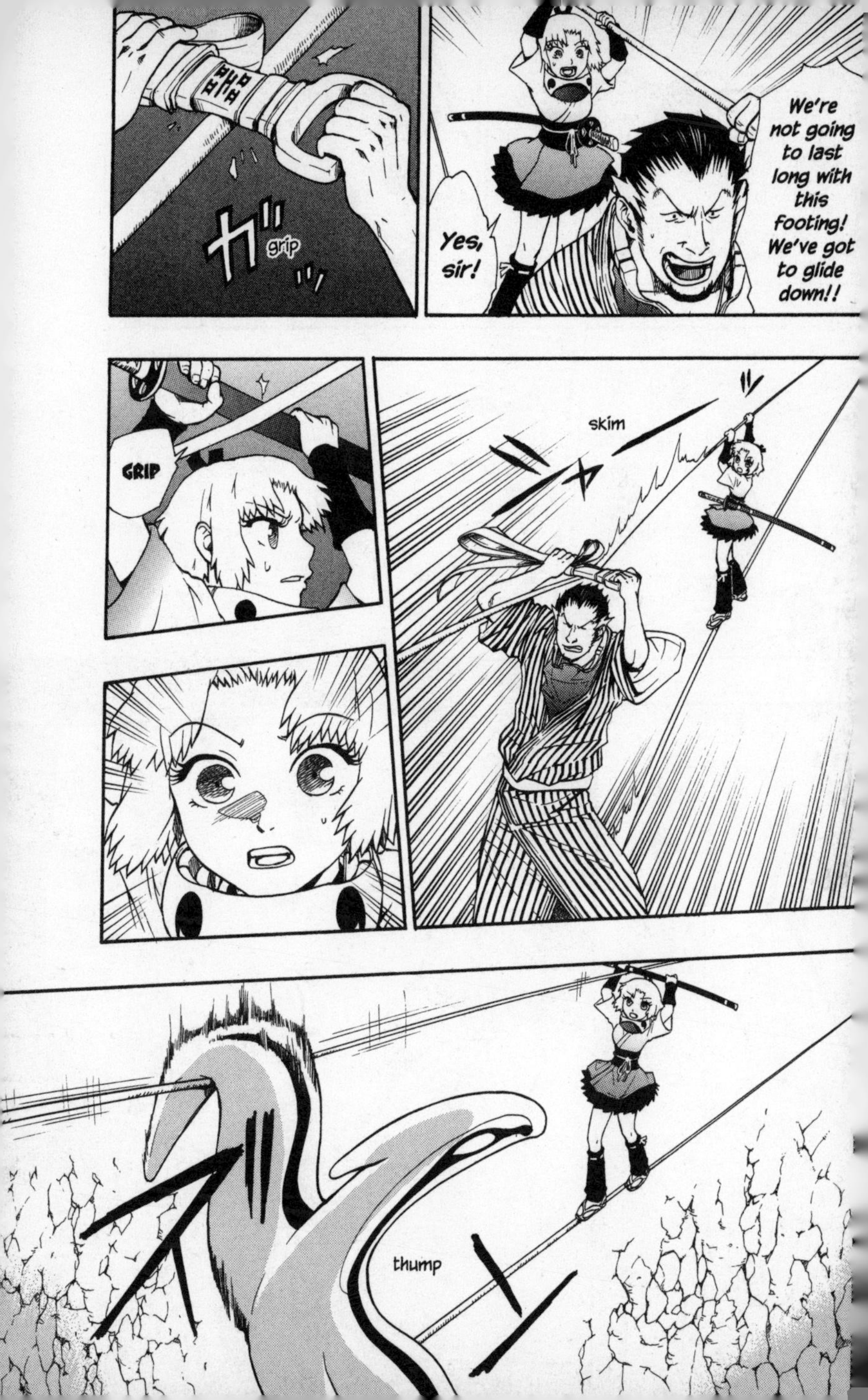
We're not going to last long with this footing! We've got to glide down!!
Yes, sir!
grip
skim
GRIP
thump

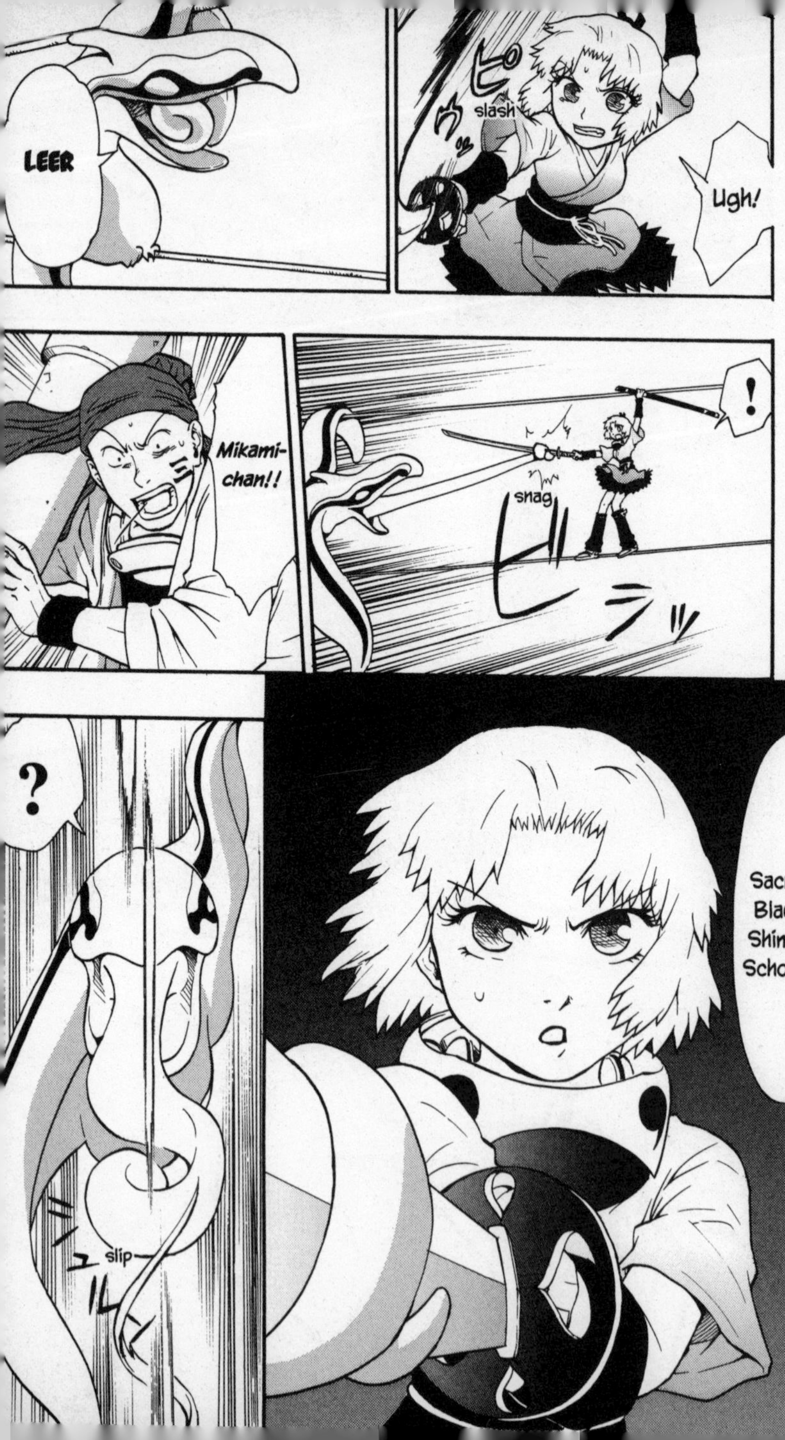
slash
Ugh!
LEER
!
snag
Mikami-chan!!
Sacred Blade, Shimon School...
?
slip

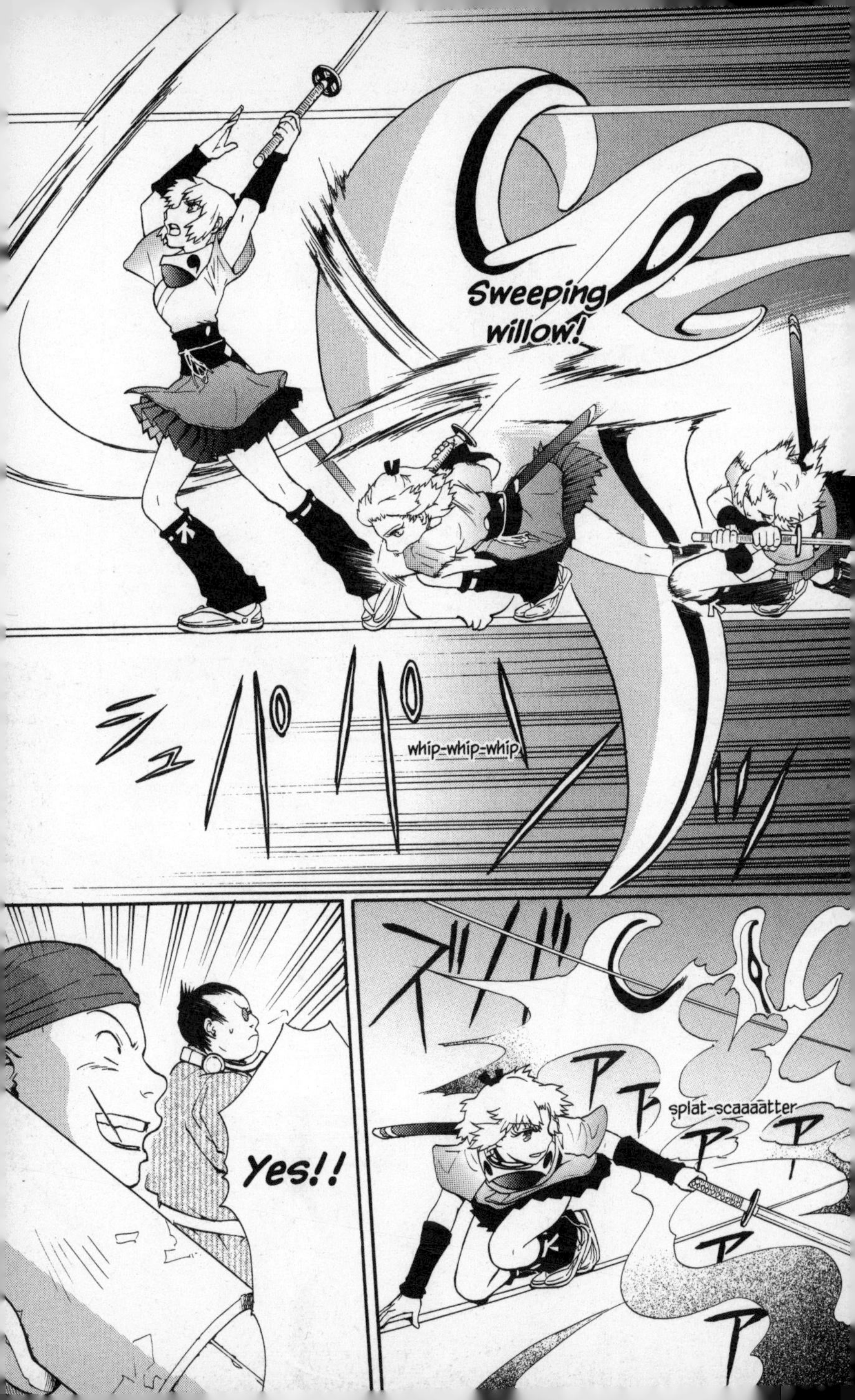
Sweeping willow!
whip-whip-whip
splat-scaaaatter
Yes!!

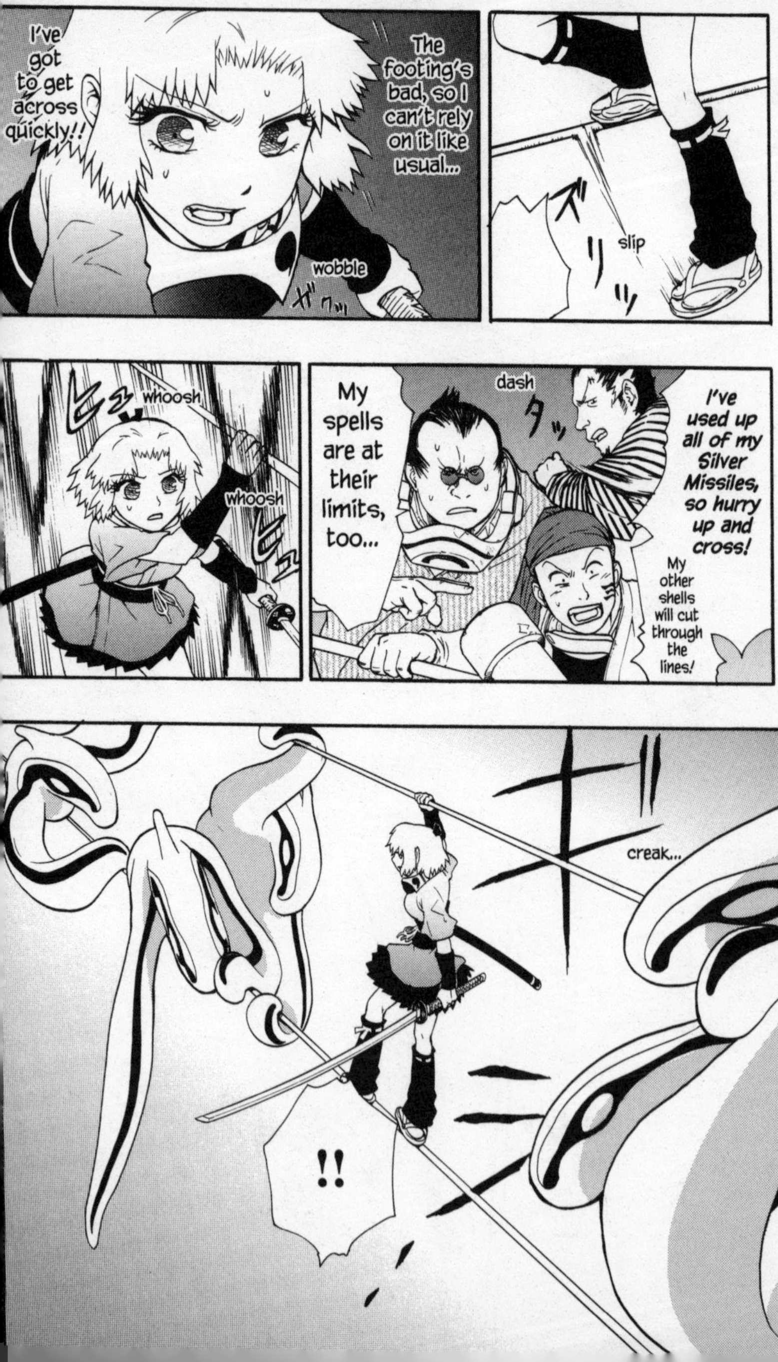
slip
The footing's bad, so I can't rely on it like usual...
I've got to get across quickly!!
wobble
I've used up all of my Silver Missiles, so hurry up and cross!
My other shells will cut through the lines!
dash
My spells are at their limits, too...
whoosh
whoosh
creak...
!!

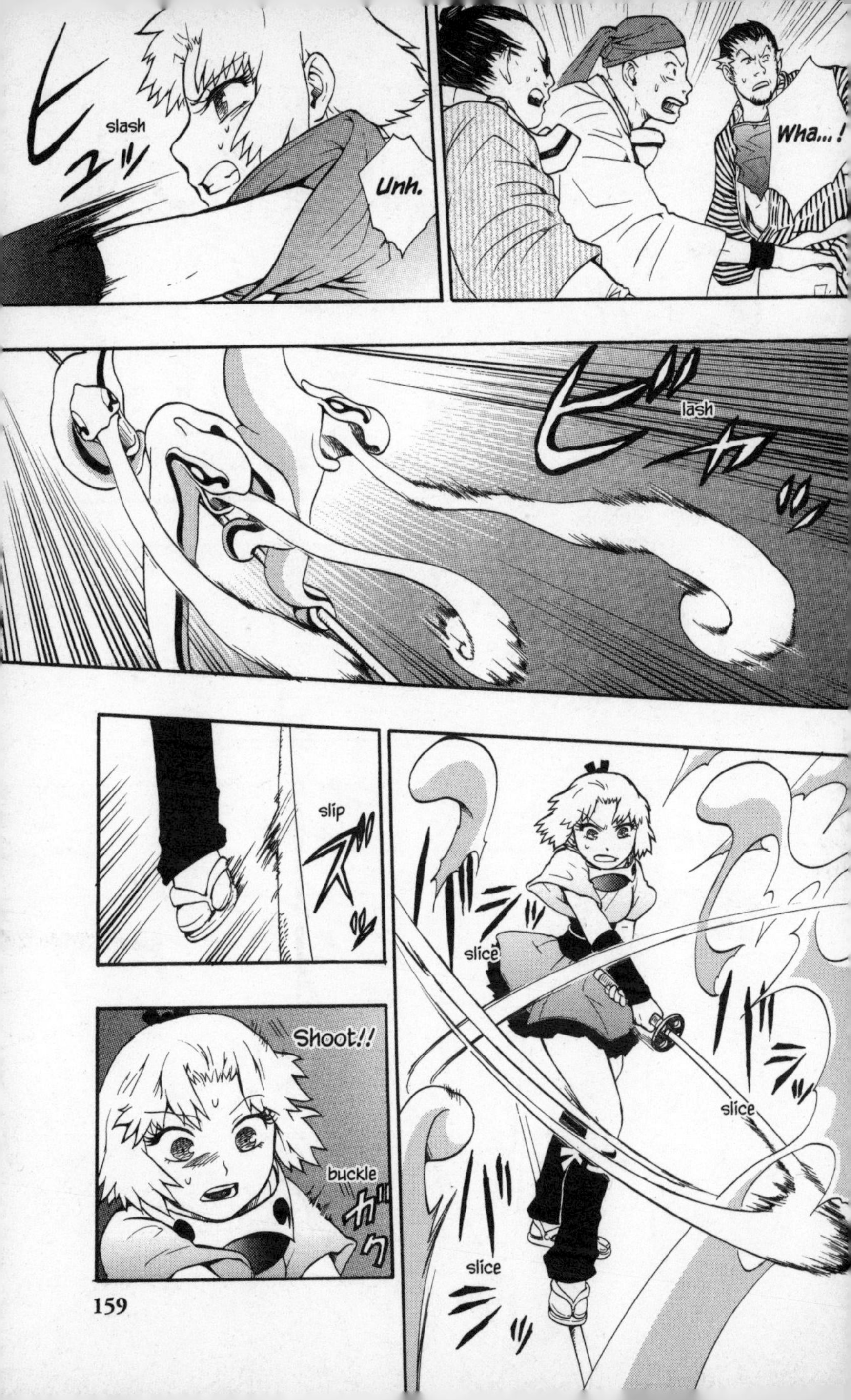
Wha...!
slash
Unh.
lash
slice
slice
slice
slip
Shoot!!
buckle

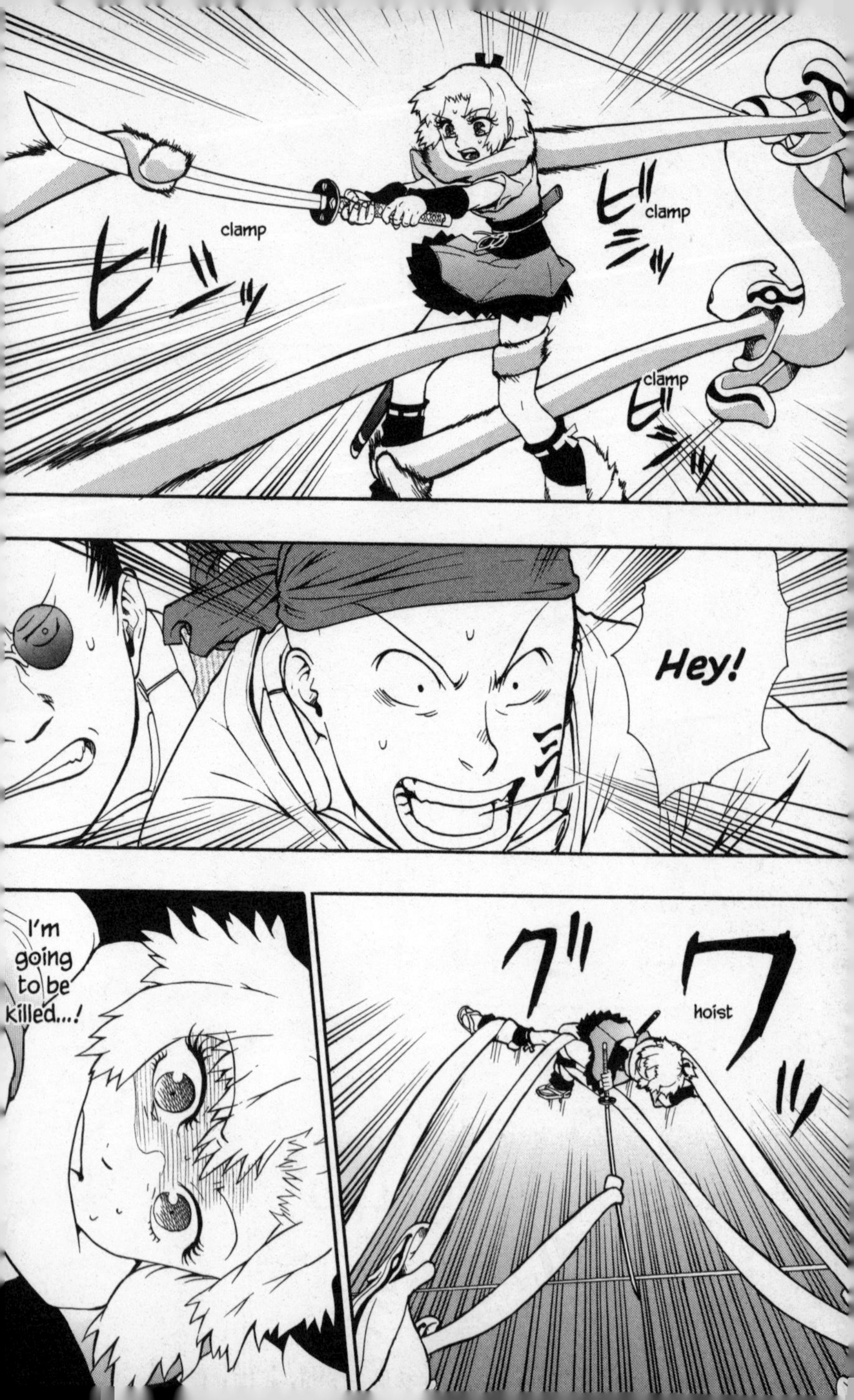
clamp
clamp
clamp
Hey!
hoist
I'm going to be killed...!

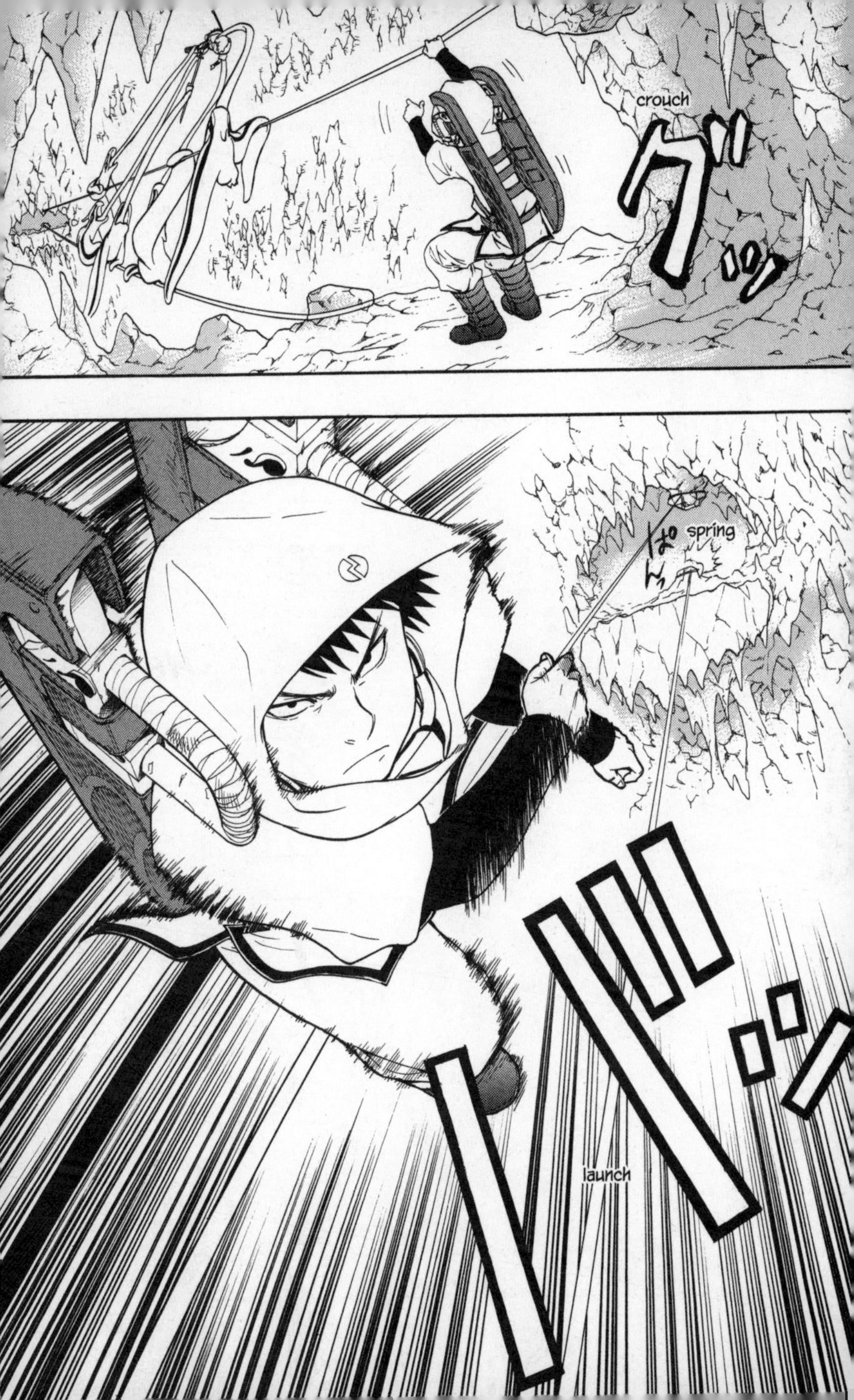
crouch
spring
launch

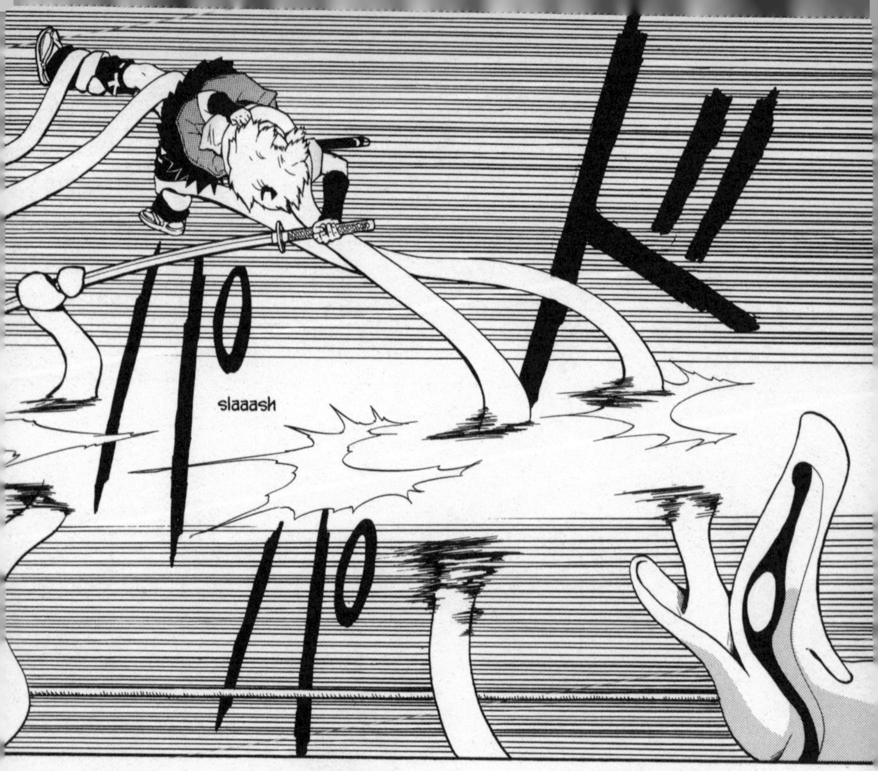
slaaash
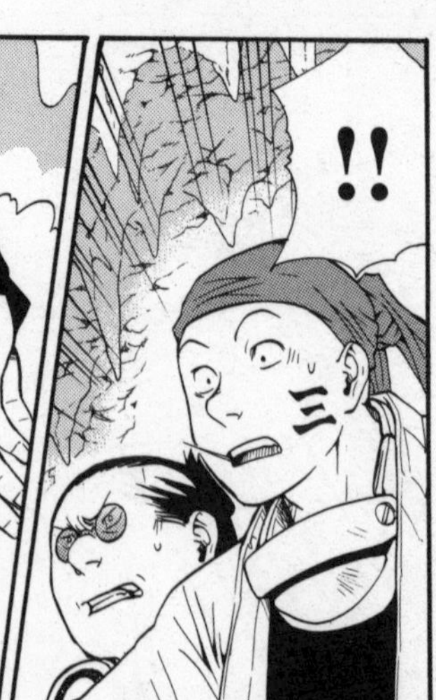
!!
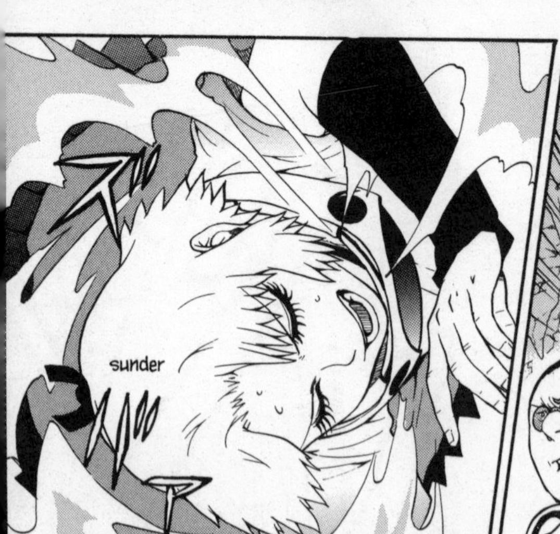
sunder

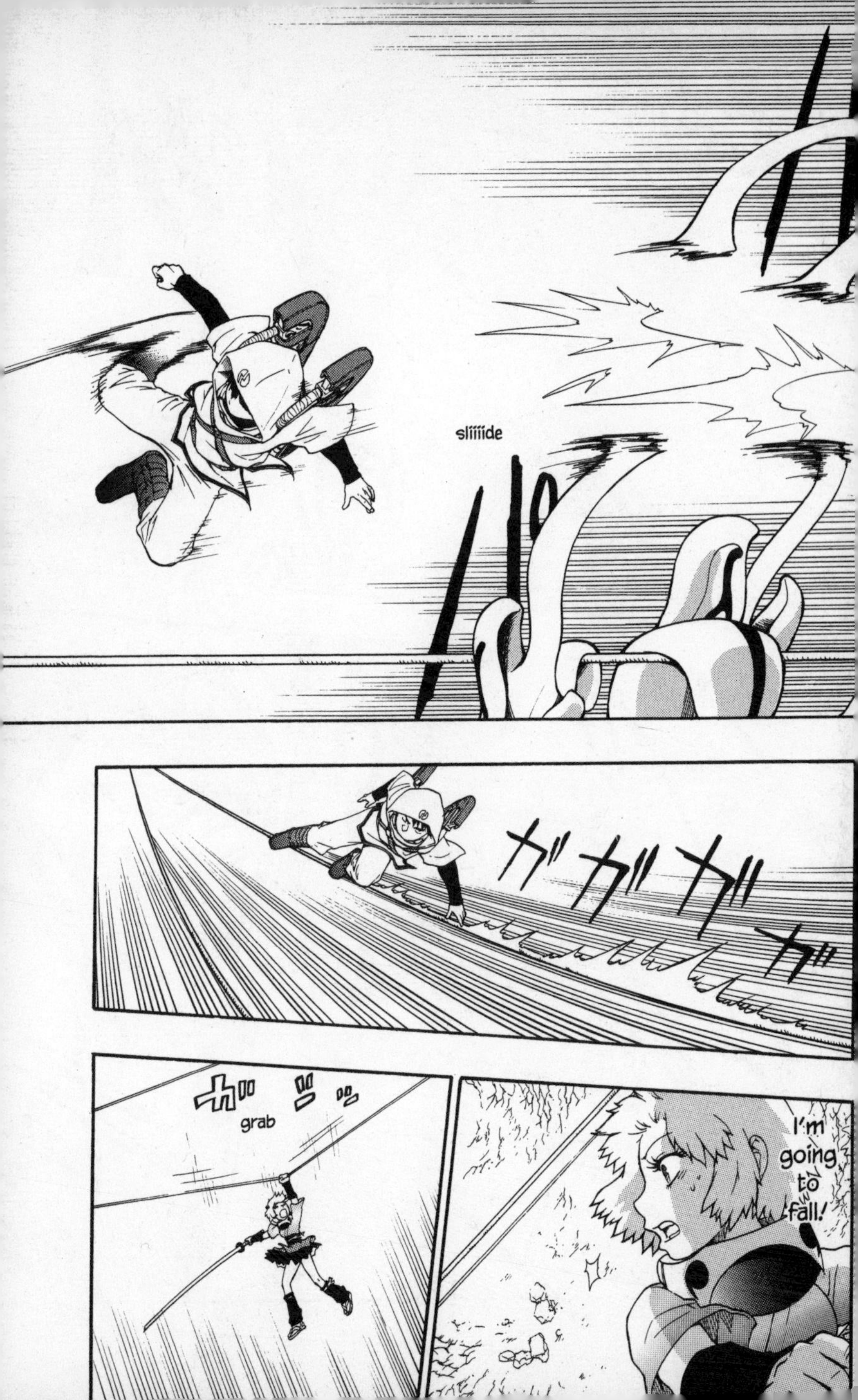
sliiiide
ガガガガ
I'm going to fall!
grab

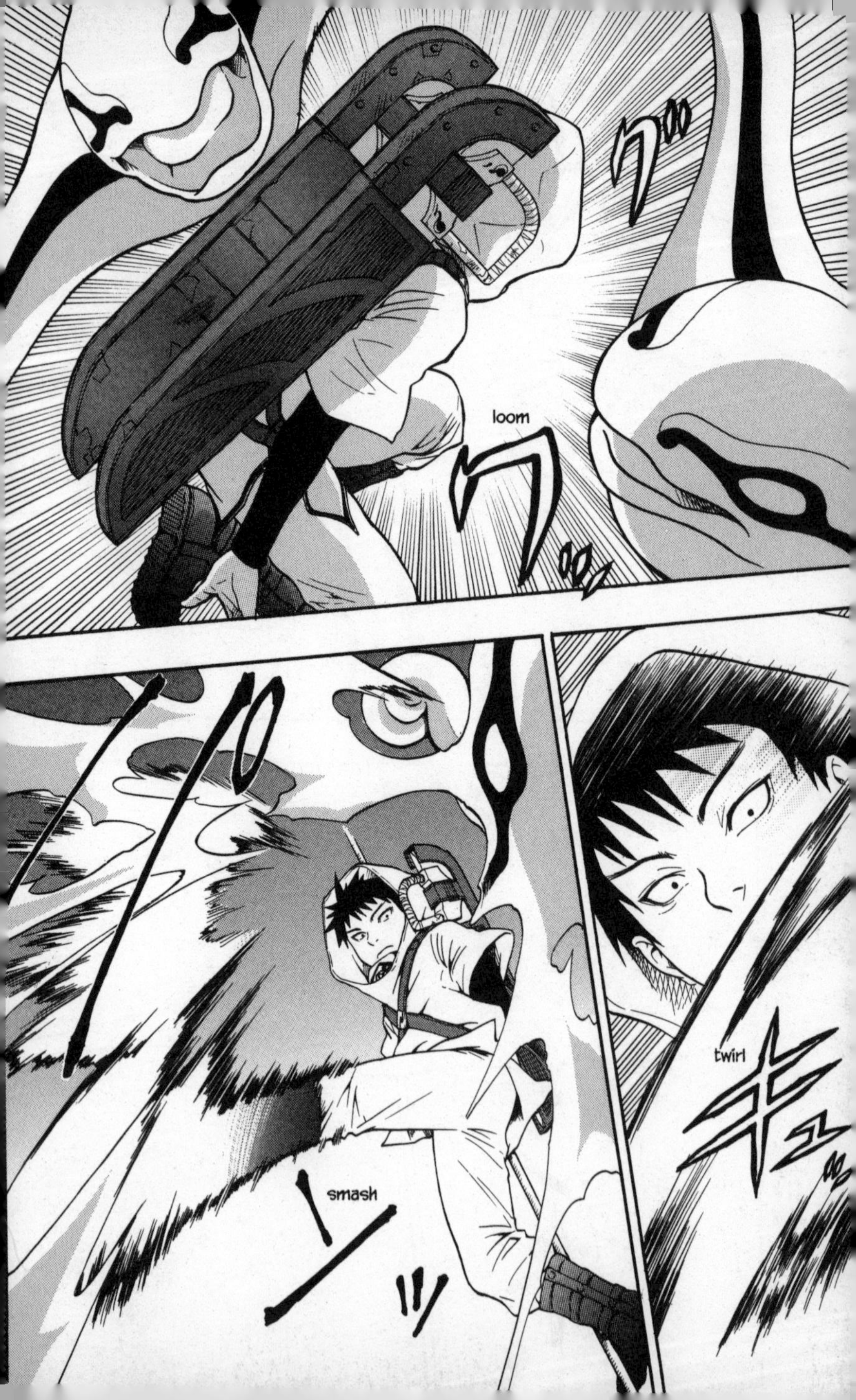
loom
twirl
smash

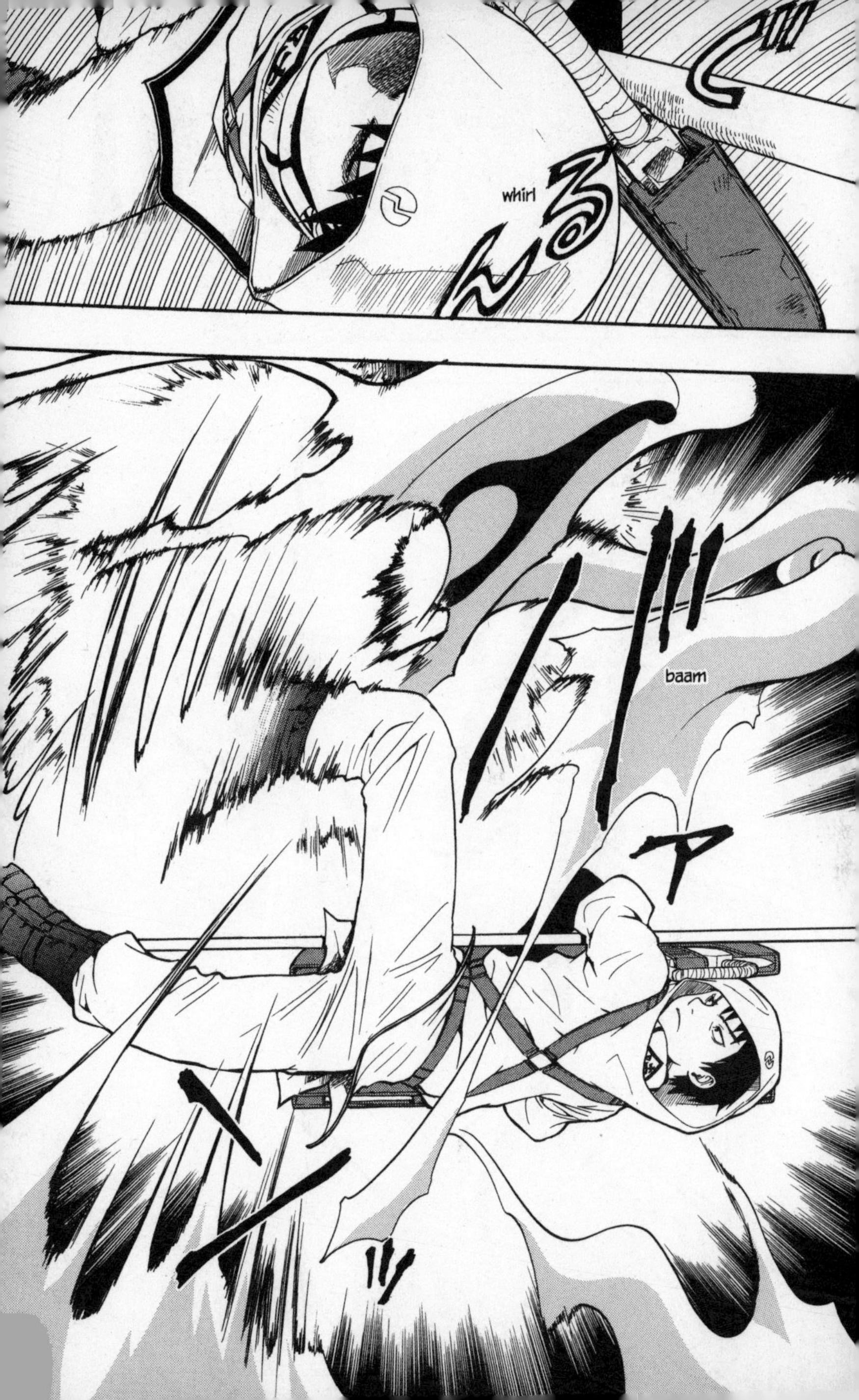
whirl
baam

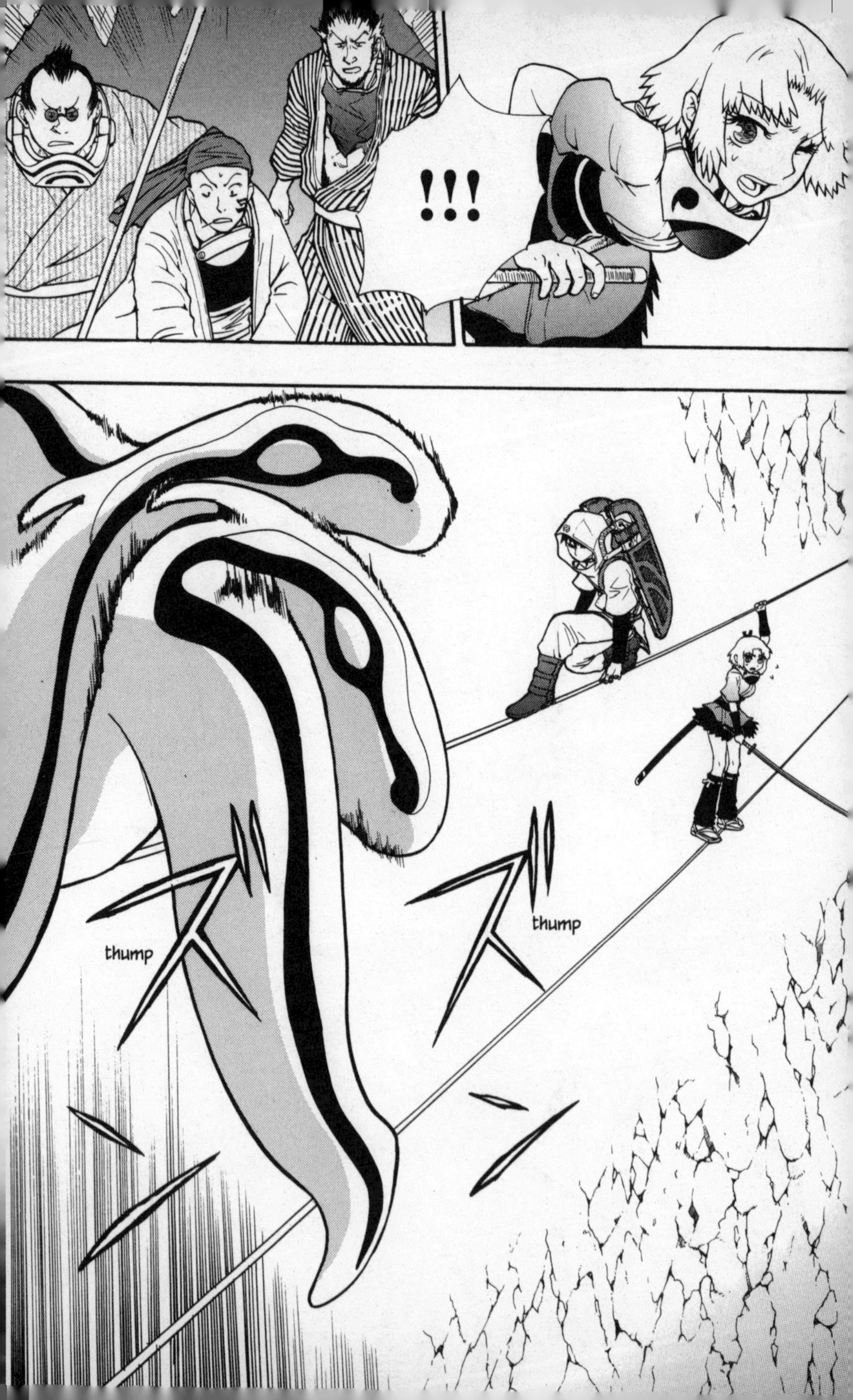
!!!
thump
thump

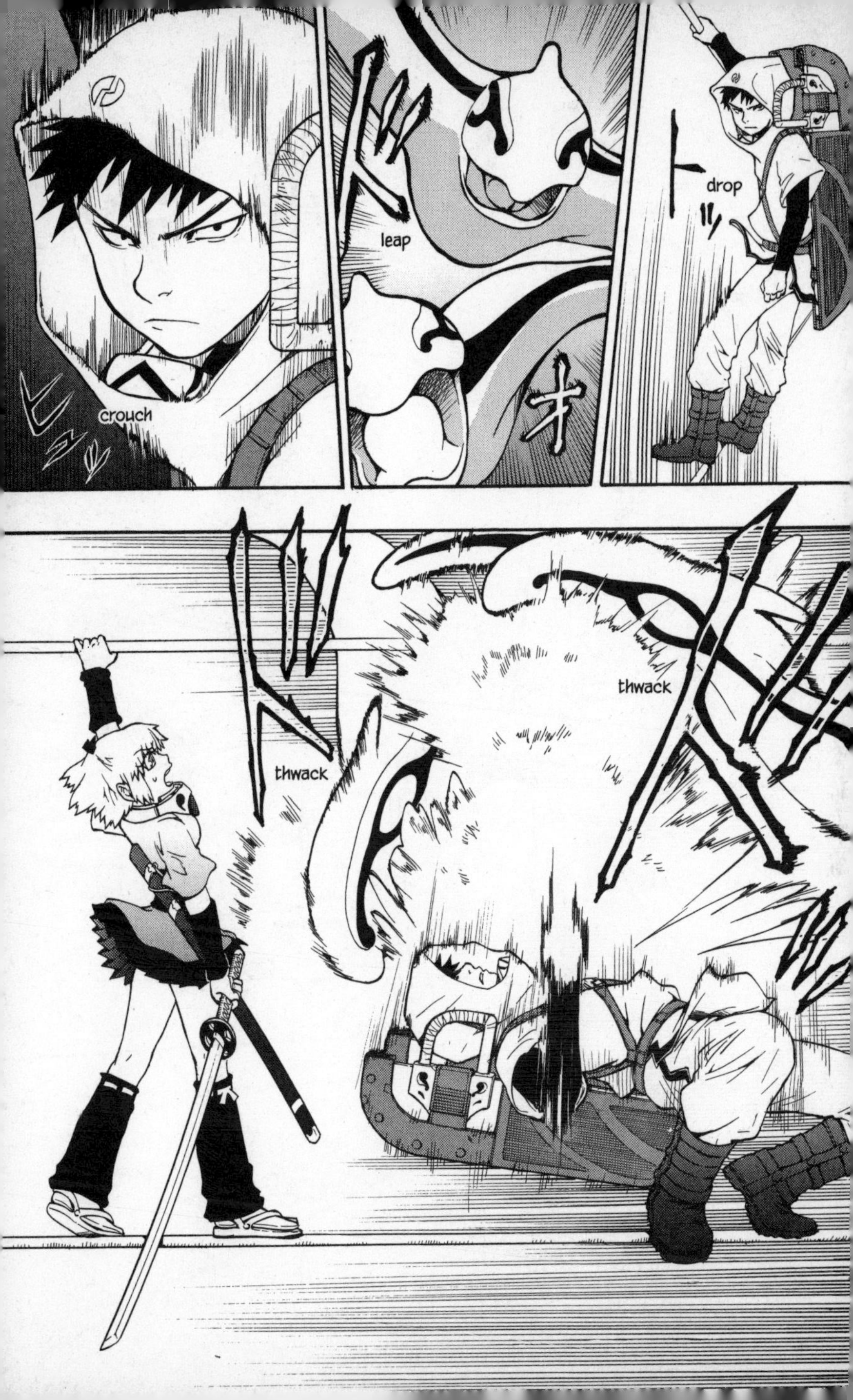
drop
leap
crouch
thwack
thwack

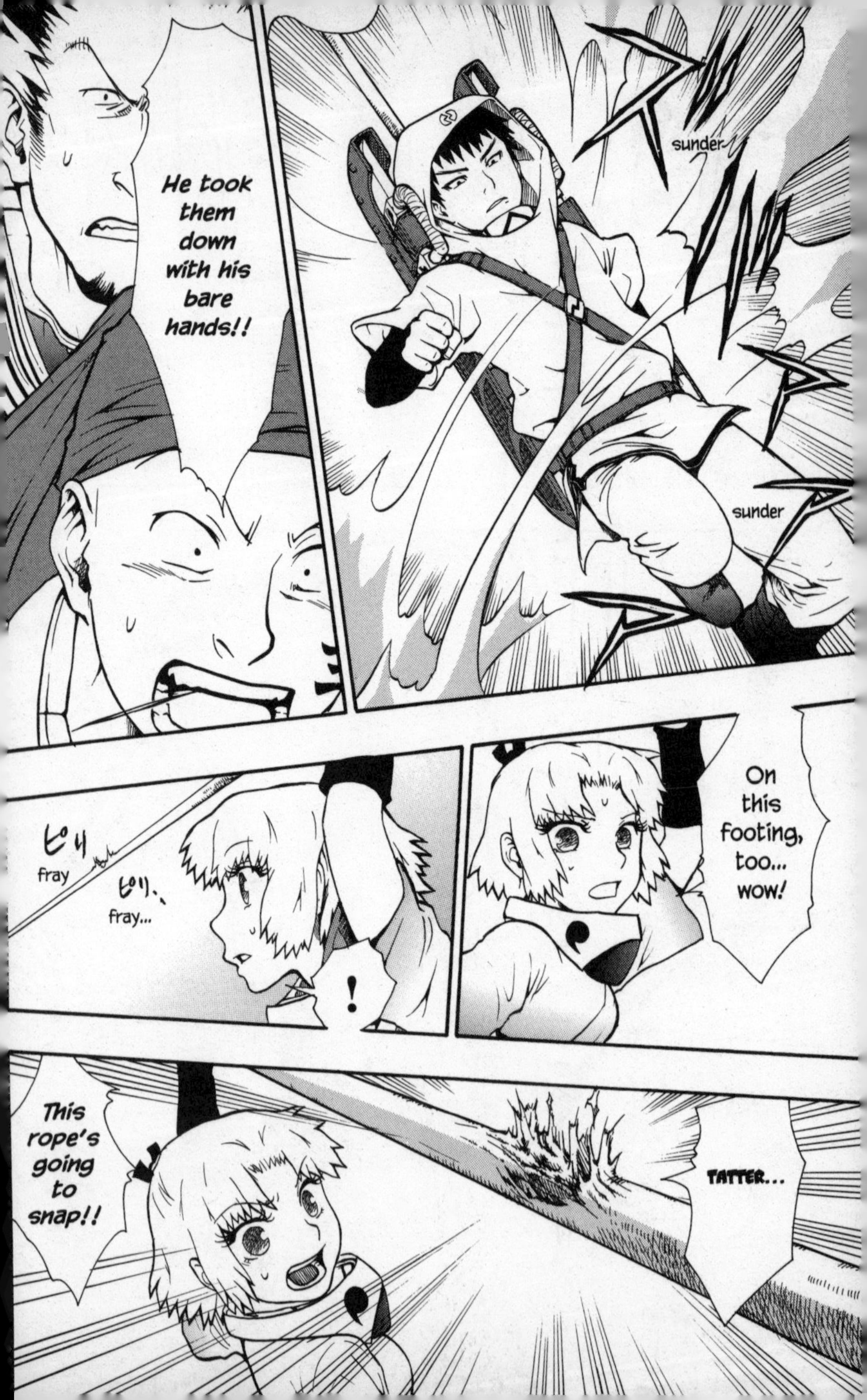
sunder
sunder
He took them down with his bare hands!!
On this footing, too... wow!
ピリ
fray
ピリ..
fray...
!
TATTER...
This rope's going to snap!!

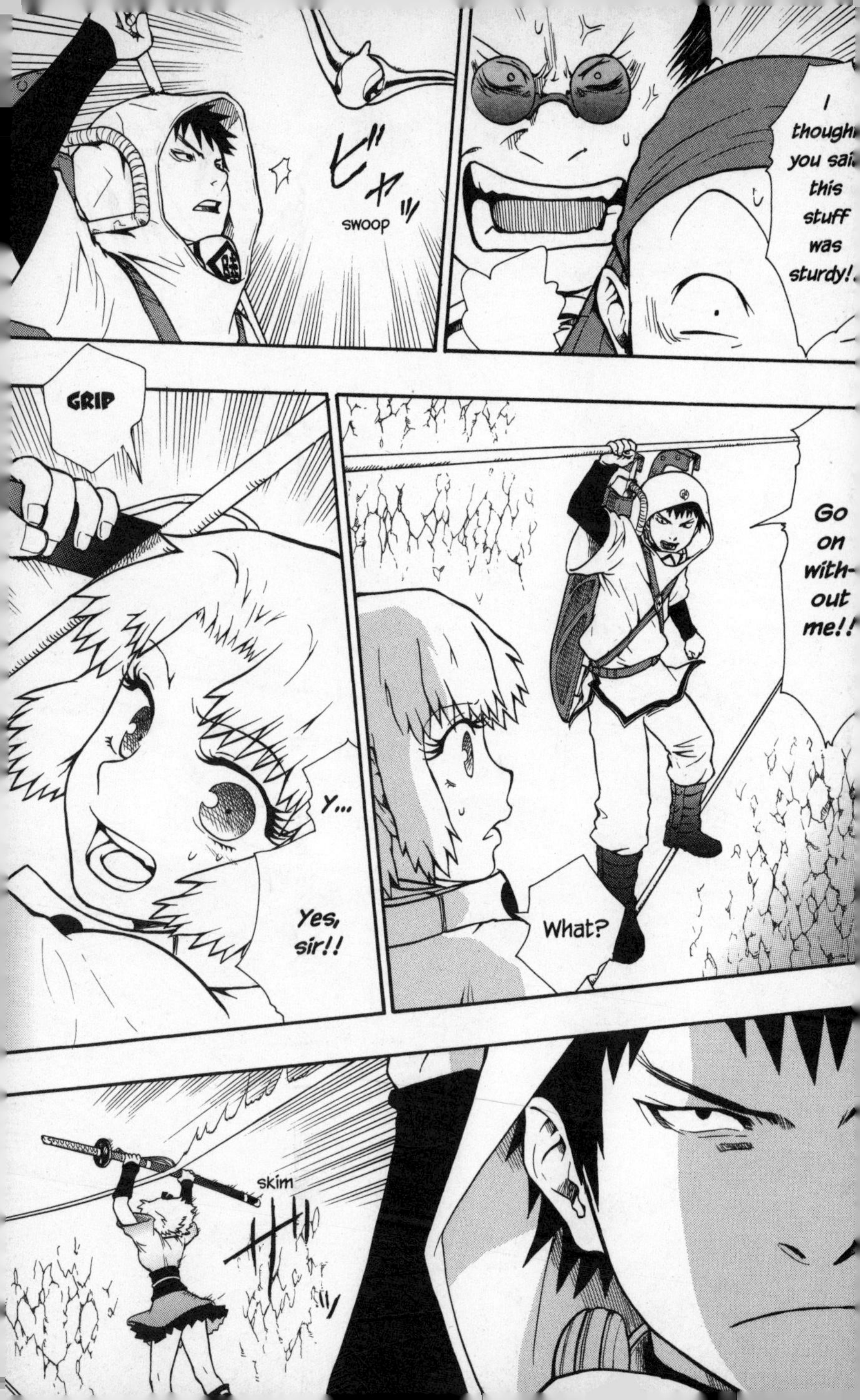

I though you sai this stuff was sturdy!!
ビャッ
swoop
Go on without me!!
What?
GRIP
Y...
Yes, sir!!
skim

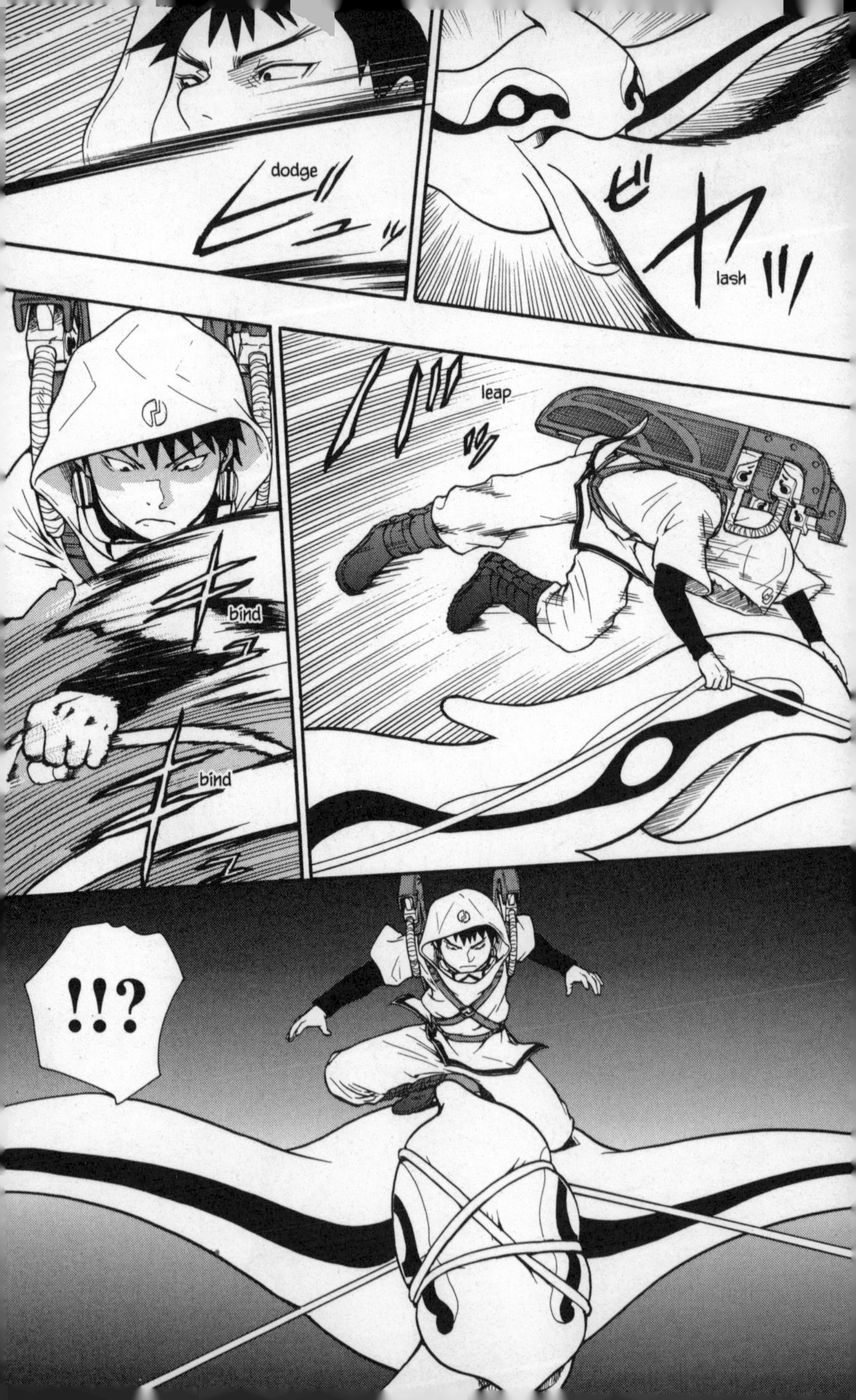
lash
dodge
ビュッ
leap
bind
bind
!!?

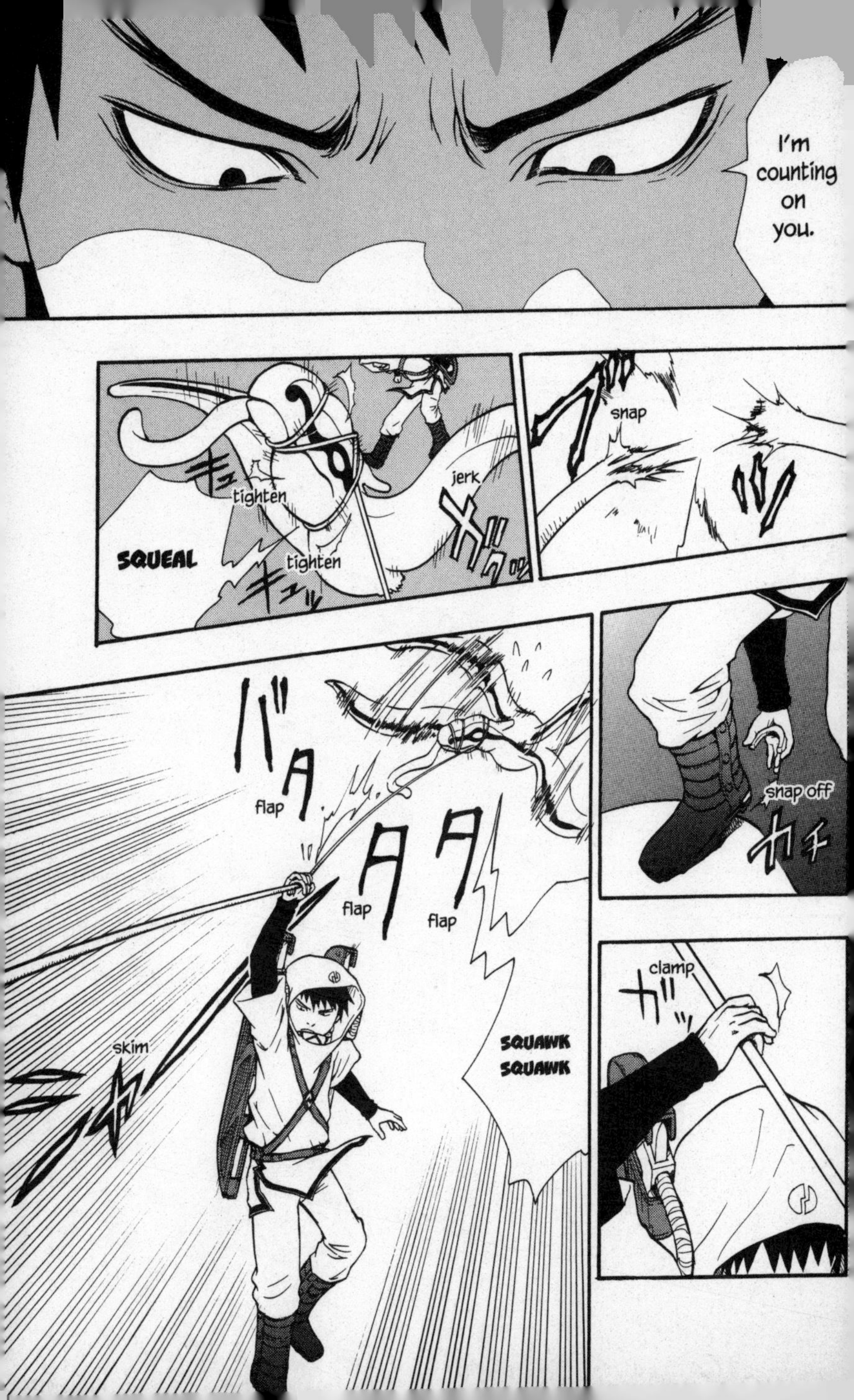
I'm counting on you.
snap
jerk
tighten
tighten
SQUEAL
snap off
clamp
flap
flap
flap
SQUAWK SQUAWK
skim

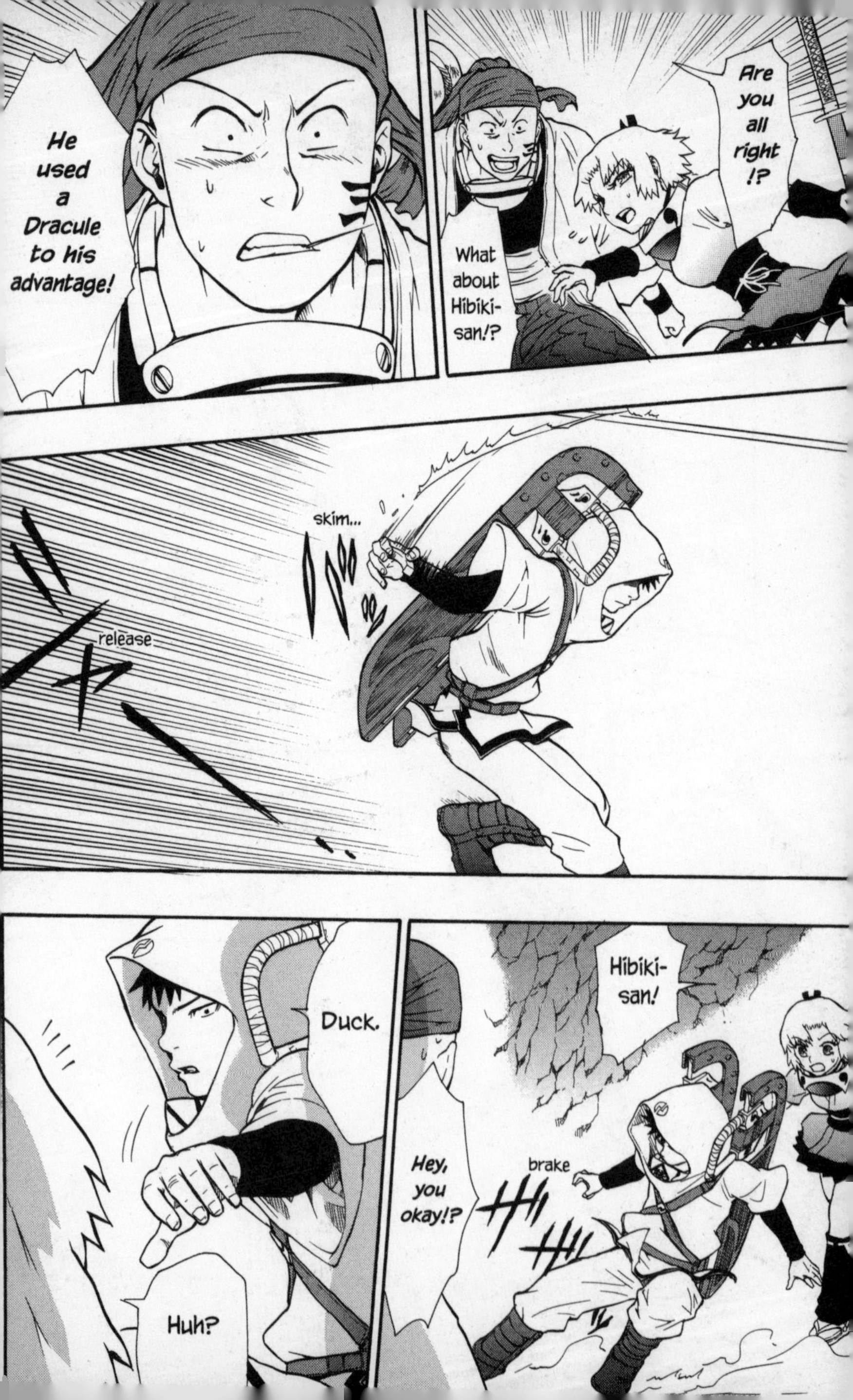
Are you all right!?
What about Hibiki-san!?
He used a Dracule to his advantage!
skim...
release
Hibiki-san!
brake
Hey, you okay!?
Duck.
Huh?

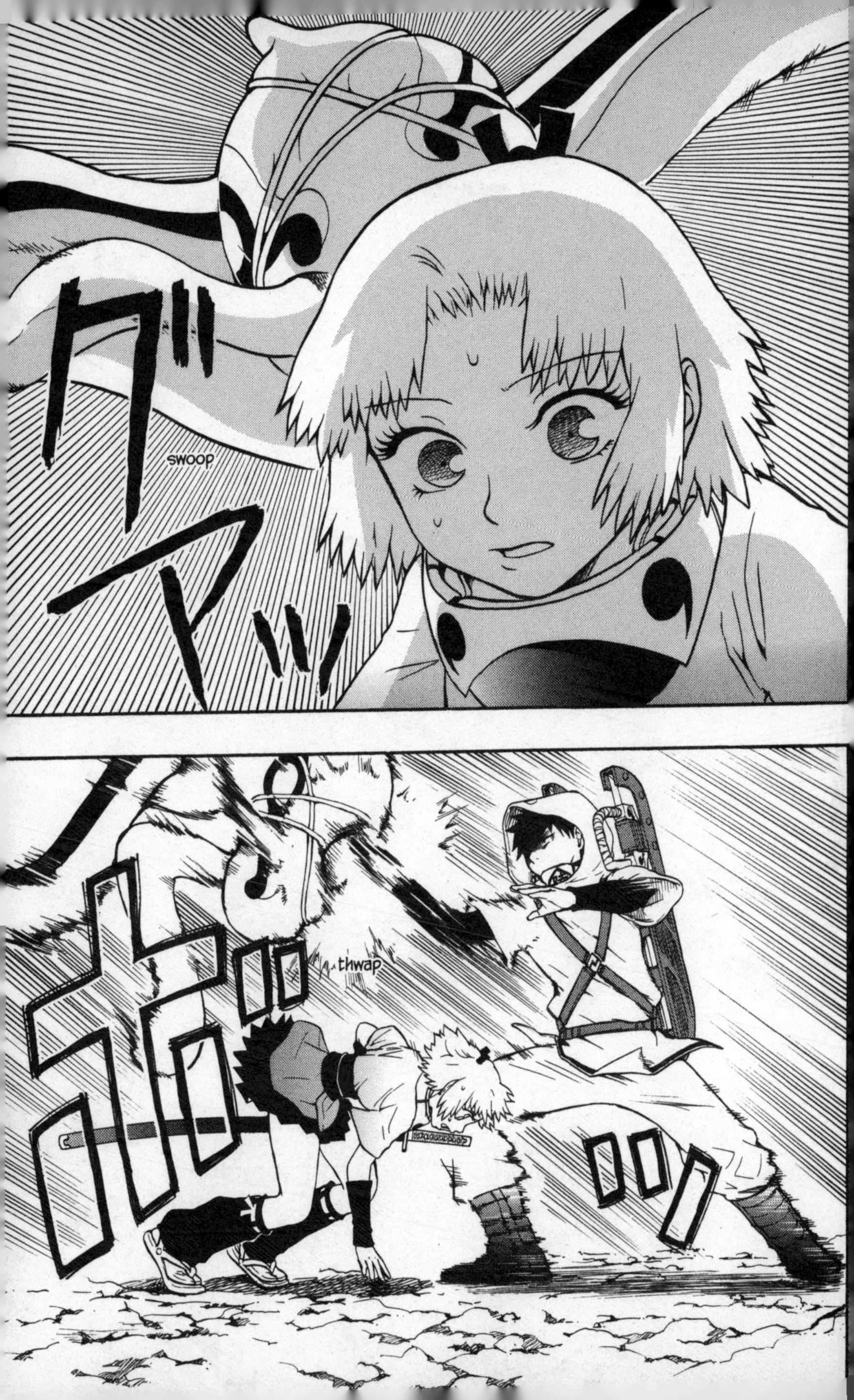
swoop
thwap

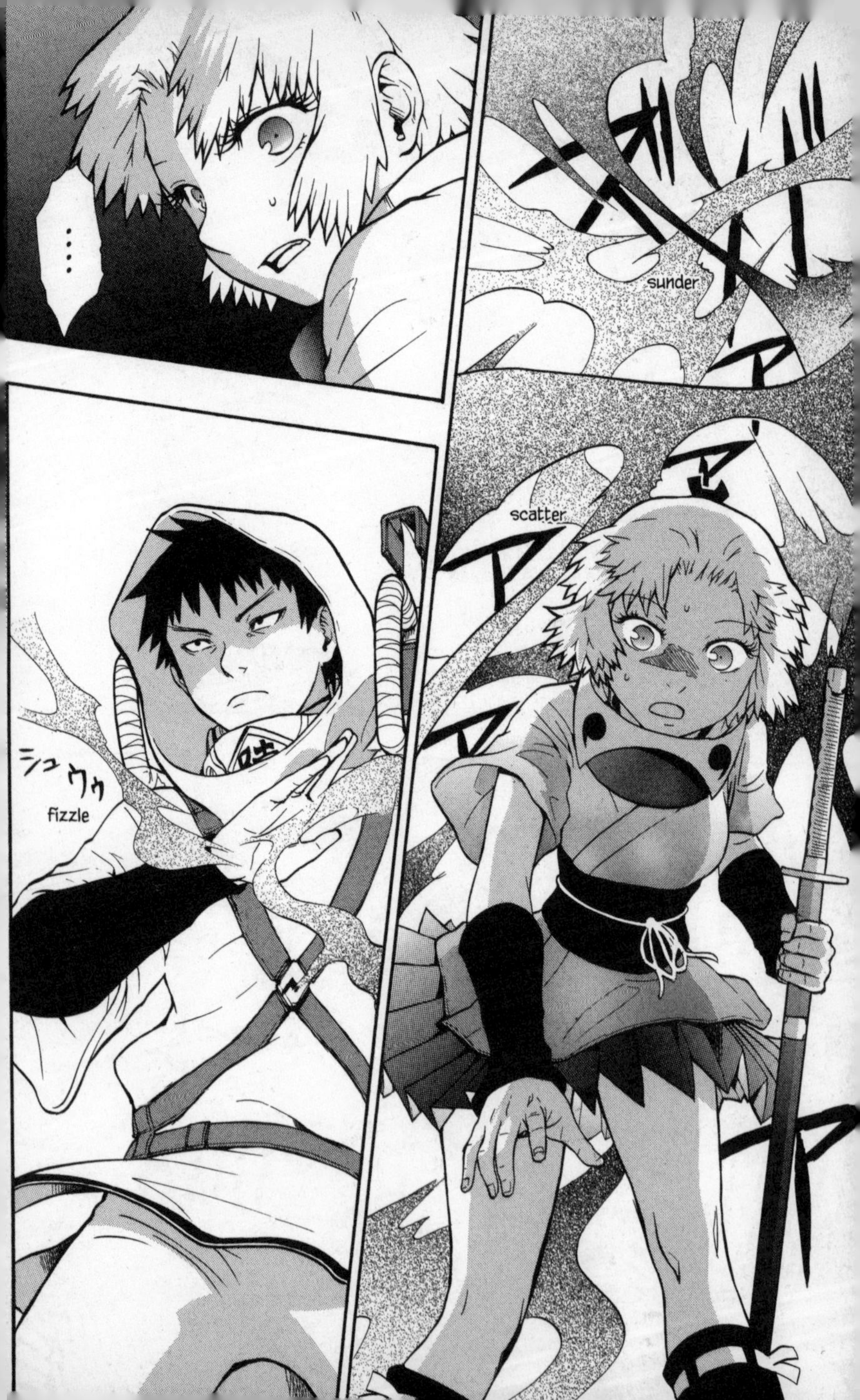
sunder
....
scatter
シュウゥ
fizzle

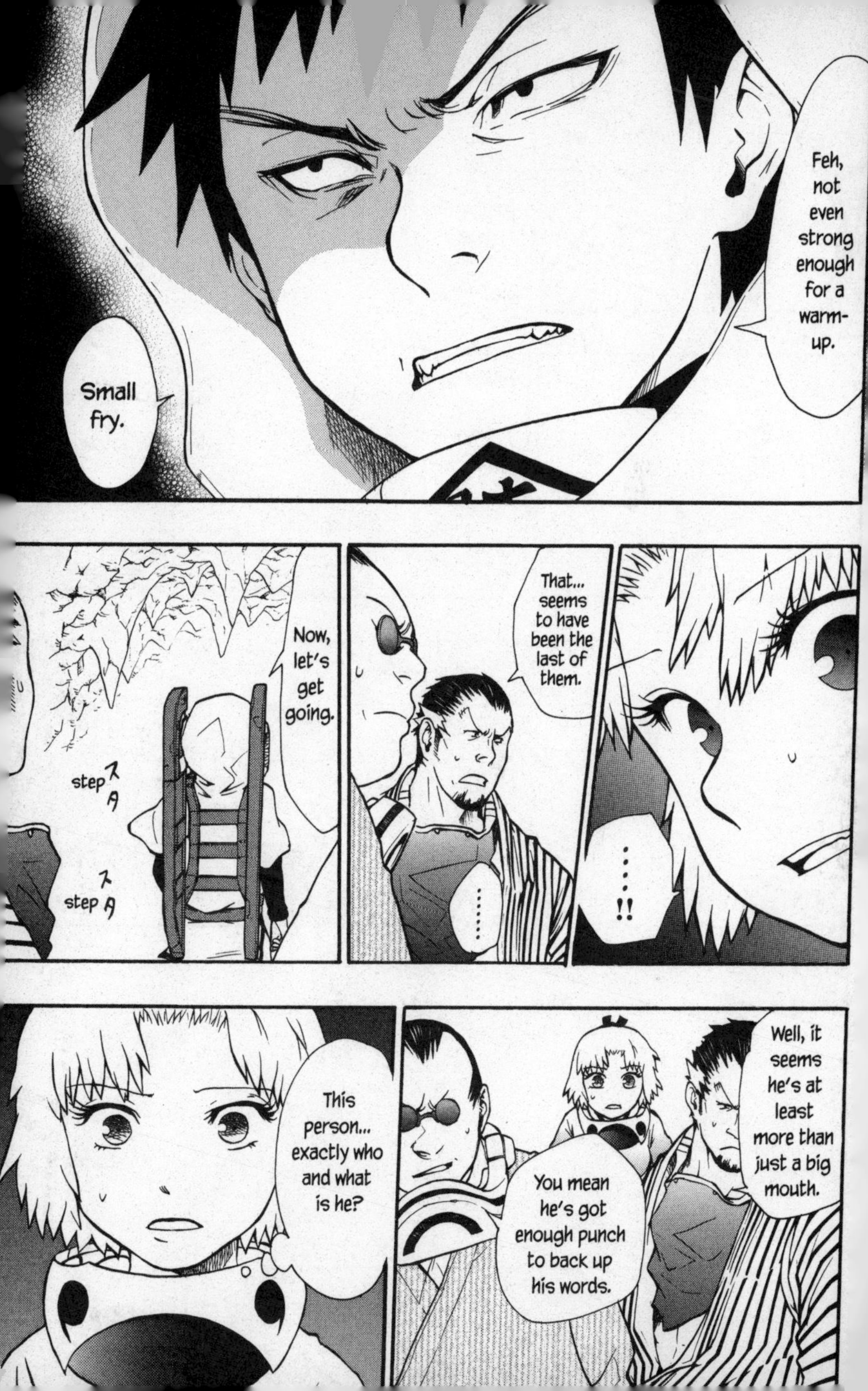
Feh, not even strong enough for a warm-up.
Small fry.
....!!
That... seems to have been the last of them.
......
Now, let's get going.
step
step
Well, it seems he's at least more than just a big mouth.
You mean he's got enough punch to back up his words.
This person... exactly who and what is he?

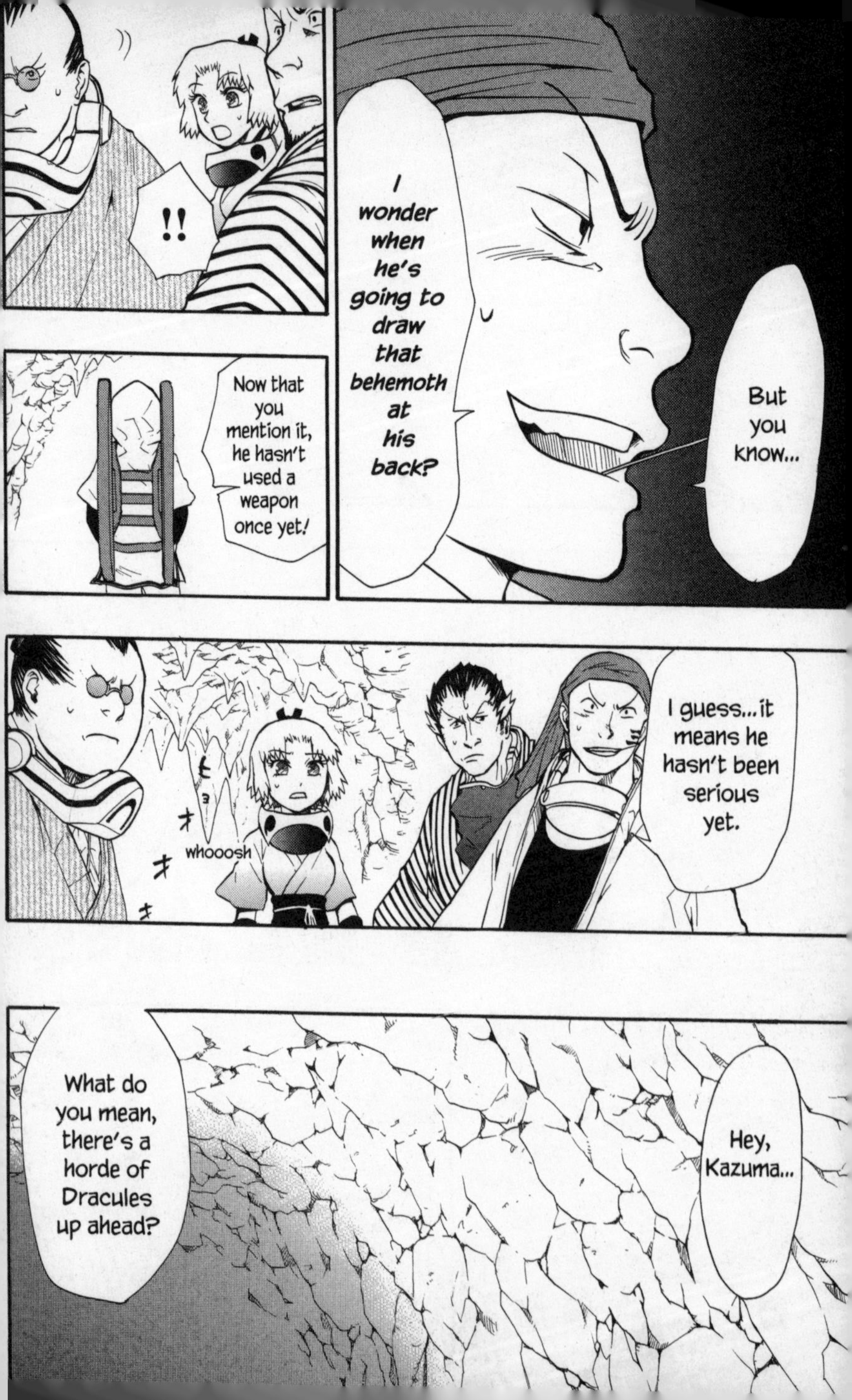
But you know...
I wonder when he's going to draw that behemoth at his back?
!!
Now that you mention it, he hasn't used a weapon once yet!
I guess...it means he hasn't been serious yet.
whooosh
Hey, Kazuma...
What do you mean, there's a horde of Dracules up ahead?

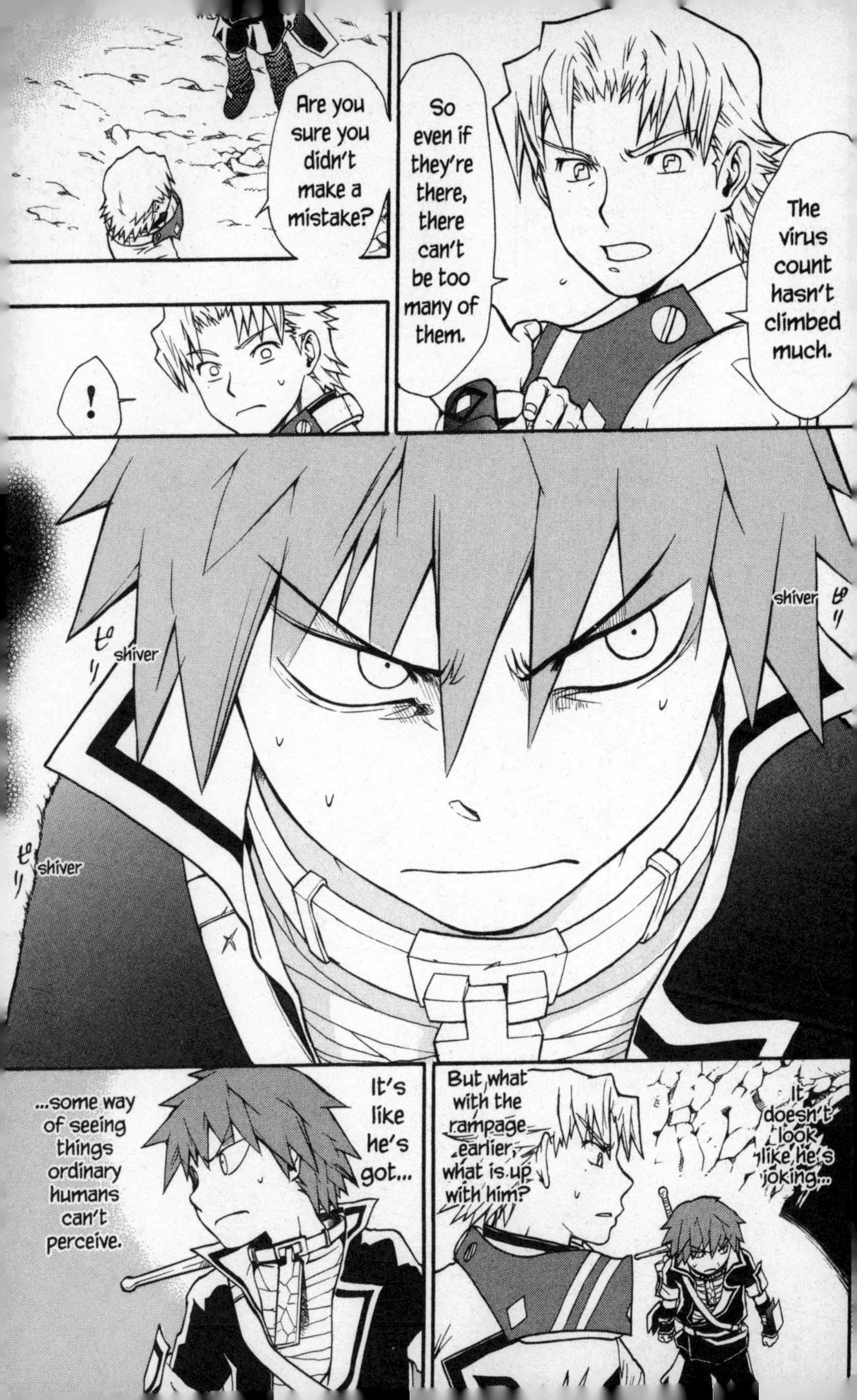

The virus count hasn't climbed much.
So even if they're there, there can't be too many of them.
Are you sure you didn't make a mistake?
!
shiver
shiver
shiver
It doesn't look like he's joking...
But what with the rampage earlier, what is up with him?
It's like he's got...
...some way of seeing things ordinary humans can't perceive.

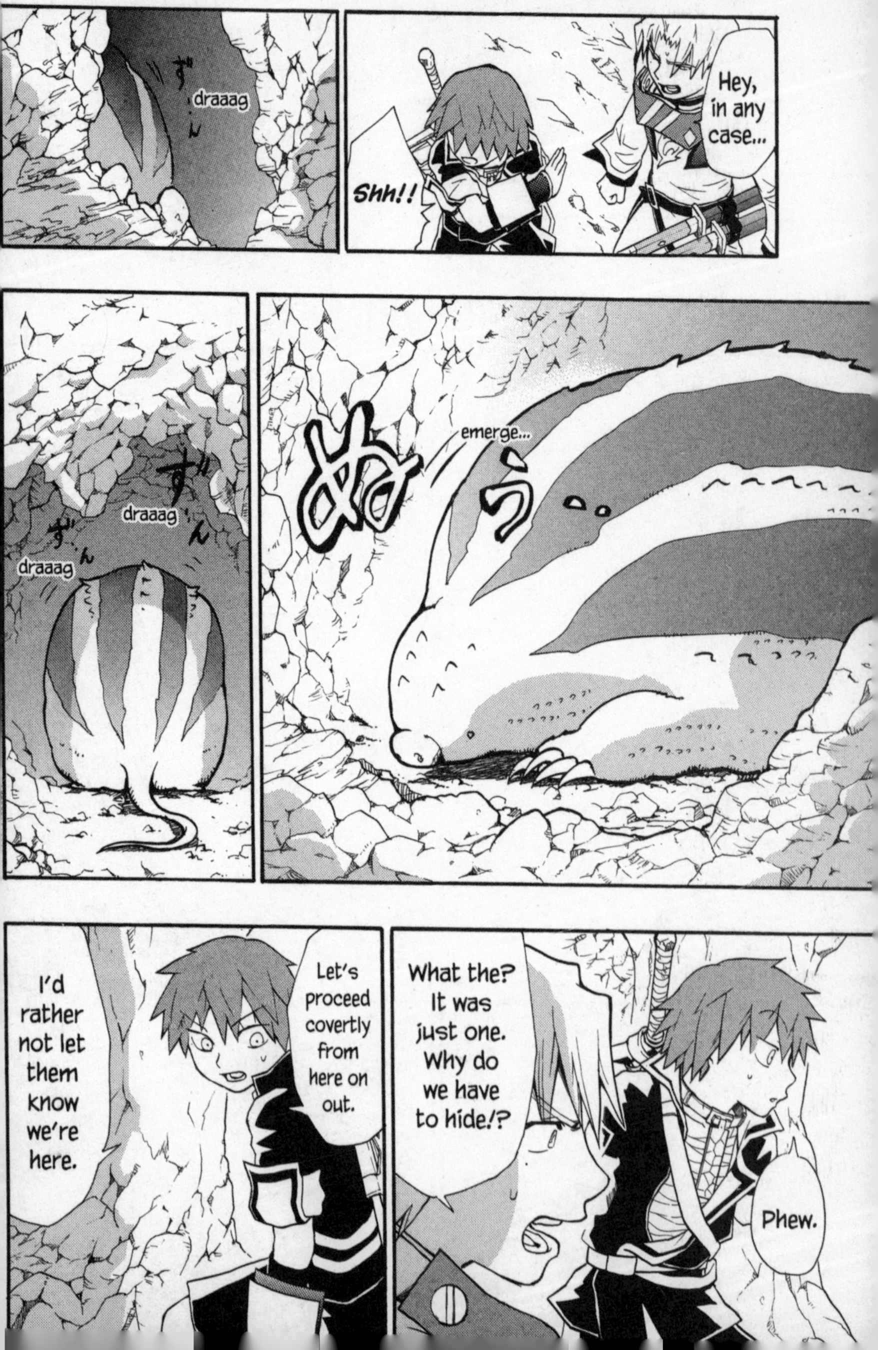
Hey, in any case...
Shh!!
ず
draaag
ん
emerge...
ぬう
ず
draaag
ん
ず
draaag
ん
Phew.
What the? It was just one. Why do we have to hide!?
Let's proceed covertly from here on out.
I'd rather not let them know we're here.

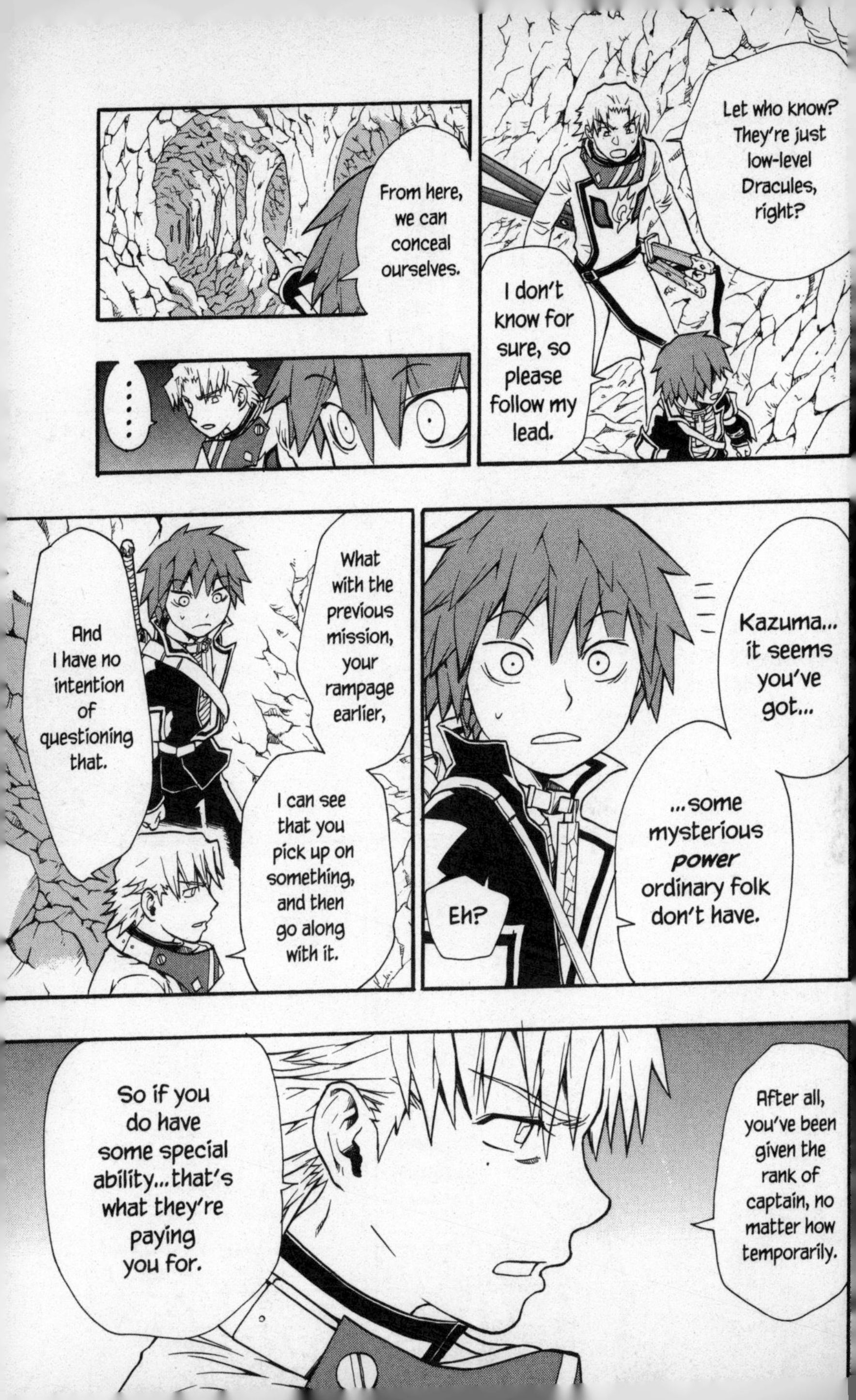
Let who know? They're just low-level Dracules, right?
I don't know for sure, so please follow my lead.
From here, we can conceal ourselves.
......
Kazuma... it seems you've got...
...some mysterious *power* ordinary folk don't have.
Eh?
What with the previous mission, your rampage earlier,
I can see that you pick up on something, and then go along with it.
And I have no intention of questioning that.
After all, you've been given the rank of captain, no matter how temporarily.
So if you do have some special ability...that's what they're paying you for.

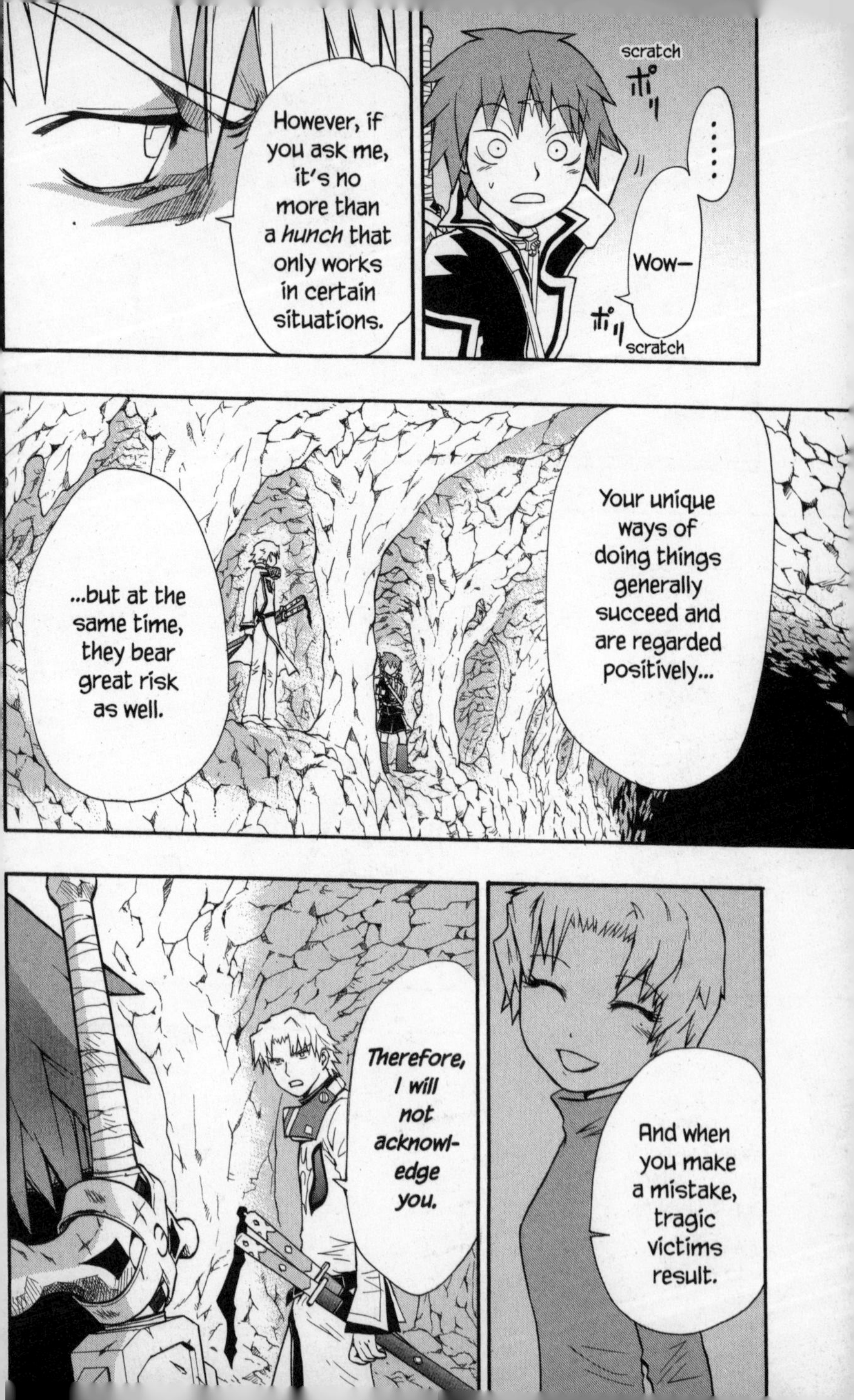
scratch
ポリ
....
Wow—
ポリ
scratch
However, if you ask me, it's no more than a *hunch* that only works in certain situations.
Your unique ways of doing things generally succeed and are regarded positively...
...but at the same time, they bear great risk as well.
And when you make a mistake, tragic victims result.
Therefore, I will not acknowl-edge you.

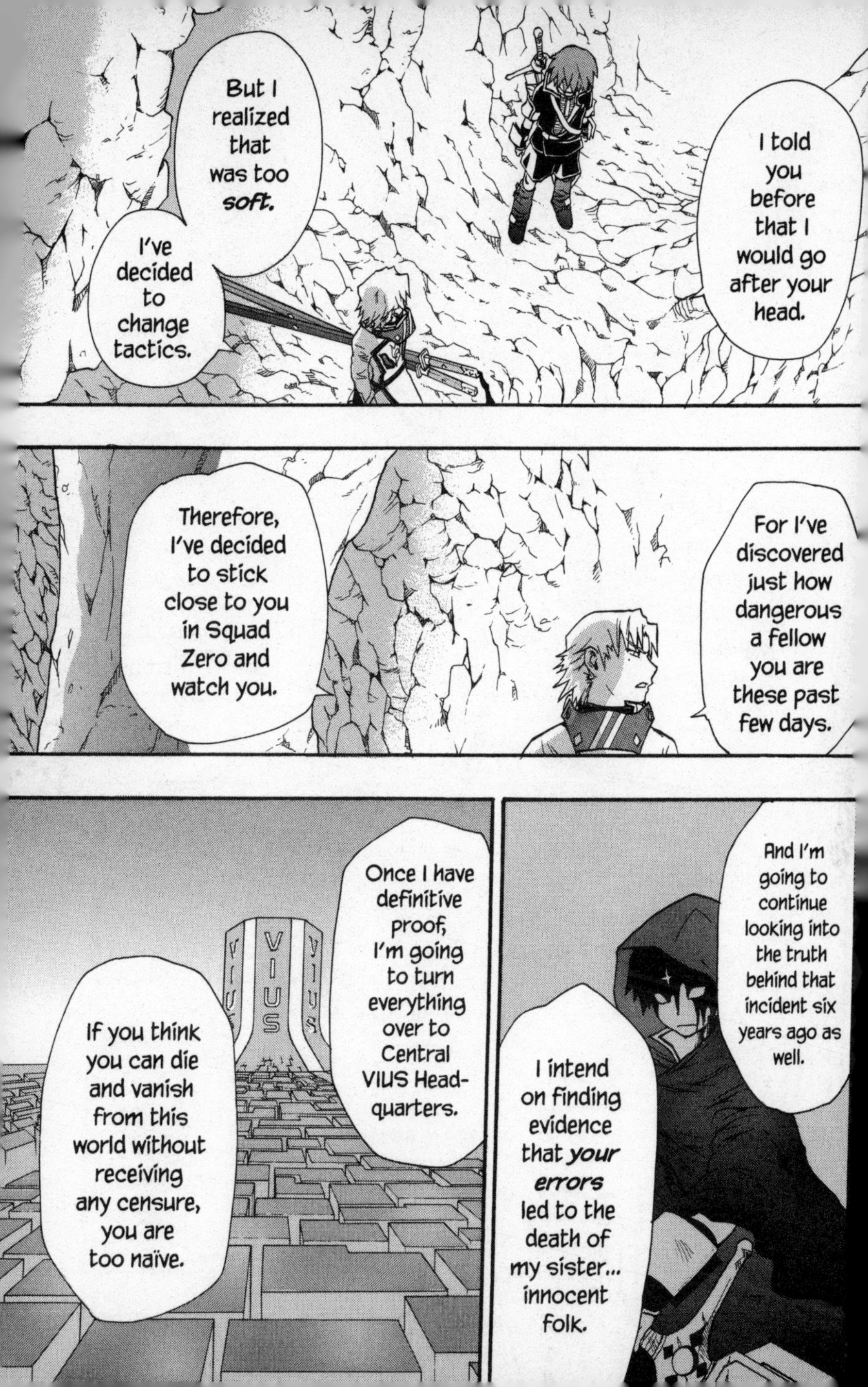
I told you before that I would go after your head.
But I realized that was too *soft.*
I've decided to change tactics.
For I've discovered just how dangerous a fellow you are these past few days.
Therefore, I've decided to stick close to you in Squad Zero and watch you.
And I'm going to continue looking into the truth behind that incident six years ago as well.
I intend on finding evidence that *your errors* led to the death of my sister... innocent folk.
Once I have definitive proof, I'm going to turn everything over to Central VIUS Head-quarters.
VIUS
If you think you can die and vanish from this world without receiving any censure, you are too naïve.

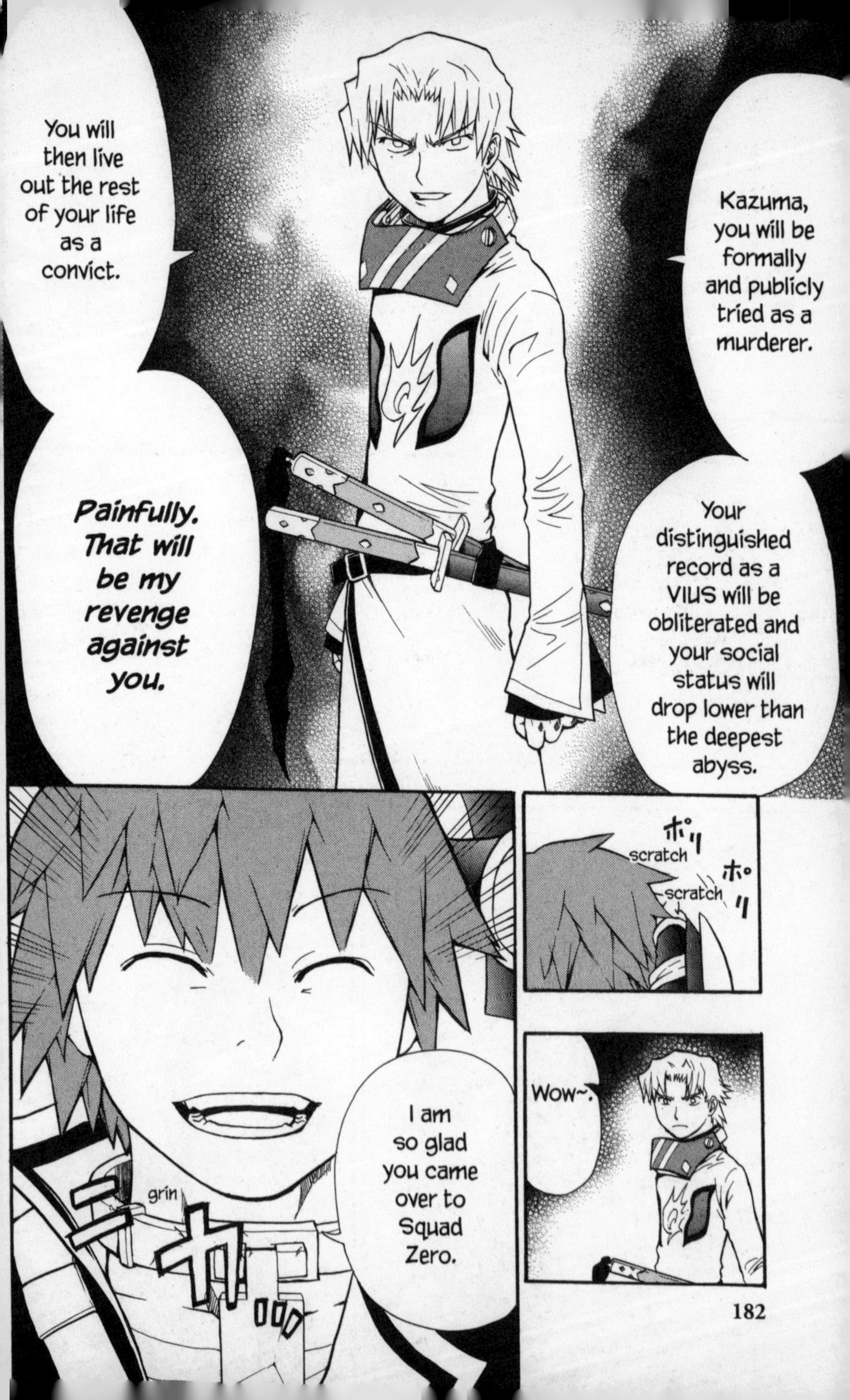

Kazuma, you will be formally and publicly tried as a murderer.
Your distinguished record as a VIUS will be obliterated and your social status will drop lower than the deepest abyss.
You will then live out the rest of your life as a convict.
Painfully. That will be my revenge against you.
ポリ
scratch
ポリ
scratch
Wow~.
grin
I am so glad you came over to Squad Zero.

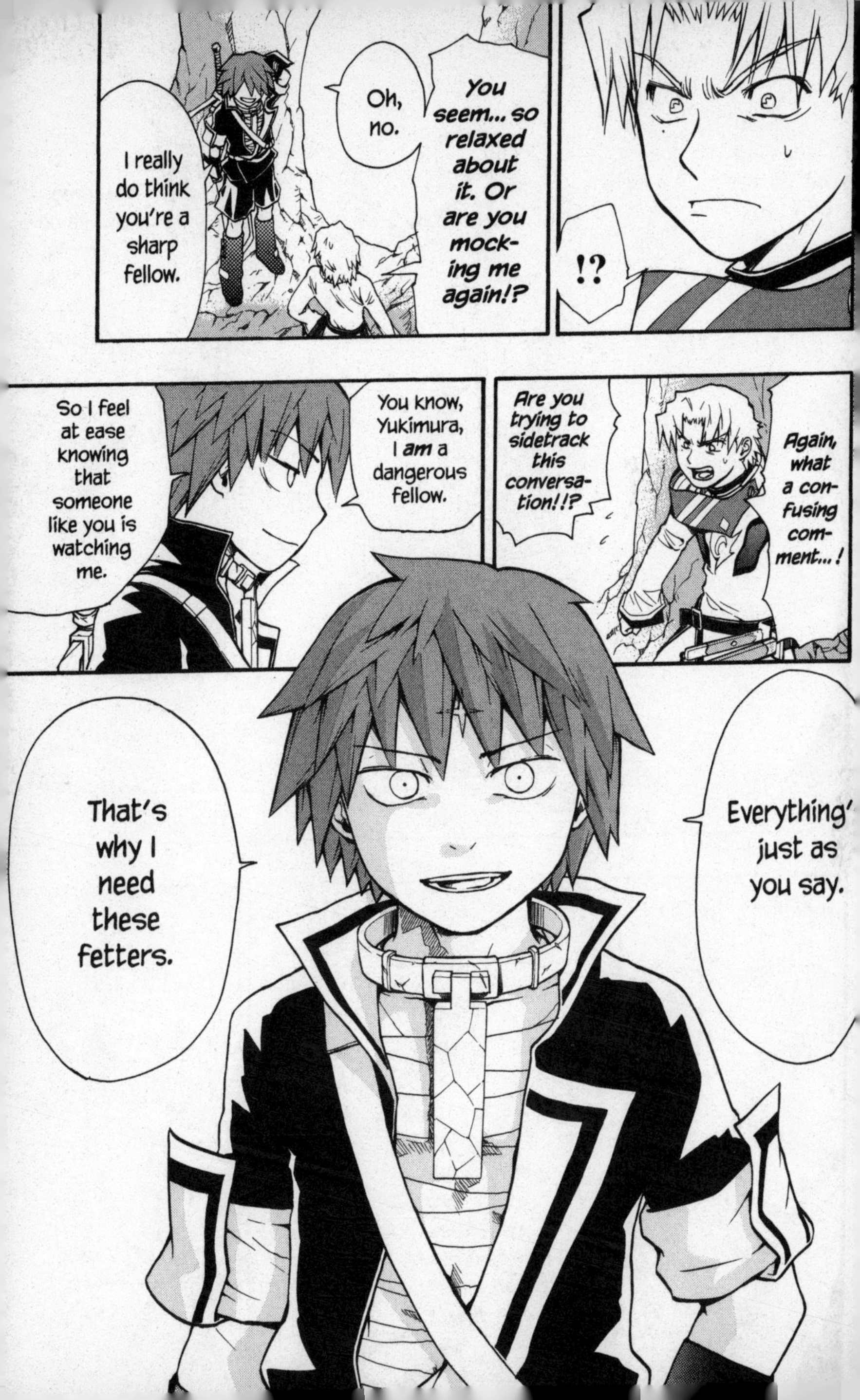
!?
You seem... so relaxed about it. Or are you mocking me again!?
Oh, no.
I really do think you're a sharp fellow.
Again, what a confusing comment...!
Are you trying to sidetrack this conversation!!?
You know, Yukimura, I *am* a dangerous fellow.
So I feel at ease knowing that someone like you is watching me.
Everything' just as you say.
That's why I need these fetters.

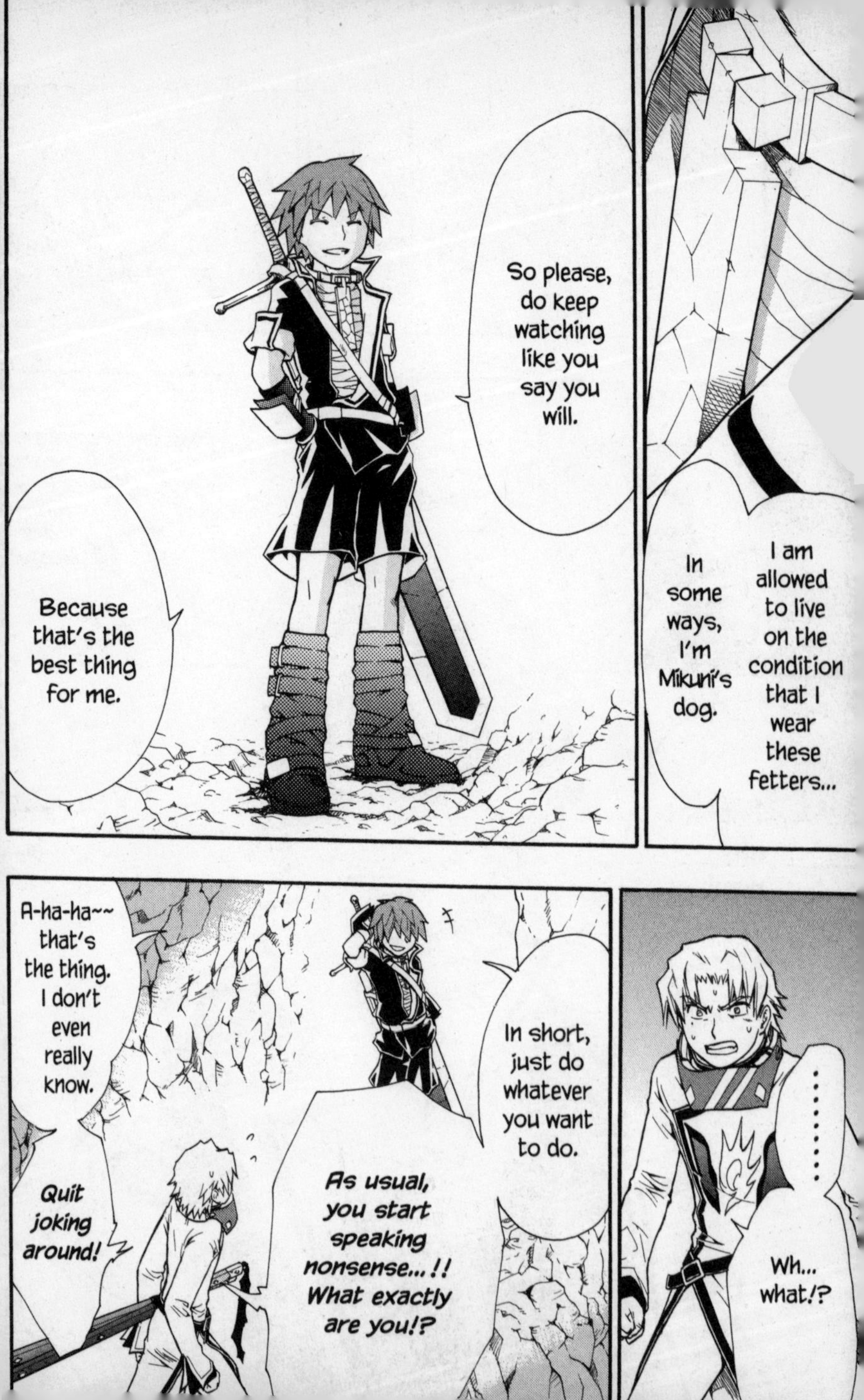
I am allowed to live on the condition that I wear these fetters...
In some ways, I'm Mikuni's dog.
So please, do keep watching like you say you will.
Because that's the best thing for me.
......
Wh... what!?
In short, just do whatever you want to do.
A-ha-ha~~ that's the thing. I don't even really know.
As usual, you start speaking nonsense...!! What exactly are you!?
Quit joking around!

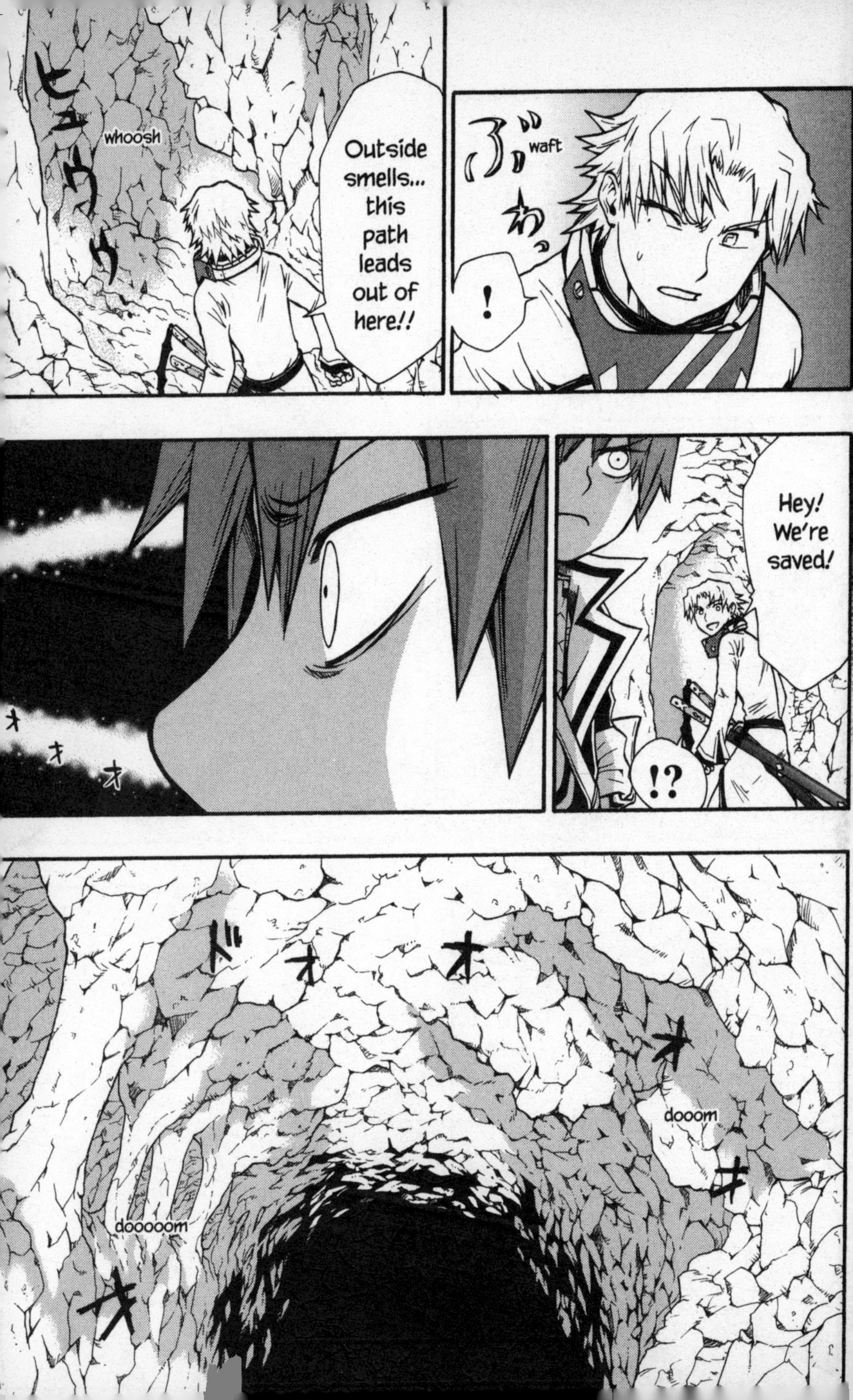
waft
!
whoosh
Outside smells... this path leads out of here!!
Hey! We're saved!
!?
dooom
doooooom

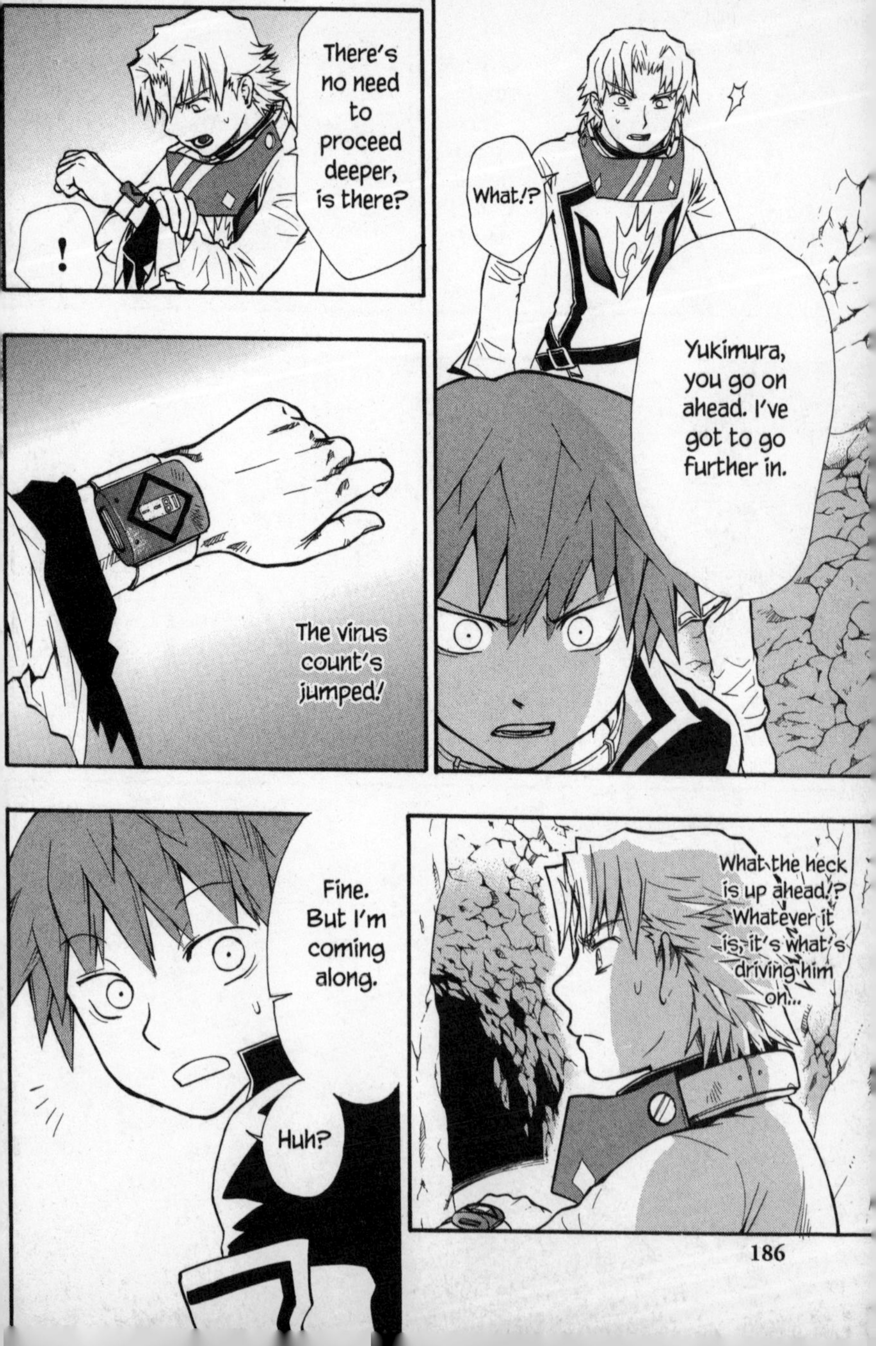
What!?
Yukimura, you go on ahead. I've got to go further in.
There's no need to proceed deeper, is there?
!
The virus count's jumped!
What the heck is up ahead!? Whatever it is, it's what's driving him on...
Fine. But I'm coming along.
Huh?

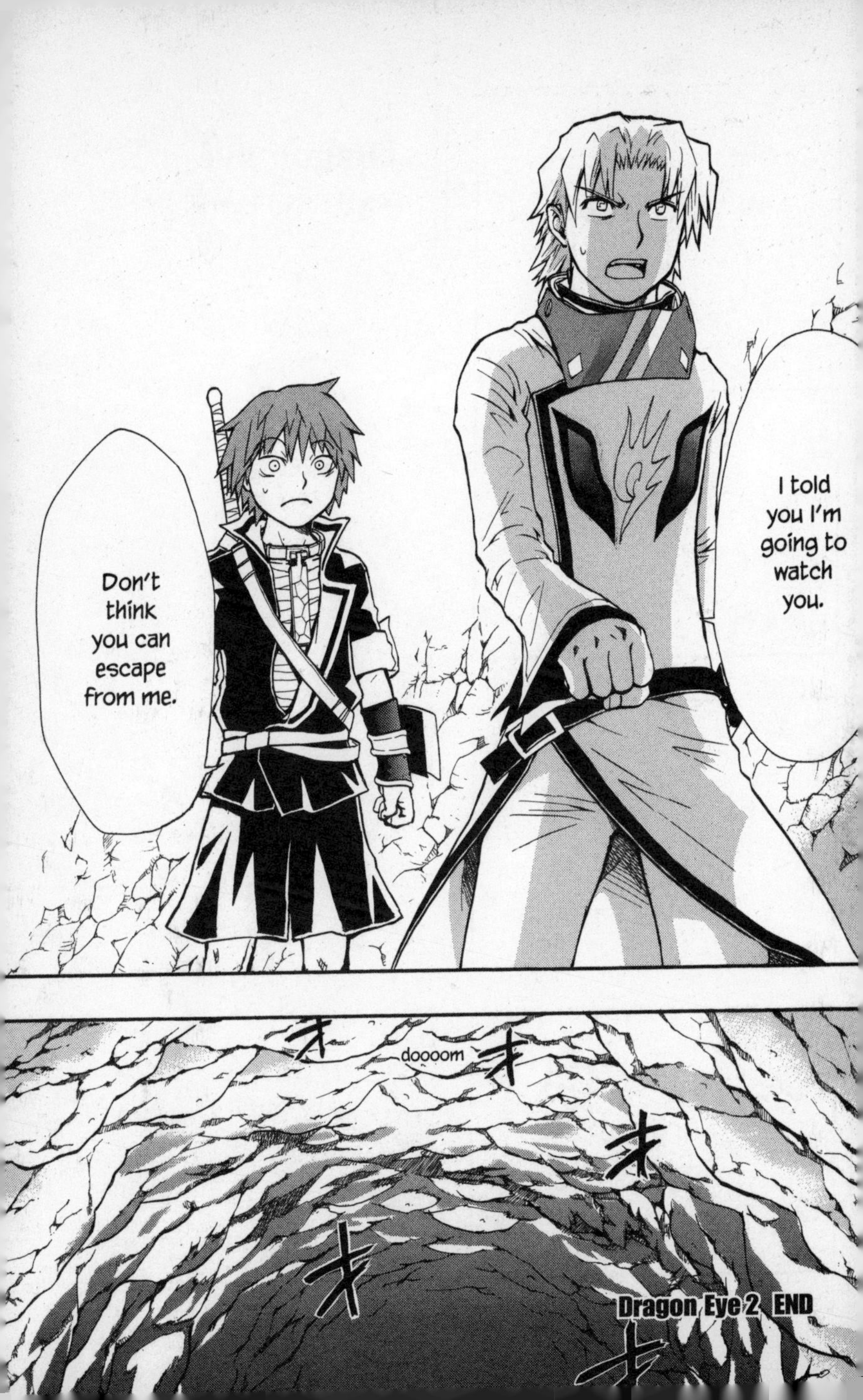
I told you I'm going to watch you.
Don't think you can escape from me.
dooom
Dragon Eye 2 END

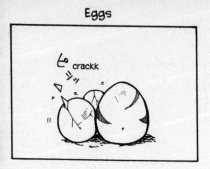

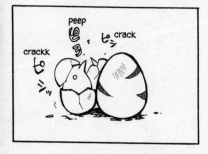

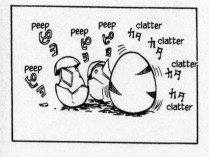

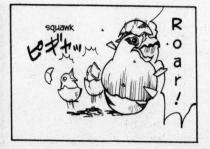

Dragon Eye
4-Cell Strip Extras

Thanks
for buying
volume 2!

Please buy
volume 3,
too.

Fujiyama

staff
- Uemura Erika
- Ueda Satomi

thanks
- Yuzuka

Eggs

ピシッ crackk
ピシ crack
ピヨ peep
ピシッ crackk
カタ clatter
カタ clatter
カタ clatter
カタ clatter
ピヨ peep
ピヨ peep
ピヨ peep
ピヨ peep
Roar!
ピギャッ squawk

Memo

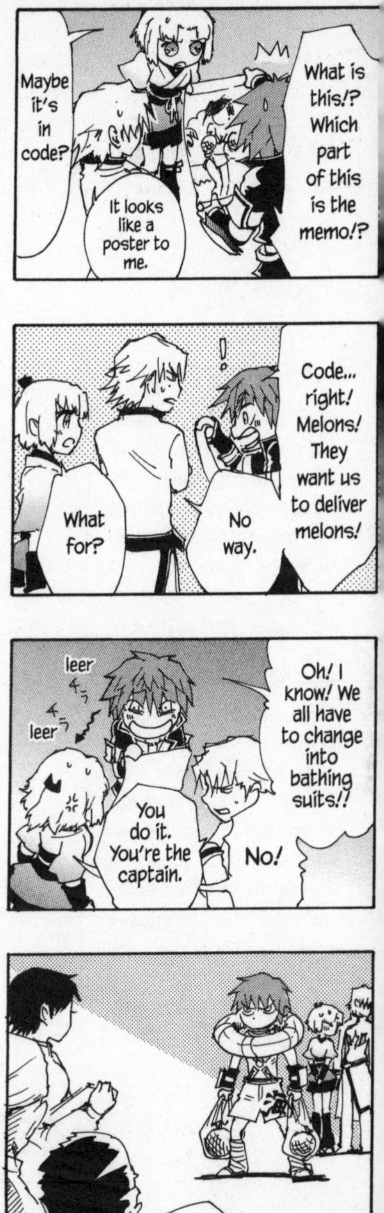
What is this!? Which part of this is the memo!?
Maybe it's in code?
It looks like a poster to me.
Code... right! Melons! They want us to deliver melons!
No way.
What for?
Oh! I know! We all have to change into bathing suits!!
leer
leer
No!
You do it. You're the captain.

Rope-walking

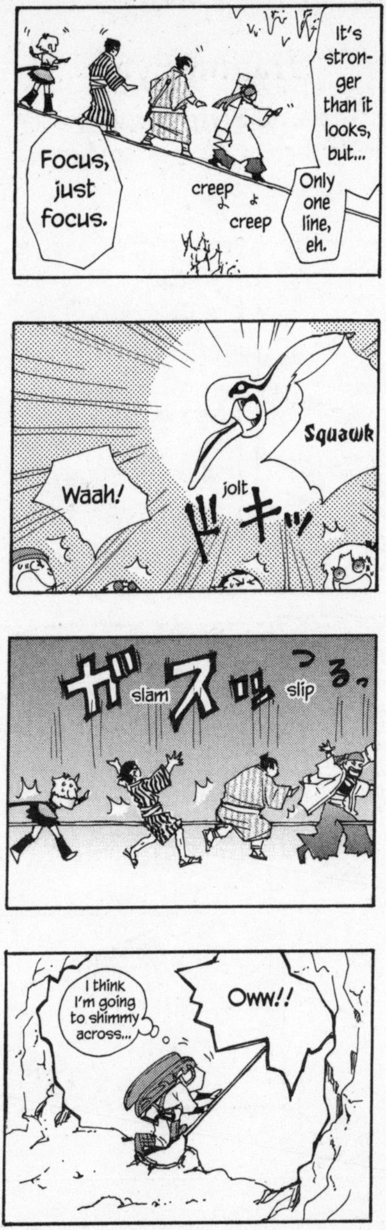
It's stronger than it looks, but...
Only one line, eh.
creep
creep
Focus, just focus.
Squawk
jolt
ドキッ
Waah!
つるっ
slip
slam
Oww!!
I think I'm going to shimmy across...

TRANSLATION NOTES

Japanese is a tricky language for most Westerners, and translation is often more art than science. For your edification and reading pleasure, here are notes on some of the places where we could have gone in a different direction in our translation of the work, or where a Japanese cultural difference is used.

Troop designation symbols, various pages

Most Vius members wear their troop designations somewhere on their uniforms, and equipment and objects sometimes bear stamps as well. For example, Sôsei, Leila, and three others wear veils embossed with 零 – "zero." Squad Five Captain Kiura wears a veil with the old form of five, 伍, on it, and Hibiki wears 陸, the older way of writing the number six, on the front of his mask. The only thing that is not yet clear is why Kajiyama has 三 (three) tattooed on his left cheek, since he is a Squad Two member (his gun has 弐 [two] embossed on it).

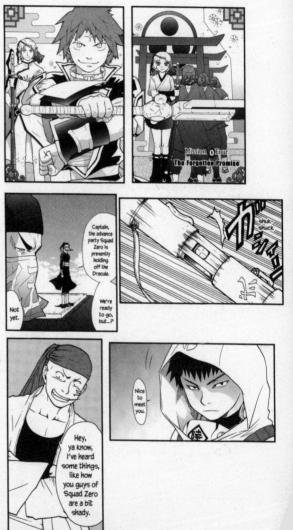

Mission Four
The Forgotten Promise
shuk-shuck
Captain, the advance party Squad Zero is presently holding off the Dracule.
We're ready to go, but...?
Not yet.
Nice to meet you.
Hey, ya know, I've heard some things, like how you guys of Squad Zero are a bit shady.

Kanikama, page 82

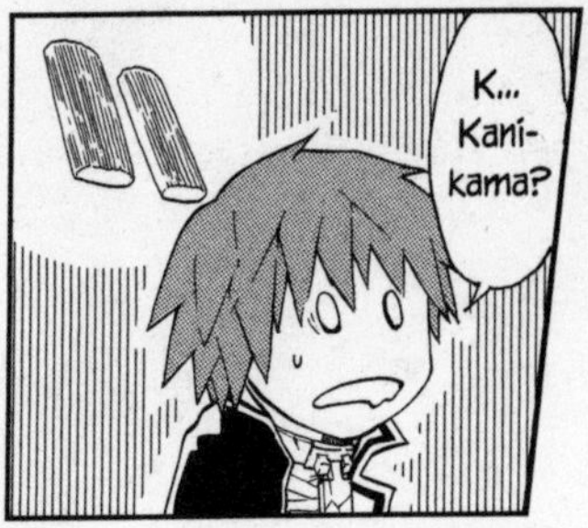
K...
Kani-
kama?

Short for *kani kamaboko*, or imitation crabmeat. Usually made from pollock or another whitefish, it is pressed into blocklike sticks or large flakes with one border artificially dyed red to look like the real thing. Most well known in America in the context of sushi (i.e. California rolls). Here, Issa mistakenly thinks Kajiyama's name is Kanikama.

Pin-up poster, page 74

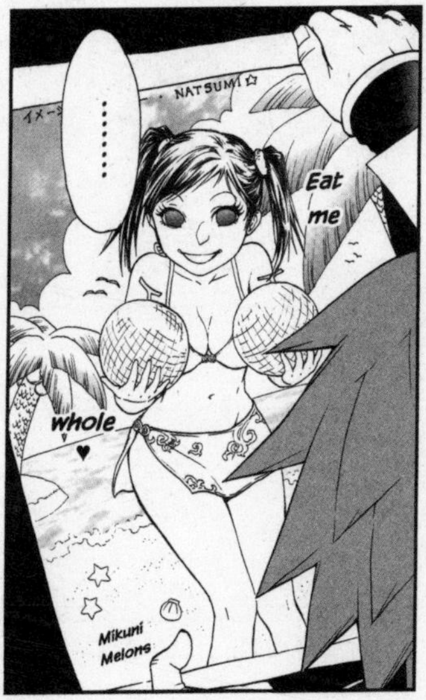
......
NATSUMI☆
Eat me
whole ♥
Mikuni Melons

Established and up-and-coming actors and singers are often hired for advertising campaigns, in this case a summer melon promotion for either a fruit farm or fruit distribution company.

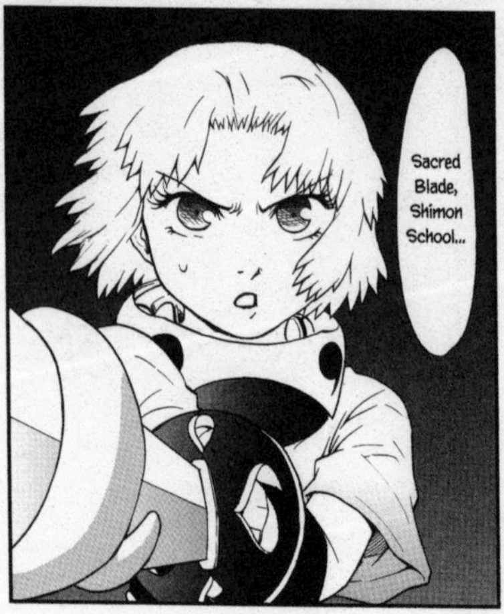
Sacred Blade, Shimon School...

Sacred Blade, Shimon School, page 156

A school of martial arts founded by Leila's pre-VIUS mentor, Master Shimon. Practitioners flow so gracefully and effortlessly through complex moves that they appear to be sword dancing.

Tonkotsu, page 84

Tonkotsu ["pork bone"] describes a type of ramen broth as well as literally what goes into making it. Supposedly originating from the Hakata area of Fukuoka City in Kyûshû, it is best when the pork bones, onions, and garlic have been stewed for many hours. Ramen noodles are added to the strained soup, which are then typically topped with sliced pork, dried seaweed, chopped scallions, and pickled ginger and bamboo shoots.

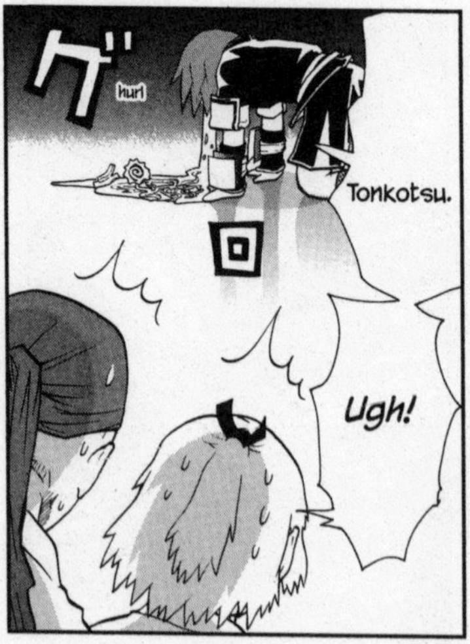
ゲ
hurl
Tonkotsu.
Ugh!

PREVIEW OF VOLUME 3 OF *DRAGON EYE*

We are pleased to present to you a preview from the next volume of *Dragon Eye*. Volume 3 will be available in English on December 26, 2007, but for now, you'll have to make do with Japanese!

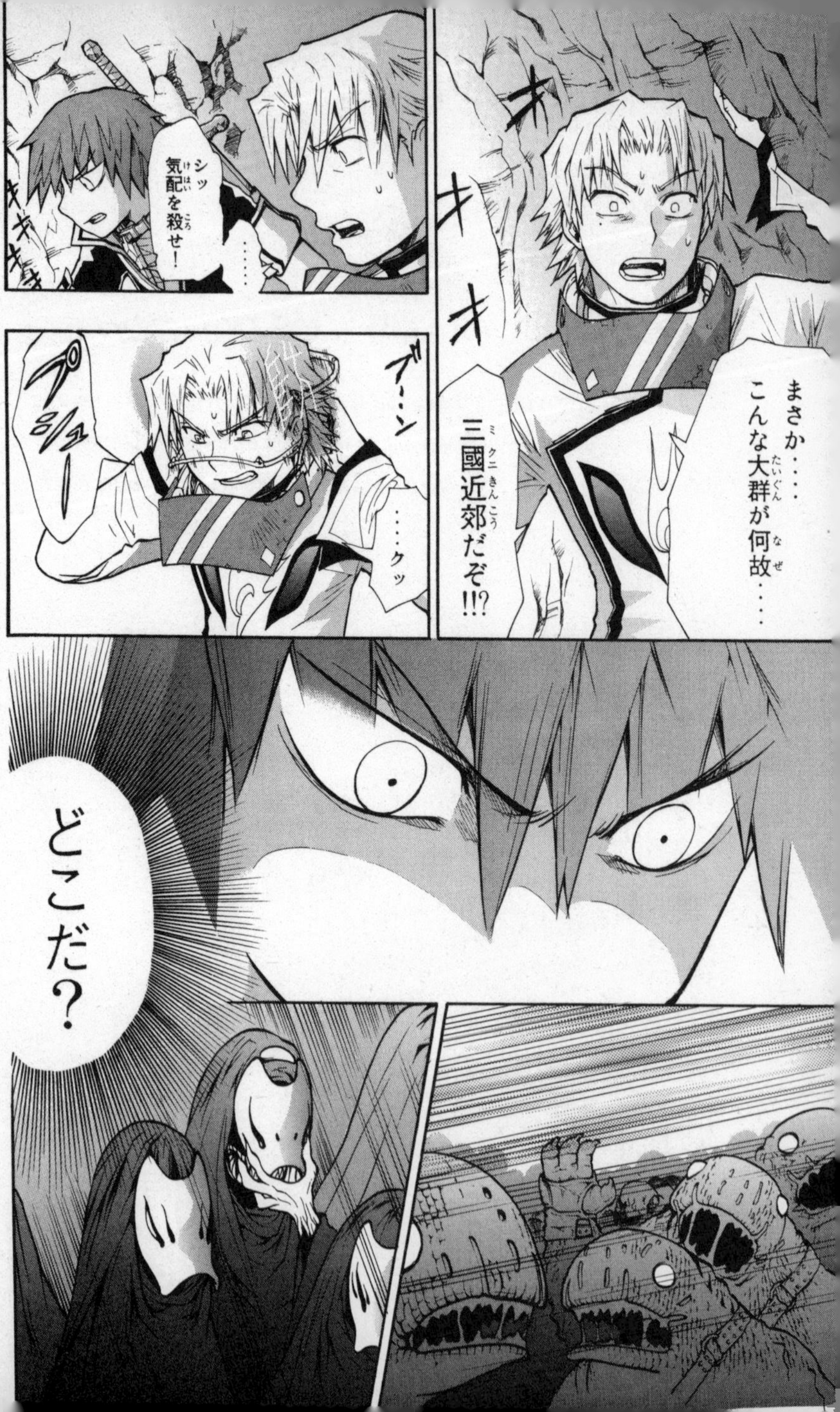
キ
キ
キ
まさか・・・・こんな大群が何故・・・・
三國近郊だぞ!!?
キキキキ
シッ 気配を殺せ!
……
プシュー
ブーン
……クッ
どこだ?

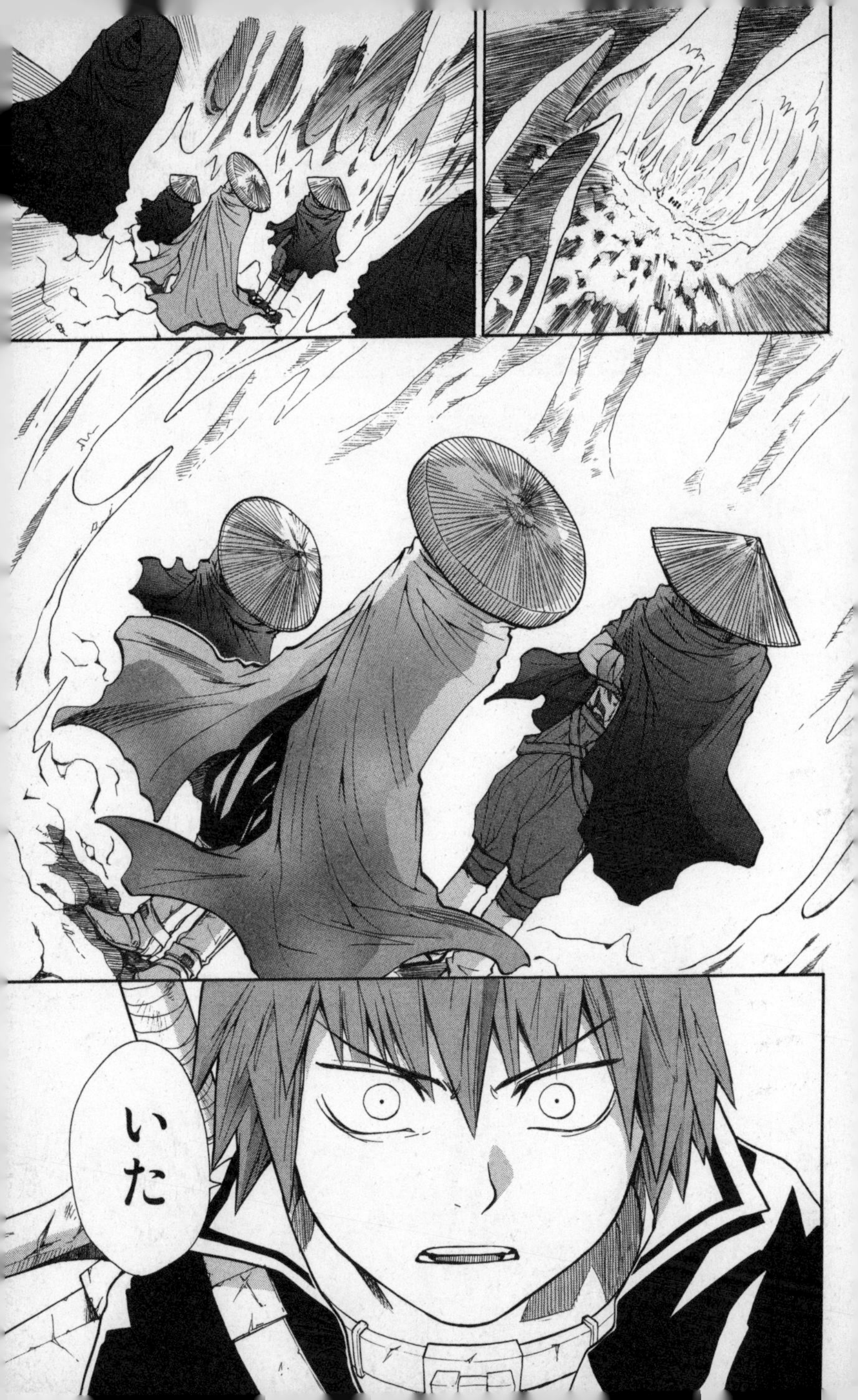
いた

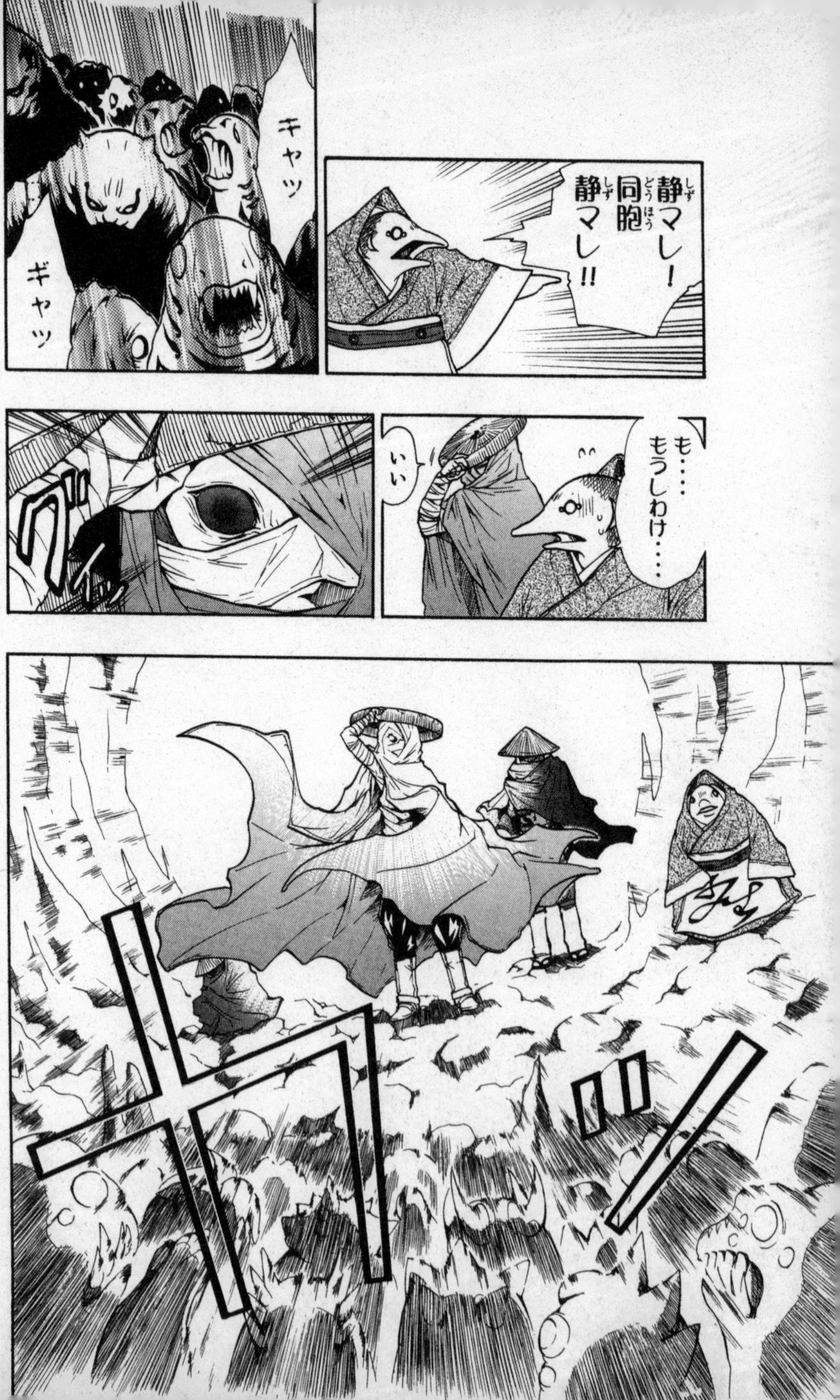
静マレ！同胞静マレ!!
キャッ
ギャッ
も……もうしわけ……
いい

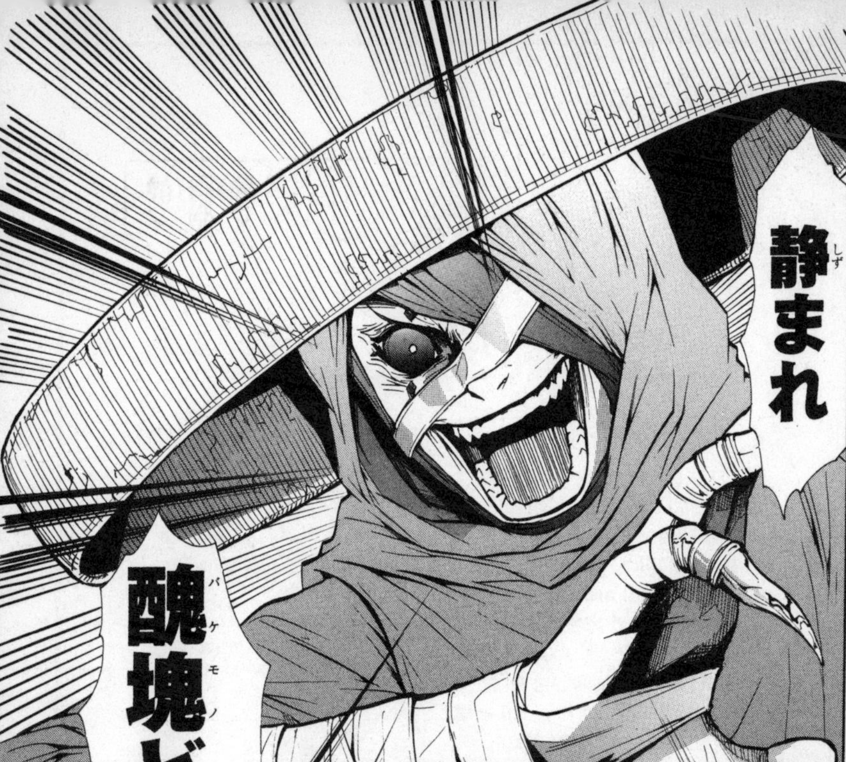
静まれ
醜塊ども！
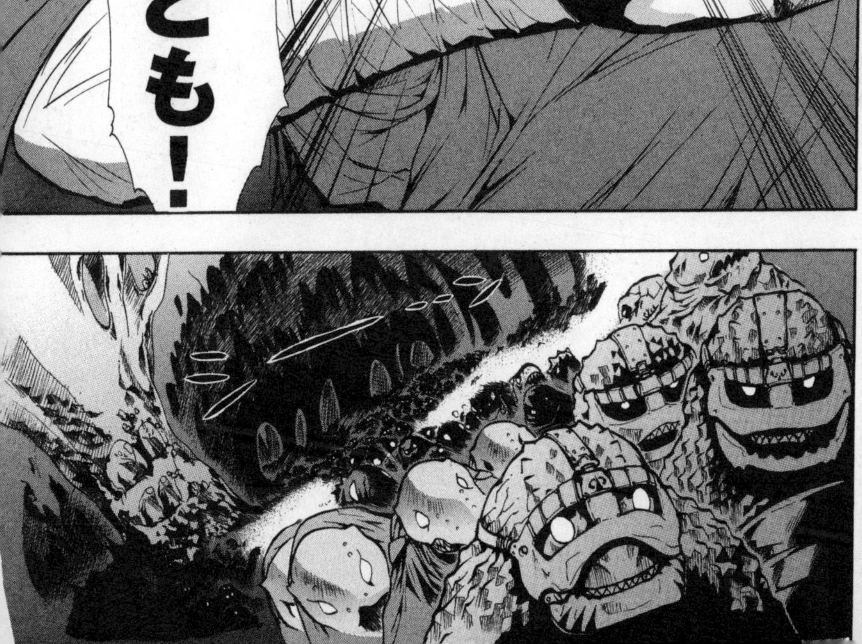

SHIKI TSUKAI

MANGA BY TORU ZEKU
ART BY YUNA TAKANAGI

DEFENDING THE NATURAL ORDER OF THE UNIVERSE!

The *shiki tsukai* are "Keepers of the Seasons"—magical warriors pledged to defend the planet's natural order against those who would threaten it.

When 14-year-old Akira Kizuki joins the *shiki tsukai*, he knows that it'll be a difficult life. But with his new friends and mentors, he's up to the challenge!

Special extras in each volume! Read them all!

MY HEAVENLY 🌫 HOCKEY CLUB

BY AI MORINAGA

WHERE THE BOYS ARE!

Hana Suzuki loves only two things in life: eating and sleeping. So when handsome classmate Izumi Oda asks Hana—his major crush—to join the school hockey club, convincing her proves to be a difficult task. True, the Grand Hockey Club is full of boys—and all the boys are super-cute—but, given a choice, Hana prefers a sizzling steak to a hot date. Then Izumi mentions the field trips to fancy resorts. Now Hana can't wait for the first away game, with its promise of delicious food and luxurious linens. Of course there's the getting up early, working hard, and playing well with others. How will Hana survive?

Special extras in each volume! Read them all!

VISIT WWW.DELREYMANGA.COM TO:
• Read sample pages
• View release date calendars for upcoming volumes
• Sign up for Del Rey's free manga e-newsletter
• Find out the latest about new Del Rey Manga series

RATING   AGES T 13+

Michiyo Kikuta

BOY CRAZY

Junior high schooler Nina is ready to fall in love. She's looking for a boy who's cute and sweet—and strong enough to support her when the chips are down. But what happens when Nina's dream comes true . . . twice? One day, two cute boys literally fall from the sky. They're both wizards who've come to the Human World to take the Magic Exam. The boys' success on this test depends on protecting Nina from evil, so now Nina has a pair of cute magical boys chasing her everywhere! One of these wizards just might be the boy of her dreams . . . but which one?

Special extras in each volume! Read them all!

VISIT WWW.DELREYMANGA.COM TO:
• Read sample pages
• View release date calendars for upcoming volumes
• Sign up for Del Rey's free manga e-newsletter
• Find out the latest about new Del Rey Manga series

RATING **T** AGES 13+

DEL REY MANGA デルレイ

The Otaku's Choice

SHUGO CHARA!

PEACH-PIT

Creators of Dears and Rozen Maiden

Everybody at Seiyo Elementary thinks that stylish and super-cool Amu has it all. But nobody knows the *real* Amu, a shy girl who wishes she had the courage to truly be herself. Changing Amu's life is going to take more than wishes and dreams—it's going to take a little magic! One morning, Amu finds a surprise in her bed: three strange little eggs. Each egg contains a Guardian Character, an angel-like being who can give her the power to be someone new. With the help of her Guardian Characters, Amu is about to discover that her true self is even more amazing than she ever dreamed.

Special extras in each volume! Read them all!

VISIT WWW.DELREYMANGA.COM TO:
• Read sample pages
• View release date calendars for upcoming volumes
• Sign up for Del Rey's free manga e-newsletter
• Find out the latest about new Del Rey Manga series

RATING T AGES 13+

The Otaku's Choice

TOMARE!

止まれ

[STOP!]

You're going the wrong way!

Manga is a completely different type of reading experience.

To start at the beginning, go to the end!

That's right! Authentic manga is read the traditional Japanese way—from right to left. Exactly the opposite of how American books are read. It's easy to follow: Just go to the other end of the book, and read each page—and each panel—from right side to left side, starting at the top right. Now you're experiencing manga as it was meant to be!